CARVED IN GRANITE

CARVED IN GRANITE

125 Years of Granite Club History

D. RODWELL AUSTIN
TED BARRIS

MACMILLAN CANADA

TORONTO

Canadian Cataloguing in Publication Data
Austin, Rod, 1927-
Carved in Granite: 125 Years of Granite Club History

Includes index.
ISBN 0-7715-7636-6

1. Granite club (Toronto, Ont.)–History. I. Barris, Ted. II. Title
GV563.A87   1999   796.06'8713541   C99–932082–3

1 2 3 4 5   FP   03 02 01 00 99

Jacket and text design by Tania Craan
Jacket photographs by Dave Starrett

We acknowledge the financial support of the Government of Canada through the Book Publishing Industry Development Program for our publishing activities.

Macmillan Canada,
An imprint of CDG Books Canada Inc.
Toronto

Printed in Canada

TABLE OF CONTENTS

About fourteen years ago I wrote to our board of directors, pointing out that the Granite Club had made an important contribution to the social, sporting, and cultural life of Toronto for more than a century. "It is time," I said, "that such a contribution be recognized and preserved. A history of the Granite Club should be written, and I believe I am the person to do it." President Walter Cassels and the board agreed and asked past presidents George Gilmour and Phyllis Parker to form a committee to work out the details. The rest, as they say, is history. Thank you, Walter and Phyllis. And a special posthumous thanks to George Gilmour whose good humour, kindness, and publishing know-how got the project off to a fine start.

The history of the Granite Club has close links with that of the city of Toronto. The club's founders and early members included many of Toronto's leading citizens and, to this day, business and professional leaders serve on the club's board and committees. More than 70 years ago *Saturday Night* said it well: "The Granite Club is a natural evolution of Toronto's growth in population, prosperity, and social activity. Few institutions have been so completely identified with the social history of its home city."

History is, at its best, biography. I have emphasized, therefore, the individual rather than bricks and mortar. I have focused on the men and women whose drive, foresight, and hard work have created and maintained such a remarkable institution.

A historian has a much easier task whenever comprehensive archival records are available. Unfortunately, official records of the Granite Club's first 50 years did not survive and I therefore have been compelled to rely on early newspapers and magazines, Toronto histories, and biographical dictionaries as my sources for the period. And so, after long years of searching through libraries and archives, and interviews with older members and staff, a reasonably complete history of the club has emerged. From this research, I have written the first 75 years of the club's history (1875-1950) and journalist, broadcaster and author Ted Barris, augmenting the research with his own lively personal interviews, has brought us up to the present day.

I wish I could adequately thank my wife, Margaret McBurney, author and social historian, who not only put up with my volatile moods during the long years of research and writing, but who also read and provided objective and insightful criticism of the manuscript's early drafts. Thanks also to Ann Schabas, freelance editor, whose precise and orderly approach kept me in line. Susan Girvan, senior editor of Macmillan Canada, provided wise and sensitive final editing, tactfully wielding her red pencil through an overabundance of data. She was heartless—but right—in consigning some of it to the "cutting room floor." I am also grateful to research assistant Donna Ivey who came up with many interesting nuggets that I had missed, and to Lenard Kotylo, hockey historian *extraordinaire*, who provided invaluable information on the club's championship hockey teams. Thanks also to director Tom Corcoran, who coordinated the project on behalf of the board, and to President Peter Singer, General Manager Peter Fyvie, Assistant General Manager Mary Elizabeth Sullivan and Karen Jury of the club's communications department, all of whom read the completed manuscript, providing valuable suggestions.

D. Rod Austin
August 1999

FOUNDERS

THE FIVE FOUNDERS of the Granite Club were remarkable men who provided the leadership and vision so necessary for this new endeavour. They created a curling and sports facility that would, within 14 years, grow to become what New York's *Outing* magazine called the "largest club of its kind in the world." And they never could have guessed that 125 years later their club would have more than 9000 members—many of them women! As club President James Hedley remarked in 1889 (by which time the membership had soared to nearly 500), "It is safe to say that the founders had no premonition of the future importance of the organization then formed."

PRESIDENT LAMOND SMITH immigrated to Canada in 1840 as an ambitious 18-year-old and settled on a large tract of land near Fergus, Ontario (then Upper Canada), that had been bought for him by his family. He soon met and married Isabella Barker, an Englishwoman, and they became parents of three daughters. As landowner, farmer, and notary public, he enjoyed small-town prosperity for some 20 years.

Lamond Smith

Then, in 1860, Smith was called to Toronto by the Bank of Upper Canada. During the boom of the early 1850s, it had speculated heavily and, as it turned out, unwisely in land and was in serious financial difficulties. In an attempt to save the bank, Smith was hired to supervise the liquidation of its land holdings. But no one could save the Bank of Upper Canada—not even Smith. It closed its doors in 1866, owing the provincial government nearly $1 500 000, most of which was never recovered. After the bank's collapse, Smith, then age 44, joined forces with accountant Benjamin Morton who had also been with the bank. Together, they formed a real estate partnership that lasted until Smith's death.

Smith was a Tory, an Anglican, and a Mason—three requisites for success in both business and society in Toronto during the last half of the 19th century. He built a fine country home, Ben Lamond, east of Toronto on the edge of what was then the village of Norway. And, in the city, he moved to the northwest corner of Church and Gloucester Streets to a large home he called Norway Place.

He was a congenial, robust, and boisterous man, and an enthusiastic athlete. In 1876 he became a founder and first captain (president) of the Toronto Golf Club—the third golf club to be established in North America. Thus, in the short space of one year, he became Toronto's leading figure in Scotland's two national sports.

Smith was destined to enjoy his beloved Granite Club for only seven years. He died in January 1882, three months after the club had made him an Honorary Member. There is little doubt that without his leadership, energy, enthusiasm, and initiative, Toronto's new "uptown" curling club would not have come into being.

VICE-PRESIDENT THOMAS MCCRAKEN was, like his friend Lamond Smith, a banker and a Mason. Unlike Smith, however, he was a Liberal and a Presbyterian. Born in 1837 in Bonaventure

County, Quebec (then Lower Canada), he was educated at the Bytown (Ottawa) Grammar School. At age 18 he embarked on his banking career, advancing rapidly to the position of cashier (general manager) of the Royal Canadian Bank in 1869. In 1876, he left banking to become the head of the lumber firm of McCraken, Gall and Company.

McCraken's move into the lumber business was not surprising. His father had been in the lumber business, and as a youth Thomas had worked for lumber firms up and down the Gatineau River and the St. Maurice. Eight years later he changed careers again and became manager of one of Toronto's largest real estate companies, the Toronto Land Investment Corporation.

Not only was McCraken an astute and successful businessman, but he also paid his dues to society. He served as treasurer of Knox Presbyterian Church and helped establish the Grand Lodge of Canada (Orange Order) of which he was an officer for many years. Prior to the founding of the Granite Club, he had been president of the Toronto Curling Club and, in 1881, he became the Granite Club's fourth president. He was also a member of the Board of Trade and the Royal Canadian Yacht Club.

Thomas McCraken

SECRETARY-TREASURER WILLIAM BAIN SCARTH was 17 in 1855 when he came to Canada. He immediately became embroiled in Conservative politics in Hamilton and London and soon attracted the attention of John A. Macdonald. In time, and despite a considerable age difference, they became close friends—a friendship that was destined to be a guiding influence throughout Scarth's life.

In 1868 Scarth moved to Toronto and within a few years he had interested a group of Glasgow merchant capitalists in organizing the Scottish Ontario and Manitoba Land Company. As its enterprising manager he was soon involved in the development of a large tract of land in the area known as Rosedale. He named two of Rosedale's streets, proud tribute to his Scottish heritage—Scarth

William Bain Scarth

Road after his family and Binscarth Road after the birthplace of his ancestors in the Orkney Islands. In 1869 he married Jessie Hamilton and they had eight children. During the early 1880s they lived on the northeast corner of Church and Gloucester Streets, directly across from his friend, Lamond Smith.

Politics was Scarth's driving interest. He joined the Conservative Association of Toronto, became its president, and was actively involved in every federal election campaign from 1875. By 1884 he had also served as a school trustee and for two terms as an alderman for the affluent St. James Ward in which he lived. But he paid a price for this single-minded devotion. In an 1880 letter to Macdonald, he confided that he suffered "continuous worry and trial" over his personal financial situation.

Bigger things, however, were in store for Scarth. In 1884, he left Toronto and the Granite Club and moved to Winnipeg to become Sir John A. Macdonald's watchdog there. That same year, he was appointed managing director of the Canada Northwest Land Company, which developed the town sites of Virden in Manitoba, and Moose Jaw and Regina in Saskatchewan. Scarth Street in Regina is named in his honour, as are the villages of Scarth and Binscarth in Manitoba. But Scarth wanted more. Crying poor, he again wrote the prime minister with an appeal for additional favours. "Like many others, I made losses in the boom and, in addition to being cleaned out of money, am daily meeting obligations from my income." It is not known what, if any, was Macdonald's reply, if indeed he replied at all. But their friendship continued. In a July 5, 1889, letter to Scarth, Macdonald wrote: "Be assured, my dear Scarth, that you have my entire confidence—as you always have had, since I first knew you."

Financial insecurity notwithstanding, Scarth persevered in his love of politics. Three years after his move to Winnipeg, he became its Member of Parliament, winning by a scant eight votes. After Macdonald's death in 1891, Scarth declined to run again. His political connections, however, were still in place and he was named deputy minister of agriculture and later deputy commissioner of patents. He died in 1902.

WILLIAM BARCLAY MCMURRICH, born in 1842, was a native Torontonian. In fact, he was the only one of the five founding members born in the city. It could be said that his interest in curling started in the cradle, for he was named after the Reverend John Barclay, DD (1813–1887), pastor of the old St. Andrew's Church on Adelaide Street and chaplain of the Toronto Curling Club. McMurrich was a bright student, attending Upper Canada College, then located at King and Simcoe Streets, and the University of Toronto, where he was gold medalist, class of 1863. He earned his MA the following year, went on to study law, and was called to the bar in 1866. That same year he married the daughter of Plummer Dewar of Chedoke, Hamilton.

William Barclay McMurrich

In 1868 McMurrich, like many lawyers before and since, leapt into the political fray—and with great success. He was elected four times (twice by acclamation) as school trustee for St. Andrew's Ward. In this role he proved to be both effective and influential.

McMurrich involved himself in the plight of the local street kids. As one writer of the day put it, "Large numbers of children [are] wandering at large in our streets and preparing for sins and crime." McMurrich, on behalf of the school board, headed for Massachusetts and New York State to survey their "industrial schools." On his recommendation, the city purchased a building near the New Gaol (now the Don Jail). It was called the House of Refuge and served as a place of shelter, discipline, and education for wayward youth.

In many ways, McMurrich was ahead of his time. He enthusiastically supported free education and was instrumental in the formation of a free library. But most of all McMurrich loved ceremonial celebrations and promoted them well—particularly when royalty, patriotism, or boosterism for the city was involved. When Lord Dufferin became Canada's governor-general in 1872, one of his

McMurrich had two younger brothers. The first, George, carried on the firm of Bryce, McMurrich and Company after the death of their father in 1883. It was one of Toronto's largest dry-goods houses and he ran it in partnership with J.S. Playfair. (The Playfair name still carries on at the Granite Club in the annual Playfair bonspiel.) The second brother, James Playfair McMurrich, was an internationally famous scientist, biologist and professor of anatomy at the University of Toronto. The Anatomy Building at 12 Queen's Park Crescent is called the McMurrich Building in his honour.

first official tours brought him to Toronto. McMurrich, then a handsome, bearded 30-year-old, was appointed chairman of the school board's reception committee and proudly arranged Dufferin's visits to Toronto's public schools. McMurrich resigned as school trustee in 1877, during his fourth term, to become the Board's solicitor—a position he was to hold for more than 30 years.

Two years after his resignation as school trustee, he was back again in politics, this time in St. Patrick's Ward, where he was elected alderman by the largest majority ever before received by an aldermanic candidate in Toronto. That year Queen Victoria's son-in-law Governor-General the Marquis of Lorne and his wife Princess Louise paid their first official visit to Toronto to open its first annual Toronto Industrial Exhibition. They were met by none other than McMurrich, who had once more been put in charge of the reception committee.

His political career continued to flourish. In 1880 he was again elected alderman and named chairman of the city's executive committee, thus becoming, next to the mayor, the most powerful man on council. Just one year later, he became mayor. One of his first duties took him to Cleveland where he attended the funeral of assassinated President James Garfield. All businesses in Toronto closed their doors for two hours that day as a mark of respect.

Mayor McMurrich initiated many civic improvements, including the consolidation, in one manual, of all city and provincial bylaws relating to Toronto. It was a Herculean task and he did it single handedly. He also ordered all contractors bidding on city projects to post performance deposits that would be forfeited if the contract was unfinished or not performed as specified—a simple proviso perhaps, but never before required.

He was a true liberal, light years ahead of his time in his opposition to racial intolerance. When a black choral group from the United States, the Jubilee Singers (most of whom were sons and daughters of slaves who had been freed just 16 years earlier), came to Toronto in 1881, they were refused admittance at every hotel they approached. Learning of their plight, McMurrich stepped in, and quickly found accommodation for them. Torontonians were obviously well pleased with their mayor, for he was re-elected by acclamation. He decided, however, against running for a third term and, ever ambitious, turned to the federal scene to contest the West Toronto riding. But this time he lost, defeated by James Beaty, Jr., QC, the man whom he had replaced as mayor two years before.

McMurrich's interests were legion. A devout Presbyterian, he was an elder at Knox Church, superintendent of its Sunday School, and a commissioner to the Presbyterian General Assembly. He also served as president of the St. Andrew's Society, vice-president of the Conservatory of Music, and a trustee at Upper Canada College. And he was a trustee, from 1883 until his death, of the Toronto General Burial Grounds (now Toronto Trust Cemeteries).

McMurrich died in 1908. He had greatly improved his city of birth in many ways. Today, the name of this remarkable man is commemorated by McMurrich Public School and McMurrich Street.

THE FIFTH FOUNDER, ROBERT CARRIE, did not achieve great fame or fortune, nor did he seek to fill any public office. He was a businessman all his life and a solid citizen.

Born in Forfarshire County, Scotland, in 1829, he was apprenticed at age 13 to a dry-goods merchant in Dundee. Fifteen years later, in 1857, he immigrated to Canada and opened a dry-goods business in St. Thomas. In 1866 he moved to Toronto and, in partnership with a Manchester merchant, founded another dry-goods business called Dobbie and Carrie. Personal tragedy followed. Carrie's wife, Isabella Cuthbert, died in 1867; a son, John, died in 1875, the year the Toronto Granite Curling Club began. That same year Carrie became one of the founding directors of the Imperial Bank along with fellow curler William Ramsay. Daniel Robert Wilkie, another Granite Club member, became the bank's general manager.

The Canadian National Exhibition was known as The Toronto Industrial Exhibition until 1912.

Robert Carrie

Carrie closed down his dry-goods firm in 1885, Dobbie having died a few years earlier, and entered the warehousing business in a four-storey brick building at 27 Front Street East.

Carrie was a Liberal and member of the Board of Trade and the St. Andrew's Society. And, of course, he was an enthusiastic curler, although he never aspired to the position of skip[*]. He was nearly 80 when he died on February 22, 1908, seven months before the death of his friend William Barclay McMurrich.

*A curling skip is the captain of a team of four players.

CHARTER MEMBERS

THE 30 MEN WHO JOINED the Granite Club in its first year were an ambitious, energetic, hard-working, entrepreneurial band of men—manufacturers, land developers, bankers, lawyers, doctors, newspaper owners, brokers, wholesalers, and lumber barons. As a close group they laid the foundations not only for the Granite Club, but also for the city of Toronto. Half a century after the club began, *Saturday Night* summed up the contribution these men made: "The [1875] list of members reads like a roll call of the men whose vision developed and built Toronto."

J. Weir Anderson

Thomas Armstrong

Robert Henry Bethune

Alexander Boyd

Robert Carrie (founder)

Archibald Hamilton Campbell

William Mellis Christie

Robert Cochran

William Davidson

W.F. Davison

James David Edgar

Remy Elmsley

Andrew Green

Arthur Harvey

Robert Jaffray

Simeon Heman Janes

John McCraken	William Ramsay
Thomas McCraken (founder)	James H. Richardson
William Barclay McMurrich (founder)	William Bain Scarth (founder)
Alexander Nairn	James Edward Smith
Stephen Nairn	Lamond Smith (founder)
John Palmer, Jr.	John Turner
John Patterson	Frederick Wyld

Historical records reveal little regarding some of these men. We do know that Anderson was rear commodore of the RCYC; Armstrong, a city alderman; Boyd, a dry goods wholesaler; Cochran, a realtor; and Davidson and Patterson, barristers. W.F. Davison, a meteorologist, became the club's third president. Elmsley was chief justice John Elmsley's grandson. Nothing has been found regarding Green, Palmer, or John McCraken. Harvey is best remembered as the developer of the Parkdale district. Ramsay, an entrepreneur in groceries, wines, and spirits, became the club's second president. Smith was a mayor of Toronto. Turner, a shoe manufacturer, was one of the founders of the Toronto Industrial Exhibition (now the CNE).

Five of the charter members were founders. In addition to these men, there are ten other charter members whose influence on Toronto, and on Canada as a whole, has kept their stories alive.

ROBERT HENRY BETHUNE was a son of the Right Reverend A.N. Bethune, protegé and successor to Bishop John Strachan, the man who ruled church and state in the first half of the 19th century in what is now Ontario. He was born in Cobourg in 1836, educated at Upper Canada College and, as an eager 17-year-old, joined the Bank of Montreal in Brockville where he rapidly gained recognition as a sound banker. He was only 34 when, to the astonishment of Ontario's financial

Robert Henry Bethune

community, he was appointed the first general manager of the Dominion Bank, a position he held until his death 25 years later. Bethune's financial acumen was legendary. He steered the bank successfully through three recessions, during which it "always reported a profit, always added to its reserves, always paid a dividend which equalled or bettered those of its competitors…the best dividend rate in the industry."

Nor was his life all bank and no play. Along with the Granite Club—he was its 12th president (1889–90)—Bethune belonged to the Toronto Club, the Toronto Cricket Club, and the Royal Canadian Yacht Club. He was an enthusiastic golfer, a keen curler, an all-round cricketer, a fine whist player—and the father of six. He served as warden of Holy Trinity Church and as a trustee of Trinity College and Bishop Strachan Schools.

In 1892, on the 21st anniversary of the founding of the Dominion Bank, the *Toronto World* reported: "The members of his staff look upon him as a father, and almost worship him. 'He is a man and a half in every way you take him,' enthusiastically announced one of them."

ARCHIBALD HAMILTON CAMPBELL was born in Stirlingshire, Scotland, and received a classical education at Edinburgh Academy and the University of Edinburgh. As the youngest son, albeit of a wealthy family, he could not hope to inherit much and so struck out on his own. He came to Canada in 1845 when he was 26 years old and settled in Montreal. At the time, the Oregon boundary dispute was at its peak and war with the United States appeared imminent. As a loyal British subject, Campbell promptly obtained a commission in the Montreal Light Infantry. After 11 years of service, he retired from the militia with the rank of captain. During those years he took part in a mining venture on the shores of Lake Huron. When it failed in 1851, he joined the Commercial Bank of Canada as manager of its Montreal branch. Five years later he married Louisa Fisher; he was transferred to the bank's head office in Kingston in the same year.

In the first half of the 19th century, "The Oregon Country" comprised Oregon, Idaho, Washington, and British Columbia. An 1818 treaty gave the U.S. and Great Britain joint occupancy of the land between 42°N latitude (the northern boundary of Spanish territory) and 54°40' (the southern boundary of Russian territory). In the 1830s and 40s American expansionists pressed to take over the whole area, by force if necessary. U.S. President James Polk negotiated a treaty with Great Britain in 1846 that set the 49th parallel as the shared boundary from the eastern border of Manitoba to the Pacific Ocean.

Archibald Hamilton Campbell

But greener fields beckoned and in 1866 Campbell left the bank to enter the lumber business in Peterborough. There he bought Nassau Mills, just north of the city where Trent University now stands. The following year, Nassau Mills produced 10 million feet of sawn lumber—20 percent of the total output of Peterborough County! The mills continued to thrive and in eight years he had amassed a fortune. He sold Nassau Mills and its timber limits and moved to Toronto.

In 1875, at age 56, he joined the Granite Club and also incorporated a new firm, the Muskoka Mill and Lumber Company, which obtained timber limits on a 300-square-mile tract on the Muskoka River. It was an expanse of virgin pine unequalled anywhere in Ontario. By 1893, the mill employed 150 men.

Two years after moving to Toronto, Campbell built a magnificent home in Queen's Park (demolished in 1932 to make way for the east wing of the Royal Ontario Museum). He called it *Carbrook*, after his family's county seat in Scotland.

The last 30 years of the 19th century was the era of the lumber barons and Campbell stood squarely in the vanguard of those entrepreneurs. He died at age 89, on June 3, 1909.

Robert Jaffray

ROBERT JAFFRAY was born a Scot in 1832 and, as one biographer rhapsodized, grew to manhood "near the celebrated battlefield where King Robert Bruce defeated the English army of invasion led by King Edward." At age 12, "he lost his father, a nail manufacturer, turned farmer, in a stagecoach accident" and, from that time, was forced to make his own way in the world. He worked for a few years as an apprentice to an Edinburgh grocer. Then, when he was 20, he immigrated to Toronto where he joined his sister's husband, John B. Smith, in a grocery and wine store on the west side of Yonge Street, south of Dundas. At the time it was the northernmost shop on Yonge. Five years later he became a partner in the business and in 1859, sole owner. Two years after that he married Mary Bugg, daughter of a Toronto alderman; they subsequently became parents of two sons and two daughters.

Jaffray expanded his business to include both wholesale and retail and, by the 1870s, he was a prosperous member of the business and political élite—respected not only for his business ability but also for his integrity. In 1874, Liberal Prime Minister Alexander Mackenzie asked him to become a director of the financially troubled Northern Railway Company, to "look after Canada's interests." Jaffray did so and still found time to become one of the Toronto Granite Curling Club's charter members the following year. He later became the club's seventh president in 1884–85.

By 1879 Jaffray had forged close political ties with fellow Reform Party stalwarts Oliver Mowat, premier of Ontario, and George Brown of the *Globe*, both of whom had been Fathers of Confederation. Together Jaffray, Mowat, and Brown wielded considerable influence, and thus were seen as tempting targets for a bizarre multiple kidnapping.

By an elaborate deception, brothers Thomas and Ross Dale lured the unsuspecting Jaffray to Playter's farm, near the Danforth, east of the Don River, where they planned to imprison him in a cave. But the 47-year-old Jaffray fought off his captors and raced to safety in a nearby farmhouse. The brothers were later apprehended; Thomas was convicted and sentenced to two years in jail, whereas Ross was discharged.

In the spring of the following year, George Brown, dying from an infected gunshot wound inflicted by a disgruntled employee,* appointed Jaffray as a director of the *Globe*. Two years after Brown died, Jaffray and financier George Albertus Cox bought a controlling interest in the paper. By 1888, Jaffray had gained control and appointed himself as president. He quickly became one of Canada's most respected press barons, tripling the paper's circulation during the 26 years he was its president.

Jaffray also served as president of the Toronto Real Estate Investment Company and as a director of a number of Canada's best-known firms including Toronto General Trusts, Sovereign Insurance Company, North American Life Insurance Company, Imperial Bank, Canada Life Assurance Company, Canadian General Electric, and Dominion Securities.

The Jaffray family controlled the Globe *for almost half a century until 1936, when George McCullough bought it and merged it with* The Mail and Empire.

*George Bennett, who at the time of the shooting was said to be "only semi-sober" was tried for murder, convicted, and hanged.

In 1906 Governor-General Earl Grey, in recognition of Jaffray's contribution to Canada, appointed him to the Senate, and in 1914, at age 82, he was named president of the Imperial Bank, succeeding his friend Daniel R. Wilkie who had died suddenly. A month later Jaffray himself fell ill and, for the first time in his life, a doctor was called to attend him, but Jaffray had suffered an aneurysm and died soon after. Among his pallbearers was Sir Wilfrid Laurier. In an editorial lamenting the death of its "Grand Old Man," the *Globe* recalled Jaffray's exhortation to his staff:

> Strive to find out what is right, and what is best for Canada. Then give that policy the very strongest support. Advocate it. Educate public opinion in favour of it. Urge it for adoption by the Liberal Party. But party or no party, if it ought to be adopted, let the *Globe* stand for it.

WILLIAM MELLIS CHRISTIE, another founding member, was a close friend of Jaffray. And yes, he *was* the man who "made good cookies." Christie began his baking career at age 14 in Aberdeenshire, Scotland. Fortunately, he kept a journal:

> 1843–12th Nov., I entered upon my apprenticeship to learn the art and mystery of baking. My pay was to be one pound sterling per year & a pair of boots…if I was a good good boy. I didn't get the boots.

William Mellis Christie

After a four-year apprenticeship and with few prospects, he immigrated to Canada. Within eight years of his arrival in Canada he had established his own bakery and by 1868 it had grown to the point where it required additional capital. His former employer, Alexander Brown, impressed with his young protegé, supplied the necessary financing and the partnership of Christie, Brown and Company was born. In 1874 they moved the bakery to the corner of Duke (now King) and

Frederick Streets and installed steam-powered machinery that allowed production to keep pace with the company's burgeoning sales. Soon the plant encompassed the entire block. This fine example of Victorian industrial architecture now serves as a branch of George Brown College, named after the man who was not only a Father of Confederation and owner and publisher of the *Globe*, but also a close friend of William Christie.

In 1878 Christie purchased Alexander Brown's interest and became sole owner of the company. Its name, however, remained the same—Christie, Brown and Company—perhaps symbolizing Christie's esteem for his former mentor, employer, and, for 10 years, partner.

In 1881 Christie, by then one of Toronto's wealthiest citizens, erected a magnificent Victorian home in Queen's Park. It was in striking contrast to the cramped quarters over the Yonge Street bakery where he, his wife, Mary Jane McMullen, and their four children had spent their first 15 years. The Christies were the first to build a home on Queen's Park Crescent and, when the legislative building was built a few years later, "the crescent…became a row of millionaires' homes and the park became the most fashionable area of Toronto."

Christie and Robert Jaffray were very close friends—so close that Christie named his only son Robert Jaffray Christie. In 1899, perhaps inspired by his friend's ownership of the *Globe*, Christie, in partnership with several prominent Liberals, bought *The Evening Star* (later *The Toronto Star*). They paid $32 000 for the enterprise, and hired Joseph E. Atkinson from the *Montreal Herald* as their editor.

As one of Toronto's leading citizens, Christie was a member of the board of trustees for the

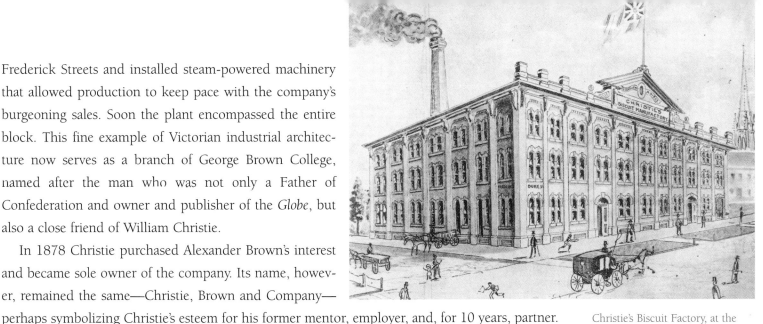

Christie's Biscuit Factory, at the corner of Duke (King) and Frederick in the late 1880's

William Christie's partners included Senator George Cox; Timothy Eaton; Lyman Jones, former president of A. Harris, Son and Co., before its merger with Massey Manufacturing in 1890; Salada Tea Company founder Peter Larkin; CPR contractor Plunkett Magann; lawyer E.T. Malone; Walter Massey, president of farm implement manufacturer Massey-Harris; and Postmaster General Sir William Mulock.

University of Toronto and a friend and confidant of Ontario's Premier Sir Oliver Mowat. At the official opening of the new Ontario legislature building in 1893, it was William Christie who, on behalf of the citizens of Toronto, presented a portrait of Mowat that still hangs there.

When Christie died on June 14, 1900, Christie, Brown and Company was worth $500 000 and employed 375 people. The company passed to William Christie's son, Robert Jaffray Christie who, 20 years later, sold it to Nabisco Brands Limited.

Among the charter members, JAMES DAVID EDGAR was unique. He was a true "Renaissance man"—poet, lawyer, journalist, businessman, author, politician, fervent patriot, and staunch Liberal. He was born in the Eastern Townships in 1841, a year after his parents had emigrated from Scotland, and received his early education in private schools there. After his father's death, he and two sisters moved with their mother to Woodbridge, Canada West (now Ontario). There he completed his schooling and went on to become a lawyer. Called to the bar in 1864 (QC 1890), he joined the firm of Samuel Henry Strong, but later left to begin his own practice, Edgar, Malone and Garvin, specializing in civil law.

His writing talent showed itself at an early age. At age 22, he was elected president of the Ontario Literary Society, and later of the Toronto Reform and Literary Debating Club. By the time he was 25 he had published three books (two on insolvency and one on contracts and real estate), and had been appointed legal editor of both the *Globe* and the *Montreal Trade Review*.

At age 24, Edgar married Matilda "Tillie" Ridout, U.E., a third-generation member of one of Toronto's "first families," granddaughter of Thomas Ridout (1754–1829), surveyor-general of Upper Canada (1810–29), and second daughter of Thomas Gibbs Ridout (1792–1861), general manager of the Bank of Upper Canada from 1822 to 1861.

Matilda Ridout Edgar was accomplished in her own right. At various times she was president of the National Council of Women, and of the Canadian Historical Association, and vice-president

James David Edgar

To celebrate Confederation, James Edgar's poem "This Canada of Ours" was set to music by E.H. Ridout, and, in 1884, at Toronto's semi-centennial, it was sung by massed choirs of school children. He published two books of poetry, plus a collection of literary sketches of political and social life in Ottawa. In recognition of all these accomplishments, Edgar was elected a Fellow of the Royal Society of Canada (FRSC) in 1897.

of the United Empire Loyalists Association. Nor was James the only writer in the family. In her mid-forties, after most of her children were grown, Matilda also became a published author. Her works include *Ten Years of Upper Canada in Peace and War* (1890), *General Brock* (1904), and *A Colonial Governor in Maryland* (1912).

James D. Edgar also enjoyed an impressive political career that began in 1867 when he was elected alderman in St. George's Ward. Five years later he won a seat in the House of Commons, acting in opposition as chief Liberal whip during the Pacific Scandal that led to the defeat of Sir John A. Macdonald's government in 1874. Edgar was elected again in 1884 and, the following year, he introduced copyright legislation in the Commons. He was persistent in his advocacy of the concept and his efforts were rewarded four years later when the Canadian Copyright Act became law. He was re-elected in 1887, 1891, and 1896, at which time Wilfrid Laurier appointed him Speaker of the House. In 1898, in spite of his long-held opposition to Canadians accepting Imperial titles, he became Sir James Edgar, Knight Commander of St. Michael and St. George (KCMG).

Simeon Heman Janes

SIMEON HEMAN JANES was born on a farm in Oxford County, Canada West, in 1843. His mother's family was New York Irish, his father's French Huguenot.* His paternal grandfather, a United Empire Loyalist, had fled to Canada after the American Revolution.

Janes moved to Toronto shortly after his marriage in 1867 and opened a retail dry-goods store on King Street. Four years later he became head of a wholesale dry-goods firm and held that position for eight years. While achieving success "in trade" Janes was also continuing his academic studies. He received his MA from Victoria College in 1872.

In 1879, discerning that the depression of 1873–80 was ending and that land could still be bought at "fire sale" prices, Janes turned his energies to real estate. A highly intelligent and daring

*In 1598, French King Henry of Navarre issued the Edict of Nantes granting freedom of religion to the Huguenot Protestants. When Louis XIV revoked the edict in l685, the Huguenots, fearing for their lives, fled to America, England, The Netherlands, and Prussia. Janes's ancestor chose Massachusetts.

Benevenuto, 1890

The Annex was given that name when the city of Toronto annexed the area in 1887.

*Janes's Benvenuto was demolished in 1931 to make way for an apartment building. All that remains is a bit of the garden wall, still visible on Edmund Avenue.

man, he purchased huge tracts of land in the city and, by adopting the business maxim "buy by the acre and sell by the foot," proceeded to subdivide them. As the population of Toronto exploded (it grew 64 percent between 1885 and 1895—from 97 000 to 159 000) the real estate market took off. By the time he was 54, the *Toronto World* declared him to be the "richest man in the city." His most ambitious project was the Annex, bounded by Avenue Road, Bathurst, Bloor, and Dupont streets. In 1887, he subdivided this area into more than 1 200 lots, and insisted on rigid building standards to ensure that the district would remain highly desirable.

Janes could spend money as well as make it. In 1890 he purchased a five and a half acre site on the west side of Avenue Road, at the top of the hill from Senator William McMaster. He then retained one of North America's leading architects, Stanford White of New York City, to design *Benvenuto*, the "most stately mansion ever erected in the city."* To remember Simeon Janes only as a businessman and land developer would overlook a great deal. Well educated, well read, and a wise observer of people and events, he took his responsibilities as a citizen seriously. He was much in demand as a public speaker and was a prolific contributor to the periodical press of the day. When the Conservatory of Music was founded in 1886, Janes was one of its first directors, along with fellow Granite Club member William B. McMurrich. He established the Janes Scholarship at the Conservatory and endowed several medals at Victoria College for competitions in philosophy, mathematics, modern languages, and the classics. He was also vice-president of Whitby Ladies' College. Throughout his life he was a patron of education and the arts. Even in death he was munificent, bequeathing his collections of classical vases and European tapestries to the Royal Ontario Museum. He was, in the words of historian Jesse Middleton, "a lover of the beautiful, and deeply appreciative of the best in art."

Simeon Janes was 69 when he died of a stroke while vacationing in England. His lasting monument is the Annex, with its handsome homes and dignified avenues—Madison, Huron, and St. George. A century later, it remains—a model urban community.

BROTHERS ALEXANDER AND STEPHEN NAIRN were among the Scots who came to Canada to make their fortune. In 1858, 26-year-old Alexander settled in Rockwood, Wellington County, opened a general store, and worked as a grain commission merchant. In 1863 his younger brother, Stephen, joined him. During the next two years they added a farm, a flour mill, and a sawmill to their holdings.

In 1874 the brothers moved to Toronto where they established A. and S. Nairn, wharfingers and coal merchants, and built one of the finest wharfs in the city, known as the Nairn Docks. They also joined the newly formed Toronto Granite Curling Club, becoming two of its first 30 members. Alexander and his wife, Elizabeth Ann, lived in a handsome Victorian home on the east side of Jarvis Street between Carlton and Wellesley. Typical of the architectural style of the 1870s, it was a large rambling house with a covered verandah that stretched across the front and along its south side.

Ten years after arriving in Toronto, the Nairn brothers dissolved their partnership. Alexander retired, but retained ownership of a group of flour, saw, and woollen mills, and continued as a director of several other companies. Stephen, then in his mid-forties, moved to Winnipeg and

Alexander Nairn

opened the first oatmeal mill in that province. Oatmeal being a staple food for the many Scots in Manitoba, the company prospered. He became president of the Winnipeg Grain Exchange in 1896 and, two years later, sold his thriving business to the Ogilvy Milling Company.

Alexander Nairn became vice-president of the Granite Club in 1885. It had been the custom since the club was founded that the vice-president of one year became president the next. Nairn, absent in Scotland in 1886, missed his chance and never did assume the office.

JAMES H. RICHARDSON was one of the few professionals and the only doctor among the charter members. At 54, he was also one of the oldest. He also had the distinction of being the only known "rebel" among the group. He was still a student in 1837 when William Lyon Mackenzie's armed rebellion ended in failure, and he and a fellow student, Henry Hoover Wright, played key roles in helping their beloved professor, Dr. John Rolph, a volatile and vocal supporter of William Lyon Mackenzie, escape to the United States. During the excitement of the rebellion, Wright witnessed the arrest of another prominent physician and alleged rebel, Dr. T.D. Morrison. Wright told Richardson and together they rushed to warn Rolph. With no time to spare, one rode Rolph's horse west along Dundas Street while the other accompanied Rolph on foot, walking quietly but purposefully along Lot Street (now Queen) to their agreed rendez-vous at the edge of town. There, Rolph mounted his horse and raced to safety in the United States. A few days later, Lieutenant-Governor Francis Bond Head proclaimed a reward of £500 for the apprehension of the "traitorous John Rolph."

Rolph settled in Rochester, New York, where he continued teaching medicine; Richardson and Wright followed him into exile to continue their studies. After the amnesty of 1843, all three returned to Toronto.* Richardson continued his studies at Guy's Hospital, London, where he earned his MRCS (Member of the Royal College of Surgeons). He returned to Toronto and became

James H. Richardson

Soon after Rolph's return to Toronto, he founded "Rolph's School," which in 1853 was incorporated as the "Toronto School of Medicine." He died in 1870.

Professor of Anatomy at both the University of Toronto and the Toronto School of Medicine—positions he was to hold for 40 years. The doctor has a place in Canadian medical history for performing one of the last operations in the country without the use of anesthetic at the old Toronto General Hospital on King Street.

When not in the operating room or classroom, Richardson was a keen outdoorsman, with a particular love for yachting, curling, lawn bowling, and fishing. He fished in streams from Cape Breton to Lake Superior.

Later in life, as well as being a distinguished professor and medical practitioner, Dr. Richardson, like many of his contemporaries, became involved in land development. He opened up Toronto's Isabella Street, naming it after his daughter, Mrs. Isabella Roaf. Richardson himself lived at 36 St. Joseph Street, an easy walk to the Granite Club, first on St. Mary Street, and later when it moved to its new quarters on Church Street.

When he died in 1912, FREDERICK WYLD was an octogenarian, married to the same woman for more than 60 years, and a partner in a prosperous dry-goods business for half a century. Born in Scotland, he apprenticed with an Edinburgh woollen merchant before moving, still in his teens, to Canada. He settled first in Norfolk County, Ontario, where he met and married Maria Louisa, daughter of Hugh Massey Barrett. At age 22, he entered the wholesale dry-goods trade in partnership with Henry Darling under the company name Wyld & Darling, in Hamilton. After 18 years, they moved to Toronto. In spite of the recession of the 1870s, the energetic Wyld and his partner Darling flourished for the next 32 years, until the fire of 1904—one of the worst in the city's history—destroyed their business.

Frederick Wyld was 72 and probably did not have the stamina to start again. That is not to say that he retired to a rocking chair—he remained actively engaged in other business, social, and

Frederick Wyld

philanthropic affairs. He was vice-president of Confederation Life and The Standard Bank, and a director of many large corporations, including Canada Permanent Mortgage Corporation, Toronto General Trusts, and the King Edward Hotel.

Philanthropically he endowed the Frederick Wyld Scholarships in English at the University of Toronto and in Latin at St. Andrew's College. An active member of St. James' Cathedral, he contributed liberally to it and many other charities.

Frederick Wyld died on August 26, 1912, survived by his wife and daughter. Historian J.E. Middleton was lavish in his praise:

> Mr. Wyld was…a successful merchant of rare merit…. His association with any company [was] almost a guarantee of its success and prosperity…. Over four-score years of life…there extended an influence and example that was a potent force for righteous and effective living, conspicuous for high-minded citizenship.

CHAPTER ONE

IN THE BEGINNING

1875

THE TORONTO GRANITE CURLING CLUB had its modest beginnings in 1875. At the time, there were three curling clubs in the city: the Caledonian Skating and Curling Club, the Dominion of Canada Four Brothers Curling Club, and the Toronto Curling Club. Times were tough. The Panic of 1873 in New York City had led to a continent-wide economic collapse that lasted seven years. Feelings were running high; as late as 1878 the city was still suffering. "We have all felt…the depression," complained one Toronto citizen, in a letter to *The Evening Telegram*. "The large number of vacant stores in the city tell a melancholy tale…not less than a hundred on Queen Street alone."

But, despite the sluggish economy of 1875, several members of the venerable Toronto Curling Club (founded in 1836), generally unhappy with the way their club was being run and, in particular, with its plan to build a lavish enclosed rink on Adelaide Street West, decided to take action.

The word "rink" has three meanings in curling. The first is the ice surface on which games are played (the space where one game is played is called a "sheet"). The second is the building that houses the ice surface. And the third is the name used to designate the four members of a curling team.

"Curling match at Linlithgow Castle"

Early Canadian curlers often played on Toronto's frozen bay, much as their Scottish counterparts played on rivers in the "Old Country"

Bloor Street, just a dirt road at the time, was the northern boundary of Toronto. The principal "downtown" residential area was south of Queen Street, just east of the business district on Duke and Duchess Streets (now Adelaide and Richmond Streets East). As the population grew, homes and businesses spread northwards on Yonge, Teraulay (now Bay), Church, Jarvis, and Sherbourne Streets— towards the "uptown" area, south of Bloor.

Curling pioneers in Ontario first used curling "stones" carved from maple or beech, banded with iron to provide the appropriate weight. Granite, readily available from the Canadian Shield, soon replaced wood. By 1839 granite stones were being advertised in Toronto at $8 a pair. Later in the nineteenth century stones were imported from Ailsa Craig in Scotland, renowned for its fine quality granite.

They were businessman Robert Carrie, banker Thomas McCraken, solicitor and local politician William Barclay McMurrich, land developer William Bain Scarth, and realtor James Lamond Smith. These five met on a warm summer day—June 30—and resolved to found a new curling club. It would be located "uptown," unlike the other three curling clubs in the city, all of which had their rinks downtown close to Lake Ontario where members often curled on the frozen bay. The founders decided to call their new club the Toronto Granite Curling Club after the granite that was, and still is, the rugged rock from which curling stones are made. All five would form the steering committee, with Smith serving as president, McCraken as vice-president, and Scarth as secretary-treasurer of the new club. Soon they were joined by another local politician, John Turner, and by lumber baron Archibald Hamilton Campbell. In December, two more were added: barrister

William Davidson and miller Alexander Nairn. The office of secretary-treasurer was then split, with Davidson becoming secretary and Scarth remaining as treasurer.

One of the first orders of business was to find and appoint a distinguished patron. An obvious choice was Sir John A. Macdonald. In 1873 Macdonald had moved to Toronto to distance himself from affairs of state following the resignation of his government precipitated by the Pacific Railway Scandal.* He practised law from an office in York Chambers in the Trust and Loan Building on Toronto Street and commuted to Ottawa whenever his presence there as opposition leader was required.

Sir John A. Macdonald, First Granite Club Patron

When approached (probably by his friend Scarth), Macdonald accepted the club's offer. And so, Canada's first prime minister (and its most famous Scotsman) became the Granite Club's first honorary patron. About the same time, Reverend R.D. Fraser was named honorary chaplain. Club records don't reveal just how long that position lasted, but it certainly does not exist today.

The steering committee wasted no time in getting on with club business. They chose a site—two lots at the southeast corner of Chapel Street and St. Mary Street, a block east of North Street (now Bay Street) and just west of one of the city's two reservoirs. The reservoir was "fifty square feet in area and surrounded by a high bank and picket fence." Chapel Street no longer exists, and the reservoir is also long since gone.

*Alexander Mackenzie's Liberals took over after Macdonald's government resigned, in 1873 and called an election. When the dust settled, Liberals outnumbered Conservatives two to one. In a letter to W.B. Scarth, Macdonald commented: "The next best thing to winning is to be thoroughly beaten." During Mackenzie's five-year reign Macdonald reorganized his party. When the 1878 election was called he had a slate of worthy candidates and a two-pronged platform for prosperity: a transcontinental railway and a National Policy of high tariffs to encourage the growth of Canadian manufacturing. He not only won that election, but held on to power until he died.

Toronto, 1878 (from Bloor to Queen and from St. George to Church Streets). Granite Rink is near the top, between St. Mary and St. Joseph Streets

By November of that first year, a five-year lease for the land had been signed and a contract let to build the rink and clubhouse—all for $700. The property was levelled and fenced and a T-shaped building erected. The stem of the T stretched south to house the two sheets of curling ice, and the crossbar on the north, fronting on St. Mary Street, served as the clubhouse. It was no beauty. Built of rough and unpainted pine boards, it still managed to serve its purpose. In those days avid curlers just wanted sheltered ice on which to play and outhouses "for the comfort of the members." Weather permitting, the newly levelled land on three sides of the curling shed could be flooded for outdoor skating.

All was ready for the 1875–76 season. The operation was quite informal. Each player simply contributed 10 cents a night to pay for the flaring gas lights that illuminated the ice, and each brought his own bottle, the fiery contents of which, it was said, "had the smell of the rafters."

The club opened with 30 members. More than half were born in Scotland. It therefore seems fitting that it was on Robbie Burns' birthday, January 25, that they established an *ad hoc* committee to draft the club's constitution and bylaws. They also chose a date—the fifth day of February—for the first Annual Club Day, at which the "Old Countrymen" would challenge the "Canadians."

The Canadians triumphed, defeating the Scots 37 rocks to 32. After the match, at the Rising Sun Hotel at 666 Yonge Street, victors and vanquished sat down to the traditional curling dinner of "beef and greens and bannocks...delicious mince collops and the stomach-trying haggis...with some pretty, tiny, kickshaws thereafter to fill up, as it were, the interstices of appetite."* Scottish beer in stone bottles and "'alf and 'alf" in pewter mugs helped wash it all down. Some years later James Hedley reminisced:

> A memorial of this first convivial gathering exists—it is pasted inside the back cover of the little, thin, ecclesiastical-looking black volume that contains the early minutes of the club.... To the credit of the diners it may be noted that, on the authority of the minutes, the members partook of the annual dinner, and *afterward* performed the business of the annual meeting, adopting unanimously the constitution submitted.

**Bannock is unleavened flat bread, round or oval; a collop is a slice of meat; and a kickshaw (from the French, quelque chose) is a sweet fancy dish in cookery.*

999 Queen Street West, Provincial Lunatic Asylum. From a sketch by John Howard

To close this memorable evening, someone sang "Hurrah for the Thistle," and all joined in the chorus until the ceiling shook. Next came a toast to "Auld Scotia, the Mither of Us A'," and finally, "Auld Lang Syne," with cross hands all around.

By 1875, Toronto had been a city for only 40 years and Canada a country for only eight. Since its inception, Toronto had been a very Tory town. (When Charles Dickens visited in 1867, he found its "wild and rabid Toryism...appalling.") Its population of 69 000 included 240 lawyers—one for every 288 inhabitants! There were almost 100 churches and more than 600 liquor outlets. "There is no city on the continent," thundered a newspaper of the day, "pestered by so many saloons and taverns."

When the Granite Club's modest quarters appeared, the city was, despite the depression, bustling with activity, and already there were a number of large and impressive buildings distinguishing it. St. Lawrence Hall was, by this time, a stately 25-year-old. The enterprising Timothy

244 Yonge Street in 1883. Robert Jaffray's retail grocery store

Eaton had opened his first Toronto store in 1869 and was now facing stiff competition from another merchant, Robert Simpson, whose store had appeared in 1872.

Architect John G. Howard had just deeded to the city his 120-acre sheep farm, now known as High Park, a gift that John Ross Robertson, *The Evening Telegram's* owner, called the "most munificent…ever made by a private individual to the public in Upper Canada."*

*John G. Howard designed several fine buildings: his home, Colborne Lodge, that still stands on a knoll in High Park overlooking Lake Ontario; St. John's Anglican Church in York Mills; and the Provincial Lunatic Asylum at 999 Queen Street West (demolished in 1976), which historian Donald Jones called the "greatest building Howard created." Built of bricks from the "famous blue clay that was once found at the top of Yonge Street south of St. Clair," it was immense, causing one waggish American reporter to comment that the "largest building in Upper Canada was a mental asylum."

By 1889, the total number of letters delivered each year exceeded three million. This did not include books, packages, circulars, postcards, or newspapers. Toronto's first telephone book, issued on June 8, 1879, by the Toronto Telephone Dispatch Company, contained forty names. Ontario Premier Oliver Mowat was the first customer, with phones connecting his law offices on Front Street West to the Ontario Legislature.

Also in 1875, Mrs. F.S. McMaster and her friends were about to open the Hospital for Sick Children, an 11-room, three-storey house occupying part of the site of today's Toronto Hospital. Because it was devoted entirely to the care of children, the hospital was unique in North America. And perhaps at the very moment that some of the first curling stones were roaring down the two sheets of Granite ice, the illuminated tower clock of St. James' Cathedral lit up for the first time— "a beacon at night to mariners coming to our port." In that same year, the first service was held at Jarvis Street Baptist Church; Knox College, that splendid example of Gothic Revival architecture, moved to its new home at 1 Spadina Circle; Woodbine racetrack opened; regular mail delivery began; and regular phone service was only two or three years away.

CHAPTER TWO

THE CLUB THAT DICK BUILT

1879 - 1889

IN THE WINTER OF 1879–80, two Granite Club skips,* W.G.P. Cassels and William Badenach, challenged each other to a series of curling matches; the loser would host a members' beer and oyster party. Cassels' team lost, and, on March 11, 1880, members arrived at his home for a dinner meeting.

During the evening they discussed the club's lease. It was due to expire and the landlord intended to increase the rent. Also on the agenda was the burgeoning membership—there were now 80—and the obvious need for a larger clubhouse with more sheets of curling ice. They all agreed that better facilities would, without doubt, attract more members. And so, that very evening, these enthusiasts formed a joint stock company and subscribed an impressive $12 000 in capital—an amount later increased to $50 000.

A skip is the captain of a team of four players.

Toronto's population grew rapidly throughout the 1880s. In 1881 it was 77 000; in 1885, it had reached 105 000. By 1890, it stood at 160 000, more than double that of ten years earlier.

The Reciprocity Treaty of 1854 removed customs duties on "grain, flour, breadstuffs, animals, meats, fish, poultry, fruit, tallow, coal, timber, and lumber." After its termination in 1866, despite many attempts to re-establish free trade, protective tariffs returned. In 1911 Canadian Finance Minister Fielding and U.S. President Taft worked out a free trade agreement in farm products and low tariffs on manufactured goods. The agreement was the main issue in the 1911 general election defeat of the Liberal government of Sir Wilfrid Laurier. Over fifty years passed before the Auto Pact; the elimination of remaining tariffs didn't come until 1989.

Within days the new company had purchased property on the east side of Church Street north of Wellesley. Directors were elected, and when the new rink was completed in time for the 1880–81 season, their names were emblazoned in gold letters carved on a red granite slab mounted on the wall:

GRANITE RINK—erected 1880

Directors

William Ramsay, *president*

D.M. McEwen, *vice-president*

William Badenach, *secretary*

Alex Nairn, W.F. Davison, R.K. Burgess, W.R. Taylor, R.H. Bethune,
W.G.P. Cassels, J. Carlyle, M.D.

Norman B. Dick, *architect.*

Contractors: J.L. Thompson, Crany and Harris.

The move to Church Street coincided with the end of the severe and prolonged depression of the 1870s and Toronto was poised to embark upon a decade of population growth, industrial expansion, technological innovation, and financial prosperity. The fledgling club would share in much of this good fortune.

In the five years that the club had been on St. Mary Street, the city's population had increased to over 75 000. The tariff of 1879 was helping promote the growth of large-scale manufacturing in Central Canada, and was drawing in American capital. New industries sprung up and existing businesses expanded. The number of industrial establishments in the city was increasing at an astonishing rate. Hart Massey moved his farm equipment company from Newcastle, Ontario, to Toronto. Lumbering operations in the Ottawa Valley, Georgian Bay, Muskoka, and the Kawarthas were also bringing great wealth to their Toronto owners. According to journalist Dean Beeby, 1880 was a watershed year—the beginning of the "transformation from a commerce and resource-based economy with small, dispersed, and water-powered factories into a modern manufacturing base, powered by steam and electricity."

Post-secondary education also took a major step forward when the Toronto Baptist College opened on Bloor Street West in 1881. Its founder and benefactor, William McMaster, had been the first president of the Bank of Canada (later named the Canadian Bank of Commerce). He died in 1887, leaving the college $900 000. In recognition of his gift, it was renamed McMaster University.

The area surrounding the Granite Club's new home—upper Jarvis and Church Streets—was rapidly becoming Toronto's most fashionable residential district. Originally granted as "park lots" to William Jarvis, the first Provincial Secretary of Upper Canada (1791–1817), and John McGill by John Graves Simcoe back in 1793, most of this land had been purchased in 1847 from S.F. Jarvis by Toronto's wealthiest citizen, William Cawthra. And, as birds of a feather, other rich and powerful men—Hart Massey, the Gooderhams, Senator William McMaster, politicians Oliver Mowat and Edward Blake, stockbrokers John Blaikie and William Alexander, and merchant John Snarr—flocked to the area to build their mansions. Snarr and his wife Emma bought land at the southeast corner of Church Street and Cawthra Avenue (now Monteith Street). The land that the Granite Club purchased was just south of the Snarrs on Church Street, a hundred-foot frontage occupied by the greenhouses and forcing beds of market gardener and florist John Ross.

In a sporting sense, as well as residentially, the second Granite Club was in good company. Seven years earlier the neighbourhood had become the centre for what was then Canada's national sport—lacrosse. Cawthra had generously given the Toronto Lacrosse Club access to the block between Wellesley and Gloucester Streets, west of Jarvis. (Toronto's first professional baseball team

McMaster University was a Baptist institution and therefore precluded by church laws from accepting state aid of any kind. It didn't enter into federation with the University of Toronto as did St. Michael's College (1881), Victoria College (1890), and Trinity College (1904). When McMaster University moved to Hamilton in 1930, its building on Bloor Street was purchased by the University of Toronto as home to its Department of Economics and Political Science. The building was taken over by the Royal Conservatory of Music in 1963.

Cawthra Avenue, originally a private lane, was named by the developer who built the 18 three-storey row houses on its north side in 1887–88. They were working-class homes but have now been upgraded to fashionable dwellings. The street name was changed to Mulock Street in 1897 and to Monteith Street in 1909. Roy Thompson (later newspaper magnate Lord Thompson of Fleet) was born in 1894 at 32 Cawthra Avenue—the son of a barber.

Jarvis Street lacrosse grounds, 1876

The lacrosse field measured 190' x 100' and on its west side Cawthra built a 2000-seat grandstand gaily decorated with a multitude of flags. The first game played on the new field was between the Tecumsehs and the Young Indians for the Junior Lacrosse Championship of Ontario. The Tecumsehs won. Several years later Alexander Street Baptist Church acquired the property and erected Emmanuel Baptist Church.

also played there, the opening game taking place on June 15, 1885.)

Club member and architect Norman Bethune Dick had been given the task of designing the Granite Club's new home. And what a home it was—two-storey red brick, 180 feet in depth, an "exuberant Renaissance Revival building,"—the epitome of Victorian grandeur. *Saturday Night* magazine described it as "handsome, commodious, costly, and artistically oriented." A 70' x 100' barrel-vaulted rink stretched out behind the clubhouse and housed four sheets of curling ice. The building also accommodated a number of clubrooms. Whenever the Union Jack flew atop the high, square, central tower of the club, it was a signal to members that there was ice that day for skating and curling.

In September 1880, the Granite Curling and Skating Company (for that was the name given to the new joint stock company) assumed all the assets and liabilities of the Toronto Granite Curling Club. And so began a new *modus operandi* between what were to be known, from that time on, as the "company" and the "club." The company was the proprietary body, controlling the purse strings, owning the land, the building, and the chattels, and bearing the responsibility for their maintenance, while the club's mandate was the management of curling activities. An agreement between the two was adopted and included such items as how ice time would be allotted between curling and skating and the amount of "rent" that the club would pay the company for the use of its facilities. This arrangement created a flexible structure that could accommodate various sporting activities without requiring the support of members who were not participants.

A membership committee composed of three members from the company and two from the club was established. W.G.P. Cassels and Robert Jaffray were the first two elected by the club to serve on it.

In some ways the club's current organization resembles the 1880 one, except the sections were known as clubs, and conveners were called presidents. Most if not all of the officers and directors of the company were drawn from the leadership of the curling club. In any event, as far as the public was concerned, it was still the Toronto Granite Curling Club, albeit at a new site.

Another difference between then and now is that skips in those early days did not hold that position for life. They were elected annually! The 16 skips chosen in 1880 were Badenach, Bethune, J.L. Brodie, Josiah Bruce, Carlyle, Cassels, Davison, James Hedley, Jaffray, Thomas McCraken, McEwan, Alex Nairn, Ramsay, Dr. Richardson, Lamond Smith, and Taylor.*

Cold weather, of course, was essential to the club's curling operations. There was no such thing as artificial ice in those days, and ice making was uncertain and difficult. The poor, long-suffering ice man would sit up night after night, waiting for the temperature to drop. When it did, he would

Granite Club on Church Street

*As club membership grew, so did the number of skips. In 1884 there were 20; 1886–24; 1887–32; 1889–40.

NORMAN BETHUNE DICK'S biography is brief, for he died when he was just 35. Canadian born, he was the son of Great Lakes steamboat captain James Dick. Just 24 in 1884, Norman Dick was the youngest of all the skips elected that year. In addition to being an ardent curler, he was also an enthusiastic sailor.

At an early age Norman decided that architecture would be his chosen field, and, almost as if he had a premonition that his life would be a fleeting one, he set out to make his mark. He studied first with Toronto architects, Smith and Gemmell. Then, in rapid succession he gained experience with architectural firms in Cleveland, Ohio, Kingston, Ontario, and Saint John, New Brunswick, returning to Toronto in 1879. He must have had an impressive portfolio by that time for he convinced the Granite Club directors to retain him as architect for their new clubhouse. He was just 20 years old. Six years later he played vice-skip (third player) on C.C. Dalton's first Tankard-winning rink.

He remained in private practice until his death 11 years later. After finishing the Granite Club he was chosen as architect for the Victoria Curling Rink at 277 Huron Street (1887; demolished 1962) and the Academy of Music, a 2000-seat theatre and music hall at 165–173 King Street (1889). That same year he became a founding member of the Ontario Association of Architects and a year later he entered into partnership with Frank A. Wickson. They had first met some 15 years before as students in the offices of Smith and Gemmell. Together they designed Olivet Congregational Church (1890) on the northeast corner of Hazelton and Scollard in Yorkville, and Oddfellows' Hall (1891–92) on the northwest corner of College and Yonge. The first Olivet Church, a wooden structure built in 1876 was moved north to make room for Dick & Wickson's splendid new red-brick edifice. The old wood church was later occupied by the Toronto Heliconian Club, a women's arts and letters organization. Norman Dick died in 1895.

throw open the large doors of the rink, don his leather gloves and high rubber boots, and begin sprinkling the floor of the rink with water, adding a little more each time as it froze, until the necessary ice thickness was achieved. Then, using warm water from a watering can, he would "pebble" the surface to produce a beautiful checkerboard appearance. Ice making in the 19th century was not only hard work, it was also an art.

For reasons lost in time, the floor of the curling rink was about twelve inches lower than the outdoor ice used for skating. According to the lore in the Francis family, who were members at the time, on cold days when the big doors of the rink were opened to admit the frigid outside air, young skaters would take great delight in skating full speed through the doors of the rink, taking off in the air like ski jumpers and landing heavily on the curling ice. Needless to say, this did nothing to improve the pebble on the ice nor, one might add, the tempers of the curlers.

Toronto's electrical era began in 1882 when young Henry Pellatt, chairman of the Electric Development Corporation, demonstrated the revolutionary new electric arc light at the Toronto Industrial Exhibition. Two years later the whole of the exhibition was lit by electricity and, for the first time, remained open in the evenings. That same year Canada's first electric railway was demonstrated on a half-mile route along Strachan Avenue to the Exhibition; 10 years later electric streetcars started to replace horse-drawn cars. In 1883 Eaton's installed its first elevator and Sir Sandford Fleming's revolutionary concept of Standard Time was adopted by the City of Toronto—but it would take 10 more years for all other countries to follow suit. Gas lights, which had made their appearance on Toronto streets in 1842, were replaced by the first electric arc lights at King and Yonge. Two years later the Granite Club, ever in the vanguard of progress, converted from gas to electricity. The light flooding from the large windows of the Granite Rink was another reminder to the homeward-bound curler in his horse-drawn carriage: "There is ice tonight."

The club's first winter on Church Street was crisp and cold. The next two years, however, were mild—disastrous for curlers and skaters. Happily, for the following five years, Mother Nature smiled

Toronto's first gas lamp was lit on December 28, 1841, to commemorate the birth of Edward, Prince of Wales (later King Edward VII).

WALTER GIBSON PRINGLE CASSELS, QC, was one of 14 children, the fourth son of banker Robert Cassels and Mary Gibbons McNab. He was born in Quebec City in 1845. Graduating from the University of Toronto in 1865, he decided that law was his field and four years later was called to the bar. He then joined the firm of Blake, Kerr & Boyd (later Blake, Lash, Anglin & Cassels; today Blake, Cassels & Graydon) and soon became one of the luminaries of the Ontario bar. In 1873 he married Susan Hamilton, daughter of Robert Hamilton, chancellor of Bishop's College, and they had two sons and four daughters.

He was created a Queen's Counsel in 1883 and was called to the Exchequer Court of Canada in 1908. The Exchequer Court of Canada was replaced by the Federal Court of Canada in 1971. He later became its President and Chief Justice. King George V honoured him with the rank of Knight Bachelor in 1917.

The *Globe* described him as "intelligent, painstaking, and upright" and the *Toronto News* as "a kindly, courteous, self-respecting gentleman, with the manners of the old school." He died in 1923 and is buried in the family plot in St. James Cemetery, Toronto. On hearing of Cassels' death, Sir William Meredith, Chief Justice of Ontario and Chancellor of the University of Toronto, told the *Globe:*

> I knew him very well. He was an able lawyer and an excellent Judge, and a man who was much respected by his professional brethren and by all who knew him. I consider his death to be a distinct loss to the community.

on the club, and only one winter was said to be mild. Aided by such good weather conditions membership soared. Large as it was, the new clubhouse could not accommodate this growth in membership. And so, in 1884, to provide additional space for its activities, the club purchased the home of broker B.F. Bostwick immediately to the south. By 1885, the Granite had 447 members, making it the largest curling club in Canada. (Curling throughout the city also prospered, with four additional clubs being formed during the 10 years after the Granite Club was founded.)

Granite curlers on the "Old Rink," 1884. The composite photograph was created by club member Josiah Bruce and donated to the club by Walter G.P. Cassels and Robert Jaffray

The Annual Meeting on March 28, 1884, with the club's sixth president W.G.P. Cassels in the chair, was a particularly lively one. Business was booming; the club was prosperous; and everyone was in a happy and expansive frame of mind. This was the event at which Cassels and Robert Jaffray (who took over the presidency the following year) presented the photograph of the 1884 Granite curlers. The wonderful composite picture was photographed and assembled by Josiah Bruce, a club member who had worked with the celebrated William Notman in Montreal. The picture hung originally in the parlour at the Church Street club, and was one of the few items to survive the 1913 fire that destroyed the main clubhouse.

In 1884, as an excited Toronto staged its semi-centennial celebrations, club charter member William McMurrich found himself back doing what he most enjoyed. The festivities began on June 30, with a spectacular parade. Cheering Torontonians lined the streets as marching bands

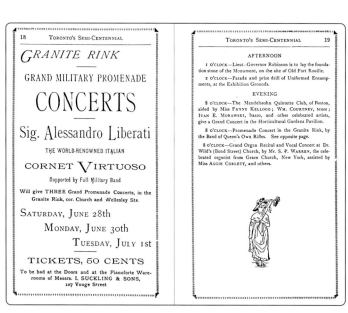

GRANITE RINK

GRAND MILITARY PROMENADE

CONCERTS

Sig. Alessandro Liberati

THE WORLD-RENOWNED ITALIAN

CORNET VIRTUOSO

Supported by Full Military Band

Will give THREE Grand Promenade Concerts, in the
Granite Rink, cor. Church and Wellesley Sts.

SATURDAY, JUNE 28th

MONDAY, JUNE 30th

TUESDAY, JULY 1st

TICKETS, 50 CENTS

To be had at the Doors and at the Pianoforte Ware-
rooms of Messrs. I. SUCKLING & SONS,
107 Yonge Street

AFTERNOON

1 O'CLOCK—Lieut.-Governor Robinson is to lay the foundation stone of the Monument, on the site of Old Fort Rouillé.

2 O'CLOCK—Parade and prize drill of Uniformed Encamp-
ments, at the Exhibition Grounds.

EVENING

8 O'CLOCK—The Mendelssohn Quintette Club, of Boston,
aided by Miss FANNY KELLOGG; WM. COURTNEY, tenor;
IVAN E. MORAWSKI, basso, and other celebrated artists,
give a Grand Concert in the Horticultural Gardens Pavilion.

8 O'CLOCK—Promenade Concert in the Granite Rink, by
the Band of Queen's Own Rifles. See opposite page.

8 O'CLOCK—Grand Organ Recital and Vocal Concert at Dr.
Wild's (Bond Street) Church, by Mr. S. P. WARREN, the cele-
brated organist from Grace Church, New York, assisted by
Miss AGGIE CORLETT, and others.

Mowat served as premier of Ontario for 24 consecutive years and was knighted by Queen Victoria in 1892. He left the premier's office four years later to enter the Senate; in 1897 he became lieutenant-governor of Ontario. The Mowat Block of the Ontario Government offices is named in his honour. The handsome Mowat Cup, donated by the premier in 1879, is still on display in a trophy case at the club.

and elaborate floats—some towering 20 feet—passed in splendour. Each float celebrated a portion of Toronto's history—wigwams, the British occupation, early settlers, the landing of Lieutenant-Governor Simcoe, the naming of York Harbour, the first parliament, and Toronto's incorporation. Politicians and other public officials were front and centre. They were followed by firemen, the York Pioneers, and several distinguished elderly citizens including theologian and historian Dr. Henry Scadding, and Alexander Muir, composer of "The Maple Leaf Forever." At the Granite Club rink the band of the Queen's Own Rifles offered three Promenade Concerts—50 cents admission.

Later that same year, Ontario Premier Oliver Mowat,* champion of provincial rights during his past 12 years in power, pulled off a colossal coup. He had pleaded before the Privy Council in Great Britain that Ontario's boundaries be extended to include the northern territories. And he had won. The federal government was furious. On his triumphant return from England Mowat was met at Union Station by a mob of some 5000 people who escorted him through cheering crowds to Queen's Park. A grand banquet in his honour was held that evening at the Granite Club. Federal Liberal leader Edward Blake presided, with Oliver Mowat seated on his right and Honoré Mercier, Liberal leader for Quebec (and its premier in 1887) on his left.

Across the country, the driving of the last spike in 1885 marked the completion of the first trans-Canada railway, the Canadian Pacific, and the opening up of the West. Tens of thousands of immigrants, every one of them needing goods and services, flooded in. And, indicative of the importance of the game of curling in those days, the Canadian Pacific Railway even offered curlers a rate reduction of two cents a mile when travelling to and from bonspiels.

Because curling was strictly a winter sport, it wasn't long before Granite members began looking for summer pastimes to introduce into the club. By 1882, members began to make use of the level grassy area behind the clubhouse for tennis. The club purchased the necessary equipment, and the sport was open to all members for a small fee. Interest in the game grew rapidly and members soon expressed the desire for a more formal organization. And so in 1884 the Granite Lawn Tennis Club was formed. Harry Suckling was its first secretary, but soon afterwards he moved to Montreal and was replaced by R.J. Tackaberry.

Tennis field, Granite Club, Church St.

The first recorded meeting of the new tennis club was on May 2, 1885, when 20 members met and elected a six-member committee: C.C. Dalton as president; George S. Crawford as vice-president; R.J. Tackaberry as secretary-treasurer; Walter Gibbs as captain; plus committee members William Badenach and A. Ford. Gibbs had just arrived from England and was an experienced and enthusiastic tennis player. He was the obvious choice as captain. It was, of course, still a men's club but lady friends of members were allowed to use the courts from 10:00 a.m. to 2:00 p.m.—a time when the courts were, in all likelihood, unoccupied by members.

It was not long before the Granite Lawn Tennis Club boasted a membership of fifty, and officers and members donated prizes for competitions—medals, a cup, a *meerschaum* pipe, and several tennis racquets. At the May 1885 meeting a tournament was planned for Dominion Day (now Canada Day) and club colours were adopted—yellow, bright red, and navy blue.

By 1886, with tennis club membership still growing, the lawn tennis committee was enlarged from six members to ten. George S. Crawford moved up to president; G.W. Meyer became

Tennis goes back to a handball game played in ancient Greece. By the 11th century it was popular in France and, by the 16th, the racquet and the rope net had been invented, and royal, or court tennis began indoors. Tennis crossed the English Channel and, a few centuries later, was adapted for outdoor play and renamed lawn tennis. The first lawn tennis match took place in Wales in 1873. Torontonians promptly adopted the new game and, in 1875 the Toronto Lawn Tennis Club was formed. The first Wimbledon championship was played in 1877.

CHARLES C. DALTON, the skip who shared the Tankard laurels with Badenach, was a successful businessman whose firm, Dalton Bros., manufactured soap and milled coffee and spices. He was also a director of the Imperial Loan and Investment Co. Limited. He was elected the club's ninth president for the year 1886–87, when vice-president Alexander Nairn, who was in line to become president, "was absent in Scotland."

His curling success in 1886 was only the beginning for him. He went on to further glory, winning the Tankard four more times over the next 14 years.* His fellow curlers in Ontario elected him president of the Ontario Curling Association for the years 1900–01. His own Granite Club awarded him an honorary life membership in 1906. And 20 years later when the club moved to St. Clair, it honoured him yet again, by appointing him as honorary patron along with Lieutenant-Governor Colonel Henry Cockshutt and Sir Joseph Flavelle.

Dalton's rinks defeated Guelph in 1886; Peterborough in 1892; Dundas in 1894; St. Mary's in 1896; and London in 1900.

vice-president; W. Gibbs was renamed captain, and he also took on the added responsibility of secretary-treasurer, with A.J. Hollyer serving as honorary secretary; the rest of the committee included William Badenach, W.H. Bleasdell, C.C. Dalton, A. Ford, B. Lacon, and J.W. DeC. O'Grady. The following years saw numerous changes; by 1892 the committee was Hon. W.P.R. Street, president; H.D. Warren, vice-president; George S. Crawford, captain; Clarence H. Badenach, honorary secretary-treasurer; committee members: D.R. Wilkie, James Strachan, W.B. Willoughby.

During the first five years of competition, Walter Gibbs was club champion three times and A.J. Hollyer twice. Matches against other lawn tennis clubs—the Toronto, the Park, Osgoode Hall, and

Ossington—were popular events. According to a Granite member of the day: "The Toronto's licked us as a rule, but…we most often beat the other fellows." In 1887 the club held a "Tennis At Home." About 1200 members and guests from other tennis clubs attended. Bleachers were erected for spectators, refreshments were served, and there was dancing to a string band. It was such a huge success that it was repeated the following year.

By 1886 the club's curling facilities (four sheets of indoor ice) were no longer enough to accommodate the demand. Two years after the expansion to the south, therefore, a decision was made to buy the rear portion of the Snarr property, north of the club and fronting on Cawthra Avenue. By this purchase, the club's property was increased to a total of one and a half acres. At the northeast corner of this newly acquired land the club erected a commodious building, 160 x 100 feet, with

Granite Tennis players, 1888 (back row, l-r) G.H. Gooderham, Mr. Brown, W. Gibbs, G.S. Crawford, W. Badenach, A.B. Lee, T. Hill, A.J. Hollyer. (front row, l-r) H.W. Pringle, Mr. Jones, R.H. Bowes, Mr. Sherwood, W.H. Bleasdell

DANIEL ROBERT WILKIE was a banker born in Quebec in 1846. His father, Daniel Sr., was a Scot; his mother Angelique Graddon, French-Canadian. He was just 16 when he joined the Quebec Bank. Five years later he became manager of its St. Catharines branch and within two years was promoted again, this time to manager of the Toronto branch.

In 1870 he married Sarah Caroline, third daughter of Senator J.R. Benson, president of the Niagara District Bank. When that bank merged with the newly formed Imperial Bank in 1875, what better person to appoint as general manager than Benson's young son-in-law, D.R. Wilkie? Wilkie was in the right place at the right time, and he carried with him an excellent 13-year track record. Under his steady and cautious hand, the bank prospered over its first 39 years, the last 14 of which he was its president. He was much honoured by his banking peers, being twice elected president of the Bankers' Association and once president of the Toronto Board of Trade.

Nor did Wilkie confine himself merely to the dry details of banking. He was president of the Niagara Falls Suspension Bridge Company and served as a director of many large companies including Confederation Life; Toronto General Trusts Corporation; and the General Accident, Fire, and Life Assurance Corporation. He also took great interest in sports and the arts. He was the 10th president of the Granite Club (1887–88); vice-president of the Toronto Golf Club; president of the St. Andrew's Society; committee member of the Granite Tennis Club; member of Lambton Golf Club; vice-president of the Toronto executive committee of the Earl Grey Musical and Dramatic Competition; honorary president of the Canadian Art Club; and member of the Canadian Society of Authors. In the philanthropic field he was chairman of the board of the Victorian Order of Nurses; a governor of the Toronto General Hospital; and a councillor of the Red Cross Society.

ample room for six sheets of curling ice. The club now had 10 sheets of indoor ice and the open ground between the two buildings could accommodate 34 outdoor sheets for large competitions. In addition to the capital costs of this expansion, operating costs also increased. And so, in his notice of the annual meeting of October 8, 1887, Secretary James Hedley informed the members:

Bowling green, Church Street, c. 1898
New rink is on the left

The popularity of most sports is cyclical and by the time the club moved to St. Clair Avenue, interest in tennis seemed to be on the wane. For some years four tennis courts adjacent to the lawn bowling green were well used, but there was no organized section. With the move to Bayview, tennis once again enjoyed a resurgence.

> In view of the enlargement of the club premises, the increased accommodation given and the variety of recreations and attractions afforded, in addition to curling—lawn tennis, bowls, billiards, whist, and the papers and periodicals to be found in the reading room, it was not to be expected that the extremely low membership fee of $10 per annum could be maintained. The annual subscription will be from November 1st, 1887, fifteen dollars, and the entrance fee to new members, ten dollars additional.

And so, just 11 years after the club was founded, it had grown to include a clubhouse, two houses, and two curling sheds. In the preface to the club's 1887 *Rules and Regulations* booklet, it was noted:

> We have now club rooms which comprise Reception, Dining, Billiard, Card and Reading Rooms, under the charge of a resident steward. THE GRANITE has now become an up-town social club, possessing all the comforts and conveniences usually found in such an establishment, while it has lost, we are happy to think, none of its former attractions as a curling club with the largest membership in Canada.

It also declared that:

> The Granite Club is…an association of gentlemen desiring to enjoy the social advantages of a club without political bias…[and] politics and religious questions of every kind are absolutely excluded from open discussion at the club.

In a letter written to Scottish curler James Brown, vice-president of the Royal Caledonian Curling Club, and published in the *Annual*, one Granite Club member got quite carried away:

> I wish you could see in summer all the intermediate space between our two brick sheds, an angle of grass, aglow at the edges with flowers, the wooden fence at the east end [abutting on Cawthra Square] lustrous with grapes and a mass of shade, the tennis players in their flannels, the bowlers in their short sleeves and Glasgow-made bowls everywhere.

Literally and figuratively, 1886 was a banner year for the Granite, for this was the year that the rinks of C.C. Dalton and William Badenach won the Ontario Tankard, the symbol of curling supremacy in Ontario. Today, the silk banner embroidered in gold, joined by many others of later years, is the most prized among the trophies displayed in the curling lounge. The victory was described in *Outing* magazine:

> Having already defeated the Scarborough Heathers…the Moss Park Rink and the Caledonians of Toronto…the Granites came into

Ontario Tankard Winners, 1886 Badenach Rink on left, standing (l-r) Norman B. Dick, vice; B. Lacon, second; seated, William Badenach, skip; reclining, R. Myles, lead. Dalton Rink on right, standing (l-r) Wilbur C. Matthews, vice; R.B. Hamilton, second; seated, Charles C. Dalton, skip; reclining, J.W. DeC. O'Grady, lead

the final competition. The surviving clubs against them were those of Listowel, Thamesville, and Guelph, the last two being especially strong teams, both appearing in the "Honor Roll of the Ontario Curling Annual." The Listowels were defeated on the first day by 57 shots to 19. Next morning on the spacious ice of the Caledonian Club, the doughty Thamesville men, too, had to succumb, being beaten by fifteen shots. In the afternoon…the quaint silent figure of "Long Tom" Dobie, pipe in his mouth, and the alert and no less well-known Alec Congalton, skips of the two Guelph rinks, contested the skill, and tried the patience of the Granite skips, Dalton and Badenach, by daylight and by gaslight…for twenty-two ends.* A great shout from the crowd announced at last the completion of the match. The Granites had won 38 shots to 32.

In January 1887, the club hosted the first official international bonspiel, at its new rink with 20 Granite teams and an equal number from New York State participating. Although it is certain that the club's hospitality was of the highest order, the Granite rinks showed no mercy on the ice, defeating the New Yorkers 312 to 224. In fairness to the Americans it should be pointed out that they were not used to curling on smooth indoor ice. In fact, one American at the time was heard to grumble, "We ain't used to playing on billiard tables, with a checker-worked ice cloth." This was the first of a series of international bonspiels that came to be held on a regular basis every five years.

That same year the Caledonian Society of Toronto offered a handsome silver cup for a city competition. The Toronto Curling Club won it the first year, the Caledonian Curling Club the second, and the Granite Club the next two.

Also in 1887, the Granite Club hosted the finals of the Ontario Tankard in which Thamesville defeated Galt 47 rocks to 30. The *Globe* reported the event at great length:

The club's 1886 curling victory was the beginning of 60 years of Granite supremacy in the Ontario Tankard competition. Granite rinks won the Tankard fifteen times from 1886 to 1945—a record that no other club has equalled. In the 19th century, games in the Tankard competition were twenty-two ends and took five hours or more to finish! The Tankard is a two-rink event (that is, two from each club), and the championship is decided by the total number of points each club scores in the two games.

*An end is the period of play during which both teams deliver four rocks in one direction, after which the score for that end is tallied. In the next end, the eight rocks are delivered in the opposite direction. This continues until the appropriate number of ends has been played or until one team concedes defeat.

WILLIAM BADENACH has been described as "one of the greatest skips who ever handled a broom." John A. Stevenson called him one of that century's 20 most famous skips and praised his contribution to the sport:

> William Badenach used to say that he liked curling on account of its healthfulness, its zest, and its complete freedom from professionalism. He had applied his intellect to a close study of the game, paying special attention to the peculiarities of ice under different conditions.... [He] rendered very conspicuous service to the Granite Club of which he was long the leading spirit.

Perhaps the highlight of Badenach's many active years of curling at the club was in 1886 when his rink, along with C.C. Dalton's, won the Ontario Silver Tankard, the emblem of curling supremacy in the province.

Badenach joined the Toronto Granite Curling Club two years after it began and promptly assumed the job of secretary—a post he was to hold for the next eight years. When the Granite Curling and Skating Company was incorporated in 1880, the professional accountant became its secretary-treasurer as well and continued to hold that office throughout the 1880s. In 1890, he was elected the club's 13th president. Another honour arrived the following year when curlers across Ontario chose him as president of the Ontario Branch, Royal Caledonian Curling Club (now the Ontario Curling Association).

When spring arrived Badenach turned to other athletic pursuits. He was an active tennis player and lawn bowler, serving for years on the committees of the Granite Tennis Club and the Granite Bowling Club. And when the weather failed to cooperate, he headed indoors for quieter competition at the whist table.

The first bonspiel between Americans and Canadians was played in 1865 on Lake Erie at Black Rock, near Buffalo, N.Y. A Toronto Curling Club team was drawn to play against a team from the Buffalo Curling Club who called themselves the "President's Rink." The Canadians (without Queen Victoria's permission) named themselves "Her Majesty's Rink" and donned cardigans of royal scarlet. From that day on they were known as the "Red Jacket Rink." Virtually unbeatable, they put curling on the front pages, both in Canada and the United States.

The curlers adjourned to the comfortable reading-room of the Granites, where the coveted trophy was surrounded by admirers. In the absence of President Davison [Ontario Branch, Royal Caledonian Curling Club] the duty of presenting the Tankard fell to Dr. [James] Ross, of the Granites, an ex-president of the Ontario Branch [1883–84]. Dr. Ross, in handing over the trophy to Mr. Jas. Ferguson, M.P.P., one of the Thamesville skips, said that he hoped the same curlers would be on hand next year to play for it…. Three rousing cheers for the Tankard winners followed and…three cheers were [also] given by the assembled company for Galt, and Mr. R. Webster [one of the two Galt skips] thanked the Granites and the Toronto curlers generally for the handsome entertainment afforded them during their visit. The visitors were particularly grateful to Mr. Robert Jaffray, who had done everything possible to make their visit enjoyable. Mr. Jaffray replied that anything the Granites could do for the furtherance of curling and the accommodation of visiting curlers they were ready and willing to do. They considered it a great honour to have the Tankard played for on their rink. Nothing was more conducive to the physical and moral development of men than this grand game. No gambling was connected with it and no drinking man could be a good curler. It was pleasant to see that while the game was Scotch it was not confined to Scotchmen. Nearly three-fourths of the members of the Granite Club were Canadians, Englishmen or Irishmen, and many of the best curlers never saw Scotland. Mr. Jaffray expressed his faith in the game and considered it as likely to become the national game of the country.

Later that year, the Granite Club made arrangements with the Montreal Thistle Curling Club:

…by which players from either club made successively the journey of 330 miles and competed on the ice of the other. In these contests the Montreal men, admirable curlers that they are, who are accustomed to curl with irons, played at Toronto with stones, and were defeated. But when the "Granites" played the return match with them in Montreal, using irons, they were in turn beaten by the "Thistles." Delicious were the breakfasts of porridge and bannocks, tawties and collops spread by the hospitable Montreal entertainers…. Notable was the flow of merriment and song when the Eastern men lunched at the Granite rooms.

Within two years other curling clubs had joined the annual "home and home" competition, with 14 Toronto rinks competing against an equal number from Montreal and Ottawa.

Asphalt paving was introduced in Toronto in 1887 and cement paving a few years later. Gradually the stone block, cedar block, and mud roads that made travel throughout the city so uncomfortable and, in wet weather, impossible, were being replaced. That same year, *Saturday Night* began publication and the Humane Society of Toronto was established "for the protection of children and animals." Four more years passed before children were cared for separately by the newly formed Children's Aid Society. Also in 1887, Toronto celebrated Queen Victoria's golden jubilee; Sir John A. Macdonald's Conservatives were re-elected; and Wilfrid Laurier, a young MP from Drummond-Arthabaska, took over the leadership of the Liberal party, a post he was to hold for 32 years.

R.K. Burgess replaced William Ramsay in 1887 as president of the Granite Curling and Skating Company (the joint stock company)—not too surprising since the two men were partners in William Ramsay & Company, merchants and brokers. C.C. Dalton took over the vice-presidency from Donald McEwen, and William Badenach stayed on as secretary-treasurer. Directors were W.G.P. Cassels, Robert Jaffray, James Hedley, Dr. James Carlyle, Walter Taylor, and E.B. Osler.

In 1888, a schism tore the club apart. Just as a group of disenchanted members of the Toronto Curling Club had founded the Granite Club 13 years earlier, so too, in 1888, 17 Granite members,* disapproving of what they considered to be excessive drinking at club curling matches, resigned to form a more abstemious club. They leased space at a rink located seven blocks away at the corner of Prospect and Ontario Streets, and called themselves the Prospect Park Curling Club. Within two years its membership had grown to 82.

Article 2 of Prospect Park's constitution read:

    The object of the club is to foster and promote the Noble Game of Curling and

    other Social Games among its members and shall consist of Gentlemen who are

R.K. Burgess

The 17 disenchanted members were David Carlyle, A.B. Crosby, John O. Donogh, Wm. Forbes, T. Gain, Joseph G. Gibson, M. Hall, W. J. Hynes, Daniel Lamb, Jos. Lugsdin, John Lumbers, John A. Mills, Jos. Oliver, N.L. Patterson, Alex. Wheeler, H. Williams, and Jos. Wright. Among the 25 additional men who joined the new club at its inaugural meeting were seven other well-known former Granite curlers — T.G. Beatty, W. Davidson, James Grand, Wm. Mowat, Wm. Petrie, O.F. Rice, and R. Simpson.

EDMUND BOYD OSLER was a 17-year-old employee when the ill-fated Bank of Upper Canada failed; Lamond Smith had taken him under his wing there. The young man, often a guest in Smith's home, married Smith's daughter, Mary Isabella, in 1868. Two sons died in infancy, and Mary Isabella herself died in 1870. Three years later, Osler married Anne Farquharson Cochran.

By the time he was 40 Osler had become a prominent stockbroker and financier. He had already founded two brokerage firms—the first in partnership with Henry Pellatt, father of Sir Henry Pellatt of Casa Loma fame; the second, with H.C. Hammond. "After forming…Osler and Hammond in 1882, he had flourished, part of a new generation of stockbrokers. Accepting shares in payment for his services, he became a director, among other concerns, of the CPR and the Dominion Bank." In 1896, E.B. Osler was elected to the House of Commons. He became president of the Dominion Bank in 1901 and was knighted in 1911. A man of few words, his maiden speech to Parliament prompted the 1913 headline: "After 17 Years in the House, Osler Speaks!"

He is best remembered for three munificent gifts to the city of Toronto. The first is the valuable collection of Paul Kane paintings of the Canadian West that Osler donated during his lifetime to the Royal Ontario Museum. The second is a pair of Reubens paintings he gave to the Art Gallery of Ontario. And the third is Craigleigh Gardens, a beautiful park sloping to the edge of the Rosedale ravine. In 1926, his beloved home, Craigleigh, was demolished and his children presented the land to the city as a memorial to their parents. "On the entrance gates is a memorial plaque with the touching inscription: 'Here amidst his children and grandchildren, his flowers, trees and birds, Edmund Boyd Osler made his home from 1877 to the date of his death, 1924.'"

desirous of engaging in Social and healthy amusement and to generate a good feeling of Friendship among its members who band themselves together to bring Credit and respect to its Membership.

And prominent in the bylaws was the edict that "no intoxicating liquor be allowed in the club." This was upheld four years later. In an attempt to mollify thirsty guests, a Special General Meeting was called to reconsider the question of serving liquor to visiting curlers. After heated discussion, R.B. Rice's motion that the "Management Committee be instructed to see that no spirituous liquors be served by the club" was carried overwhelmingly.

The Granite Club's four-sheet "old rink" came to be used mostly for skating. It was also leased to other curling clubs. During the warmer months, the "new rink" was often rented out for various group functions.

One such artistic event took place on May 7, 1888, when the Granite Rink was the venue for the first Royal Canadian Academy of Arts exhibition. Its first president, prominent Toronto painter Lucius O'Brien,* occupied the chair, and honoured guests included Lady and Governor-General Lord Lansdowne. Having just been elevated to the vice-regal throne of India, he and his wife were on a farewell visit to Toronto. (Next day, he officially opened Lansdowne School on Spadina Avenue.)

A year later, a raucous political gathering of more than 3000 angry Orangemen met at the

Invitation to the 1888 opening

Lucius Richard O'Brien (1832–99) studied art at Upper Canada College under John G. Howard. He practised civil engineering until 1872 when he became a full-time professional artist. Sponsored by the CPR, he painted magnificent landscapes in the Rockies and along the Pacific coast.

The Orangemen considered themselves to be upholders of Protestant
ascendancy. From the year of incorporation until well into the 1920s,
Toronto, often referred to as the
"Belfast of North America," was controlled by the Orange Order. Between
1834 and 1923 only 13 elected may-
ors were not Orangemen; in 1923,
four out of twenty-three members of
Council were not connected to the
Order. The number of members of
the Orange Lodge in Canada grew
from 100 000 in 1870 to 300 000
in the 1920s.

"Bowling was not the game of tenpins
played with much noise and perspi-
ration in a wood-floored alley," as
James Hedley in 1889 hastened to
point out, "but the game of lawn
bowls... a sort of summer curling."

*In 1903, Dr. B.E. Hawke succeeded
Thornton as secretary of the lawn
bowling committee. Hawke was also
a prominent curler, playing vice-skip
on Ontario Tankard winning rinks in
1909, 1910, and 1911.

Granite Rink and filled the hall to overflowing. They were there to protest a Quebec bill that offered compensation to the Jesuits for huge tracts of land confiscated by the British Crown in 1773.

Throughout the 1880s, both the club's membership and its real estate holdings increased. The variety of activities offered its members also flourished. For those seeking less strenuous pastimes, the Granite Chess, Draughts and Whist Club was founded in 1886. The following year marked the formation of the Granite Bowling Club. Five years earlier, at the request of a few members, the club had imported a set of bowls. Initially, however, there was no organized play. Members just bowled when they felt like it, on payment of a small fee. Lawn bowling had yet to become a popular sport in Toronto, although it was sometimes played on the breezy lawn of the Royal Canadian Yacht Club and at one or two other private grounds. Since the two sports, curling and lawn bowling, are in many ways quite similar, it should come as no surprise that Granite curlers took to lawn bowling quickly and enthusiastically. It was also convenient that the acre of level turf between the old rink and the new one provided an ideal site.

Within days of the formation of the Granite Bowling Club, 60 members had joined, and a committee was set up to draft rules and regulations. It used as its guide a Scottish textbook, *Mitchell's Manual of Bowling*. Thomas Taylor, a Glasgow bowls manufacturer, also gave a great deal of helpful advice. A few members wrote to Samuel Gunn, a veteran bowler in Glasgow, and induced him to visit the club in 1888. During his stay, he taught members many of the finer points of the game and also the proper care and treatment of the bowling green.

The first lawn bowling committee included Dr. James Carlyle as president; John C. Kemp as vice-president; and W.O. Thornton as secretary,* along with W.M. Merritt and William Badenach. Although lame in one leg and the proud owner of a gold kneecap, Badenach still managed to become one of the best curlers and bowlers of the century. John Kemp took over as president the following year and remained in that office well into the 20th century. W.H. Bleasdell, secretary of

Toronto Granite Club Bowlers, 1889 (l-r) W.O. Thornton, Ralph K. Burgess, T.H. Bull, W.H. Bleasdell, Jim Robertson, George Musson, Dr. Adam Henry Wright, William Badenach, John C. Kemp, W.M. Merritt, William A. "Bill" Littlejohn, Willoughby Crooks, Charles C. Dalton

the Granite Club, also assumed the vice-presidency of the bowling club. Within two years of its founding, the Granite Bowling Club boasted 80 members and 12 teams.

Granite bowlers were not long in proving their mastery of the game. As one of 12 Ontario clubs competing in an 1889 tournament hosted by Toronto's Victoria Club, the Granites easily won first prize, capturing four gold medals. The next best performance was by the Walkerton Club, which won two silver. Fourteen years later, *Saturday Night* magazine awarded the club this high praise:

> The Granite has done more than any other club to popularize the game of bowls in this country, and their green has always been considered the best in Toronto.

By the end of the decade, Toronto's population had reached 160 000 and Granite Club membership was close to 500.

Evidence has been found in an ancient Egyptian tomb that bowling was popular in 5200 B.C. The Romans first developed the game and brought it to Britain—originally two people played by rolling round stones or pebbles towards a stationary object. Manuscripts from the 13th and 14th century depict a game played much as it is today. The Southampton Town Bowling Club opened in 1299. The Scots formulated rules in 1849 and there has been little change since. Scottish colonists took the game to North America and a park remains on lower Broadway [in New York City] called Bowling Green.

JAMES CARLYLE, MD, was born in Dumfries, Scotland, into a highly intellectual family. His uncle was the celebrated writer, philosopher, and teacher Thomas Carlyle, lifelong friend of John Stuart Mill and Ralph Waldo Emerson. James Carlyle came to Canada as a boy in 1837 and, following in his uncle's footsteps, chose teaching as his profession. He graduated from the Provincial Model School in 1855 and for the next few years taught at Brantford Central School. His career then took off. He was offered the position of principal at the Provincial Model School, one of the most prestigious schools in Ontario. During his 13 years there he somehow found the time to study medicine and graduated with his MD from Victoria Medical College. In 1871 he was promoted to the position of mathematical master of the Normal School*. and for the balance of his career he was a highly regarded and much loved teacher of teachers.

When the club moved to Church Street in 1880 he was chosen as one of the 10 directors of the new Company. He was an enthusiastic curler and lawn bowler and was elected president of the Toronto Granite Bowling Club in 1887.

*The Normal School was founded in 1847 as a teachers' college at the instance of Egerton Ryerson. It moved in 1858 to the corner of Gould and Victoria Streets.

CHAPTER THREE

THE END OF THE VICTORIAN ERA

1890–1900

AS THE 1890S BEGAN, Toronto's population stood at 160 000—more than twice what it had been when the Granite Club first opened the doors of its tiny St. Mary Street clubhouse 15 years earlier. The Club's splendid "new" building on Church Street was 10 years old and already a landmark in the city. Bloor Street, located a few blocks farther north, was little more than a narrow country road marking the northern boundary of the city. "The Granite Club," enthused New York City's *Outing* magazine,* "with premises covering an acre and a half, having a clubhouse, two covered [curling] sheds, a spacious lawn for the enjoyment, summer and winter, of between 400 and 500 members…[is] the largest club of its kind in the world."

The decade got off to a bad start when fire gutted the entire east wing and more than half of the south wing of University College, including its museum and invaluable library—35 000 books and documents were destroyed. One witness recalled that:

*Outing *magazine was a periodical devoted to sports activities, published from 1883 until the 1920s.*

A.H. WRIGHT, PRESIDENT, 1891–1892

Adam Henry Wright, a prominent obstetrician and gynecologist, became president in 1891. Born in Brampton, Ontario, in 1846, he earned his BA in 1866 and his MB in 1873, both at the University of Toronto. Following his marriage to Flora Cumming of Trenton, Ontario, he completed his medical studies in England and became a Member of the Royal College of Surgeons (MRCS) in 1877. Returning to Toronto, he opened a practice and was a lecturer at the Toronto School of Medicine for eight years. He then became professor of obstetrics at the University of Toronto—a position he was to hold for the next 25 years. During that period he was on staff at the Toronto General Hospital and also sat on the senate of the university. He was elected president of the Ontario Medical Association in 1900 and of the Canadian Medical Association nine years later. Despite such a busy life, he somehow found time to write and publish *Lectures on Obstetrics*, in 1905.

Wright and his wife lived with their five children at 30 Gerrard Street East and his practice was located in his home.

The scene during the fire, in the early evening of February 14th, was one that onlookers will not readily forget. It was the date of the Annual Conversazione, and had the guests arrived before the flames broke out many deaths must have resulted. As it was, the burning of the venerable-looking pile presented a vivid spectacle to the thousands who surveyed it from carriages and neighbouring streets and buildings.

Other events that occurred that year include the death of John G. Howard, the munificent donor of High Park; the re-election of Oliver Mowat as Ontario's premier, with a greater majority than he had ever before enjoyed; and the affiliation of Cobourg's Victoria College with the University of Toronto. Two years later Victoria College moved to its present site in Toronto.

Throughout the decade, a series of epidemics ravaged the city. The problem was that Toronto's sewage simply drained into the bay. As a result, the city's tap water was turbid and polluted. Back in 1873 the city had tried to solve the problem by extending a four-inch wooden water-intake pipe far out into Lake Ontario. In 1890, this pipe had become plugged with sand and was replaced by a longer five-inch steel pipe that soon developed leaks and rose to the surface. In no time a disastrous typhoid epidemic broke out.* Later that same year a diphtheria epidemic devastated the city and the Sisters of Saint Joseph turned their Bond Street hostel for young women into an emergency hospital (soon to become St. Michael's).

But in spite of these calamities, the city continued to grow. The Hospital for Sick Children moved from the house in which it began to nearby new premises at the southeast corner of Elizabeth and College Streets, and a cornerstone was laid for a "new" City Hall at Bay and Queen Streets. Further north, the expensive and controversial Provincial Parliament Building at Queen's Park officially opened for business. As well, the city was rapidly becoming electrified. A five-year contract was signed with the Toronto Electric Light Company to "provide not less than eight hundred arc lamps of at least one thousand candlepower each. For that the city was to pay twenty-four and a half cents per lamp per night." Two farm-implement manufacturing firms merged to form Massey Harris, the largest such company in the British Empire. In other parts of the world, Thomas Edison applied for a patent on the first motion-picture machine and an initial study was made of a way to link Prince Edward Island to the mainland.

Known originally as the Victoria Hospital for Sick Children, the hospital's massive Richardson Romanesque structure was designed by architects Darling & Curry. It was E-shaped to provide cross-ventilation and maximum light to its wards. The building was financed, in large part, by the philanthropy of John Ross Robertson, owner-editor of The Evening Telegram. *He served as chairman of the board of trustees of the Hospital for Sick Children for thirty-five years and, when he died in 1918, he bequeathed it his whole estate. The hospital moved to its present quarters on University Avenue in 1949.*

Hart Massey's eldest son, Charles Albert, died of typhoid fever in 1884. In his memory, his father built Massey Hall.

A.R. CREELMAN, PRESIDENT, 1892-1893

The distinguished Adam Rutherford Creelman, QC, was the Club's 15th president. Born in New Brunswick in 1849, he received his early education there, then left to study law in Toronto. He was called to the bar in 1875. Two years later he married Margaret Cumming Jennings, daughter of Rev. John Jennings, DD, of Toronto. Adam and Margaret lived in a fine house at 13 Queen's Park Crescent. A partner in the firm of McCarthy, Osler, Hoskin & Creelman (now McCarthy Tetrault), he was named Queen's Counsel in 1889.

Just before his vice-presidential year at the Club, Creelman took on the formidable task of revising the Club's bylaws, rules, and regulations—the first revision since the original constitution introduced at that convivial dinner meeting at the Rising Sun Hotel back in 1876. The new bylaws were adopted at the Club's annual meeting on October 10, 1891.

In 1901 Creelman moved to Montreal as chief solicitor for the Canadian Pacific Railway (CPR). Called to the Quebec bar the following year, he was appointed its general counsel in 1908 and two years later was elected a director.

Creelman was "much devoted to clean and manly sport," according to one biographer, and he enthusiastically pursued these sports at a host of clubs in Toronto, Montreal, and Ottawa. In politics Creelman was a Liberal; in religion, a Presbyterian. He retired as general counsel of the CPR in 1913 and died soon after. His law partner Britton Bath Osler, QC, deemed Creelman a "splendid man of business."

In 1891 the country's first prime minister, Sir John A. Macdonald, died, shortly after winning his last election; that year the economic boom of the 1880s plummeted into a five-year depression. A U.S. dispute with Britain over the borders of Venezuela brought the parties to the brink of war and caused a major stock-market panic in 1895 to make matters worse. But, although the economy as a whole was gloomy, there were some bright spots. On August 15, 1892—it was Toronto's Civic Holiday—Granite members were excited to see the city's first electric streetcar glide past the club on its inaugural run. The Toronto Railway Company proudly published a souvenir booklet advising: "The Church streetcars...pass the Public Library, the Normal School, Athenaeum and Granite Club Houses." The line led from its terminus at the City Hall in the St. Lawrence Market, along Front Street to Church; turned north to Bloor; east to Sherbourne; then up Sherbourne and across the bridge to its northern terminus in Rosedale. Next day the *Mail* reported:

It was nearly 3:30 p.m. before the first electric car left in front of City Hall.... Among the party on board were several aldermen and ex-aldermen and some prominent citizens in addition to several city officials. The progress of the car was watched by crowds at several intersecting points, and twelve minutes after the start it reached the bridge at Sherbourne Street.... After arriving at the terminus the party adjourned to a large marquee where they were welcomed by officers of the company, which had provided solid and liquid refreshments.

And the *Globe* wrote that:

The new cars are wider than the old horse cars, and a man of ordinary dimensions can sit reasonably cross-legged in them without his boot on the shin of his

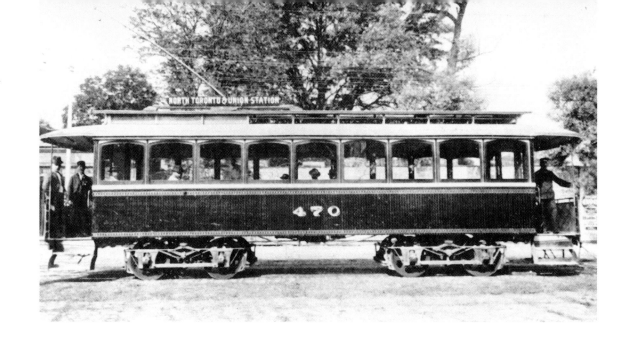

The sample Palace Trolley Car— the prototype for the new cars for the Toronto Railway Company, 1894

travelling companion on the opposite side. They have a fresh, store-like appearance and are as bright inside and out as the new paint on the City Hall door. The springs and padding in the cushions are in perfect order, and long rows of commodious and upholstered straps hang invitingly from the roof for the suspension of standing passengers. Everything connected with the trip was auspicious, even the weather.

Charles Z. Zwick of Rochester, New York, had the dubious honour of being the first person to be hit by a Toronto electric streetcar. Zwick, on the day following the inauguration of the Church Street line, was riding in a horse-drawn carriage when he saw an electric streetcar approaching and, to get a better look at it, "stretched over too far, lost his balance and fell in front of the electric car, which struck him on the shoulder and inflicted an ugly scalp wound," reported the *Mail*. "Dr. [Alton Huyck] Garratt was called in, and the injured man was removed to St. Michael's Hospital, where he is reported to be doing as well as could be expected." City Council decreed that the maximum speed of electric streetcars could not exceed 12 miles per hour and that they must not cause alarm or jeopardy to horses or vehicles.

By 1893 the conversion to electricity was complete and horse cars were seen no more. That same year, 1893, the University Avenue armouries opened and Gladys Marie Smith, later known as Mary Pickford, was born, not far from the armouries, at 211 University Avenue.

In 1895 the Mendelssohn Choir under the direction of Dr. Augustus Stephen Vogt had its first concert in the superb new Massey Hall; fire broke out in the *Globe* building, at the southwest corner of Yonge and Melinda Streets. It spread rapidly and destroyed all of the principal buildings on King Street—the worst fire to that date in Toronto's history. Then another tragedy struck when yet another epidemic hit the city. This time it was smallpox and countless Torontonians died. The following year might have been even more devastating had it not been for quick action on the part of the city's Office of Public Health, which imported, just in time, a large quantity of vaccine from the Pasteur Institute in Paris.

The big news of 1896 was Wilfrid Laurier's decisive election victory. His Liberal cabinet included such powerful members as government leader of the Senate (and former Ontario premier) Oliver Mowat, former premier of Nova Scotia William S. Fielding, North York MP William Mulock, and *Winnipeg Free Press* owner (and former attorney general of Manitoba) Clifford Sifton.

In 1897 Queen Victoria, as part of her diamond jubilee celebration, conferred knighthoods on Oliver Mowat and Wilfrid Laurier. In Toronto, voters finally approved Sunday streetcars.

In 1898, the United States went to war with Spain—a war that ended four months later, with the United States annexing Guam, Puerto Rico, and the Philippines. And during the last year of the

W.C. MATTHEWS, PRESIDENT, 1895–1896

Wilbur Cassius Matthews was born in Vaughan Township in 1846. He had little formal education and remained on his father's farm until he was 19, receiving whatever education district schools provided in those days. On leaving the farm, he attended one term at a commercial college in Toronto and then went to work for the Registrar's Department in Ottawa. After two years, perceiving little future for himself in the civil service, he joined Dun, Wiman & Co. (now Dun and Bradstreet), a firm providing businessmen with information about the financial standing of their customers. He advanced quickly and, after a few years, was appointed manager of its Memphis, Tennessee, branch. The following year he was again promoted, this time to general manager of the firm's Canadian operations, with offices at 13 Wellington Street East, Toronto.

Matthews was a superb athlete, excelling in curling, lawn bowling, and lacrosse. Four times he played vice-skip on an Ontario Tankard-winning rink: with C.C. Dalton in 1886, and with T.G. Williamson in 1892, 1894, and 1896. Three years later he won the Dominion Bowling Association championship and its magnificent Hiram Walker & Sons' trophy. As well as being the 18th president of the Granite Club, he was also president of the Toronto Athletic Grounds and vice-president of the Toronto Lacrosse Club.

century, a much longer and bloodier conflict—the Boer War—broke out. More than 3000 Canadians enlisted to fight for the mother country. Closer to home, Toronto's impressive new City Hall at Queen and Bay officially opened amid controversy, lawsuits, and investigations. It had cost the taxpayers an astronomical $2.5 million.

And what was going on at the Granite Club during those 10 tumultuous years? For one thing, the Granite Club was helping to establish hockey as Canada's national sport. According to *Saturday Night*, "In 1891 the Granite Hockey Club* was born as one of the pioneer organizations in its field." Pioneer, certainly, but the Granites hockey team had been on the ice three years before that—and two years before the Ontario Hockey Association was founded.

An account of that game—possibly the first recorded game in Toronto—appeared in the *Globe* on February 17, 1888:

> GRANITES DEFEAT CALEDONIANS. The first hockey match of the series was played at the Granite Rink last night…. The play was very exciting, and this sport is sure to become popular. [C.G.] Crawford scored the first goal for the Granites in five minutes after play began. [J.E.B.] Littlejohn and [D.] Donaldson also scored for their side before half-time closed. In the second half-time the Caledonians scored their only goal…. The Granites won another, the score at the close standing— Granites, 4 goals; Caledonians, 1.

An account of a later game appeared in the *Mail* on January 27, 1890:

> The season opened Saturday night, when the St. George's and Granite Hockey Clubs met on the Victoria rink. The match started at 7:15 before a large and fashionable audience…. The boys played hockey from the word go. Some pretty play was done on both sides and…the match [ended up in] a draw…. For the Granites Messrs. H. Green, C. Crawford, and W. Meharg played the best game. If

"Hockey on the ice" was first recorded in Kingston, Ontario, in 1843. The first indoor game of hockey recorded was played in Montreal in 1875, using a block of wood rather than a ball. Formal rules for the game were published in 1877 by J.G.A. Creighton, a Haligonian enrolled at McGill University.

*In 1892, the officers of the Granite Hockey Club were H.D. Warren, president; C.A.B. Brown, vice-president; W.E. Meharg, honorary secretary-treasurer; members of the executive committee, C.G. Crawford, James S. Garvin, and J.E.B. Littlejohn.

Granite Ladies Hockey
Team, 1892

*Not to be outdone, a group of women
formed the Granite Ladies Hockey
Team in 1890. One member of that
team was Janet Nicholson, daughter
of Tankard-winning skip C.C. Dalton.*

the number of spectators is any criterion the public have already caught on to the game. If the weather holds out numerous matches will be played.

Two weeks later, the *Toronto World* gave an account of yet another Granite Club game. This time the opposition came from Ottawa—the Parliamentary and Vice-Regal Hockey Team, nicknamed the Rideau Rebels. Two of Governor-General Lord Stanley's sons, Arthur and Edward, were on the team. Arthur was considered to be its most valuable player, and it was he who had organized the Rideau Rebels/Granite match, as well as games in Lindsay and Kingston. Anyone who assumes that violence on the ice began only in recent years might be surprised to learn that fights were far from unknown a century ago.

Hockey is one of the most popular winter games in Ottawa, Montreal, Quebec, and other eastern cities, while in Toronto the game has not been extensively played. There can be no doubt that the matches played on Saturday will have the effect of popularizing the game in this city so long as it is kept free from such objectionable features as took place in the afternoon game at the Granite rink. It is greatly to be regretted that in a game between amateur teams some players should so forget themselves before such a number of spectators, a good proportion of whom on the occasion referred to being ladies, and indulge in fisticuffs and the action of some of the spectators in rushing on to the ice is also to be condemned…. Apart from [this]…the afternoon game was most enjoyable, and the excitement towards the close was intense. [The visitors won the match 5 to 4.] Garvin played a grand game, showing the best play of the match. Green and Meharg were also prominent for good play…. After the match the teams were dined by the president of the Victoria Hockey Club, Col. Sweeney…. Those present included…J. Miles, H. Green, J. Littlejohn, Jas. Garvin, and E. Badenach, of the Granites.

On January 10, 1896, *The Toronto Star* reported, with disgust and dismay, another donnybrook at the Granite Rink:

> If the game of hockey is to continue in this country as a popular sport, roughness and rowdyism must be eliminated…there is no necessity for slugging and free fights…. Last night, Toronto spectators saw the first ungentlemanly match of the season…. The Victorias met their old rivals, the Granites, at the Granite Rink…. The Victorias were hissed and the Granites applauded, the latter team having by far the greater number of friends in the crowd…. Johnson [Granites] and Forsyth [Victorias] started to fight early in the game. Some spectators interfered and held Forsyth, then his team rushed to the rescue, so did the Granites, and in a moment a large part of the crowd surged out on the ice. There was swearing and scuffling on all sides, and the scene was disgraceful. For the welfare of the game this match should be investigated by the Ontario Hockey Association and the guilty parties punished.

H.D. Warren,
Granite Hockey Club president,
and president of the Ontario
Hockey Association, 1892–4

The Victorias went on to win that game eight goals to three. *The Toronto Star's* reporter, however, showered lavish praise on one James Macdonald—the Granite's "chrysanthemum-headed star [who played] the best game of the evening."

From the outset, the Granite Club took an active role in the Ontario Hockey Association (OHA). Nine delegates, including Granite Hockey Club captain H. Green, attended the organizational meeting held at the Queen's Hotel on November 27, 1890. Other organizations that sent delegates

Teams were made up of seven players. "Point" and "cover-point" were defencemen, the point playing about 15 feet in front of the goalie and the cover-point, fifteen feet in front of him. The four forwards were today's left wing, right wing, and centre with the fourth as a "rover." At face-offs, the rover stood behind the centre. The rover could skate anywhere, looking for the best position to receive a pass. There was no substitution—except in case of injury.

were the Royal Military College and Queen's University from Kingston; the Athletic Lacrosse Club; the St. George's Club; the Victoria Club; C. Company, Royal Canadian Infantry; and Osgoode Hall, all of Toronto; plus a representative from the town of Bowmanville. Two years later, Granite Hockey Club President H.D. Warren became the Association's second president (1892–94) and after him, C.A.B. Brown, also of the Granite Club, its third (1894–96). Granite members J.S. Garvin and George Irving also served on the OHA executive committee. Thus, for four of the first six formative years of the OHA, a Granite Club member sat in the president's chair.

In the first year of the Association's existence an Ottawa team won the championship, and repeated its win the following year by defeating Osgoode Hall's Legalites by a score of 10–4. That game, played at the Granite rink, attracted an estimated 2500—more than the building could accommodate. Later, at a banquet honouring the victors, a letter from Governor-General Lord Stanley was read in which he offered a cup for the hockey championship of Canada—a proposal that was promptly and enthusiastically accepted. Thus began more than 100 years of Stanley Cup competition—amateur from 1893 to 1910, and after 1910, professional.

The Granite Club's team drew praise from W.A.H. Kerr in *The Dominion Illustrated Monthly*:

> [The Granites] play a hard game, and impress one with the idea that they mean to win if sticking to it will do it. Their defence with Meharg and Carruthers at point

and cover-point will be an extremely strong one, and the game played by Walker and Shanklin on the forward line is bound to bother most defences they will be pitted against. Walker is a very dodgy skater and is adept at getting the puck out of a tight place. He passes well to Shanklin, and the latter goes down the ice towards his opponent's goal doubled like a ball. He, Shanklin, is such a strong stick handler and so firm on his feet, that, although he may be momentarily checked, he seldom loses the puck till it's time to pass across in front of goal for a shot. Walker then generously turns up to shoot. Carruthers, quite a lad, gives great promise. His shooting and quick lifting at cover point are as good as one sees.

In the 1893–94 OHA Junior series, the Granites reached the finals, but lost disastrously to the Peterborough Hockey Club, 14–0. But by the following year the Granites had improved. They won the OHA Junior City Championship to become, once again, Ontario finalists. The final was a squeaker, Peterborough defeating the Granites by the more respectable score of 7–6. In 1896 the Granites triumphed at last, winning the OHA Junior Championship, defeating Peterborough 7–3. And then the Granite Hockey Club, for reasons unknown, abruptly resigned from the OHA. It would be 23 years before the club rejoined the Association. Members of that 1896 championship team were Carlyle, goal; Davis, point; C. McArthur, cover-point; and for-

Twice around the park as consolation after a serious loss at lawn bowls at the Granite Club, 1900

wards C.G. Crawford, F. Dixon, W. Lillie, and H. Johnson. The latter was considered at the time to be "one of the best junior forwards in Toronto." Crawford had played on Granite hockey teams every year since 1887, and became a member of the Granite Hockey Club executive committee in 1892.

G.R. HARGRAFT, PRESIDENT, 1898-1899

George Ross Hargraft was born in Cobourg in 1856; he was the eldest son of Margaret and William H. Hargraft, MPP. At age 25, he married Rachel Macnachtan, also of Cobourg. Hargraft first worked for the Bank of Toronto but soon moved into the insurance field, joining the Toronto office of the Commercial Union Assurance Company of London, England. In 1900 he was appointed their general agent for the Toronto district. Soon after, Hargraft founded his own company to represent Commercial Union as well as other companies.

Not only was he president of the Granite Curling Club (1898–99), but he also served as president of six other organizations: the Granite Bowling Club, the Ontario Lawn Bowling Association, the Ontario Curling Association (1917–18), the Rosedale Golf Club, the Toronto Board of Fire Underwriters, and his own insurance agency, George R. Hargraft & Company. He was also a warden of St. Paul's Anglican Church. He curled on two Ontario Tankard-winning rinks, first in 1896 and again four years later. As an avid lawn bowler, he donated a trophy in 1905 for competition among the clubs of Toronto and vicinity. He also belonged to the National Club and the RCYC.

The names of other Granite Club hockey pioneers should not be forgotten: H. Fletcher, W. Lamont, and F. Nelles who played on the 1889–90 team; George Higinbotham who played coverpoint, 1891–93; Joseph Irving, goal, 1892–94; and H. Livingstone.

Hockey, of course, was not the only winter sport at the club during the 1890s. Curling continued to attract over 300 enthusiastic members.

In 1890 the Royal Caledonian Club bonspiel, an event at which 14 rinks from its Quebec branch took on an equal number from Ontario, made headline news:

ONTARIO SCORES A HANDSOME VICTORY OVER QUEBEC

The visitors left the East Friday night and arrived here at an early hour the following morning. Play began at eleven o'clock and was concluded at three o'clock when the returns showed a hard-earned victory for the Ontario stone-pushers by 49 shots.... The visitors were handsomely entertained...by their opponents. They returned home by the evening train, well pleased with their visit, and although beaten, as confident as ever in the superiority of the iron over the granite stone. The return match will be played in Montreal on March 1.

Granite rinks comprised six of the fourteen from Ontario. The skips were Wilbur C. Matthews, William Badenach, James Hedley, W.F. Davison, Charles C. Dalton, and Alex Bertram. They won five of their six games, Matthews being the only loser.

Throughout the decade most winters were ideal for the roaring game—crisp and cold—except for the 1891–92 season when mild weather delayed play until mid-January. The weather continued to be dreadful that year—rain, slush, and mud for most of the ensuing months. Granite curlers were dismayed.

The second International Bonspiel was hosted by the Prospect Park Curling Club in 1892. (The Granite Club had hosted the first, back in 1887.)

A Toronto Granite rink, skipped by the President of the O.C.A., Mr. Wm. Badenach, opened the fray against an American rink skipped by Major Peattie,

For almost 150 years, Quebec curlers used "stones" made of iron. "Irons" originated in Quebec City after its capture by British forces in 1759. Scottish soldiers melted down cannon balls and added handles as they moulded something suitable for curling. The running surface was ground and polished.

Quebec curlers eventually switched to granite. Players initially owned their own stones and carried them to each game. The size and weight of stones varied. Finally a standard was established as to size, material, and weight (44 lbs.) and curling clubs across Canada began to provide uniform stones for use by members and guests.

President of the Grand National Curling Club of the United States, and, after a keen contest lasting three and a half hours, defeated it 25 to 18. And this initial superiority was so well maintained by the other Canadian rinks that they won the contest very comfortably with an aggregate score of 567 shots against 418.

Later that year the Granite Club celebrated yet another curling victory. Six years after winning his first Ontario Tankard, C.C. Dalton did it again, this time in the company of fellow skip, T.G. Williamson. Not only that, but the talented Dalton repeated the feat in 1894, in 1896, and again in 1900.

From today's perspective, the cost of curling in those early years appears very reasonable. Minutes of the 1892 annual meeting of the Toronto Granite Curling Club show that annual fees amounted to three dollars for skips, two dollars for vice-skips, and one dollar for other players. The minutes also took great pains to once again remind curlers that:

One of the rules most constantly violated is that which prescribes the position of players during a match. None but the skips should stand within the rings; and the place of sweepers is somewhere between the two hog scores.

The club customarily held an in-club bonspiel on New Year's Day, with the president heading up one group of teams and the vice-president another. A record was set in 1895, unequalled previously by any other club. It was the largest turnout of club members ever to play at one time on their own ice. One hundred and twenty-eight Granite curlers, 32 rinks in all, played under the leadership of President Arthur Brindley Lee and Vice-President Wilbur C. Matthews. Competition was keen, with Matthew's 16 rinks defeating Lee's by a total score of 199 to 190.

City-wide competitions were also popular in the 1890s. And although members of Prospect Park had separated from the Granite Club in 1888 in a dispute over the question of liquor consumption, relations between the two remained amicable. Hence, in the Prospect Park minutes of December 4, 1891, we find:

> Mr. Carlyle reported on the meeting held at the Queen's [Hotel] on the 3rd inst. of the Joint Committee re The Curling Trophy. The Granite Club was represented by Messrs. Dalton & Jaffray; Toronto [Curling Club] Messrs. McGow & Wilson; Prospect Park Messrs. Carlyle and McCulloch. The Committee were unanimous as to the advisability of having a trophy to compete for. Mr. Dalton presented a number of designs, one of which, a very elegant one (and which was shown to the club at this meeting), the Committee decided upon, and [named it] The Toronto Challenge Cup. All the City Clubs eligible to compete for same with 8 rinks, 2 home and home matches to be played with each club. The club winning 3 consecutive seasons to become the owner. The cup, though a $500 one, could be purchased for $150 and the 3 clubs named contribute an equal share to procure same. It was provided that should any other City Club this season enter with the requisite number of rinks they should contribute their proportion.

This cup remained in competition until 1896. Its whereabouts 100 years later are unknown. We do know that in the Prospect Park minutes the following appeared:

> October 4th, 1895…. Letter was read from Sec'y Granite Curling Club stating that Messrs. Hiram Walker & Sons Ltd., Walkerville had offered through Mr. W.C.

The members of those Tankard winning Granite rinks were:
1892: Skip Charles C. Dalton, W.J. McMurtry, D.L. VanVlack, J. Kilgour; Skip T.G. Williamson, Wilbur C. Matthews, H.W. Williamson, C.N. Candee.
1894: Skip Charles C. Dalton, W.J. McMurtry, G. DeC. O'Grady, J.W. Carroll; Skip T.G. Williamson, Wilbur C. Matthews, E.A. Badenach, J.W. Gale, Jr. 1896: Skip Charles C. Dalton, R. Watson, J. Kilgour, G.M. Higginbothan; Skip T. G. Williamson, Wilbur C. Matthews, H.W. Williamson, G.R. Hargraft. 1900: Skip Charles C. Dalton, Jos. Irving, E.A. Badenach, G.M. Higginbothan; Skip G.H. Gooderham, G.R. Hargraft, W.E. McMurtry, Dr. C.V. Snelgrove.

W.A.J. LITTLEJOHN, PRESIDENT, 1899–1900

William A.J. Littlejohn was the president who ushered the club into the 20th century. A civil servant, he dedicated some 50 years to the City Clerk's office. He had started in 1874 as a $1.50-per-day junior, moved up to assistant clerk eight years later, and became, in 1900, city clerk—a position he was to hold well into the 1920s. He was acclaimed for organizing the department "to deal rapidly and efficiently with the vast increase in business commensurate with the remarkable growth of the city."

Littlejohn's Scottish ancestors had emigrated from Inverness in the 18th century and settled in North Carolina where he was born in 1857. When William Littlejohn was 10, his father died and his mother decided to emigrate once again. She brought him, his brothers James Edward and John, and his sister Mary, to Toronto in 1869. All three boys attended Upper Canada College.

As a young man Littlejohn was an avid rower, secretary of the Toronto Rowing Club, and president of the Canadian Association of Amateur Oarsmen. Later in life, golf at the Lambton Golf Club and lawn bowling and curling at the Granite Club were his principal recreations—and he was said to be one of the city's best billiard players. He also belonged to the National Club, the Athenaeum Club, and the RCYC.

His brother James Edward B. Littlejohn also became a member of the Granite Club and was a member of the executive committee of the Granite Hockey Club in 1891–92. He scored one of the first three goals in what was likely the first recorded hockey game played in Toronto: Granites vs. Caledonians, February 17, 1888. In business, James was vice-president and treasurer of the Rapid Electrotyping Company.

Matthews, Vice President of the Granite Club a handsome…challenge trophy for Annual Rink Competition among the curlers of Toronto. 4 gold medals to be given annually to the winning rink. The generous offer of Messrs. Walker was gladly accepted.

Walker Cup

Prospect Park's scruples regarding alcohol obviously did not extend to refusing a trophy funded by the profits from the sale of liquor. The first Walker Cup match took place in 1896, and during nine years of competition, the famous Rennie rink won five times and Ernie McMurtry's Granite rink once.

Nor were Prospect Park and the Granite Club destined to remain apart forever. In September 1896, at a special meeting of the Prospect Curling Club, the minutes concerning the discussion of rental of ice time and clubroom space from the separate Prospect Park Company read:

R.B. Rice, Chairman of that Committee, stated that the Committee had interviewed the P.P. Co. Directors and had not been able to procure any better terms but had received a written offer from the Granite Club which was read to the meeting. The offer being in substance, with a guarantee of 60 members, the annual fee of $15.00 to be paid which includes the privileges of the Granite Club curling and bowling.

The Rennie rink comprised three brothers, Thomas (skip), John (vice-skip) and Robert (lead) with A.B. Nichols as second. W. Ernest McMurtry had with him: J.W. "Will" Gale, P.J. Edwards and D.T. Prentice Jr.

The meeting voted to accept the offer, provided that "good ice be guaranteed, weather permitting." And so the dissidents returned to their old home, renaming their group the Queen City Curling Club. Its first meeting was held at the Church Street building on November 8, 1896.

J.C. Kemp, president,
Granite Bowling Club

Obviously the two clubs got along well together, for they ratified a five-year agreement the following year. And a year later the agreement was amended to give Queen City exclusive use of the "old rink" with its four sheets of ice. The Granite Club then curled exclusively on the six sheets of the "new rink."

Other sports were enjoyed at the Granite Club in the nineties. "The Wanderers" were a group of vigorous young members addicted to cycling across the countryside. (H.T. Wilson was president and H.S. Macnamara was secretary.) Billiard tournaments were held annually, "the club boasting some of the best players in the city including Messrs. W.A. Littlejohn, H.J. Child, and W.F. McGee." And whist, a card game which evolved first into auction bridge and later into the contract bridge played today, was one of the more popular indoor pastimes.

On warm summer days, members turned to lawn bowling. All through the nineties the Granite Bowling Club flourished under the capable leadership of its president, J.C. Kemp. The Ontario Bowling Association was formed at the beginning of the decade and the Granite Bowling Club was one of the first to join. Hiram Walker & Sons Ltd. donated a handsome silver trophy, this time for the Association's annual competition at Niagara-on-the-Lake. Granite Club bowlers won it so many times that it became the Club's permanent possession.

Looking back on the final decade of the 19th century, *Saturday Night* magazine commented, "Much of the success of the [Toronto Granite Curling] club has undoubtedly been due to the capable presiding officers." They had come from all walks of life: from the professions—a physician, a lawyer and an accountant; from business—a manufacturer, a wholesaler, and an insurance agent; from the field of finance—a banker and a credit agency executive; and from the civil service—a city official. All shared an affection for the club where they could meet like-minded men for social and athletic recreation. Like so many members to this day, they "paid their dues" by serving on the club's board and committees.

By the time the century came to a close, the Granite Club was a dignified 25 years old and had already achieved a unique status among the leading clubs that played a significant role in the city's stratified social life. Looking back from the middle years of the next century, one writer noted that in Canada, for a man to become successful, "membership in the 'right' clubs and associations, even though he may rarely appear there, [was] considered useful, if not essential, to validate the male career." Certainly that held true in Toronto, and the Granite Club had become one of the "right" clubs.

CHAPTER FOUR

PRELUDE TO WAR

1900 – 1914

THE EXUBERANT CROWD at Queen and Bay cheered as the three huge bells of the new city hall rang in the 20th century. Torontonians had every reason to be happy and optimistic. Their city was booming. The wheat-fuelled expansion in the West was spurring employment growth—not only in agriculture, but also in natural resources, construction, and industry—and much of this new employment was centred in Toronto. By 1900 the city's boundaries had expanded westwards to High Park; eastwards beyond the Don River to Kingston Road; and northwards into the Poplar Plains area.

The Granite Club was also thriving. According to architectural historian Patricia McHugh, "By the 1900s, the Granite Club could boast the biggest membership of any club in Canada." This, after only 25 years.

Queen Victoria died on January 22, 1901, after more than 63 years on the throne. It had been a glorious era for Queen and Empire. During her reign, maps and globes were filled with vast areas

R.L. PATTERSON, PRESIDENT, 1900–1901

Robert Lawrence Patterson had the honour of being the club's first president of the century. He was an Irishman who, before he had been long in Canada, had become as enthusiastic a curler as any Scot. He came to Canada in 1858 as a 12-year-old, and at age 16 became an apprentice under George Brown at the Globe Printing Company. After seven years he left to set up his own business as the Canadian representative of an Edinburgh printing-press manufacturer, Miller and Richard Company.

Patterson retired in 1907, leaving two of his sons to run his company. He continued as vice-president of the Manufacturers Life Insurance Company and director of both the Dominion Guarantee & Accident Insurance Company and the Ottawa Light & Power Company, but these two positions were not onerous and he had more time to enjoy his favourite sports, curling and lawn bowling.

In addition to being the 23rd president of the Toronto Granite Curling Club, Patterson was also president of the Granite Bowling Club and the bowling section at the RCYC. He also held frequent, informal bowling tournaments on the spacious grounds of Fernwood, his home in the village of Todmorden in the Don Valley and took a special interest in a bowling league for newspaper men, donating the Fernwood Cup for their tournaments. He was a nature lover and maintained a sanctuary for peacocks, deer, and other animals on his property. Patterson also belonged to the National Club and the Canadian Art Club. At his death in 1917, *The Globe* eulogized him as a "man known far and wide for his genial personality."

of pink marking the countries of the British Empire on which the sun never set. Toronto, renowned for its imperialistic zeal, held a memorial service on February 2, and every shop and office closed. With Edward VII's coronation, the brief Edwardian era began. At the end of the year, Guglielmo Marconi successfully transmitted the first long distance wireless telegraph signal from Cornwall in England to Signal Hill in St. John's, Newfoundland. It was now clear to everyone that long distance wireless telegraphy was feasible.

The Boer War, which had begun three years earlier, finally ended in 1902. It had lasted longer and had taken more lives than anyone had anticipated. And in Toronto, the age of the automobile had begun. City council passed a bylaw permitting motor cars to travel on city streets.

Another event, not of earth-shattering importance nor even of wide general interest, was noted in the *Toronto World*. Perhaps it was a slow news day for the paper because the article described, at some length, the annual general meeting of the Granite Curling Club:

GRANITES ELECT OFFICERS

Church Street Curlers Have Large Attendance at Enthusiastic Meeting

The annual meeting of the Granite Curling Club was held Saturday night and, if enthusiasm and large attendance count for anything, the season of 1902–1903 will

SAMUEL GEORGE BEATTY

Samuel George Beatty was president of the Granite Curling and Skating Company Limited (the proprietory company) in 1901. Born in Hastings County, Ontario, in 1843 and educated there, the ambitious Beatty was in his teens when he left for New York City and a course at Claflin's Business College. He was only 19 when, convinced that a similar college would thrive in Canada, he proceeded to establish one—in Belleville. He had to borrow money from friends, one of whom was Mackenzie Bowell, then owner of the Belleville *Intelligencer* and later prime minister of Canada. Within six months the school had become so successful that Beatty was able to repay all his debts.

Twenty-two years later, the prosperous and middle-aged Beatty sold his school, came to Toronto, and married Annie M. Eastwood. They moved into a splendid, three-storey Victorian house, Oakdene, at 168 Isabella Street, just west of Sherbourne. There, three sons and two daughters were born. In the 1990s, Oakdene still stood, somewhat shabby and forlorn, almost dwarfed by surrounding high-rise condominiums and commercial buildings.

Not surprisingly, after so many years in business education, the field of publishing caught Beatty's eye. He became manager, and later, president of the Canada Publishing Company where "he revised the whole school book system of Canada and modernized the entire curriculum." Beatty remained with Canada Publishing for about 30 years, during which time he also became a vice-president of the Manufacturers Life Insurance Company (along with his friend Robert Patterson, Granite Curling Club president) and a director of many financial concerns including the Canadian Mortgage Investment Company and the Bank of Hamilton.

be a record one…. The officers elected were: President, Mr. C.P. Smith; vice-president, Mr. George H. Gooderham; hon. secretary, Mr. A.E. Trow; hon. treasurer, Mr. Spencer Love.

The article went on to list every director, each member of the committee of management, and all the elected skips. Even bowling prize winners saw their names in print!

During George Gooderham's first term as club president in 1903–04, James Baird, KC, was president of the joint stock company, the Granite Curling and Skating Company Limited. After 25 years, the club's founding generation was less active, and, with expansion plans in the wind, Gooderham, Baird, and other influential members of the club decided it was time to reorganize. Some of the original shareholders had died and their shares were held by widows, children, or estates. Other shareholders may have felt they were too old to participate financially in any new building projects. It was a risky situation, since active members might lose control of the club to those shareholders who were inactive. A new company, Granites Limited, was incorporated to shift the ownership to the active members, and its first shareholders meeting was held December 30, 1903. Two weeks later, Granites Limited purchased from the Granite Skating and Curling Company its lands, premises, goods, and chattels for $29 315.05—part cash, with the balance covered by a 10-year, five percent mortgage. The entrance fee for the new club was $25–$10 for shares plus $15 for annual dues.

The first officers of the new company were president, James Baird; vice-president, Robert L. Patterson; and secretary-treasurer, J.M. Macdonald. Directors were S.G. Beatty, C.C. Dalton, J. Todhunter, James Hedley, C.P. Smith, and George R. Hargraft. The House Committee consisted of A.F. Rutter (chairman), George H. Gooderham, Spencer Love, E.F. Garrow, P.L. Bailey, A.J. Russell Snow, J.W. Seymour Corley, and Charles Reid.

C.P. Smith, President, Granite Club, 1902–3

J. Baird, President, Granites Limited, 1903

G.H. GOODERHAM, PRESIDENT, 1903–1904 AND 1906–1907

George Horace Gooderham became president in 1903. Independently wealthy, he was a third-generation scion of the distilling family. His grandfather, William Gooderham, and his great-uncle, James Worts, founded a flour mill at the mouth of the Don River in 1832. Worts died in 1834; three years later, William decided to build a distillery to use up the surplus and second-class grain. By 1914, Gooderham and Worts was the largest distiller in the British Empire.

George H. Gooderham was born in Toronto in 1868. He was just twenty when he married Maude Northrup and they first lived in a magnificent red sandstone Romanesque Revival style home at the northwest corner of Cawthra Square and Jarvis Street, a block east of the Granite Club. Gooderham particularly loved curling, lawn bowling, and sailing. As a curler, he and fellow skip C.C. Dalton won the Ontario Tankard in 1900.

He was active in the family firm and president of two insurance companies plus many others, including Canada Permanent Mortgage Corporation, Colonial Investment and Loan Company, Imperial Trusts Company of Canada, and the Toronto Hotel Company. He was also civic-minded, serving as president of the Canadian Zoological Society, director of the Children's Aid Society, and governor of the Toronto General Hospital. During his term as chairman of the Toronto Industrial Exhibition from 1909–1911, he donated the magnificent fountain that sparked the expression "Meet me at the fountain."

Gooderham was an active politician, first at the school board level, where he served as trustee from 1899–1903, and, the following year, as chairman. Putting his money where his mouth was, he donated 25 scholarships for students in Toronto's public schools. In 1908, he ran successfully for provincial office, becoming MPP for South Toronto.

The years 1903 and 1904 marked several important events in the life of the city and the province. In 1903 the King Edward Hotel opened. That was also the year that saw the death of Sir Oliver Mowat. He had been a Father of Confederation, premier of Ontario, senator, and lieutenant-governor of Ontario. His funeral cortege, one of the largest ever seen in Toronto, proceeded from Government House at King and Simcoe north to Mount Pleasant Cemetery. The following year was the year of the Great Toronto Fire, which destroyed almost everything east of York Street, south of King—one of the worst in the city's history.

On the evening of April 19, smoke was seen drifting from a building on Wellington Street between Yonge and Bay. Moments later, flames leapt from its elevator shaft and, fanned by high winds, spread rapidly through the city's commercial district, engulfing an area 500 feet wide and a quarter of a mile long. More than 200 firefighters from Toronto, and eventually Hamilton, Buffalo, London, and Peterborough, could not contain the fire that at times leapt 100 feet into the air. By the next morning 122 buildings had been gutted and more than 6000 people saw the firms for which they worked go up in flames. All that remained was 14 acres of smouldering ruins. Total financial losses exceeded $13 million.

Bruce West quotes eyewitness J. William Gerred, a Toronto streetcar motorman, one of the thousands of Torontonians who poured into the

Wyld, Grasett & Darling Warehouse before and after the Great Toronto Fire, 1904

J.M. Macdonald,
Secretary-Treasurer,
Granites Limited, 1903

In 1986 the Annex was designated as a property of architectural and historical interest under the Ontario Heritage Act. The designation states: "The property at 519 Church Street is recommended for designation for architectural and historical reasons. The Granite Club built this building as an addition to their clubhouse in 1906. It was designed by Edward R. Babington and was the only part to survive a 1913 fire. . . . The entrance hall and stair to the second floor are important features of this prominent community building in a City park."

downtown area that night, as he watched the warehouse of Granite member Frederick Wyld succumb to the flames:

> Everything was burning on both sides of Bay, both above and below Wellington, with one exception: a huge stone building on the southeast corner of Bay seemed to resist all the fire could do. It was surrounded by flames, and for what seemed an interminable time it held out…. Suddenly, as from an explosion, all floors seemed to be a blazing inferno in a single instant. This building had been the centre of all eyes, as if the vast throng was willing it to survive; but when the explosive blast ran through it, the entire mass of people gave a long drawn expression of 'Ah….'

After purchasing the assets of the Granite Skating and Curling Company in 1904, the directors of Granites Limited recognized the need to expand the facilities once again to provide for the club's growing membership. They decided to build a 56-foot-wide, three-storey annex, on the south side of the clubhouse, in a style consistent with that of the handsome 1880 original. It was to be attached so that members could go from one building to the other without venturing outdoors. Architect Edwin R. Babington was retained. Although his addition reflected the original design, what had succeeded for the first building—an "exuberant, Renaissance Revival building with flags set flying from a high centre tower," didn't quite work for the Annex. What members got was an uninspired, "dour clubhouse" with matching red brick, round-topped windows, and an ungainly front entrance—the doors flanked by skimpy granite columns that supported a massive projecting arch. (The Annex may well have appeared visually more attractive when anchored to the original clubhouse. It now stands alone, and adds little to the city's architectural heritage.)

There is nothing on the public record about the Granite Club in 1905, but it *was* the year of Eaton's first Santa Claus parade. It was also the year when scientists began to reassess their thinking when Albert Einstein published his *Theory of Relativity*.

The Annex was completed in December 1906. To celebrate its opening the directors organized a reception to be held on December 29. One

The Annex

hundred dollars was allotted for entertainment and light refreshments for the members, ladies, and friends who arrived to tour the new facility. At the annual meeting three weeks later the board passed a vote of thanks to Charles Reid, chairman of the building committee, "for his untiring energy and faithful devotion in carrying out the completion of the New Club Building." At about the same time C.C. Dalton and James Hedley were named honorary life members.

The year 1906 also marked the beginning of a bonspiel that was to become, if not the largest in the world, certainly the largest confined to one municipality. And by the time it came to an end 88 years later, it was incontestably the oldest.

In 1904, representatives from the Granite, Toronto Victoria, and Prospect Park curling clubs met at the Granite's Church Street clubhouse to organize a single-rink competition for Toronto

The First Canada Life Trophy winners, 1906 (l-r): J.W. Gale, vice skip; D.T. Prentice, Jr., lead; P.J. Edwards, second; W.E. McMurtry, skip

Charles Reid,
Building Committee Chair, 1906

curlers. They needed financial backing for such an ambitious enterprise and approached the Canada Life Assurance Company for sponsorship. Canada Life agreed and two years later those four clubs, joined by the Parkdale, Aberdeen, and Lakeview curling clubs, entered an impressive 81 teams in the inaugural event. (Of all these early clubs, only the Granite survives today.) A Granite rink skipped by W. Ernest McMurtry was that year's winner.

In 1909, former club president Robert Patterson sailed for Scotland with a contingent of 10 Canadian curlers to take on their traditional and congenial Scots rivals. Financier and diplomat Lord Strathcona, then president of the Royal Caledonian Curling Club, had presented a cup for competition between Scotland and Canada six years earlier. The Canadians won handily by an aggregate majority of 214 in three matches and the Scots were invited to pay a return visit to Canada three years later.

In 1910 the Granite Club again won the Canada Life Bonspiel. Of the 90 rinks competing, an impressive 23 came from the club. A record was also established that year that would never again be equalled—not that anyone would ever care to do so. Under ordinary circumstances the Canada Life Bonspiel lasted for a week. That winter the weather was so mild, it took more than a month to play all the games. In the final game Tom Rennie and Tom Wilson, fellow skips from the Granite Club, faced each other on their home ice and Rennie emerged victorious.

Rennie and his rink won three more Canada Life competitions between 1911 and 1917. With five victories since the competition's inauguration, the rules of the competition gave the Granite Club permanent possession of the trophy, a handsome 18-karat gold cup with miniature curling stones and brooms positioned on either side, "with a [pale green] solid marble base. Lifting it is a major problem." Twelve gold plaques affixed to the base bear the names of the winners. It can still be seen today, proudly displayed in the club's trophy case.

The highlight of the club's next five years was the remarkable achievement of the Rennie and Wilson curling teams in Tankard competition. These memorable rinks won the Ontario Silver Tankard for three consecutive years,

In 1904, Charles Boeckh became president of the Granite Curling Club. He was a partner in one of Canada's largest and oldest brush manufacturers, Charles Boeckh & Sons, established by his father in 1856. By the 1890s their large factory on Adelaide Street west employed more than one hundred skilled workmen and its brushes, brooms and wooden ware were sold from coast to coast in Canada and in Newfoundland and England as well.

Ontario Tankard Winners, 1909, 1910, 1911 Left: Rennie Rink (seated, l-r) John Rennie, vice skip; Thomas Rennie, skip; (standing, l-r) A.B. Nichols, second; C.O. Knowles, lead. Right: Wilson Rink (seated, l-r) H.T. Wilson, skip; Dr. B.E. Hawke, vice skip; (standing, l-r) R.J. Hunter, second; F. Tremble, lead.

CHARLES OSWALD KNOWLES, Granite Member and Champion Curler

Knowles was born in Guelph in 1875; early in his working life he had a brief stint as a hardware store clerk, then he became a "printer's devil" (errand boy) at the *Guelph Mercury.* One day the editor needed someone to cover a political meeting and young Knowles, the only employee in sight, was assigned. His career in journalism took off and before long he was made city editor. Moving to Toronto at the turn of the century, he worked briefly for *The Mail and Empire*—one of seven dailies in the city—then joined *The Evening Telegram,* where he was to spend most of his working life. Slim and keen-featured, he sported large, black horn-rimmed glasses that soon became his trademark.

Knowles left the paper for a brief period to help organize the Canadian Press news service and become its general manager. He returned to *The Evening Telegram* in 1920 and 12 years later was appointed editor-in-chief, a position he held until his retirement in 1948. A year earlier, in honour of his 50 years as a newspaperman, Lieutenant-Governor Ray Lawson, along with city councillors, representatives from the Toronto Police Association, the Canadian Press, the Toronto Press Club, and members of his staff gathered at City Hall to pay tribute to his remarkable career. Even his political opponents were there—a token of their grudging respect for the fierce independence of his editorial pages. An illuminated address, read by Mayor Leslie Saunders, proclaimed: "In you we recognize a doughty champion and a true guardian of the liberties of the people."

using the same eight players each time—a record no other club has achieved, before or since. They defeated Ingersoll in 1909, Grand Rapids, Michigan, in 1910, and Lindsay in 1911. And perhaps to make their accomplishment even more impressive, those were the days of five-hour-long, 22-end games, played on natural ice.

For the Rennie rink, Thomas was skip, his brother John, vice-skip. Their father, William (who, in 1870, established the William Rennie Seed Company* on Adelaide Street East, near Jarvis), had been a prominent curler. In 1872, three years before the Granite Club opened its doors, he had been a leading spirit in the founding of the Toronto Caledonian Curling Club. Married in 1862, he and his wife, Sarah Glendinning, began producing their own family curling team—four sons: Robert, William Jr., John, and Thomas. The Rennie boys had begun curling on a rink at the George Street Public School on Wilton Crescent, playing with wooden blocks, for what they called the "backyard championship."

In 1894 the Rennie brothers won the Mowat Cup and, although William Jr. defected the following year to become a missionary in Japan, the remaining brothers (joined by A.B. Nichols) won it again in 1895—and so often thereafter, in 1905 it became theirs to keep. They also won the

Thomas Rennie in action

William Rennie saved the log cabin that John Scadding built in 1792. Scadding came to Upper Canada with John Graves Simcoe and was father of Henry Scadding, the first rector of Holy Trinity Church. In 1879 the cabin was slated for demolition, but Rennie, as president of the York Pioneers and an officer of Toronto's Industrial Exhibition, intervened. He supervised the loading of the cabin onto a primitive ox cart, then proudly drove the oxen along King Street to the cabin's present site where Toronto's oldest building remains—in the grounds of the Canadian National Exhibition.

*The company prospered for 91 years. It was bought in 1961 by the Steele-Briggs Seed Company.

Mowat Cup

Walker Gold Cup for the single-rink championship of Toronto in 1896, 1897, 1900, 1903, and, for their permanent possession, in 1904.

The lead and second for the Rennie rink in the Tankard were both newspaper men. A.B. "Bert" Nichols was superintendent of the composing room of the *Toronto World*, and Charles Oswald Knowles (known to everyone as "C.O.") was, at the time, news editor of *The Evening Telegram*.

The second triple-crown Tankard rink was skipped by another fine competitor, Holcombe Thomas Wilson (known to all as Tom), part owner of the highly successful Grocers Limited. His partners in the firm were Granite curlers Harold E. Beatty and W. "Ernie" McMurtry. Wilson's wife, also a champion curler, played three times on a winning Ladies' Tankard team. One of Wilson's great loves was his air-cooled Franklin motor car, a familiar sight on the streets of Toronto in the early 1920s. The Wilsons' son, Harry, began his business life as an office boy at National Trust—and ended up as its president. His grandson, Michael Wilson, served as Canadian finance minister in Brian Mulroney's Conservative government.

According to Harry Wilson, his father "was the *best* curler in Canada, without a doubt…very steady." He and Thomas Rennie established a record unequalled in the 125-year annals of the Ontario Tankard competition. It could be argued that Rennie was the better of the two, since he was on a winning Tankard rink eight times, while Wilson won just half that number. And it might be argued as well that, in 1910, when they competed against each other in an all-Granite Club final of the Canada Life Bonspiel, Rennie came out on top. Nevertheless, they were both all-star curlers who brought honour to themselves and to the club.

And what of the other members of Tom Wilson's formidable Tankard team? Vice-skip Benjamin Elmore Hawke was a physician who lived around the corner from the Granite Club at 21 Wellesley Street. Born in Waterloo County, he grew up in Berlin (now Kitchener) and attended Trinity Medical College, Toronto, graduating in 1887. After earning a post-graduate degree at the New

York City Polyclinic, he practised in Stratford for 10 years. Dr. Hawke also began his curling and lawn bowling career in Stratford. Moving to Toronto in 1901, he promptly joined the Granite Club. The second position on Wilson's rink was capably filled by R.J. "Bob" Hunter. He was in the flour and feed business in the west end, and his firm supplied the city cattle market. Wilson's lead, Fred Tremble, was proprietor of the Victoria Exchange Hotel on Victoria Street.

During the century's first decade, Toronto's population soared from 200 000 to 342 000. One of the highlights of those years was the opening of the Royal Alexandra Theatre in 1907. That same year there were 1500 automobiles bumping along Ontario's roads—and, in Toronto, police issued their first traffic ticket. As well, in its ongoing drive to keep the youth of "Toronto the Good" from slipping into moral decay, city council declared it illegal to toboggan in city parks on Sundays.

In 1908, thanks to a generous donation of $350 000 from American steel tycoon Andrew Carnegie, the Central Reference Library opened; and in 1909, Governor-General Earl Grey donated a trophy for the Canadian football championship. The first Grey Cup game was played in what is now Rosedale Park, between Toronto Varsity and Toronto Balmy Beach. In 1910, after only nine years on the throne, Edward VII died, aged 69, bringing the Edwardian era to an end. His son, George Frederick, succeeded him as George V.

As the second decade began, vast mineral resources discovered in Northern Ontario created a flood of wealth that flowed into the city. The "means of transporting electric energy long distances by high tension cable was being perfected [and] Toronto was less than a hundred miles from Niagara, the source of boundless and cheap power…. Under their silk hats, the business leaders of Toronto began to feel large ideas stirring. New buildings, new factories, new residential suburbs sprang up." By 1913, power from Niagara was flowing to Toronto.

Varsity Stadium opened in 1911 and construction began for the first home of Women's College Hospital at 18 Seaton Street. It had only seven beds when it opened in 1915 and owed its very existence to the efforts of a few determined women doctors who had been denied accreditation in other Toronto hospitals. During those same years Casa Loma rose in all its opulence and splendour atop the escarpment overlooking the city, and the Timothy Eaton Memorial Church, the Eaton family's enduring legacy to the city in which their fortune had originated, opened its doors.

In 1912 the Toronto Harbour Commission began its vast landfill project south of Front Street. Until this ambitious project was begun, Front Street did just what its name indicates—it "fronted" on Lake Ontario. (Everything south of Front Street is on reclaimed land.) The following year the new General Hospital on College Street was officially opened by Lieutenant-Governor John Gibson and a streetcar line began operating between Bathurst and Yonge on St. Clair Avenue, then little more than a rutted mud road.

As Toronto prospered, so did the Granite Club. In 1910, Alexander Archibald Allan became president of Granites Limited, a post he held until his death in 1922. He was just the man the club needed to see it through the turbulent years that lay ahead. Born in the Orkney Islands, Allan had

The Granite Club after the fire of 1913

come to Toronto as an infant. He became a successful businessman, president of the firm A.A. Allan & Co. (wholesale hats and furs), a director of the National Club, and a member of the Ontario Club.

Other than the two Toms—Rennie and Wilson—skipping their curling teams to their second and third Tankard win in 1910 and 1911, nothing of great note happened at the Granite Club during the first few years of the century's second decade. Then came 1913.

At 3:20 p.m. on October 3, 1913, alarm bells clanged in fire halls across the city and fire engines raced to Church Street. But "it was twelve minutes before the first stream of water was turned on to the fire which by this time had made marvellous headway." Dozens of hoses under the personal direction of Fire Chief Thompson and Deputy Chief Noble soon joined in—all to no avail. By 3:50 p.m., a mere half-hour after the first alarm sounded, the 1880 Granite clubhouse and rink on Church Street had been reduced to smouldering ruins.

For quite some time, the club had not used the main floor where the fire had started. Four years earlier the board of directors had decided that, with the Annex fully operational, the rink and the main floor of the original clubhouse were no longer needed. The latter was rented to Gibson's Electric Ltd. for offices and a showroom, while the rink area in the rear was leased to A.L. Spalding for an automobile repair shop. The fire began in the office area and was attributed to defective wiring. No one was there at the time and the fire spread undetected until a passerby on Church Street saw flames leaping out of the transom above the front door. Up on the second floor, club member S.J. Murphy saw smoke in the billiard room and, with great presence of mind, slammed shut the fire doors leading to the Annex. Murphy's prompt action undoubtedly saved it from destruction, but the reading room, the billiard room with its four English billiards tables,* and the steward's quarters, all on the second floor of the old building, were lost. The Annex suffered only water damage.

Once it got going, the blaze raced along the T-shaped building's 180-foot length. Nine automobiles in Spalding's repair shop were destroyed and gas tanks exploded. One lucky fireman narrowly escaped being "buried under a mass of debris when one of the walls fell immediately after the explosion of one of the cars."

There were, fortunately, no human casualties, but birds and dogs fared less well. Jennie, a prize whippet valued at $300 and owned by club steward G.D. White, refused to leave her rooftop kennel and was asphyxiated. Blue Prince, in an adjoining kennel, managed to escape and was last seen

*English billiards tables are larger than regulation-size snooker tables, and have no pockets.

high-tailing it up Church Street. And Merlin Clubins, a neighbour at 513 Church, was more than a little upset at losing a dozen valuable pigeons, "smothered by smoke in their cots."

Other frightened neighbours raced to save their houses and their belongings. "People in the homes to the south between the club and the drug store at the corner of Church and Wellesley streets began taking the furniture out of their houses, and the sidewalks and lawns were covered with bed clothes, tables, pianos, and all kinds of household furnishings." Just east of Church Street, at 84 Wellesley, Cottage Hospital was also threatened by the blaze, since its building extended northwards to within 30 yards of the old rink. Patients were evacuated on stretchers and taken by ambulance to the brand-new General Hospital that had opened on College Street just four months earlier. Ten newborn babies were carried to the Chinese Mission on Wellesley Street and to neighbouring homes. Doctors Primrose, Copp, and Milner stayed behind at Cottage Hospital to extinguish fires that kept flaring up on the roof, the awnings, and the exterior woodwork—fires ignited by sparks and the intense heat. For hours dense smoke hung over the neighbourhood. Streetcars were rerouted along Sherbourne Street between Bloor and King and thousands of curious spectators were held back by cordons of police, some on horseback.

The curling rink at the northeast corner of the property was fortunately unharmed. That evening, with the fire engines barely out of sight and the old clubhouse a pile of rubble, a game of indoor baseball proceeded at the rink, as scheduled.

Club Secretary James M. Macdonald estimated damages at $65 000, but the club was, he said, "pretty well covered by insurance." The directors wasted no time in dealing with the emergency. Just 10 days after the fire, they met with architect and club member William F. Sparling to consider a rough sketch of a new building that he had prepared. After much discussion, they decided to build a two-storey addition to the east end of the Annex rather than rebuild on the site of the old clubhouse. Sparling's firm, Curry & Sparling, was retained to draw plans for the "addition of a building sixty-six feet by fifty feet, of a uniform width of the rear part of the present building." It was to include a large auditorium, a billiard room, a kitchen, and staff quarters. Sparling magnanimously offered to waive his fee. Two months later, the directors accepted a bid of $13 675 and construction began. At a later meeting, the directors decided to add bowling alleys.

The directors went on to approve a tender of $308 from Goldstick & Company to remove the debris left by the fire. And, reluctantly, they decided to sell the south portion of the club's property (an area of about 66 by 125 feet), since the insurance payable on the loss of the old clubhouse would not be sufficient to finance the new addition and its furnishings. The property was duly listed with the real estate firm of Sinclair & Sinclair. (By June of the following year, it remained unsold and realtor R.B. Rice of the Queen City Curling Club, and Gibson Smith Realtors were retained with a commission of 2.5 per cent to be paid on sale.) The final item on a very full agenda that evening was a motion, passed unanimously, to send a cheque for $2500 to the Firemen's Benefit Fund "for the efficient work of the firemen in the discharge of their duties at the recent fire of [the] Granite Rink."

CHAPTER FIVE

LAST YEARS ON CHURCH STREET

1914–1925

IT TOOK A LITTLE MORE than a year to complete the addition and renovations of the club. The grand opening took place December 17, 1914, and *The Globe* greeted it with a glowing report:

> HIS HONOR OPENS NEW GRANITE CLUB
>
> The new premises of the Granite Club, so extensively and handsomely remodelled that old-timers would hardly recognize the interior of the big Church Street organization, were opened last night with great *éclat*.... Lieutenant-Governor Hendrie was the guest of honor. The presentation of an address by President E.L. Williams, and his Honor's reply, were the chief formal features, and the Lieutenant-Governor was made an honorary member of both the club and the curling section. He promised to take a hand in the winter's games, and Miss Hendrie will play with

Three thousand one hundred
Torontonians were killed in the
course of the First World War.

the ladies' club that has been organized. The new big billiard room with six English tables, and a fully equipped bowling alley are some of the additional attractions for members.... There has been a large increase in the membership, which is now close to the waiting list.

War had broken out in Europe four months earlier, but Canadians, with an ocean separating them from the conflict, felt safe. As C.L Burton had so aptly put it, they "had not the faintest premonition of what was in store.... Canada had been in a definite slump during 1913 and the months of 1914 prior to the declaration of war. The year 1913 marked virtually the end of the great railroad building era which, for more than a generation, had been the basic construction enterprise...[leaving] Canada as a whole at a loss to know what to do next. The war provided the answer, terrible though it was in the loss of 60 000 Canadian lives and the maiming of over three times that number...." The industrial community promptly geared up for the production of munitions of all kinds. The war overseas was an unprecedented horror, but, "at home, individual companies...had never been better off.... The four war years...put a firm economic foundation under all legitimate businesses and brought a new standard of living to all who worked. While others gave their lives, and some gave up any prospects of ever making an adequate living...[those] at home fared rather shamefully well." (Burton may well have been thinking of Simpson's vice-president, Sir Joseph Flavelle, who, as president of the British Empire's largest pork packer, William Davies Company of Toronto, was accused of profiteering from wartime sales of bacon.)

Nor did the Granite Club suffer unduly from the war. Members, of course, did join the tens of thousands of Torontonians who volunteered to serve overseas. Leaves of absence were granted to those who enlisted and membership revenues declined accordingly. It is probably no coincidence that it was then that women (wives, daughters, and sisters) were invited to join the club for the first time. And join they did; during the first year of the war, the Ladies' Granite Curling Club was founded. As Lieutenant-Governor Hendrie mentioned in his opening remarks, his daughter would "play with the ladies' club." Curling as a game for women was an idea whose time had finally come.

It had once been said, perhaps in jest, that the "hand that rocked the cradle would never cradle a rock."

Granite Lady Curlers, circa 1915

In a similar vein, Rev. John Kerr, a well-known Scottish curler, had stated patronizingly in 1890 that women "find the curling stone too heavy for their delicate arms." But it wasn't just Victorian male attitudes that had prevented women from curling. There had been physical constraints as well—whalebone corsets pulled as tight as possible, voluminous layers of petticoats, and long, heavy skirts, to mention but a few. Women's dresses in the 19th century were designed to attract attention and hamper movement—hardly an encouragement for any athletic endeavour. But the 20th century brought new freedoms for women.

The Granite Club cannot, however, take credit for introducing Canadian women to curling. At the turn of the century, 80 spirited women had formed the Montreal Ladies' Curling Club and, in their very first year, organized an "At Home" event in which six "mixed" teams played.

By 1910 Ontario had witnessed the founding of three women's curling clubs—in Belleville, Kingston, and Peterborough. Three years later, the Toronto Ladies' Curling Club, which had been founded in 1911, joined these three to form the Ladies' Ontario Curling Association (LOCA). In 1915 the Ladies' Granite Curling Club joined the association, with 31-year-old Marian Elizabeth Suckling (née Myers) as the club's representative at that year's annual meeting. Tragically, she died just seven years later and, in her honour, the Marian Suckling Trophy was inaugurated at the Church Street Granite Club in 1924. It has been in continuous competition ever since.

The association's constitution and bylaws, drafted by the Granite's Emma Robertson and the Toronto Curling Club's Mrs. George Biggar, were adopted in 1918. A year later, Granite member Mrs. H.T. Wilson, wife of legendary curler Tom Wilson, became LOCA's president.

A man well ahead of his time, James Andrew Macfadden, the Ontario Curling Association's president in 1914–15, welcomed women to the "roaring game" and presented them with a handsome trophy, the Ontario Ladies Tankard. To this day, winning the Tankard is Ontario's top curling honour for women. The Granite Ladies first won it on their "home ice" in 1917. The ecstatic skips were Mrs. E.B. Nettlefield and Christina (Mrs. Charles) Bulley. The following year, Bulley triumphed

*Skips Christina Bulley and Mrs. E.B.
Nettlefield's team mates were Marian
Suckling, Mrs. Cork, Mrs. Mills,
Mrs. H.T. Wilson, Mrs.George H.
Shaw, and Miss Boomer.*

Granite Ladies Team, 1919, Winners
of Ontario Ladies Tankard (front
row, l-r) Miss Blanche Rennie, skip;
Mrs. Ziba Gallagher; Mrs. George H.
Shaw, skip; (back row, l-r) Betty
Alexander; Mrs. Charles W.W.
Archibald; Mrs. J.Lindsay Graham;
Mrs. Cork; Mrs. Frederick F. Myles;
Marion Suckling.

again—this time with Blanche Rennie, who was following in the footsteps of her famous father, Thomas. Skips Mrs. George H. Shaw and Blanche Rennie won for the Granite Club for the third, consecutive time, in 1919. In 1921, having served two years as the LOCA president, Mrs. H.T. Wilson curled on one of the Granite Club's Tankard winning rinks. The winning skips that year were Mrs. Cork and Mrs. Shaw. In addition to a miniature Tankard trophy, each winning curler received a beautiful Crown Derby cup and saucer. Runners-up had to settle for Aynsley. These prizes were donated by the Granite Club, a practice continued until 1936 when the Association took over.

While Granite women were busy garnering curling honours during the war years, other people were involved in a variety of pursuits, many of which had nothing to do with the war effort. In 1914, for instance, Canada's Governor-General, the Duke of Connaught, officially opened the Royal Ontario Museum. Later that year, at Maple Leaf Park on Toronto Island, the legendary George Herman "Babe" Ruth hit his first home run as a professional.* That year as well, the federal government suspended gold conversion for its currency, and soon the printing presses at the Mint were running overtime. Inflation, which had been running at a comfortable rate of 2.5 per cent per year from 1900 to 1914, soared to 20 per cent due to minimal taxation and heavy government borrowings to finance the war effort.

On February 4, 1916, the *Globe's* morning headlines reported that a spectacular fire had destroyed the Centre Block of the Parliament Buildings in Ottawa: "The most picturesque public building in North America is a shapeless ruin…fire believed to be work of the enemy…dramatic end of Commons sitting." The House was in session when the fire was discovered and members fled without retrieving their hats and coats. Within three hours the building was almost totally in ruins and the main tower a furnace of flames. Seven lives were lost. Later investigation established that the fire had been caused, not by the incendiary work of enemy agents, but by careless smoking in the reading room.

Four of the 1918 Tankard winners, Christina Bulley, Mrs. H. T. Wilson, Mrs. Cork, and Mrs. Frederick F. Myles had curled with the victorious Granite rinks the year before. (Myles was the former Miss Boomer.) The other four curlers were new: Blanche Rennie, Betty Alexander, Mrs. Charles W. W. Archibald, and Mrs. J. Lindsay Graham (née Heintzman). Between 1917 and 1942 Christina Bulley skipped eight Granite rinks to victory in the Ladies Ontario Tankard competition.

The winning Tankard curlers in 1919 were the same as the previous year, except that Christina Bulley and Mrs. Wilson were replaced by Marian Suckling and Mrs. Ziba Gallagher.

Ruth was pitcher for the Providence Grays, a farm team of the Boston Red Sox, playing against the Toronto Maple Leafs in the International League.

Also in 1916, cries of dismay were heard in some quarters when Sir William F. Hearst's Conservative government passed the Ontario Temperance Act and Prohibition was ushered in. The sale of all alcoholic beverages was banned—ostensibly to induce breweries and distilleries to produce industrial alcohol to help the war effort.* Hearst, however, was a zealous temperance advocate and there was a well-founded suspicion that Prohibition had more to do with lobbying by the Women's Christian Temperance Union than with the demands of war. "But it was never forbidden to *make* alcoholic beverages in Ontario—for export purposes only, of course—and respectable distillers and brewers enhanced their fortunes when their goods were shipped to the United States—and, often, back into the province." Liquor could be consumed legally in one's home and, by extension, in one's club, but the problem remained—where to buy it? The other provinces followed suit within the year, except for Quebec, which waited until 1919 and then banned only liquor sales, not beer or wine. The United States also enacted prohibition legislation in 1916, passing the 18th Amendment to their Constitution. Bootlegging thrived in both countries.

In 1917 Ontario became the fifth province to give women the right to vote, and in 1918 women won the federal franchise. For the first time in history, the federal government introduced income tax—proclaiming the Dominion Income War Tax in 1917 as a "temporary measure" to finance the war. That same year a munitions ship collided with another vessel in the Bedford Basin at Halifax. The ensuing explosion destroyed most of the surrounding area and left 1800 dead and 4000 injured. On April 6, 1917, the United States entered the war.

The tide of the war began to turn in the Allies' favour and in August 1918 Canadian soldiers broke through the enemy lines at Amiens. The armistice was signed in November of that year. But, as the Great War ended, a new scourge loomed on the horizon—the virulent Spanish flu that killed "25 million people in six months and was likened to the Black Death. It was responsible for the deaths of twice as many people as the First World War and in only one-eighth the time…. In

*By 1927, when the Act was discarded, only 15 of the 54 breweries in existence in 1916 remained.

Canada (population eight million), it sent one of every six citizens to their sick beds and killed 60 000 people." What made matters even worse was that, for some reason, the virus infected mostly young people—26- to 30-year-olds. War casualties and deaths from flu inflicted a loss on Canada of 120 000 people in five years—the better part of a generation. Ten thousand people perished from the flu in Ontario alone and, in Toronto, 150 000 were infected and 1750 died. Toronto's Medical Officer of Health, Charles J. Hastings, decreed that "after Saturday, October 19th, 1918, all Moving Picture Shows and other places of amusement, including Pool Rooms, Billiard Rooms and Bowling Alleys, throughout the city shall be closed during the period of the Influenza Epidemic, and shall not be opened until further notice." The 1919 Stanley Cup playoffs, between Montreal and Seattle, were cancelled in mid-series. People were terrified, and for good reason. It was the deadliest pandemic in history.

In August 1919, the Prince of Wales (later Edward VIII and, after his abdication, the Duke of Windsor) arrived in Toronto for a three-day visit, during which time he laid the cornerstone for the new RCYC clubhouse. Three months later, Hart House, a cultural, social, and athletic centre at the University of Toronto, was officially opened—for the use of male students only. Vincent Massey, later Canada's first native-born Governor-General, had conceived the idea when he was an undergraduate at Oxford and his family financed the project. He supervised every detail of its construction and, when it was finished, named it after his grandfather, Hart Massey, founder of the family firm. Soldiers' Memorial Tower was added to Hart House in 1924 to commemorate students and alumni who had lost their lives in the war.

After the armistice, soldiers flocked home and some began to play hockey again, just as they had done in their university days before the war. The Granite Club had not had a hockey team since 1896 but now, with renewed enthusiasm, the club's athletes took to the ice once again. The Granites rejoined the Ontario Hockey Association where the sports editor of *The Toronto Star*,

Toronto Granites: OHA Senior Champions, 1920. (front row, l-r) Donald J. Jeffrey, forward; Hugh J. Fox, defence: (middle row, l-r) Hugh R. Aird, forward; Henry "Harry" Ellis Watson, forward; P.G. Campbell, manager; H.E. Beatty, president Toronto Granite Hockey Club; D.T. Prentice, treasurer, Toronto Granite Hockey Club; Dr. W.J. "Jerry" Laflamme, defence; Alex. E. Romeril, forward; (back row, l-r) H. Westerby, trainer; Wilfred F. Wright, forward; H.A. Fowler, forward; T.A. Clark, sub. goal; F. Carroll, coach; (absent) G.D. Addison, goal

William A. Hewitt (father of hockey broadcaster, Foster, and grandfather of Bill) was secretary. Hewitt also served as manager of the Granite Club hockey teams.

It didn't take long for the new team to return to the championship form of their 19th-century predecessors. In 1919–20, their first year together as a team, they won the OHA Senior Championship for the coveted John Ross Robertson Cup. In the finals between the Granite Club and Hamilton Tigers, the Granites lost 2–1 on Hamilton ice. In the return game in Toronto they won 5–0, winning the round 6–2. "The Granites had a very aggressive and determined team, with a strong defence, and they measured up well with the champions of former years."

The following year the Granites were runners-up for the OHA Senior Championship, defeated 7–3 in the two-game finals by the University of Toronto—the first year in OHA history that Varsity had won the championship.

In 1922, for the second time in three years, the Granites won the OHA senior championship, defeating Aura Lee of Toronto in the two final games by a total score of 16–5. At left wing, Harry Watson scored four goals in the second game. In the two-game finals for the Allan Cup (donated by Sir Hugh Montagu Allan in 1910 and emblematic of Canadian amateur hockey supremacy), "Granites outclassed Regina Victorias, Western champions winning the first game 6–2 and the second 7–0.... Granites played good clean hockey all winter and the honors won by them were well deserved."

During the war, the number of players on a team had been reduced from seven to our present day six. This decision was made by the OHA because of "the way all clubs had been depleted of players [by the large numbers who had enlisted in the armed forces] .... John Ross Robertson, approaching eighty at the time, and not well, pushed himself to his feet, was recognized by the chair, and spoke in favour."

In 1921, Hugh Aird, Hugh Fox, Donald Jeffrey, Alex Romeril, and Harry Watson were the only remaining players from the previous year's Granites championship team. Jerry Laflamme moved up to the manager's position, replacing P.G. Campbell, and John Ross Roach replaced G.D. Addison in goal. The other new players were Jack T. Aggett, Ernest J. ("Ernie") Collett, Clarence Hicks, Albert J. ("Bert") McCaffery, and Duncan B. ("Dunc") Munro.

In 1923 the Granites once more became OHA senior champions. "The victory of the Granites marked their third in the last four years, a remarkable record." A *Globe* reporter described their impressive two-game win over the Hamilton Tigers:

Watson, Munro and Cameron Provide Brilliant Play.

The 1922 Granite team remained pretty much the same as the 1921 version, except that Ernie Collett was promoted to manager, Bert McCaffery to forward captain, and R. Fred Anderson replaced Roach in goal. Hugh Aird and Clarence Hicks left the team and the new players were Dr. J.M. "Mac" Sheldon on defence, and H.S. Reginald ("Hooley") Smith and Frank G. Sullivan on the forward line. Frank Carrol was the coach and H. Westerby, the trainer.

The 1923 Granites had kept their team intact from the previous year except for three new players: Jack Cameron, who replaced Anderson in goal, and Beattie Ramsay and J. Murray Rutherford who took over from Sheldon and Sullivan.

Granites are champions of the Ontario Hockey Association senior series for the second consecutive time…. The score on the round is 6-4…there is no doubt as to the better team…but they have goalkeeper Cameron to thank…at least eight times the Tigers beat the defence only to have the former St. Andrew's College star coolly block the shot. Six thousand fans jammed their way into the arena…. At 6 o'clock in the morning the fans began to line up at the standing room entrance, and fully a thousand were on hand before the game commenced…Harry Watson, rated as a "bad man" in the "Ambitious City" scored the first goal…. The work of Watson, Munro, Cameron and Smith deserves special mention…. After a season of ups and downs, "Dunc" Munro came into his own last night and showed that he is rightly rated one of the best defence men in the sport… "Hooley" Smith…did a lot of useful checking and proved tricky on the attack. McCaffery, Jeffrey, Ramsay and Fox were also effective.

As they had done the year before, the Granites went on to become Canadian hockey champions, winning the Allan Cup. They handily defeated the University of Saskatchewan by a two-game total score of 11–2.

Having won the Allan Cup two years in a row, the Granites were chosen to represent Canada at the first Olympic Winter Games, to be held in Chamonix, France, from January 25 to February 5, 1924. Six of the players were unable to make the trip (Aggett, Fox, Jeffrey, Rodden, Romeril, and Rutherford) and Cyril "Sig" Slater and Harold McMunn were added to the nine-player roster as substitute left and right wings. To get in shape, the team played eight exhibition games against the best amateur teams in Ontario and Quebec, finishing up with a 4–1 win against the Maritime champions, the Charlottetown "Abegweits" in Saint John, N.B. The Granites left for England the next day aboard the RMS Montcalm for an eight-day Atlantic crossing. In a report filed with *The Evening Telegram*, Harry Watson described the voyage:

> Jan. 11, 1924—The trip started in a not too promising manner as the Bay of Fundy was on its bad behaviour and certainly showed its mean disposition with a wind, rain, and fog storm from the time we set sail till the morning of Jan. 12. The result was that almost all of us remained on deck till pretty late. Hooley Smith had bet me $10 that he wouldn't be seasick, but about 11 p.m. was counted out by Referee P.J. Mulqueen. At this time Hooley's main cry was "And we've got to come back!" Breakfast on the 12th was a very sad affair, as Jack Cameron, Ramsay, Rankin, and myself were the only members to appear. This was the day of Dunc Munro's famous quotation: "Why the — don't they hold the games at Oakville?" He was afraid he was going to die; the next day he was afraid he was not going to die.

Calm seas and warm sunny weather, however, soon arrived to cure their ills. The remainder of the voyage passed quickly and pleasantly with shuffleboard and deck tennis tournaments, evening concerts, and bridge games. The players kept in shape by throwing a medicine ball, skipping, and jogging around the deck. Arriving in London at the Hotel Cecil* on the Thames embankment, they set off for a day's shopping, followed by a sumptuous dinner at Simpson's-on-the-Strand—famous for its roast beef served from a trolley at tableside—and a play at the Winter Garden theatre.

A beautiful oil painting of the Hotel Cecil hangs in Peacock Alley at the club. The hotel was demolished in 1930.

Paris was the next stop, with box seats at the Folies Bergères. "A great time was had by all," enthused Harry Watson, "and the best parts…I will withhold until I hear from the censor."

Then on to Chamonix and six games that were to make hockey history. When they arrived, Hewitt, the team's general manager, cabled *The Toronto Star*:

> One and all agreed that there was no more picturesque spot anywhere…. The village is about 5000 feet above sea level, but set down in a beautiful valley surrounded by towering mountains, which reach into the clouds. The most famous peak is that of Mont Blanc, 16 400 feet high, which throws its shadow down the Chamonix valley. There are several glaciers with thousands of tons of ice which shift on an average of from 30 to 40 feet per year. A rushing mountain stream, 30 feet in width, bisects the village…. The stadium is about twice as large as the University of Toronto stadium, and has seating accommodation on both sides in bleacher form for about 5000 people.

Because of his short stature—he was just 5'4"—Hewitt didn't have much opportunity to play hockey. But he loved the game with a passion, and it became his life. He was sports editor of *The Toronto Star* from 1900 to 1931. He served as secretary of the Ontario Hockey Association (OHA) for an amazing 60 years—from 1903 to 1963. He also helped to found the Canadian Amateur Hockey Association in 1914 and was its registrar-treasurer from 1924 to 1961. Confirming the high regard in which he was held, more than 500 sports celebrities attended a testimonial dinner held in his honour in 1953 on the occasion of his 50th anniversary as secretary of the OHA.

In another report from Chamonix for the *Toronto Star*, team captain Duncan Munro informed the folks back home that:

Mr. Hewitt has the boys under strict discipline. They are to retire at ten o'clock and rise for an eight o'clock breakfast. I may say that by ten o'clock they are all glad to go to bed, as the wonderful air here makes you very tired.... Chamonix is the St. Moritz of France. There are many things to do here, but most of them are out of bounds until after we win the world's championship.

The games were played on natural ice out doors, on a European size rink—185 x 90 feet—"quite unfamiliar to Canadians who were used to smaller confines that created a more physical game. Also, the boards were only about a foot high, thus preventing the Canadians from using them with the skill they did back home, particularly for hitting and passing.... From the time the Granites arrived, the weather varied in the extreme, from warm sun to heavy rains. These conditions were not ideal for hockey."

In spite of these obstacles, the Granites could do no wrong. They covered themselves with glory, winning every game they played. They shut out Sweden, Czechoslovakia, and Switzerland; crushed Great Britain 19–2; then defeated the U.S. in a hard-hitting final, 6 to 1. "The weather for that game was perfect—clear and cold—producing hard fast ice." Harry Watson was knocked unconscious in the first 20 seconds of play. He not only recovered, but went on, with blood in his eyes, to score the first two goals. After the game, Beattie Ramsay remarked that the "U.S. players evidently intended

Hooley Smith leading the Canadian delegation at the 1924 Olympics in Chamonix, France

Beattie Ramsay takes a shot on goal during Olympic competition

to stop our star forward if possible because they figured, with his goal scoring ability lessened, their chances would be improved. But it only tended to make Watson play all the harder."

The Granites were heading home in triumph, bearing the Olympic Gold Medal. Congratulatory messages poured in. The Prince of Wales wired his "hearty congratulations," as did Prime Minister Mackenzie King who expressed the country's delight: "All Canada is proud of this latest feather in her cap." Ontario's Premier George Howard Ferguson was equally enthusiastic: "You have not only brought great credit to yourselves, but to your country." From the chairman of the French Olympic Committee: "Le Compte Justinien Clary presents his compliments to Mr. Hewitt with all his admiration for your splendid hockey team and your brilliant final victory." And from the Granite Club, "Congratulations. You sure did it."

On their return to Paris, the Granites agreed to play an exhibition game against Great Britain. A weary Hooley Smith confessed that it was the most exhausting game of the entire tour: "Between the champagne parties, excursions to the Folies Bergères and the like," he complained, "we were pooped out, and the only way we could get a rest during the exhibition game was to shoot the puck up among the champagne drinkers at the tables surrounding the rink. It was messy but effective." A dinner and dance at the posh Claridge Hotel, sponsored by Canada's T. Eaton Co. Ltd., no doubt added to the athletes' fatigue—as, quite possibly, did their visits to the Temple of Beauty, 7 à 9 Rue de Hanovre, that advertised "bains de luxe, ouvert jusqu'à 3 heures du matin, English spoken."

Back in London, the red carpet was rolled out. The team was welcomed at St. James Palace by the Prince of Wales, given passes to the Distinguished Visitors Gallery in the House of Commons, and entertained by the Canadian Club of Great Britain at a St. Valentine's Day dance, held at British Columbia House. At the dance, the players, who had taken up a collection among themselves, presented gold watches to manager Bill Hewitt and coach Frank Rankin to express their appreciation. Tired but triumphant, the Granites sailed for home at the end of February on the S.S. *Matagama*.

No. 19 S

DANCE

in honour of the

CANADIAN OLYMPIC HOCKEY TEAM

AT

BRITISH COLUMBIA HOUSE, 1, REGENT STREET, S.W. I

(CHARLES STREET ENTRANCE)

ON

St. Valentine's Night, Thursday, 14th February, 1924

Dancing from 8.30 *p.m. to* 1 *a.m.*

Single Ticket, 12/6 (*To be presented at the door.*)

Beattie Ramsay did not linger with the team to enjoy the celebrations in Paris and London. Back in Toronto, his wife was expecting their first child, and the birth was imminent. By ship and by train he raced home from France, arriving in Toronto just seven minutes before his son, Beattie Ramsay Jr., was born, on February 14. Seventy years later, that son donated a replica of his father's gold medal to the Granite Club. It can be seen, along with a photograph of the team, in the club's lobby.

The Granites' Olympic win was celebrated with a dance party in London, England, on the way home

The City of Toronto proudly welcomed its conquering heroes with a gigantic parade. Mounted police, pipers, floats, and silver bands marched up Bay Street from Union Station to City Hall, to the cheers of thousands upon thousands of excited fans. In the procession were members of the Beaches Girls' Hockey League carrying a 180-foot banner. They were followed by the Granite athletes, accompanied by civic and provincial officials—all seated in decorated open cars. Only the elements failed to

Olympic gold medal, 1924

Toronto Granites, Olympic Hockey Champions, 1924: (front row, l-r) Peter G. Campbell, team manager in Canada; Harry Ellis Watson, left wing; William A. "Billy" Hewitt, general manager; Duncan Brown "Dunc" Munro, team captain and defence; Frank J. Rankin, coach; (back row, l-r) Harold McMunn, right wing; Albert J. "Bert" McCaffery, right wing; Reginald Joseph "Hooley" Smith, centre; William Beattie Ramsay, defence; Ernest J. "Ernie" Collett, goal; Cyril "Sig" Slater, left wing; Jack A. Cameron, goal.

*CFCA, Toronto's first radio station had begun broadcasting in 1922. In 1923, attesting to the popularity of the new station, Ernest Hemingway, at the time a reporter for the Star, exclaimed "Canadians … are in a hurry to get home to their supper … and their radio sets." Radio quickly became a "crucial part of the everyday lives of Canadians. They did their homework, cooked meals, fell in love, worried about the weather — and all to the sound of radio." (Stewart, Sandy, A Pictorial History of Radio in Canada, Gage Publishing Limited, Toronto, 1975.)

cooperate and the players, marchers, and spectators were soon soaked to the skin in a cold, steady, March drizzle. But no matter. When the procession reached City Hall, the mob surged along Queen Street and completely filled the area from west of Bay all the way east to James Street. The crowd roared its approval as the team was joined by dignitaries on a floodlit platform and the cheering seemed to go on forever. Mayor W. W. Hiltz and the Hon. Charles McCrea, KC, MPP, offered official congratulations while the *Toronto Daily Star* radio station CFCA* broadcast the celebration to points outside the city. Finally, as the happy noise died away, massed police bands struck up "The Maple Leaf Forever." The crowd, with bared heads, joined in the chorus.

But there was more to come, as it became the Granite Club's turn to honour its returning heroes. On March 6, 1924, directors unanimously passed a motion that each player "be given a five year

Banquet

TENDERED BY THE CORPORATION OF THE
CITY OF TORONTO

AND

THE PRESIDENT AND DIRECTORS OF THE
GRANITE CLUB

TO THE

OLYMPIC
HOCKEY CHAMPIONS

GRANITE CLUB, TORONTO
THURSDAY, MARCH SIXTH
NINETEEN TWENTY-FOUR

Menu

OLYMPIC COCKTAIL
"I could a tail unfold."—Cameron

DAINTIES
McMunn and Slater

SOUP A LA RIVIERE
Harry Watson

FRENCH BROILED CHICKEN
"I love them all."—Collett

POTATO PUCKETTES
Romeril's favorite dish

FRENCH PEAS
"Big or small, he stops them all."—Munro

FOX SALAD
With Holy "Hooley" dressing

CHEESE BALLS
"High or Low, I love them so."—Ramsay

GRANITE PUDDING with RUTHERFORD SAUCE
"Lead me to it."—McCaffery

FRUITS from OVERSEAS
WORLD'S CHAMPIONS

COFFEE
"Grounds for reflection."—Jeffrey

membership in the club, 1924–1929 inclusive, and that a suitably inscribed instrument be presented to each…setting forth the same." Later that evening, dignitaries from the City of Toronto, along with the club's president, directors, members, and guests sat down to a celebratory banquet. A memorable adjunct to this happy evening was a printed menu poking gentle fun at each member of the team. Entertainment after dinner included a series of boxing matches, a repeat of some of the better bouts from a boxing smoker held three weeks earlier at the club.

It had been a glorious five years of hockey for the club. After the Olympic victory, however, the team disbanded and the game was never again played officially on Granite ice. But the team, one of the best of the 1920s, was not to be forgotten. As Ted Reeve, sports columnist for *The Evening Telegram* for almost half a century, wryly commented years later, "Granites were probably as strong as any pro club when they reached their peak between 1922 and 1924. The Granites could beat the Leafs on their lunch hour."

A Globe *article on February 14, 1924, reported that "The Granite Club are [sic] holding a boxing smoker on Thursday February 21, when the Granite colors will be worn for the first time in this branch of athletics. Secretary [E. E.] Cottingham is arranging the bouts. The best of the bouts will . . . be repeated in the presence of the distinguished company at the banquet in honor of the Granite Hockey team on their return from France." Boxing became fashionable during World War I when it was found useful for physical conditioning of the troops.*

Most of the Granite players moved on to careers in business or the professions, but a few chose the world of professional hockey. After the Olympics, Beattie Ramsay coached Princeton University's hockey team in the Ivy League from 1924 to 1926. The next year saw him playing defence (alongside Hap Day and Ace Bailey) for Conn Smythe's Toronto Maple Leafs during their first year in the National Hockey League. But in 1928 Ramsay returned to his Regina home where he pioneered a successful road contracting business. His love of hockey, however, never flagged. For the rest of his life he devoted his energies to fostering junior hockey in Saskatchewan. Many a young player received financial help from him, as did the Regina Junior Pats. He served as president of that club until shortly before his death in 1952.

Another Granite player, Bert McCaffery, joined the Toronto Maple Leafs and played in the NHL for eight years—four with Toronto, two with Pittsburgh, and two with the Montreal Canadiens. Montreal Maroons signed brawny, barrel-chested Dunc Munro and he played defence for them from 1924 to 1931, and for the Montreal Canadiens from 1931 to 1932. Because Harry Watson was regarded as "without a peer in the sport...one of the fastest skaters in the game...[and] a brilliant stick handler," Conn Smythe offered him $5000, as a bonus, to sign with the Toronto Maple Leafs, but Watson decided he did not want to turn pro and turned the offer down.

The prize player of them all, the irrepressible Hooley Smith, turned professional in 1925, played in 12 NHL play-off series, won two Stanley Cups, was voted all-star centre for the 1935–1936 season, and ended his 17-year career in 1941 after scoring his 200th goal. Smith played three years with the Ottawa Senators, nine with the Montreal Maroons, one with the Boston Bruins, and four with the New York Americans. "There never was anybody in the league who was much better than Hooley," claimed Hap Day. "Brother, he was aggressive." Smith, Harry Watson, and coach Frank Rankin have all been inducted into the Hockey Hall of Fame.

Three other athletes carried the flag for Canada at the 1924 Olympics in Chamonix. One was speed-skating champion Charles Gorman, the others were figure skaters Melville Rogers and a talented young woman from Toronto, Cecil Eustace Smith. Cecil was only 15 and was accompanied by her mother and her older sister, Maude.

The Smith sisters were tomboys—a feisty pair. Maude's nickname was "Jim." As children they had organized a girls' hockey team that, they claimed, had beaten every team it ever encountered, including those from Branksome Hall and Havergal College. No doubt this was true—perhaps in part because in 1916 the Smith sisters scandalized their opponents by wearing trousers! Maude was just 11 at the time, Cecil, seven.

Then fate, in the person of Mrs. Scott Griffin, stepped in. Mrs Griffin lived across the street from the Smiths on Clarendon Avenue and regularly welcomed neighbourhood kids to her backyard rink. She belonged to the Toronto Skating Club (TSC), whose published aim was "to promote figure skating among amateurs." And so, while she didn't actively *discourage* the children's hockey games, she encouraged Maude and Cecil to practise figures as well. By 1920 both girls were skating at the Toronto Skating Club (TSC), which had just purchased shares in the Winter Club on Dupont Street, one of the first in the city to install indoor artificial ice. (The Granite Club did not enjoy this luxury until it moved to St. Clair in 1926.) The determined Smith sisters practised six hours every day—three before classes at Bishop Strachan School and three when classes were over. So by 1921, to no one's surprise, they had won the TSC junior pair championship. In the following year Cecil went on to win the TSC junior ladies competition and, by 1923, she was ready to contend for national honours. On her first try, she became runner-up in the Canadian Junior Ladies Figure Skating Championship— and won a place on the Canadian team for the 1924 Winter Olympics—the first woman ever to represent Canada in an Olympic event. There were 13 competitors in ladies figure skating that year, and young Cecil did well to finish sixth, edging out Sonja Henie, who came eighth. The 1924

Cecil and Maude Smith at the Olympic Games, St. Moritz, 1930

Cecil Smith, the first woman to
represent Canada in an Olympic
event in 1924, posed for a 1931
Granite Club skating show

*Between 1908 and 1927, Henry
Ford sold over 15 million "Model
Ts." In 1918, R. S. McLaughlin sold
his Oshawa company (founded in
1907) to General Motors and
became its Canadian president. He
served in that capacity until 1945
and then as chairman of the board
until his death in 1972.*

Olympics marked the beginning of a long and illustrious skating career for the Smith sisters. Soon after, they joined the Granite Club and brought fame to themselves and recognition to the club's fine skating program.

"The twenties in Canada, as elsewhere, were years of optimism and promise that ended in disillusionment and economic crisis." The pent-up demand for products unobtainable during the war years produced an inflationary boom and the early years of the decade brought marked technological advances, especially in the fields of communication and transportation. The telephone had "begun to establish itself as part of the mainstream of Toronto life. According to *Might's Directory*, there were only 7242 telephones in the city in 1900...by 1921 [there were] 101 531." Automobiles like the McLaughlin Buick and the Model T Ford were by this time no longer a rarity, and gradually the city's muddy, rutted streets became paved. The Toronto Transportation Commission was created in 1921, when the ownership of the street railways was taken over by the city. Tickets went on sale at four for 25 cents—a price that remained in effect for the next 30 years! That may sound like a bargain today, but Torontonians at the time were outraged because the TTC increased the rates by 40 percent over the price that had been in effect when the company was privately owned.

Toronto's population grew slowly during the early years of the "Roaring Twenties" and some visitors regarded the city as smug, dull, and provincial. Anyone looking for exciting night life had to drive all the way to Buffalo. And of course, on Sundays everything was shut down tighter than a drum. But in spite of this reputation for blandness, there really was quite a lot going on in "Toronto the Good."

In June 1920, from her Rosedale mansion on Glen Road, Mrs. Ambrose Small offered a reward of $50 000 for information on the whereabouts of her husband, "a womanizing impresario whose Grand [Opera House, near Adelaide and Yonge] had a secret room with a bar and bed." He had disappeared six months earlier, having just sold his chain of theatres in seven cities for $1.75 million. He put the money in the bank, walked off into a snow storm, and was never seen again except in fiction where he made an appearance in Michael Ondaatje's novel, *In the Skin of the Lion*. (Police officially closed the case 40 years later, in 1960.) Also in 1920, Loew's Uptown Theatre opened on the west side of Yonge Street, south of Bloor and excited Torontonians flocked there to see the glamorous, albeit silent, moving pictures. Loew's second theatre—downtown on Yonge Street—provided two movie houses: Loew's at street level and the elegant Winter Garden upstairs.* These two, along with Shea's Hippodrome on Bay Street (now the site of Toronto's City Hall), combined vaudeville with movies. And Mary Pickford, born in the city in 1893, had become "Toronto's first great gift to the emerging dream factory in Hollywood."

The winter of 1920–21 was an exceptionally mild one and this meant little curling. But in spite of the weather, A.E. Dalton and W. Austin Suckling still managed to skip their rinks to victory in the Ontario Tankard. This was the 12th time that the Granite Club had won this prestigious event. And 13 Granite teams entered that winter's Canada Life Bonspiel for the men's curling champi-

Both theatres have been restored to their original splendour. The Winter Garden's name remains the same; Loew's has been renamed the Elgin Theatre.

During the winter of 1921–2 insulin was discovered at the University of Toronto by Dr. Frederick Banting and Dr. Charles Best, under the direction of J.J.R. Macleod. In 1923 Banting and Macleod received the Nobel Prize in Medicine for their work. Banting generously gave half his prize money to Best. Banting was awarded a life annuity from the Canadian government, and a life membership in the Canadian Club, and was knighted in 1934.

onship of Toronto, which the club won as well. Granite women won their Tankard that year too—for the fourth time since its inception seven years earlier. Mrs. Cork and Mrs. G.H. Shaw were the winning skips.*

In 1922, the Royal Winter Fair was inaugurated in the newly built Coliseum. That same year, the 200-acre Sunnyside Beach Amusement Park, on the waterfront west of the CNE, was officially opened by Mayor Alfred McGuire. It was a real crowd-pleaser, greeted with enthusiasm by Torontonians hungry for fun and frivolity after years of war and devastating influenza epidemics. Excited visitors lined up to ride the giant roller-coaster, the merry-go-round that revolved at break-neck speed, and a host of other heart-stopping rides. The park's terraced tea gardens and Easter Parade boardwalk were equally popular. (Although the park was replaced by the Gardiner Expressway in 1956, the merry-go-round lives on at Disneyland in Anaheim, California.) Other Toronto attractions included the Parkdale Canoe Club (now the Boulevard Club), the Palais Royale dance hall, the Seabreeze outdoor dance pavilion, and the Sunnyside baseball stadium. A huge swimming pool was added later and, during July and August, children travelling to and from the pool could ride for free on TTC streetcars.

In January 1923 Granite director Frank Shannon, on behalf of the club, hired 12 pipers and five drummers, at a cost of $30, to meet a group of curlers arrived from Scotland for the Strathcona Cup, and escort them from Union Station to City Hall. Later that year, 156 members attended the 53rd Annual Meeting of the Granite Curling Club. Boxing matches (not, we trust, among the directors) followed, as the evening's entertainment. This was also the year of Canada's last bank failure—that of the Home Bank of Canada. Sir Henry Pellatt, its major shareholder, found himself in severe financial difficulties and could no longer afford to keep his spectacular home, Casa Loma. He moved out, never to return. An auction sale of its contents—valued at more than a million dollars—raised a mere $140 000. The Granite Club bought a few exquisite pieces of furniture which are still in use at the club 75 years after the sale.

*Their teammates were Mrs. Blackburn, Mrs. Gallagher, Mrs. Smith, Mrs. Soules, Mrs. Thomson, and Mrs. H.T. Wilson.

In 1924 Toronto elected, as alderman, its first Jewish politician—Nathan Phillips—who, after several decades on city council, became "mayor of all the people" in the 1960s and was immortalized by the new city hall square being named in his honour. The Toronto Symphony, disbanded during World War I, was re-established in 1924 and the Granite Club decided that better and more long-lasting curling ice could be made on ground rather than on the existing board floor. At a cost of $150, the wood floor was torn up. Once again the weather refused to cooperate and many curling competitions had to be cancelled due to the unseasonably warm winter. In December 1925, the Toronto Curling Club proudly invited their less fortunate Granite brethren to curl on its newly installed artificial ice. Also in 1925, Trinity College opened its doors on Hoskin Avenue in premises that replicated, in almost every detail, its original 1851 building on Queen Street. And the city, in an attempt to cope with the growing number of automobiles on its busy streets, installed the first automatic traffic light at Yonge and Bloor.

By the mid-1920s, speculation in the commodities and stock markets was on the rise, fuelled by lax regulations that allowed huge purchases on payment of a low margin of 10 per cent. Optimism was king and the markets continued their dizzy ascent. The economy grew exponentially, especially in the second half of the decade. Canada was prosperous and its cities even more so. People flooded into Toronto, attracted by new jobs in the manufacturing and service industries. The city's population grew by 32 percent in 10 years.

Meanwhile, in the Granite Club's Church Street boardroom, a small group of men, headed by President Frank Shannon and Chairman E.B. Stockdale, were formulating optimistic plans of their own—exciting ideas that would see the club move from its pleasant but somewhat ordinary clubhouse into a new, spacious, and handsome facility—one that *Saturday Night* would exuberantly hail as "the *dernier cri* [the last word] in clubdom."

The Sunnyside Bathing Pavilion, with its 350 x 75-foot pool, was restored at a cost of $1 100 000 and officially reopened in 1980. Its impressive front gates, with Lake Ontario in the background, have continued, over the years, to provide a popular romantic setting for wedding photos.

CHAPTER SIX

THE MOVE TO ST.CLAIR

1926

THE TWO DISASTROUSLY MILD WINTERS of 1923 and 1924 had all but eliminated curling activity in Toronto—and curlers were reminded of the song, "Lament for John Frost," composed by Granite member John Douglas back in 1884.

Cheery winter's noo awa'
Johnnie Frost far North has gane;
Gane is a' the ice and snaw,
Rink and brooms and curling stane.

Chorus
Will ye no come back again,
Will ye no come back again?
Better freens ye canna hae
Than Granite Rink o' curling men.

Scotland was about 20 years ahead of Canada in the development of artificial ice. Some time in the years 1903–06, the Scottish Ice Company was formed and it built at Crossmyloof about three miles from the heart of Glasgow a commodious rink, equipped with a first-rate modern refrigerating plant. Its ice space, oblong in shape and covering an area of 1525 square yards, made it larger than the big curling rink of the Toronto Granite Club and provided room for six full-sized curling rinks.

FRANK SHANNON, PRESIDENT, 1925–31

Frank Shannon was a friendly, idealistic, dignified and successful businessman—president of Automatic Paper Box Company Limited, and an active member of numerous clubs in the city. He and his wife Edith lived at 89 Roxborough Drive.

Indefatigable, Shannon provided dynamic leadership as club president on Church Street in 1925 and 1926 and for five additional years on St. Clair, followed by two more as honorary president. (Edith, in her role as the president's wife, felt it her duty to keep a vigilant eye on the housekeeping at the club during this period and was often observed running her white-gloved hand along shelves and window sills, checking for dust.)

Frank Shannon's portrait by Kenneth Forbes, RCA, hangs beside the fireplace in the Bayview club's lobby. His memory also lives on in the Shannon trophies, now awarded to the winners of the annual Shannon Invitational Bonspiel, an annual two-day rated bonspiel for thirty-two rinks. The ladies' trophy is thought to be the oldest women's curling trophy in continuous play in North America, donated by Frank Shannon in 1927 for the Ladies' Single Rink Championship of Toronto—then a week-long competition with twelve-end games.

Shannon was an active member of the board for forty years until he died in 1964, at eighty-four. A solemn high requiem mass was held for him at St. Michael's Cathedral.

By 1925 the situation was no longer a laughing matter. All across the city, curlers were resigning from their clubs in disgust. It was then that the Toronto Curling Club had "decided to install artificial ice—the first in Canada for curling purposes." It soon became obvious, to anyone who gave it half a thought, that those clubs that did not have artificial ice would soon lose members to those clubs that did.

Granite President Frank Shannon was not only aware of this, he also had a dream—a dream he had been discussing with his fellow directors for several years. He envisaged an exclusive uptown athletic and social club, located in the centre of the population from which it would draw its membership—a club with state-of-the-art facilities for a wide variety of sports, whose membership would be open, not just to men, but to their wives and children as well. He even proposed exclusive ladies' quarters, hitherto unknown, and lounges where both sexes could meet and socialize— a concept nothing short of revolutionary! Shannon was convinced that many of Toronto's 777 000 residents would support such a facility and that the Granite Club, with its prestigious membership and distinguished 50-year history, was uniquely positioned to succeed in such an undertaking.

Shannon was also aware that, while the Church Street area had been one of the leading residential districts of the city in the 1880s, it had, by the mid-1920s, lost its original character. Church and Wellesley was no longer a suitable area for a club like the Granite. Many members had moved north of Bloor Street to the tree-lined avenues and crescents of Rosedale or to prestigious St. George Street. Some had even moved above St. Clair Avenue to Moore Park, Deer Park, and Forest Hill. The Hill district, which extended from the CPR tracks north to Burton Road, and from Yonge Street west to Bathurst, was becoming one of the residential areas

Frank Shannon Trophy

The Toronto Curling Club laid pipes in sand for five sheets of curling ice in time for the 1925–26 winter season. The first major North American curling competition played on indoor artificial ice was the Montreal City Championship for the Edinburgh Trophy that took place at the Montreal Forum nine months earlier on March 5, 6, and 7, 1925.

Frank Shannon donated two curling trophies still in active competition. The first Shannon Trophy is awarded annually to the men's Club Champions. The other, thought to be the oldest women's trophy in continuous play in North America, was donated in 1927 for the Ladies' Single Rink Championship of Toronto—a week-long competition with 12-end games. Allie May Agar skipped her Granite Club rink to victory the first year, aided by Mrs. Charles W. Archibald, Mrs. William Dutton Copp and Mrs. Victor H. McWilliams. The trophy is now awarded to the winners of the annual Shannon Invitational Bonspiel.

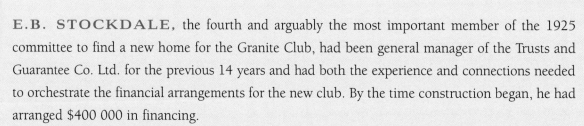

E.B. STOCKDALE, the fourth and arguably the most important member of the 1925 committee to find a new home for the Granite Club, had been general manager of the Trusts and Guarantee Co. Ltd. for the previous 14 years and had both the experience and connections needed to orchestrate the financial arrangements for the new club. By the time construction began, he had arranged $400 000 in financing.

Stockdale loved sports—curling and lawn bowling at the Granite Club, golf at the Rosedale Golf Club and fishing, with his friend Foster Hewitt, on Lake Simcoe near Beaverton where they both had cottages. In 1904 he married Ethel Thomas and they had two sons and three daughters. Soon after his marriage he purchased and subdivided a large tract of land in North Toronto. The gates, still standing at Alexandra Boulevard and Yonge Street, were the entrance to this development. He built a magnificent tile-roofed house at 184 Alexandra Boulevard near Avenue Road which, to this day, overlooks the bowling greens he had constructed "for friends, relatives and prospective property purchasers … On July 12, 1912, the North Toronto Bowling Club was established. Mr Stockdale was the first president."

Honoured by a life membership in the club he loved, E.B. Stockdale died, at 69, on November 27, 1951. His wife Ethel died eight years later.

of choice for well-to-do Torontonians. It was reasonable to assume that new members would come from that vicinity as well.

The timing for such a move could not have been better. The economy was booming and optimism was in the air. Spurred on by Shannon's drive and enthusiasm, the directors consulted privately with a number of members whose opinions they respected. The response was over-whelmingly positive. Thus encouraged, they called a special meeting for June 24, 1925. Naysayers, of course, argued that it was a mistake to move the club so far north. Others feared that such a vast project could not be readily financed; however, the membership supported the move. A four-man steering committee, chaired by President Shannon, was appointed "with full power to act on behalf of the Granite Club in securing a site, formulating plans for the new club and carrying the project through to completion." Shannon chose board chairman E.B. Stockdale to handle organization and finance and G. Herbert Rennie to look after publicity. He assigned H.E. Beatty to help him with the daunting task of enrolling the requisite number of members.

It was a powerful committee. Shannon and Stockdale were joined by men such as Herbert Rennie, assistant general manager of the Robert Simpson Company, who was "well-known in business and sporting circles."

Harold Eastwood Beatty, secretary-treasurer of skip Thomas Wilson's firm, Grocers' Limited, was a long-time member of the club and son of past president Samuel George Beatty. He had been a Tankard-winning skip in 1916 and again in 1919, and president of the Granite Hockey Club from 1919 to 1923. Under his leadership the Granites had won the OHA Senior championship three times in four years, and the Canadian senior championship for the Allan Cup twice.

As trustee for the company to be incorporated for the new venture, one of the first things Frank Shannon did was to purchase, from Granites Limited, the curling rink, clubhouse, furniture,

Toronto, June 11, 1925

SPECIAL GENERAL MEETING

Dear Sir :

You are requested to take notice that the above meeting will be held in the Granite Club, 519 Church Street, Toronto, on Wednesday evening, June 24th, at eight o'clock.

The Special General Meeting is being called for the purpose of considering the advisability of securing a new Club site with buildings for artificial ice for Curling and other Club activities.

This question is important and demands your attendance. Be sure to come.

Respectfully yours,
WM. F. KELLY, Hon. Sec.

chattels, and lands on Church Street for $81 000—payable by the assumption of an existing mortgage of $33 000 and by stock in the new company for the remaining $48 000.

During the next three months, the steering committee looked at all available sites in the Hill district. They finally settled on a 3.5-acre property owned by Havergal College and occupied by Havergal-on-the-Hill.* Negotiations with the college proceeded through August and September and were concluded on October 1, 1925, with a signed contract "between Havergal College of Toronto and F. Shannon as Trustee for the Company...to purchase for $125 000.00 land on the south side of St. Clair Avenue...just west of Yonge Street, having a frontage of 279 feet on St. Clair Avenue by a depth of 330 feet, and an adjoining block in the rear 150 feet by 180 feet." The deal was negotiated for a $5 000.00 deposit and $10 000.00 per month for 12 months, commencing December 1, 1925, with interest at six per cent payable half-yearly. There were two houses on the property. One was the prep school that would become the property of the club when the kindergarten and junior grades moved to Havergal's new premises. The second was a substantial brick building, known as "Brown House," which would be available, if required, as temporary club premises. To allow for future expansion, an option to purchase the remainder of the school site, 150 feet of frontage by 150 feet deep, was secured. (The option was exercised on November 12, 1926, for $54 347.95.)

Having settled on the new location, Shannon's committee presented a progress report to a select group of proposed directors that included John D. Hayes, Harry McGee, Col. J.G. Weir, William H. Alderson, Frank Kennedy, Thomas Rennie, Chas. Stark, R.C. Davison, Frank Littlefield, F.L. Ratcliff, and I.H. Weldon. Perhaps to ensure privacy, they met at the Rosedale Golf Club on a Tuesday evening, October 6, 1925. Shannon began with a summary of the reasons for the new club and progress to date. He then called on Stockdale to present a confidential memorandum covering, in minute detail, "the proposed objects of the club, the scope of the project, the financing thereof, and the expected earning power thereof." The new club was to contain "spacious lounge

*Havergal-on-the-Hill had opened in 1912 as a prep school. The senior school was located at 354 Jarvis Street. In 1923, Havergal had purchased 27 acres at Lawrence and Avenue Road as a site for a combined prep and senior school and proceeded to sell Havergal-on-the-Hill and its other properties to finance this new project.

rooms, card rooms, dining room, reading room, billiard and locker rooms, as well as one floor of bedrooms; …ten sheets of ice for curling and…sufficient floor area [for] a standard sized arena rink; a swimming pool; six indoor bowling alleys; badminton, hand ball, squash courts and golf drives." On the grounds outside there would be "lawn bowling greens, tennis courts and private parking accommodation for the members, as well as reasonable lawn and terrace space." The ice provided for curling was not only artificial, it was twice the size of the Toronto Curling Club's facilities.

St. Clair Avenue in 1919, before the Granite Club moved into the neighbourhood

The steering committee stated confidently "that a full quota of members can be obtained.… Approximately 300 prominent citizens have intimated to the Committee their desire to secure admission to the club." They were sure that at least 200 of the present club members would join, making a total of 500—and this prior to any formal solicitation. An attractive two-colour, 16-page, illustrated booklet would be mailed to 5000 additional prospects, and the committee forecast that not only would the membership target be achieved, but that by the time the club opened its doors, there would be a substantial waiting list.

The committee proposed five classes of membership, each with a maximum limit: Senior Male — 1200; Senior Lady — 350; Non-resident — 250; Junior (sons, daughters, sons-in-law, and daughters-in-law, 18 to 25 years) — 250; Juvenile (children of members, under 18 years) — 150. When these limits were reached, a waiting list would be established. Recommended stock requirements were: senior males — $200.00; senior ladies and non-residents — $50.00. Proposed annual dues were: senior males — $60.00; senior ladies and non-residents — $25.00. Curling and lawn bowling section fees would be extra, ranging from $2.50 for juniors to $10.00 for senior men.

Stockdale next presented the capital budget. Estimated capital expenditures were $570 000: $125 000 for the land; $300 000 for the clubhouse, ice plant, and other equipment; $50 000 for

JOHN D. HAYES was general manager of the Laura Secord Candy Company and also honorary president of the Kiwanis Club of Toronto. In 1933, as the Depression deepened, he decided to sponsor a picnic for about 300 Cabbagetown kids from the Gerrard K Club on Sumach Street. Along with the usual picnic goodies, he gave each youngster $1.00 in a bank savings account and, not surprisingly, a box of chocolates to take home to their families. The picnic became an annual event. Some years later, Hayes became president of both Laura Secord and its American counterpart, Fanny Farmer, and commuted between Toronto and Rochester on a regular basis. The Association of American Confectioners named him Candy Man of the Year in 1955.

Hayes not only helped found the new Granite Club, he was also founding co-chairman of the Canadian Council of Christians and Jews. Following up on his work with inner city youth, he established a $1000 award for any underprivileged boy who reached a top position in the city. Hayes accomplished all these good works in spite of being virtually blind since the mid-1930s. "His correspondence was read to him by a secretary and daily newspapers by his wife." He and his wife Cecil (née McKenna) lived at 111 Lyndhurst Avenue with their daughters, Mary and Cecilia Maureen, moving in the mid-1930s to 15 Hillholme Road. Despite his handicap, Hayes lived a long and productive life. He died, at 83, in 1966.

Laura Secord Inc. was founded by John Hayes' brother-in-law, Frank O'Connor, when he opened his first store on the southwest corner of Yonge and Elm streets in 1913. Three more stores opened within the year.

furniture and furnishings; $25 000 for landscaping; and $70 000 for sundry expenses such as legal and architectural fees, interest, taxes, and so on. These expenditures would be financed in three ways: first, by the sale of $270 000 in common stock to members; second, by the sale of $250 000 (later increased to $275,000) in first-mortgage bonds to the public; and third, by $50 000 in

second-mortgage bonds to be given as partial payments to the architect and general contractor. The first mortgage bonds were to be underwritten by Colonel J.G. Weir's firm, McLeod, Young, Weir. The trustee for the bondholders, not surprisingly, would be the Trusts and Guarantee Company, Limited, of which E.B. Stockdale was general manager. The committee members were of the opinion that the estimate of capital costs was a liberal one and that some savings would be effected. A first-year operating budget forecast a net operating profit of $73 530 and a net profit after depreciation and bond interest of $34 655.

—Granite Club promotional booklet

Several architects had already submitted cost estimates. Members of the steering committee, in view of their extremely heavy workload, requested that three additional persons be appointed to review these plans, recommend an architect and, as an additional task, draft the new club's bylaws, rules, and regulations.

The 15 proposed directors enthusiastically and unanimously approved the project as outlined and authorized an application for a charter to be prepared by the club's solicitors, Kilmer, Irving, and Davis. And, as requested, three new members were added to the steering committee: Colonel J.G. Weir, one of Ontario's leading bond dealers; Thomas Rennie, president of Wm. Rennie Co., Ltd.; and John D. Hayes, general manager of the Laura Secord Candy Co., Inc. (The two Rennies on the committee were not related.)

COL. J. GORDON WEIR was born in West Flamboro, Ontario, attended Hamilton Collegiate, earned a BA at the University of Toronto, and an MA at Harvard. He then worked at the *Financial Post* for a year or so before joining A.E. Ames, investment dealers, in 1910. At the outbreak of war, he took a leave of absence and enlisted in the army. He served overseas with distinction and returned home, a hero, having won both the DSO and Military Cross for his leadership and valour as commander of the Second Canadian Machine Gun Company. He rejoined Ames, but left, two years later, to form McLeod, Young, Weir.

At one time Weir's family owned all the land stretching from Yonge Street to Bayview Avenue—east of the old town of Eglinton. He built his home there on a piece of the property at the northwest corner of Blythwood and Mount Pleasant, a few blocks east of his friend and fellow steering committee member, Herbert Rennie. Although Weir never did become an officer of the club, he continued to serve on the board until 1946.

The proposed directors met about two weeks later, this time at the Ontario Club. Shannon announced that, since the last meeting, five others had agreed to join the board: D.J. McDougald, head of the financial firm D.J. McDougald & Company; W.K. Pearce, assistant general manager, Dominion Bank; John A. Tory, Supervisor, Sun Life Assurance Company; W.J. Northgrave, president and general manager, City Dairy Company, Limited; and C.L. Burton, general manager, Robert Simpson Company, Limited. The directors then elected officers: Shannon as president,

Stockdale as chairman of the board, Thomas Rennie as first vice-president, W.J. Northgrave as second vice-president, Burton as third vice-president, and Frank Kennedy as honorary secretary-treasurer. Sir Joseph W. Flavelle, Charles C. Dalton, and Colonel Henry Cockshutt, Lieutenant-Governor of Ontario (1921–27), were appointed as honorary patrons.

—Granite Club promotional booklet

Stockdale reported that an advertising agency, A. McKim, Ltd., had been retained to produce the promotional booklet that described the club as "pleasantly and conveniently situated in the heart of the residential Hill Section," and, although the new club was to be a "family club," the agency seemed to have some difficulty in coming to grips with that concept. A "comfortable lounging chair, a cheery fire, soft lights and congenial friends, await a 'Granite' man within its friendly rooms," the booklet asserted and went on to state that a "Lad and his Dad is an ideal companionship. The loyalty of one to the other is inspiring. If Dad's a 'Granite' man, Son will be certain to want to follow in Father's footsteps." Women received scant mention in the text, and appeared in only one of the many illustrations. On the last page, however, it was acknowledged that "wives and daughters as well as sons…would be eligible for membership having the full privileges of the club during certain specified hours."

Submissions from five architectural firms were studied and "after a very full discussion," Annex designer (and club member) William F. Sparling was chosen. The Board then appointed a five-man building committee—Shannon, Stockdale, Beatty, G.H. Rennie, and Harry McGee—to work with the architect to finalize the plans and specifications during the winter months. Three days after this meeting, on October 24, 1925, a charter was granted to Granite Club, Limited, by letters patent. The capital of the company was $500 000, divided into 50 000 shares of $10 each.

JOHN ALEXANDER TORY was a member of a dynasty founded by Loyalists James and Christiana Torey (the original spelling) of Aberdeen, Scotland. They immigrated to North Carolina in 1770, where James fought for the British in the American Revolution, then fled to Canada and settled in Guysboro, Nova Scotia, in 1783. John A. Tory was their great-grandson and one of four sons and a daughter born to Robert Kerr Tory, a Methodist minister, and his wife, Honora. The other sons were H.A.T. Tory, a professor at Harvard University; Henry Marshall Tory, BA, BD, MA, DSc, LL.D., FRSC, a minister, prominent academic, founding president of the University of Alberta, and chairman of the National Research Council; and James Cronswick Tory, Lieutenant-Governor of Nova Scotia from 1925–30. Historian Michael Bliss described James and John as "brilliant salesmen" who pioneered the early growth of the Sun Life Assurance Company of Canada. Both were elected directors of the company. James remained in Nova Scotia, while John moved to Toronto to become supervisor of Sun Life.

John promptly became a dynamic member of his new community and president of four organizations: the YMCA, the Life Underwriters Association of Canada, the Toronto Industrial Commission, and the Toronto Board of Trade. After World War I, he organized the Remembrance Day Poppy Fund, which carries on each November. He remained an active member of the Granite board past his eightieth birthday. He died February 11, 1950.

John had married Abbie Buckley of Guysboro back in 1898 and they had two sons, one of whom was John Stewart Donald Tory, founder of J.S.D. Tory & Associates in 1941 and, 10 years later, Tory, Miller, Thompson, Hicks, Arnold & Sedgewick. He was the principal fundraiser for both the provincial and federal Conservative parties, a close friend of Ontario Premier Leslie Frost, the "legal wizard" for Argus Corporation and, like his father and uncle, a director of Sun Life.

The hard-working building committee met many times during the winter of 1925–26, some-times at Sparling's offices in the 21-storey Metropolitan Building located at the southwest corner of Victoria and Adelaide. It had just been completed and was, at the time, the tallest building in the British Empire. On other occasions the committee met at Stockdale's office in the Trusts and Guarantee Building at 302 Bay Street. And they often met in E.B. Stockdale's living room at 184 Alexandra Boulevard. Sparling had been the architect for both the office buildings and also for the Stockdale house.

By early spring in 1926, plans and specifications had been approved and tenders were called. But when the bids from 10 general contractors were opened by the building committee on May 4, 1926, every tender exceeded the budgeted $300 000. Sparling was therefore instructed to revise (in consultation with six of the bidders) the plans and specifications, so that the cost of construc-tion would not be greater than the budget. Revised tenders were received four days later and, after checking references of the three lowest bidders and investigating their financial integrity, the com-mittee awarded the contract to Witchall and Son, the second-lowest bidder at $232 840. The refrigeration plant, estimated at $40 000, was to be a separate contract. Canadian Ice Machine Co. and Refrigerating Engineers, Limited, would be invited to submit tenders. Mr. Witchall was called into the meeting where he stated with confidence that the "club would be completed [and] ready for occupation before the 15th of November, and that the rink building, if required, could be com-pleted [and] ready for use by October." He pointed out that "as the time for completion is short, every day that can be saved at this time was of the utmost importance." A Mr. Carswell of Carswell Construction Company was appointed as associate engineer to work with Sparling, and a survey of the property was ordered from Messrs. Wilson and Brunell, land surveyors.

The very next day, a few directors gathered at the St. Clair site to watch President Shannon turn the first sod. True to his promise, contractor Witchall remained on schedule and, six months after

Turning the First Sod, May 15, 1926: (l-r) G. Herbert Rennie, director; Harold Beatty, director; E.B. Stockdale, chairman of the board; Frank Shannon, president; William Sparling, architect; Col. James G. Weir, director; unidentified; unidentified; unidentified; Harry McGee, vice-president; D.C. Haig, hon. secretary-treasurer

the contract was awarded, the clubhouse was ready for the laying of the cornerstone. Lieutenant-Governor Henry Cockshutt, one of the club's three honorary patrons, performed the honours on September 16, with Shannon acting as chairman of the ceremony and Rev. Trevor Davies pronouncing the invocation and the benediction. Vice-president C.L. Burton gave a short outline of the plans for the future of the club, claiming not only that it would it be self-supporting but also that income would amply provide for interest charges, depreciation, and a small surplus. The sports building was to be ready for use towards the end of October, and the main clubhouse between mid-November and early December.

Nearly half a century later, long-time member John Scott recalled watching the construction and playing on the site as the building progressed. He was 10 at the time and living nearby at 123 Warren Road:

Laying the cornerstone, September 16, 1926

Yes! It was quite a sight—the large stone and brick building taking shape on St. Clair Ave. To a very small boy, it was awesome. But it was a great place to play, in those days before watchmen and guards. From a vantage point in Alice's Garden, across the street from 63, I could see the club beginning to rise. The cemetery* was still visible, but was out of bounds to all the neighbourhood kids. St. Clair was lined then with tall elm and maple trees and the open trollies, electric in 1926, ran as far west as Bathurst Street, on a boulevard in the centre of St. Clair. Flowers and grass grew beside the tracks. We were civilized then. We had sidewalks which stretched all the way from the bridge east of Yonge St. to Spadina Ave. The roads were kind of paved, but there was no salt or sand on them in the winter time, so we could skate to school. Sweet smelling Hunt's store was on the northwest corner of St. Clair and Yonge and there was a barber shop on the south side of St. Clair, in the basement, where a haircut cost 15 cents, with a stick of Wrigley's [chewing gum] thrown in. The water in the horse trough at St. Clair and Avenue Road was always pure and cold, and the drivers in the district used to stop there to water their horses, and perhaps we would snitch a small piece of ice from the ice cart.

*St. Michael's Cemetery today provides a peaceful vista for residents on the south side of the Granite Place condominiums, built on the site of the St. Clair club. The cemetery was created in 1855 when St. Paul's, on Queen Street east of Parliament, was filled—mostly by victims of typhoid and smallpox epidemics. This second burial ground of 19th-century Roman Catholics — mostly Irish — is accessible along a footpath leading in from the west side of Yonge Street, south of St. Clair. By 1900, after some 27 000 burials, the cemetery was virtually full.

CHARLES LUTHER BURTON was the St. Clair club's second vice-president. Born in 1876, he was one of seven children whose sole support was their father's tiny corner grocery store near Bathurst and College. He had to leave Toronto Collegiate (now Jarvis) at 14 because his family could no longer afford to send him there. Luckily, he found work with Harris H. Fudger, the owner of Fancy Goods Company of Canada,* a wholesaling enterprise. Fudger befriended Burton and became his mentor.

Burton had been with the firm for about 10 years when he married Ella Maud Leary. During the early years of their marriage he was a travelling salesman, peddling the firm's stock-in-trade to retailers across Canada.

Burton spent over 20 years in the wholesale business, gradually assuming more and more responsibility in the firm's operations, including many buying trips to Europe.

In 1912 Fudger, who was also president of the Robert Simpson Company Limited, offered the position of assistant general manager in that firm to his 36-year-old protégé. Burton jumped at the opportunity. Seventeen years later, with the financial backing of investment dealer J.H. Gundy, he led a group of employees in a takeover of the company from its owners—financier and Granite skip Sir Joseph W. Flavelle, H.C. Cox, and Harris Fudger. Burton took over the presidency from Fudger and within a quarter century had transformed "the modest dry goods store into a corporation with assets totalling more than $100 000 000."

In 1948 Burton became chairman of Simpsons and his son Edgar was elected president. Five years later, the company's mail-order business merged with Sears and a new merchandising giant, Simpsons-Sears Limited, burst upon the Canadian retail scene. Burton remained on the Granite's board of directors for more than a quarter of a century.

In 1926, John became a Juvenile or "Privileged" member of the club—a gift from his aunt.

Jack Brunke, who chaired the Granite Club swimming committee in the mid-1960s, and who had attended Brown School and Upper Canada College with Scott, recalled other details:

> As a "Privileged" contemporary of John Scott in 1927, let me gently correct his observation that "sweet smelling Hunt's was on the northwest corner of Yonge and St. Clair." As I recall, that spot was occupied by Liggett's Drug Store (milkshakes 10 cents and 15 cents). Hunt's, next door, sold their excellent chocolates at "50 cents the pound" sustaining their slogan, "be thrifty—pay fifty." A few doors along, the Queen's Royal Theatre charged us 10 cents for the Saturday matinee that included Pathé News, a comedy (*Our Gang*), serial (Pearl White), and a feature (Tom Mix). Other reminiscences of that period (1925–9): ogling lovely Eleanor (not yet Phelan) O'Meara as she cut her ice figures under the watchful eye of her father, who attended most of her practice sessions [and] admiring the dives of Alf Phillips in the pool.

As the clubhouse and sports building neared completion, the board met frequently to review progress, approve extras, confirm the sale and removal of the Brown House, award contracts for furniture and furnishings to Eatons and Simpsons, select conveners, and ratify the hiring of senior staff. The following conveners were appointed: alley bowling, W.G. Lumbers; badminton, E.W.J. Kerr; curling, Charles Bulley; fencing, F.A. Moore; golf, John Rennie; handball, H.W. Phelan; skating, H.W.D. (Walter) Foster; squash, C.D. Henderson; swimming, E.A. Chapman.

On September 27, the directors approved a request that the City Badminton Championships be held on the club's courts on December 16, 17, and 18, and also agreed to allow the McDonald

Until 1921 students were required to pay fees to attend high school in Toronto; secondary education was then declared open and free to all who had attained the necessary qualifications for admission.

Fancy goods included such items as watches, combs, clocks, hair brushes, toys, mouth organs, tobacco, and pipes.

Tobacco Company to hold the first Canadian curling championship, the McDonald Brier, on the club's ice in March 1927.

The most important staff appointment at the new club was, of course, the general manager. The club's expansion meant that there was a need for a seasoned professional to handle administration and the directors chose Hector Donnelly. They chose well. They had become acquainted with him a year earlier when David C. Haig, honorary secretary of the club (1926–1931), recommended him to the steering committee as an advisor on the drafting of the operating budget—especially with regard to "revenues available from cards, refreshments, cigars…and dining room." Donnelly was, at the time, manager of the Mississauga Golf Club, and Haig was a director and chairman of its house committee. Informal and formal negotiations progressed during the next several months, culminating in Donnelly's official appointment on October 1, 1926. His terms of employment had likely been settled earlier in the year since he was one of those invited to attend the "turning of the sod" ceremony in May.

Churchillian in manner, Hector Patrick McCambridge Donnelly was a strict, yet fair, disciplinarian, and members and staff grew to love and respect him. He would set the tone for the club's first quarter-century on St. Clair.

Donnelly immediately surrounded himself with a staff of competent professionals. He first chose James A. Lyons as assistant manager and sports secretary. Lyons had been, for the previous two years, secretary at the Church Street facility, and for the two years before that, secretary-treasurer of the Parkdale Canoe Club (now the Boulevard Club). He was to remain with the Granite Club until 1933, when he moved on to greener pastures as secretary-manager of the Ontario Club.

Emma McCoskie ("Miss Mac") was the second key figure hired. A close friend of Donnelly's, she had worked with him at the Mississauga Golf Club and followed him to the Granite, first as accounts receivable manager and later as office manager—a position she held well into the 1950s.

Next James Johnston, Canadian Professional Golf Champion in 1926, was chosen to teach at the club's winter golf school. Donnelly then appointed a tall, ruddy-faced, powerfully built Scot, Johnnie Walker, as swimming director. It was an inspired choice. Walker was just one year away from becoming the world's most famous swimming coach—the man who trained world marathon swimming champion George Young, hailed internationally as the "Catalina Kid."

Swimming was Johnny Walker's life. In Scotland he had been 50-yard and 100-yard champion, and for 16 years he taught swimming at England's Tunbridge Wells, a pool rated by *The Toronto Star* as the "finest open-air tank in the world." Coming to Canada in 1910, Walker coached at the Sunnyside pool, interrupting his career in 1914 for a four-year stint in the 4th Canadian Hospital Corps, serving at Salonica, Greece. Not long after his return from the war, he became swimming instructor at the West End YMCA. Within a few years, he had developed its swim team into Canada's finest—winning 22 out of 24 Canadian Championships in 1925, and the all-round American Senior Pentathlon as well. He had been coach at the West End Y for seven years when the Granite Club lured him away. He prophesied that he would "produce a swimming team for his new club that will be as well-known as his crack West End team." *The Mail and Empire* agreed: "It would not be a surprise for the swimming fans of Canada to see the Granite Club possess the finest swimming team in Canada."

Six years before moving to the Granite Club, Walker had made an amazing prediction as he chatted beside the YMCA pool with W.T. "Tommy" Munns, sports writer for the *Globe*. "See yon lad," he remarked, "the short, stocky one in the corner there? You mark my words, Tommy, he'll be champion of the world some day." And he was as good a prophet as he was a coach. In 1927, George Young "threshed through kelp strewn tides of Catalina [Strait], to win the world's first world's professional marathon swimming championship." With the win came the Wrigley prize of $50 000—a fortune in those days!

In April, 1928, Miss Mary Casson of the Granite Club held every Canadian swimming title from 50 yards to 3 miles. She swam a Canadian 100 yard victory in a time of 1.09 2/5. Miss Casson was followed by record breaking Betty Edwards. Both girls were pupils of the famous Johnnie Walker, trainer of the great Ernst Vierkotter who won the first Canadian National Exhibition 21 mile swim.

JOHN FIZALLEN ELLIS was president of Barber-Ellis Limited and "one of Canada's most successful businessmen." (He and his fellow Granite Club directors Frederick Ratcliff and I.H. Weldon were all presidents of paper companies.) At eighty, Ellis had more energy and enthusiasm than most men half his age. Until two weeks before he died, he was at his office every day, managing the firm's far-flung empire in Toronto, Winnipeg, Calgary, Vancouver, and a manufacturing plant at Brantford, Ontario.

He was born in 1845 in the village of Mount Pleasant, Ontario. His mother, Janet Carlyle, was a first cousin of Dr. James Carlyle, charter member and director of the club when it opened on Church Street in 1880 and, in his professional life, principal of the renowned Toronto Model School from 1857–71. Young Ellis spent his early school days there under his cousin's watchful eye.

Ellis established his paper company with John R. Barber in 1876. Over the next two decades it grew and prospered and Ellis was honoured by his peers from across Canada when they elected him as president of the Canadian Manufacturers' Association for the years 1898–1900. He next became president of the National Club, 1901–02, and of the Toronto Board of Trade, 1902–04. Two years later he was a delegate to the Sixth Imperial Trade Conference in London, England where he was presented to King Edward VII. After more than half a century in the vanguard of the paper industry, he died at his home, on Old Forest Hill Road, in 1928.

Grit and determination were two of Young's sterling qualities. He had ridden his motorcycle all the way from Toronto to Los Angeles to take part in the event and was the only entrant to finish. "'It's not a surprise. I knew he could do it if he would,' Johnny [Walker] remarked with a smile when Young finished the long grind between San Pedro [Los Angeles] and Catalina Island." Four years later, again under Walker's tutelage, Young won the prestigious 15-mile CNE Marathon.

Fate had a hand in the hiring of the next professional. On a sunny day in May 1926, a young Englishman, Alf Ablett, found himself on St. Clair Avenue where he noticed a group of distinguished-looking people, a steam shovel, and a photographer. Curious, he stopped and asked one of the men standing there what was going on. As luck would have it, the person he spoke to was none other than Hector Donnelly, soon to become general manager of the Granite Club. Donnelly explained that they were witnessing the turning of the sod for a new sports and social club. Ablett then told Donnelly about his experience as a racquets professional at the Princess Club, Knightsbridge, in London, where he had coached the Prince of Wales in squash. Impressed, Donnelly told him that there would likely be an opening for someone of his experience and suggested that Ablett contact him later that summer. Ablett did, and thus began 45 years of dedicated service to the club—a record that spanned the years from the opening of the St. Clair facility until the move to Bayview. Among his badminton pupils, two stand out: Rod Phelan, who became Canadian champion, and Jack Storey, who won the Ontario championship.

Johnny Walker (with cap and cigarette), George Young, and one of Toronto's finest

When Ablett retired in 1972, he recalled that, in 1913, a lot at Yonge and St. Clair had sold for $500 and that St. Clair was a "sand road that resembled the Sahara Desert when the wind blew." He also remembered "working fourteen hours a day and seven days a week in the early 1930s." And he remembered that, during the early years on St. Clair, Edith Shannon, the president's wife, felt it was her duty to keep a vigilant eye on the housekeeping at the club. And so, on her way to badminton lessons with Alf, she would run her white-gloved hand along shelves and windowsills, checking for dust. Older members recall Ablett as a bit of a contradiction. He was irascible yet lovable, difficult to deal with but dependable. Above all, he was a faithful and dedicated professional. The Granite Club was his life.

Donnelly also chose the doorman—the first person whom members met on entering the club—with care. William J. Bourke at 51 was a tall, good-looking Irishman with flowing white hair and a white moustache. His posture, erect and straight as a ramrod, put one in mind of a company sergeant-major. In his white gloves and uniform, "he would bend over almost double when people arrived at the club." He was flowery but not obsequious. Ron MacFeeters, a "privileged member" in 1926 (along with John Scott and Jack Brunke) and a club member ever since, recently recalled this fine Irish gentleman:

> "Privileged" members entered the club through a door on the west side that was down a narrow alley and came in by the skating rink, but when we moved up a category it was possible to enter through the Front Door. For years the guardian, custodian, greeter was a distinguished…Mr. Bourke who knew most of the members by name and always called them by name as he held the door for them to enter or leave…. Mr. Bourke was often the staff member chosen to take special guests or visitors on a tour of the club. He had a delightful ritual with the large painting, *The Young Visitor* which…hung on the east wall of the men's reading room…. In the prewar and early post-war years, it was not uncommon for the half dozen readers and snoozers to hear a knock on the door—then see Mr. Bourke open it a bit as he asked: 'May I show these visitors into this room, gentlemen?' He

would lead the couple or small group into the room and in a whispering voice describe the room and then in a reverent hushed tone point out THE PAINTING. I heard him so often I can still recall most of his description: 'This is our most beautiful painting. It is called *The Young Visitor*—(If you would just stand over here, madam, I think you get the best view,' he would say as he led the woman over to the right of the picture). 'You see it is the little daughter from the castle who has come

"The Young Visitor"
by James Hayllar

for tea with the gardener and his family in his cottage. See how demurely she crosses her ankles and sits so primly nursing the cup which is probably the gardener's prized china that goes with the precious teapot they have got out for the occasion. See how sweetly proud the old couple is to have the lord's daughter on a visit and how their shy little boy is hanging back at the same time—he wants to be included in the party—and notice how the afternoon light is coming through the window—we think it is a wonderful painting. Now if you will just come with me, we will move to another room.' He would usher the visitors out the door as

WILLIAM H. ALDERSON was one of the original St. Clair directors but, for reasons unknown, he was no longer a member of the club after its first year at the new location. He had been manager of the Ontario division of Gutta Percha and Rubber Company Ltd. for about 20 years, and had been president of the Toronto Board of Trade in 1921. He was what we would call today, a workaholic—not just in business, but in the field of community service as well. The *Star Weekly* had this to say about him: "Mr. Alderson has no hobbies and has no time for any. His greatest relaxation is to get into a suit of old clothes and 'potter around.' On Thanksgiving Day for example he dressed thus and spent most of the day cutting down dead trees on some property of his on King Street."

Alderson began his social service work with the Big Brothers movement, having "received his first impetus in this direction from his home environment and from his mother who was a woman of many good works." A founder of the Rotary Club of Toronto, Alderson later became its president and was one of five men on the Canadian Advisory Board of the International Rotary Clubs that launched the Rotary movement in Australia and New Zealand. During the Depression, Ontario's Conservative government of George Stewart Henry (1930–34) appointed him supervisor of unemployment relief for Northern Ontario. He had previously been chairman of the Northern Ontario Fire Relief Committee which distributed $1 000 000 to forest-fire victims a few years earlier. In its laudatory profile of Alderson, the *Star Weekly* went on to describe him as a "type of the twentieth century style of citizen who does not believe in living just for himself…but gives himself whole-heartedly to any movement which is for the good of his community and the betterment of his fellow man."

he turned to the members still reading their magazines: 'Thank you gentlemen!' I seldom walk down Peacock Alley without thinking of Mr. Bourke and *The Young Visitor* and that old reading room which took so much space for so long and was so little used.

Meanwhile, back on Church Street things were winding down. Sports and other activities continued, but at a reduced level. A few members who disapproved of the move to St. Clair resigned. Others, discouraged by the mild winters, also left the club. However, before the doors closed on Church Street in 1926, two noteworthy events took place—the Dominion Lawn Bowling Tournament, played on the club's bowling greens from August 16 to 20 with more than 120 bowlers from across Canada taking part, and the Canadian curling team's tour of Scotland to contest the Strathcona Cup.*

Granite Club members W. Defoe and Charles Bulley joined eight other Ontario curlers and 14 from the rest of Canada for the trip to Scotland. A seasoned skip and auditor for the Ontario Curling Association (OCA), Bulley was elected vice-captain of the Canadian team. The competition for the Strathcona Cup was held alternately in Scotland and Canada every five years and took place over a period of two months. On the eve of their departure, Granite skip Thomas Rennie, president of the Ontario Curling Association, organized a farewell dinner for the Ontario contingent. During the course of the evening, a multitude of toasts challenged the sobriety of the guests. First Rennie toasted the Toronto team, and Mayor Thomas Foster responded. Then S.B. Gundy, president of the Board of Trade, raised his glass to Canada, and the Honourable Joe Thompson, speaker of the Ontario Legislature replied. Next came a toast to curling by Sir William Mulock and a response from Sir Joseph Flavelle. And finally, not to be outdone by the members of his flock,

*The Strathcona Cup remains the world's oldest international curling competition. The first ... match was held in the winter of 1902–03". More recently, in 1992–93, 28 Scottish curlers challenged Canadian curlers in every province except Newfoundland, with the final games taking place in Toronto on January 28, 1993.

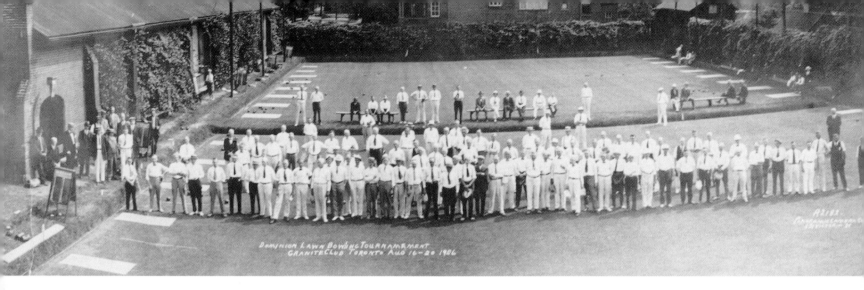

Dominion Lawn Bowling
Tournament at the Granite Club,
held at 519 Church Street,
August 16–20, 1926

OCA chaplain the Reverend J. W. Pedley proposed toasts to the entire Canadian team. There were, undoubtedly, other toasts that went unrecorded. In any event, the Ontario delegation was exuberantly escorted to the North Toronto railway station at Yonge and Summerhill and they were soon en route to the next party in Montreal, followed by yet another in Saint John, N.B. The bibulous group then sailed for Scotland. Bulley described their trip:

> We sailed about 1 p.m. on the good CPR ship *Montrose*…. The Bay of Fundy was kind to us and it was not until we were well out, close to Newfoundland, that any meals were missed. We had some rough weather, but the team, as a whole, did pretty well…. We arrived at Greenock…and our reception was characteristically Scotch and very damp. The rain just poured down but, notwithstanding, the pipers played and the whistles shrieked their welcome…. Here a special train was waiting to take us to our comfortable quarters at the North British Hotel, Edinburgh.

Canada's curlers won 33 games that year, tied one, and lost seven. All games were played on artificial ice in Edinburgh or Manchester. In spite of their somewhat lopsided victory, the Canadians acknowledged that the Scots' curling had improved considerably since the last competition.

Edward, Prince of Wales, was president of the Royal Caledonian Curling Club that year and requested that he meet the Canadians. Bulley described the reception:

> After the schedule of games in Scotland and England, we proceeded to London, where the Prince of Wales received us at York House.... The Prince shook hands with each member of the team and congratulated...them...on the success of their tour. He was particularly interested to find out how representative the team was of

The Canadian Team in Scotland in 1926. Charles Bulley is in the front row, third from the left; Defoe is in the fifth row, fourth from the left

the various parts of the Dominion, coming, as they did, from towns stretching from the Pacific to the Atlantic coasts.... The Royal President was asked to accept a replica of the badge which each member of the team was wearing. The emblem was especially made in gold and was ornamental with the Prince's crest.

Bulley then concluded his report:

> No words of mine can adequately express the great warmth and wonderful hospitality extended to us, both in Scotland and in England, all through the tour. To our hosts, the Royal Caledonian Curling Club, we are particularly grateful...and we shall look forward, with great pleasure to the visit of the next team to Canada.

Charles Bulley

Bulley, at 51, was a successful builder and brick manufacturer—a self-made man who had begun his working life as a bricklayer—first in various Ontario towns and then in Cleveland and Chicago. This rolling stone returned to Toronto in his late twenties, married Christina McIntosh of Meaford, and proceeded to develop most of the Riverdale district, providing the city with more than a hundred buildings—factories, schools, churches, and houses. In 1910, in association with Dr. G.J. Steele, he founded the Standard Brick Manufacturing Company, Ltd., and, three years later, shut down his contracting business to work full-time at Standard Brick. Its modern, efficient, 12-acre plant on Greenwood Avenue was soon producing 12 million bricks per year. Bulley seemed to find time for social pursuits as well, and not only at the Granite Club. He belonged to the Rosedale Golf Club, the Kiwanis Club, the Canadian Club, and the YMCA.

By the summer of 1925, the new St. Clair clubhouse was almost completed and the club's days on Church Street were coming to an end. But what was to become of the old buildings that had served the members for so many years? In 1924 the steering committee had reported that it had "received a number of inquiries for the purchase of the…property. Some of these appear substantial and…it is reasonable to expect that a sale can be made…at a fair price within a reasonable delay." Unfortunately this was not to be the case. The curling rink at the northeast corner of the property was sold to the York Badminton Club in 1928. (At the beginning of the Second World War, the rink was rented to the Department of National Defence as an enlistment centre and, when hostilities came to an end, for demobilization. In 1967, the York Badminton Club sold it to a developer who razed the old rink except for part of the north wall that still stands. The City of Toronto wisely stepped in and purchased the land from the developer and it eventually became part of a municipal park.)

More than two decades would pass before the Annex building was sold. Finally, on February 27, 1940, the Ulster Football Association purchased it for $25 000. In 1949 the Association resold the building to the 48th Highlanders militia regiment who occupied it for 25 years and then sold it to the city of Toronto.

Piece by piece, the city picked up all the parcels of land and buildings previously owned by the Granite Club and transformed this historic site into a busy community centre surrounded by Cawthra Square Park, where Toronto's AIDS memorial was unveiled in 1993. The 519 Community Centre, housed in the former Annex building, opened its doors in 1976, and became the core of the Church and Wellesley St. area's gay community, North America's third-largest "behind only San Francisco's The Castro and New York's Greenwich Village."

CHAPTER SEVEN

EARLY YEARS ON ST. CLAIR

1926–1929

PROMPTLY AT SEVEN ON THE EVENING of November 12, 1926, the club's officers, in evening dress, and their wives in their most expensive finery formed a receiving line at the main entrance of the new Granite Club to greet the first arrivals. By 8:45 the clubhouse was filled to capacity, its parking area jammed and, according to *The Mail and Empire*, "St. Clair Avenue from east of Yonge Street to west of Avenue Road, as well as the adjoining streets, was lined on either side with automobiles…. At one time the congestion became so great that the police shut the doors and refused to allow any more people to enter until part of the crowd had left for home." Talk about a "crush lobby!" *Saturday Night* declared that "over five thousand of the best-known people in Toronto," attended the gala opening.

Main Entrance

The city's journalists vied with each other for superlatives to describe the new facility. The *Telegram* dubbed it "a modern sporting palace." The *Globe* proclaimed it the "answer to a sportsman's prayer." "Unique," gushed *Saturday Night*, "the only 'family club'…on this continent, or perhaps anywhere." Not to be outdone, the *Toronto Star* rhapsodized:

> If anybody wanted to realize just how big a city Toronto is getting to be, they had but…to go to the opening of the palatial new Granite Club on St. Clair Avenue West…. Fifteen hundred were expected, and at least five thousand must have 'dropped in' during the evening…. Though the Granite Club is not expected to be finished until December 10, last night's guests' first glimpse of it overwhelmed them with its beauty and completeness. Its swimming pool is the finest in the city. If ever infinite variety of Canadian life was ever illustrated in one spot it surely was in the sports wing of the Granite Club last night. On one floor girls in one-piece bathing costumes thrilled members by their exploits. Nearby star skaters, including Canada's feminine representatives at a world's skating competition, pirouetted on a superb rink. Across a runway hundreds danced in the badminton court, which is one of the city's biggest dancing floors. A peep at the big white dining room and lounges and lovely quarters for feminine members made the evening's guests even more enraptured.

John Scott, who had so avidly watched the construction as it progressed, described the opening from an 11-year-old's perspective:

> The night being cool, I was allowed to wear my new plus-fours, but with a jacket, tie and Eton collar. The new club was an awesome sight. Flowers abounded everywhere. There was a reception line that I was not too keen on, but the sparkling washrooms amazed me. Imagine, silver hairbrushes with the Granite crest engraved on them. They were all misplaced the first night. The steps going down to the sports section were a mile wide and the swimming pool was two miles long. I remember some heated discussion among the 'elders' that the plaster plaques by the pool were obscene—and should the figures not have clothing on them? Curling in those days was played with rocks belonging to the members, and were much greater in diameter than those used now. All the gentlemen curlers had their own wooden boxes in which they stored their stones between games and these boxes were arranged neatly in a line at the end of the ice. Skating at the club was a great success, but small boys were urged to doff their tube skates and don figure skates. Hockey was discouraged as being too dangerous, both to the figure skaters and to the glass. The dinner on opening night was a huge success. I don't remember what I ate, but I do remember going home about 9:00 p.m. feeling that the night had been memorable.... We were "privileged" members and it was, and is, an honour to belong to such a magnificent club.

The enthusiastic crowds were amazed by the rink—the "largest single covered expanse of artificial ice on the American continent." The curling and skating areas were side by side and, in days

WILLIAM FREDERICK SPARLING

The talented William Frederick Sparling was an architect who, before he began work on the Granite Club, had already designed several other familiar Toronto buildings, including 302 Bay Street with its classical columned façade and exquisite marble and plaster-work banking hall; the Metropolitan Building at Victoria and Adelaide Streets; the recently restored Masonic Temple with its round sculpted corner overlooking the corner of Davenport and Yonge; 105 Bond Street; 1140 Yonge Street, formerly the "Toronto flagship dealership for the luxury Pierce-Arrow motor car"; and Loblaws office and warehouse at the northeast corner of Lakeshore Boulevard and Bathurst Street. Sparling also designed the Foy Building on the north side of Front Street between Yonge and Bay; the fondly remembered "old lady of Melinda Street"—*The Evening Telegram* building—at the southeast corner of Bay and Melinda; and his own home at 132 Glen Road.

His most daring venture was the purchase of Sir Henry Pellatt's Casa Loma. He planned to transform the unfinished mansion into a luxury hotel. When Sparling took it over in 1925, the great hall and entrance were still lined with scaffolding, and the billiard room and third floor were unfinished. The first guests arrived in 1927 (including the Prince of Wales), but Sparling could not get approval for the additions that were necessary to make the project viable and a padlock went on the door in June 1928.

Like most successful men in Toronto, Sparling belonged to a group of social, sports, and fraternal organizations. At the Granite, he was a keen lawn bowler and curler. In 1935, he skipped a rink to victory in the third event of the Canada Life bonspiel. His teammates were W. Cockburn, vice-skip; J.W. Burgess, second; and Dr. D.M. Ross, lead. In the final game Sparling defeated another Granite rink skipped by John Rennie with H.R. Smith, vice-skip; T.J. Smith, second; and C.H. Boomer, lead.

Curling Rink

Swimming Pool

to come, many a crucial shot would be missed when a curler's eye was distracted by lovely young skaters in revealing costumes pirouetting nearby. Plate-glass windows lined the south end of the sports lounge, giving spectators a clear view of the area, and those who had the foresight to bring skates had the thrill of being among the first to glide, to the strains of a waltz, across this vast expanse of indoor ice.

"Without a doubt the finest…in Canada," affirmed *The Mail and Empire*, referring to the tiled, "regulation-size," five-lane swimming pool—its water "kept clean and fresh by special hygienic treatment." It was 75 feet long and 25 feet wide; 4 feet deep at the shallow end and 9 feet 6 inches at the deep end. Eighty thousand gallons of water were required to fill it. Next to the pool were showers and men's and women's locker rooms, with separate sections for juveniles. (The demand for lockers was greater than expected and the directors promptly had to have a new structure built to house additional locker rooms.)

Badminton

Bowling Alley

Billiards

Driving Range

The new club also boasted seven badminton courts—four with bleachers for spectators; a sound-proofed room with eight five-pin bowling alleys; two full-size squash courts; golf practice courts; six billiard tables; and several card rooms. At the rear of the building, spacious verandas and terraces were provided for members watching the action on the lawn bowling greens and tennis courts.

Services provided included a beauty parlour for the ladies, a barber shop and shoe shine for the gentlemen, and two therapeutical departments featuring steam baths, electric cabinet baths, ultraviolet ray applications, diathermic (radiant heat) treatments, and massage therapy.

Three lounges provided a genial setting for conversation, reading, or quiet snoozing. The main lounge was furnished with opulent oriental rugs, comfortable furniture, fine paintings, antique wall hangings, and hammered brass and wood carvings (including a four-foot model of a British man-o'-war—accurate in every detail). Soft, indirect lighting shone from behind carved sconces and, in the immense fireplace, a cheery log fire bestowed a warm welcome on all who entered the area. The overall effect was one of old-world charm reminiscent of a continental chateau. The men's

Former racquets professional Alf Ablett recalled that "the B.C. fir floor of the original badminton courts had been laid the wrong way … [and] many twisted ankles resulted from the mistake…. A second floor was laid directly over the original.

Lawn Bowling

Beauty Shop

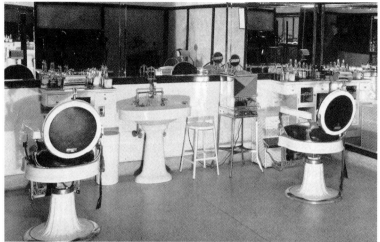

Barber Shop

Therapeutics

reading room, secure behind its large dark wood doors, was a sanctum where one spoke only in whispers and where the reading material was mainly a collection of English magazines including *Punch, London Illustrated,* and *Town and Country*—all in leather binders. It was furnished with overstuffed leather chairs, oak side tables, oriental rugs, and lots of ashtrays. In contrast, the ladies' lounge had an appropriate feminine ambience with soft pastel walls and wicker furniture.

The main dining room could seat 200 people, with two adjoining rooms to handle any overflow. Several smaller rooms were also available for more intimate dinners.

The entire upper floor was devoted to living quarters for men who chose to live at the club. There were one- or two-bedroom bachelor apartments, 26 in all, each with an adjoining bath or shower. Long-term room rentals ran from $60 to $100 per month. Shorter rentals by the week or

Main Lounge

Men's Lounge

day could also be arranged. At the foot of the stairs leading to these rooms, a discreet brass plaque gravely warned: "LADIES MAY NOT BE TAKEN ON THE GENTLEMEN'S BEDROOM FLOOR."

On that gala opening night, each sports section proudly demonstrated the prowess of its top athletes. The crowd that surrounded the swimming pool was treated to an exhibition by some of the country's finest swimmers and divers, and the excitement was palpable. In 23 events, they competed to establish new records, as officials from the Canadian Amateur Swimming Association stood by to adjudicate and affix its official stamp of approval. That evening 23-year-old Tommy Walker,* son of the club's swimming professional, Johnny Walker, broke the Canadian 100-yard backstroke record. Four other marks also went by the board. Canadian diving champions Laura Little and Alf Phillips thrilled the crowd with their high- and low-board diving feats. And a toddler, the wonderfully named Peter Puddy, galvanized the crowd when he jumped into the deep end. Peter, two-and-a-half years old, was Johnny Walker's youngest pupil.

*In 1923 Tommy Walker had won the U.S. all-round championship with four firsts and one second — all in one afternoon! Twenty-six years after his father was appointed swimming professional at the Granite Club, Tommy Walker took over the same position.

Ladies' Lounge

Hall leading from the Men's Lounge

Over at the rink, National Fours Champions Cecil and Maude Eustace Smith,* Jack Eastwood, and Montgomery Wilson thrilled the audience with their brilliant exhibition of skating talent. The badminton courts also presented the city's best, featuring players from the Carlton and Badminton and Racquet Clubs, including Canadian champion Mrs. E.F. Coke and city champion Arnold B. Massey. Canadian squash champion Jack Chipman and Toronto senior handball champions Harry Phelan, Frank Seyers, and Bill Curry also displayed their exceptional skills in a series of exhibition games.

*Cecil Smith had also won the Canadian Ladies Singles Championship that year.

Dining Room

On the bowling alleys, "four teams from the RCYC and four from the Granite Club enjoyed a friendly series of games," and in golf, well-known professionals and amateurs gave exhibitions of driving off the tee in the canvassed enclosure. Even fencing was demonstrated.

By 10:00 p.m. the demonstrations had come to an end and guests drifted into the badminton courts where they danced until midnight "to the lilt of Chas. Bodley's orchestra." It was a fitting end for a memorable evening. *Saturday Night* provided the final stamp of approval: "The historic Granite Club," it intoned, had found a "magnificent apotheosis as the first institution of its kind in America."

The Granite Club's first year on St. Clair witnessed a surge in membership that was nothing short of spectacular. A roster published on September 15, 1926, recorded 937 members—243 of them curlers. Six weeks later membership had risen to 1600 and, by the end of the club's first fiscal year, it had soared to 2606. Many younger members had joined with their parents and, to

A two-room apartment
at The Granite

The 1926 Tankard winners were
Mrs. Moorehouse and Mrs. E. B.
Nettlefield, skips, with Allie Agar,
Mrs.C.W. Archibald, Mrs. Lucas,
Mrs. Victor McWilliams, Edith
Pepall, and Emma Witchall. The
1927 victors were: Allie Agar and
Christina Bulley, skips, with
Mrs. C.W. Archibald, Mrs. W.D.
Copp, Mrs. Gallagher, Marguerite
Grantham, and Edith Pepall.

introduce these young people to the "roaring game," champion curler John Rennie, eight times an
Ontario Tankard winner, volunteered to be on the ice every Saturday from 10:00 a.m. to noon to
give lessons to junior members. Many of the leading Granite skips of the 1930s and 1940s owed
their success to his fine coaching. Granite women curlers were Ontario Tankard champions in
1926 and 1927, which gave the club the enviable record of having won the competition six times
out of fourteen.

Also during the year, the club purchased all the remaining Havergal College property, giving it
a total frontage on St. Clair Avenue of 439 feet, with a depth of 330 feet. The additional land was
to be used temporarily for free parking for members, pending a decision as to its ultimate use.

In 1926, Thomas Rennie, vice-president of the Granite Club and president of the Ontario Curling
Association, called together a group of prominent curlers from Montreal, Ottawa, Toronto, and
Winnipeg to discuss the creation of a national curling championship. They met at the Granite

Club, agreed that it was high time that such a competition be organized, and sat right down and drafted its rules and regulations. The MacDonald Tobacco Company, which had donated a trophy for the curling championship of Western Canada a year earlier, became first choice as sponsor for this new Canada-wide event.

The first MacDonald Brier was played on Granite ice in March 1927. Fans and curlers alike marvelled at the new artificial ice. Both the Canadian National and Canadian Pacific Telegraph companies installed special wiring in the club to "broadcast" running scores of the games via the miracle of Morse code telegraphy to fans across the country. Professor Murray Macneill and his rink from Halifax were the first Brier champions, winning six games and losing only one. (It would be eight years before the East won again. Western Canada dominated the Brier competition for the first 16 years, with Manitoba and Alberta winning a total of 13 times.) Macneill's win was in the days of 14-end games. The number of ends was reduced to 12 by the second year. The Brier was held at the club for the 13 consecutive years—1927–39.

On December 2, 1927, members packed the club's huge auditorium for its first annual meeting at the new facility. They learned that the Toronto district badminton championships would once again be held at the club later that month and the Canadian amateur figure-skating championships would be held there the following February. It was also announced that an outdoor rink would be provided for the club's more robust members—those who preferred to skate in the open air, not indoors on artificial ice.

Financially, the initial year's operations had been an unqualified success. Net operating profit was \$49 773; assets had climbed to \$933 071; and equity was \$399 313. The club was not one to hide its light under a bushel—it proudly published its financial statements in *The Mail and Empire*, *Saturday Night*, and the *Toronto Star*. The latter paper reported that "Frank Shannon's…untiring efforts have resulted in a most gratifying financial statement," and summed up the feeling of the

"Brier" is not an old curling term, as some people might suppose. It was a brand name—MacDonald's Brier tobacco. Its trademark was a small heart stamped into the plug of tobacco that was advertised as "the tobacco with heart." Picking up on this image, each provincial champion was awarded a purple heart-shaped crest to wear on his sweater. When MacDonald's dropped the sponsorship in 1979, Labatt's took over and retained the Brier name for the event. The "purple heart" crest also continues.

meeting with excerpts from a stirring speech by First Vice-President Thomas Rennie in which he paid tribute to his fellow directors:

> The success of the club was remarkable. It was the first major venture as a club for the whole family and the wisdom of having it as such has been amply demonstrated by its use and enjoyment. The success of the club has not been accomplished without a great deal of hard work on the part of those chiefly interested in its formation…. It is only fair to those who have been actively interested to say to all here present that the efforts of these gentlemen has been entirely gratuitous, and that the sale of stock has not cost the club one dollar for commissions.

The election of officers followed. To no one's surprise, Frank Shannon was unanimously re-elected as president and E.B. Stockdale as chairman of the board.

The phenomenal success of the new Granite Club provided further verification for what was then the common wisdom—that the 1920s were the beginning of a golden age of prosperity. Nothing seemed impossible. Charles Lindbergh had just flown across the Atlantic! And what about the grocery clerks who had never before in their lives invested a nickel—mortgaging their homes and insurance policies, plunging into the stock market, buying shares on margin, and becoming wealthy overnight—at least on paper. Even the visiting Prince of Wales, according to *The Toronto Star*, could do the impossible:

> The Prince of Wales performed a Toronto miracle today [August 6, 1927]. He opened the new Union Station. The Prince's coach was pulled into the station and he became the first passenger to step off a train and come to Toronto by way of

The 25-year-old mail pilot Charles Lindbergh, dubbed "The Lone Eagle," flew his plane "The Spirit of St. Louis" solo from New York to Paris on May 20–21, 1927, and won a prize of $25 000 for being the first to do so. The 5790 kilometre journey had taken 33 hours and more than 300 000 cheering French men and women greeted his arrival at Paris airport. The New York Times paid him $250 000 for the rights to his story.

Union Station. An official party, including the mayor of Toronto and the prime minister of Canada, Mackenzie King, greeted him, while a choir of soloists from every major church in the city sang "Land of Hope and Glory."

Completed in 1920, the saga of Union Station had been one of much hope but little glory. For seven long years that magnificent structure had sat empty, while the railways, deadlocked in a disagreement with the city, refused to build viaducts over York, Yonge, and Bay Streets to replace the level crossings where so many pedestrians and motorists had been injured, often fatally.

The Ontario Temperance Act was replaced by the Liquor Control Act, and the first liquor store opened in Toronto on June 1, 1927. This undoubtedly added to the euphoria of the times as the province was among the last to choose government control of alcohol over prohibition. The year 1927 was also Canada's diamond jubilee year and everyone was in a party mood.

Next year the Prince Edward viaduct was completed, allowing traffic to flow across the Don Valley from Bloor Street East to Danforth Road. And there was great rejoicing at the Granite Club when Thomas Rennie and Dr. Victor H. McWilliams won the Ontario Tankard curling competition and brought home the coveted purple banner to hang in the curling lounge. And in the Brier's second year on Granite ice, McWilliams's team of Eddie Brower, John Brandon, and Bob Hamilton ended up in fourth place.

Also during the year, R.C. Davison and J.D. Hayes resigned as directors and the deaths of J.F. Ellis, R.B. Rice, and I.H. Weldon left three additional vacancies on the board. William Inglis; Frederick J. Neale; T.N. Phelan, K.C.; George Henry Ross; and G. Harrison Smith were their replacements.

Harrison Smith, the fifth new director, served for almost 20 years, 17 of them as second vice-president. In business he was president of both Imperial Oil and International Petroleums Limited.

Rennie's winning 1928 rink included A.E. Dalton as vice-skip, W. Austin Suckling as second, and C.O. Knowles as lead. E.H. Brower played in the vice-skip position on McWilliams' team, with J.W. Brandon at second and R. Hamilton at lead.

William Inglis was 61 at the time he became a Granite Club director, and had been president for the past 30 years of the John Inglis Company, Limited, Canada's foremost manufacturers of boilers, tanks, machinery, engines, pumps, and just about anything else that could be fabricated from steel plate—a business founded by his father. Its modern plant at 14 Strachan Avenue in Parkdale covered eight acres and employed 1200 workers.

GEORGE ROSS

Born in 1880, George Ross joined the Bank of Ottawa as a teenager; within about 10 years, he became inspector of its more than 100 branches, from Montreal to Vancouver. In 1915, he moved to Toronto to manage the bank's main branch. He became active in as many clubs and organizations as possible, becoming president of the Kiwanis Club. He also served as honorary treasurer of the YMCA and the Canadian National Committee for Mental Hygiene, and was appointed to the board of governors of the University of Toronto.

When the Bank of Ottawa merged with the Bank of Nova Scotia in 1919, Ross resigned to become a partner in J.G. Beaty and Co., a large brokerage house with a seat on the New York Stock Exchange. Twelve months later, Thomas L. ("Tommy") Church, popular mayor of Toronto during World War I and for a few years after, offered Ross the prestigious appointment as treasurer and commissioner of finance for the city. Ross accepted. It had been just five years since he had arrived in Toronto.

Almost before Ross could catch his breath in his new job he was elected, by the unanimous vote of 708 delegates representing more than 900 clubs from every state of the Union and all the provinces of Canada, as president of Kiwanis International.

By the time Ross joined the Granite board in 1929 he was back in the brokerage business—in charge of the Canadian operations for the Chicago investment house, Thomson & McKinnon—a position he held for the rest of his life.

Ross served as chairman (1932–33) and honorary president (1934–36) in his more than 20 years on the Granite board and remained a director until the day he died in February 1950.

In 1929 the club embarked on its first major building project since the grand opening. Its facilities, more than acceptable back in 1926, had become inadequate for a membership that was approaching 3400. The directors called a Special General Meeting of Shareholders to approve the construction of an additional four badminton courts to the east of the rink building plus additional locker room space, offices, service and store rooms, and a larger billiard room; further work included the conversion of the men's card room into a grill room and the existing billiard room into a new men's card room; the extension of the ladies' locker room, with a new hair-dressing room, a ladies' rest and therapeutic room and improved coat-checking facilities; and the creation of an enlarged kitchen. Capital costs were estimated at $135 000, to be met by $50 000 cash on hand and the issuing of additional second-mortgage bonds for the balance. Operating costs for the additional space would be covered by an increase in senior men's annual dues from $60 to $75. Shareholders enthusiastically approved the proposal and construction began shortly after.

Just before the new building was completed the roof of the rink fell in. It was a mild winter day, about 10:00 a.m. Skaters practising their figures heard a loud crack and, looking up in horror, saw the ceiling begin to buckle. With just seconds to spare they fled the area as the steel girders gave way and the roof collapsed under a heavy load of melting snow and ice. As soon as the Granite Club directors learned of the accident, they called an afternoon meeting and a second meeting that evening with representatives of the company that had built the roof. "Sister curling clubs on hearing of the misfortune also immediately went into session and [offered] certain nights and afternoons to be given over to Granite members." In the meantime, Manager Hector Donnelly, composed and efficient as usual, promptly assembled a crew to clear away the debris and shore up the walls. Skating and curling resumed that evening, albeit under starry skies. Two days later, the curlers' annual New Year's Day buffet luncheon and spoon-draw competition was held as scheduled. The badminton courts took a little longer, but Donnelly had them in action again within the month.

In spoon draws, rinks were drawn at random, by position, and sterling silver teaspoons were awarded to each member of the rink that had won by the largest margin. John D. Arnup in his history, The Toronto Curling Club 1836–1957, *claimed that that club had inaugurated spoon games in 1930. Not so. The Granite Club had begun the practice three years earlier. In later years, despite the substitution of other prizes, such as steaks or turkeys, and the name changed to "tag draws," many older members still insist on calling the games by their original name—"spoon draws."*

For almost four decades, the Auto Show was the most popular event presented at the Exhibition. It was discontinued in 1967 because new cars were being introduced after the fair had ended.

Rehearsals for the club's first annual carnival starring Maude Eustace Smith and Jack Eastwood, Canadian Olympic Pair; Stewart Reburn, Canadian Junior Champion; Cecil Eustace Smith, Canadian Singles Champion; and Leah Croger Muller, Granite Club professional, were also resumed without undue delay and members and guests were enthralled at its two performances on March 22 and 23.* And the third Brier competition was held at the club with Granite skip Eddie Brower's team of Jack Brower, Stan Beatty, and Harry Howard capturing third place. The ladies fared somewhat better, winning the Tankard for the fourth consecutive year. Mrs. C.W. Archibald and Christina Bulley were the successful skips. Their teammates were Allie Agar, Edith Kearns, Mrs. Lindsay, Mrs. Victor McWilliams, Edith Pepall, and Mrs. Reid.

Meanwhile, the stock market continued to soar and Toronto's construction boom kept pace. "In February, the National Motor Show was held on the upper four floors of the newly constructed eight-storey addition to the Robert Simpson store at Bay and Richmond…. Later that year, the $1-million Automotive Building at the CNE was officially opened by Premier Howard Ferguson," and the Royal York Hotel by Governor General Viscount Willingdon. And, up Yonge Street, the Pantages Theatre welcomed Toronto playgoers to its opening production.

Then the bubble burst. The New York stock market collapsed and markets around the world plunged in unison. It was "Black Tuesday"—October 24, 1929. Sixteen million shares changed hands on the New York Stock Exchange and billions of dollars in paper values suddenly disappeared. Brokers closed out clients' margin accounts and grocery clerks and financiers alike were wiped out. The stock-market highs of 1929 were not seen again until the 1950s. The golden age had come to a harsh end. The Great Depression loomed, and a financially chastened decade was about to begin.

*Others in the show included Mr. and Mrs. D.M. O'Meara, and their daughter, Eleanor; former Granite hockey star Dr. J.M. ("Mac") Sheldon in a comedy role; D.M. Bullen; Dorothy and Hazel Caley; Betty and Peggy Stockdale; and Eleanor Wilson.

CHAPTER EIGHT

THE GREAT DEPRESSION BEGINS

1929–1934

"IN CANADA, AS ELSEWHERE, the crash was assumed, at first, to be temporary…. Company presidents and politicians alike, and undoubtedly most other Canadians, agreed with Edward Beatty, the president of the CPR who, after reviewing the economic problems of 1929, concluded, 'It is probable that, when the temporary adverse effects of each [problem] shall have run its course, Canadian economic conditions will be that much more soundly based, and it will be found that the way has been cleared for a more vigorous and better balanced forward movement than has been experienced in the past.'" How wrong he was.

Eaton's optimistically launched its College Street store although the Depression and construction difficulties intervened and the seven-storey 1920s Art Deco building was much less ambitious than the 40-storey-plus skyscraper that was originally planned. The Granite Club proudly published its financial statements in three of Toronto's four daily newspapers—the *Globe, The Evening*

Ontario Ladies Tankard Winners, 1930 (back row, l-r) Christina Bulley, skip; Edith Kearns; Edith Pepall; Mrs. C.W. Archibald. (front row, l-r) Allie Agar, skip; Mrs. Lindsay; Mrs. Victor McWilliams. Absent: Mrs. Mitchell.

Ontario Ladies Tankard Winners, 1931 (back row, l-r) Edith Pepall; Edith Kearns, Mrs. Medland. (front row, l-r) Mrs. Lindsay; Christina Bulley, skip; Allie Agar, skip; Marguerite Grantham.

Telegram, and *The Mail and Empire.* "Notwithstanding the unfavourable condition of trade and business," the club's operating profit for the year ending October 31, 1930 was $71 218—six per cent more than the preceding year. A disquieting note, however, was that membership had also fallen by six per cent. But the phenomenal success enjoyed by the club in its first four years at St. Clair had made members euphoric and no one brought this negative fact to the attention of the Annual Meeting.

It was also a bountiful year for the club in the realm of sports. Cecil Eustace-Smith won the silver medal in the World Figure Skating Championships in New York. She finished behind Sonja Henie, who won the gold medal in 1930. Although Cecil Smith outshone Henie in compulsory figures, Henie won out on overall points. And for the eighth time in 17 years, the Granite Club won the Ontario Ladies Curling Tankard. Christina Bulley and Allie Agar skipped the winning rinks.

The second year of the Depression was financially successful for the club as well. Granted that operating profit was down a bit from the previous year, it was still sufficient to cover depreciation, interest on bonds and mortgages, with a little left over for the surplus account. Membership, however, had plunged precipitously—down 11 percent from the previous year.

Curling continued to be the club's number one sport. Charles Bulley and his rink of John W. Brandon, T.S. Kerr, and A. Ross combined forces with skip Eddie Brower, John Rennie, Jack Brower, and Robert Hamilton to win the Ontario Tankard in 1931. The latter team also took second place in the fifth consecutive Brier held at the Granite Club. Women curlers were every bit as invincible, perhaps even more so. For the ninth time, they captured the Ladies' Tankard. Skips

Ontario Men's Tankard Winners, 1931 (back row, l-r) Robert Hamilton; Jack Brower; T.S. Kerr; A. Ross; (front row, l-r) John Rennie; E.H. Brower, skip; Charles Bulley, skip; John Brandon.

Howard Nicholson, 1931

Christina Bulley had played on six of those winning rinks, Allie Agar on five.

The badminton section was equally busy—hosting the Ontario Championships for the first time and the Toronto and District Championships for the fifth consecutive year.

In skating, John C. (Jack) Eastwood, Canadian Fours Champion in 1926 and 1927, won the 1931 Canadian Waltz championship. General Manager Hector Donnelly, always on the lookout for excellence in his staff, hired British professional champion Howard "Nick" Nicholson as the club's skating instructor. Nicholson had previously taught at St. Moritz and at the renowned Ice Club of London. He directed the next three Granite Club skating carnivals and performed a solo exhibition in each. In 1932 he published a book providing complete illustrated instructions for 41 school figures. It was, for its day, the definitive book on figure skating. In 1934 Nicholson moved on to become skating instructor at Rockefeller Centre in New York City and one of Sonja Henie's coaches. During her career she won the gold medal in three Winter Olympics and 10 consecutive world championships. She went on to star in the *Hollywood Ice Revue* for 18 years and in numerous movies.

In the early 1930s things had yet to grind to a halt in the city—in spite of the Depression. The 34-storey Canadian Bank of Commerce head office building at King and Bay was completed and it dominated Toronto's skyline. At 476 feet, it was the tallest building in the British Empire. Hockey impresario Conn Smythe took his Toronto Maple Leafs out of the Mutual Street Arena, and moved them to the newly completed Maple Leaf Gardens. University Avenue was extended southwards from Queen Street to Front. Ernest MacMillan (*Sir* Ernest after 1935), the 38-year-old principal of the Toronto Conservatory of Music and dean of University of Toronto's Faculty of Music, took over as conductor of the Toronto Symphony Orchestra—a post he held until 1956. And in New York City, the Royal Canadian Mounted Police premiered their Musical Ride in the United States at the International Horse Show at Madison Square Garden.

With 1932 came the changing of the guard at the "sporting palace." After seven years as president Frank Shannon stepped down and Thomas Rennie took over. Shannon became honorary president for two years, and continued to serve on the board until the day he died in 1964.

Rennie was one of the province's most esteemed curlers—he and his teams had won permanent possession of the Mowat Cup and the Walker Gold Cup, and secured the Canada Life competition trophy while playing under the Granite's banner. The Rennie families later donated the two cups and they joined the Canada Life trophy on display at the Granite.

By 1919, Thomas Rennie had also skipped Granite rinks to victory eight times in Ontario Tankard competitions* and was runner-up an additional three. In 1927, he passed on the torch to the next generation of curlers by establishing an annual single rink event, "open to juniors under twenty-two years of age"—the Ontario Junior Tankard. In its first year, the finals were held at the club and "group winners [from] Unionville, Lindsay, Colborne, Barrie Thistle, Allenford, Fergus, St. Thomas, Thornhill, Toronto Oakwood, and Penetanguishene" were "entertained at dinner…by Thomas Rennie, donor of the trophy."

Thomas and his brother John Rennie were inseparable. They worked together as partners in the William Rennie Seed Company after their father's retirement in 1889, curled together, and even lived next to each other—John at 25 Elm Avenue, on the southwest corner of Elm and Sherbourne, and Thomas in a similar house immediately to the south at 10 North Sherbourne.

*Tom Rennie won the double rink Tankard competitions with skips H.T. "Tom" Wilson in 1909, 1910, 1911, and 1914; Harold E. Beatty in 1916 and 1919; W. Austin Suckling in 1921; and Dr. Victor H. McWilliams in 1928. Strictly speaking, Rennie skipped only seven Tankard winning rinks. In 1916, Thomas gave his brother John the opportunity to skip the team, and they won just as handily.

THOMAS RENNIE, PRESIDENT, 1910–11

When Thomas Rennie began his two-year term as club president he was 64 and had already lived a rich and rewarding life—in business, in sports, and in the sphere of community service. He had been president of the William Rennie Seed Company for 43 years and was a past president of the Canadian Seed Trade Association.

Rennie also found time for community involvement and served on the board of the Toronto Harbour Commission for 26 years, eight of them as chairman. His substantial contribution was recognized in 1951 when the new 1000-passenger, diesel-powered, double-deck ferry, *Thomas Rennie,* was launched.* In 1999, almost half a century later, the dependable *Thomas Rennie* continued to ply the waters of Toronto Bay from the mainland to the island.

In sporting circles, Thomas Rennie was elected president of the Ontario Curling Association in 1925–26, chairman of the McDonald Brier in 1928, and honorary life member of the Canadian Branch of the Royal Caledonian Curling Club in 1932.

John didn't achieve quite as much fame as his brother. His contribution to the game of curling was, however, recognized in October 1939, when he was elected an honorary life member of the Ontario Curling Association.

The Rennie brothers were, to no one's surprise, accomplished lawn bowlers as well. Playing doubles, they won 32 lawn bowling trophies in Ontario and Thomas was "captain of the victorious lawn bowling team that went to England [in] 1913." And somehow, between curling and lawn bowling, they managed to find time for golf. Both belonged to the Rosedale Golf Club and the Muskoka Lakes Golf and Country Club, and Thomas at one time served as president of the Canadian Seniors' Golf Association. John was a life member of the Canadian Seniors' Golf Association; at the age of 84 he played his last game at Rosedale Golf Club, shooting an impressive 39 for nine holes.

One of the first appointments made by the board in 1932 was to name 71-year-old James Nicholson as the new curling convener. He had served on the curling committee ever since the new club had opened on St. Clair and for the five preceding years on Church Street.

A 1932 grant from a Granite curler established the Robertson Bonspiel, originally the ladies' single rink curling championship of Ontario. The donor of the trophy was candy manufacturer William Robertson, whose three sisters and three nieces curled at the Granite Club, as did his two brothers and his cousin Alexander Robertson and his wife Josephine—10 curlers from one family, seven of them female!

Robertson Bros. had been founded in 1864 by Thomas Robertson and his four brothers. Thomas, although twice married, had no children. When he retired at the beginning of the 20th century, he turned the company over to three of his nephews, Alexander, Edward and William. The company was one of Canada's largest confectioners, renowned for its chocolate bonbons. During the 1890s, it employed more than 125 workers in a spacious five-storey brick factory at 107–113 Queen St. East. Thirteen travelling salesmen sold its products "from Vancouver to Labrador."

In 1956, the Southern Ontario Ladies Curling Association (SOLCA) decided to take over the competition, change its name to the Provincial Competition, and establish a new trophy. The

The ferries were built by former Granite director William Inglis's company. There was a fleet of five— three of them named after Granite Club members: the William Inglis (1935), the Sam McBride (1939) and the Thomas Rennie (1951). Sam McBride was a Granite Club member, father-in-law of W. Reg. Shaw, club president (1950–51), and mayor of Toronto in 1928–29 and again in 1936.

JAMES NICHOLSON

Born in Scotland in 1861, Nicholson was educated at a private boarding school, then apprenticed to a Liverpool architectural firm. He set sail for Canada at 30, and settled in Toronto four years later. Nicholson was both a successful businessman and a brilliant scholar. He was the manufacturer of Brock's Bird Seed, still remembered for its trademark—a yellow canary, with its head tilted upwards, in full song. The business not only made Nicholson personally wealthy but also enabled him to provide funding for a project dear to his heart—the *Dictionary of Canadian Biography* (*DCB*). In 1999, the DCB included 14 volumes—with at least nine more planned—containing thousands of biographies of Canadians from all walks of life—a host of memorable and fascinating characters, famous and infamous.

Not only did Nicholson serve on the Granite curling committee for 25 years, 15 of them as convener, but he was also honorary secretary of the Empire Club's curling section. He became an honorary life member of the Ontario Curling Association in 1942 and when he stepped down as convener in 1946, curling members elected him as honorary life curling convener and established a trophy in his name. He was then 85 years young—so young in fact that he was elected to the club's board of directors and served the club for six more years.

Nicholson died in his ninety-second year in June 1952. Along with his provision for the endowment of the *DCB*, he left a much smaller bequest to his fellow Torontonians—$10 000 to purchase "seats and benches for the benefit of the public. Such seats to be placed in open spaces, whether public parks, streetcar intersections or as otherwise or shall best serve the public in Toronto." And to the club he loved so well for so many years he left a "substantial [number of] securities, the income from which is to be used in the purchase of curling prizes."

Robertson continued, however; it began a new life as one of the province's most prestigious bonspiels for women, held annually at the Granite Club.

In 66 years of competition, Granite Club rinks have won the Robertson trophy 26 times, with half of those winning rinks skipped by the incomparable Emily Woolley.

In men's curling, the 1932 MacDonald Brier and the finals for the Ontario Tankard were both held at the club. Hamilton Thistles defeated Barrie to win the Tankard. In the Brier, Charlie Bulley's rink of Jack Brandon, Tom Black, and Dan Defoe came third.

In March of that year, the club also hosted the Canadian Amateur Figure Skating Championships and held its fourth annual Skating Carnival directed by Howard Nicholson with music supplied by Ross Brown and his Granite Club Orchestra. Solo performers included Canadian Singles Champion Cecil Eustace Smith, Club Junior Champion Eleanor O'Meara, and Dorothy and Hazel Caley.

In April the club received a fascinating offer, news of which was first leaked to the public in a feature article in the *Globe* headlined: "Granite Club May Buy Glen Mawr Golf Course."* The article contained one particularly prescient remark—65 years ahead of its time: "The proposal presented to the Granite Club is that the golf course…would be an inducement to the club in maintaining the interest of its members during the summer and early fall in their club."

Granite Chairman George H. Ross had received the offer from the president of the Ontario Golf Association, Lewis M. Wood, CBE—a highly respected businessman, financier, and philanthropist. Wood was largely responsible for the founding of the Canadian National Institute for the Blind, where he served as president for 36 years.

But those were depression days and the Granite Club was facing severe financial difficulties. Resignations had soared and operating revenues declined. Membership had plunged to 2422, down 27 per cent from its peak in 1928. And—horror of horrors—the club had defaulted on the

In 1930 the Bayview Golf Club had sold its original property for a residential development, constructed a new 18-hole golf course northeast of its previous premises, and changed its name to the Glen Mawr Golf and Country Club.

EMILY WOOLLEY

Born in Sarnia in 1899, Em Woolley was a granddaughter of 1839 Sarnia pioneer W.B. Clark who had founded a coal, marine-supply, and shipping business. In June 1920, Em, as she was known to her friends, married American businessman LeRoy (Roy) Woolley. The Woolleys were original members of the Granite Club on St. Clair. Emily Woolley's curling career began in 1932 when, after a game of badminton, she paused to watch a team of visiting Scottish curlers. Intrigued with the game, she joined the curling section where the renowned Allie Agar became her mentor and friend. One year later, Woolley found herself a member of Agar's Tankard winning team and, before long, she became a skip. Her rink, composed of her sisters Dadie, Jane, and Cathleen, won the Tankard in 1939 and again in 1941. Even when Cathleen left the rink, the remaining sisters went on to win the Tankard five more times during the years 1945–54, and the SOLCA Provincial Championship five times as well. In all, Woolley curled on 14 Tankard winning teams, seven times as skip.

As her curling career continued, honours poured in. She became an honorary life member of the Granite Club and in 1964, on the floor of the legislature, Ontario Premier John Robarts awarded her the province's Achievement Award "in grateful recognition of her distinguished contribution in the field of fitness and amateur sport." It cited her "superb curling ability…exceeded only by her modesty and her graciousness, her consideration, and her charm. Particularly is she known for her kindliness in helping new players to learn the game."

Emily Woolley died in 1967. In her honour, the Southern Ontario Ladies Curling Association established a seniors competition for the Emily Woolley trophy. A second Emily Woolley trophy, sponsored by her daughter Jane and son-in-law Jack Carruthers, is awarded annually to the Granite Club Ladies Champions. In 1975 the Canadian Curling Association elected her to the Curlers Hall of Fame.

principal repayments on its second-mortgage bonds—a default that continued over the next two years. Interest, however, had been covered, and both principal and interest payments on the first-mortgage bonds had also been paid. It was not the right time to be buying a golf club, even though a few directors were mildly impressed that Glen Mawr's chef had previously served for 14 years in Buckingham Palace. Ross

"Mother lived life to the full…she was a positive person, seldom angered and very modest. I often heard her exclaim, 'It takes four people to win a game.'"
—Jane Carruthers, on her mother, Em Woolley

bluntly told the board that, "he was personally opposed to anything being done which would in any way involve the present financial position of the Granite Club, Limited…. The Board was unanimously opposed to the proposition, and the Chairman was authorized to advise Mr. Wood of their decision."

World news items of 1932 included Amelia Earhart's solo flight from Harbour Grace, Newfoundland to Ireland. She was the first woman to fly the Atlantic alone, duplicating Charles Lindbergh's 1927 feat. And Charles Lindbergh and his wife Anne suffered terrible tragedy when their first son Charles Augustus Jr. was kidnapped and brutally murdered.

The Depression continued to inflict more and more suffering across Canada and throughout the world. Close to 700 000 Canadians were unemployed—65 000 laid off by the railways alone. Many who kept their jobs were forced to accept wage cuts as high as 30 per cent. Canada's steel mills were operating at less than 20 per cent capacity. By 1932, there were no doubts left as to the serious nature of the situation.

Emily Woolley Trophy

In an attempt to staunch the flow of resignations and attract new members, the directors took some unprecedented steps. On October 22, 1932, they offered 250 special-category memberships that waived not only the requirement to buy shares in the club but also reduced initiation fees by

Eleanor O'Meara (centre) with the Caley sisters (Hazel, left; Dorothy, right)

50 per cent. And, for the first time, members would be allowed to spread the payment of annual dues over a four-month period, rather than pay the whole sum in advance. A number of applicants took advantage of the offer and as late as 1999 there were still a few who joined during those dark days and did not own shares in the club.

At the 1932 Annual Meeting in December, Chairman of the Board George Ross had words of praise for the dedication shown by his fellow directors during a difficult year. President Thomas Rennie then shared his concerns with his fellow members: "We have passed a very difficult operating year.... Revenue suffered a sharp decline in 1932.... Your club has suffered the loss of many valuable members.... Severe financial reverses, owing to the existing conditions, made their withdrawal from the club necessary." But he concluded his address with an upbeat piece of oratory to rally the troops for the battle ahead:

We approach 1933 in faith and hope that as the year progresses, we may find general business conditions somewhat improved and it is with confidence we expect to maintain and perhaps improve our position. The old Granite Club of Toronto largely owed its proud position in the sporting world, to the brilliant record of its curlers dating back as far as 1875. The names of the most outstanding citizens of Toronto—outstanding in commerce and in the professions—adorn the banners which draped its walls. But the new Granite Club, while not departing from the ancient traditions, has widened its scope, just as the city has grown from a small town, to the proud position of second largest city in the Dominion. Today the Granite Club is not merely a sporting organization. It is an institution which plays an important and beneficial role in the social life of the city. It enjoys the reputation of being one of the finest equipped and best managed organizations of its kind on the American continent. As in days of old, its members embrace the most prominent and influential citizens in the community…As a convenient place for entertaining friends, or business connections from other cities, it has no equal. Not only the members of the club, but the citizens generally, have reason to be proud that this city is the home of a club so wide in its scope, so strong in its affiliations, as the Granite Club of Toronto.

But in spite of such high hopes, economic conditions failed to improve. In fact, they got worse. In spite of an aggressive membership campaign at the club, resignations outstripped the number of new members The club realized a small operating profit for the year ending October 31, 1933, but again it was not sufficient to meet principal repayments on the second-mortgage bonds, although interest was paid when due.

With fewer members and mounting losses, it was a fairly quiet year at the club. Members' morale did receive a boost, however, when Canada's Governor General Sir Vere Brabazon Ponsonby, 9th Earl of Bessborough conducted a tour of inspection of the building and "many branches of sport were presented for the entertainment of the vice-regal party, followed by a reception in the delightfully decorated ballroom."

The club, that year, elected Alfred Edward Dyment, a colourful and successful entrepreneur, to take the place of Frederick Ratcliff who had died during his sixth year as a director.

Women curlers managed to stir up some excitement in 1933 by winning, for the 10th time, the Ontario Tankard. The two winning rinks were skipped by Christina Bulley (with Edith Kearns,

ALFRED EDWARD DYMENT

Born in 1869 and educated at Upper Canada College, Dyment had joined the frenzied excitement of the northern Ontario lumber boom of the 1890s and had made a fortune. He then turned his considerable energies to politics and was elected, aged 27, to parliament in the Laurier sweep of 1896. Re-elected in 1900 and 1904, he went down to defeat in 1908—but hardly paused to catch his breath. He sold his timber limits and lumber mills, and co-founded a Toronto brokerage house, Dyment, Cassels and Co. By 1909 he was a member of the Toronto Stock Exchange.

Dyment loved horses and was a highly successful breeder of thoroughbreds at his Brookdale farm at Hillsburgh, Ontario—a village between Guelph and Orangeville. Horses from his stable won the King's Plate at Woodbine in 1903, 1904, 1912, and 1921. He was a governor of the National Association of Breeding, president of the Ontario Jockey Club and a director and member of the executive committee of the Toronto Hunt.

He was also an avid curler and was elected president of the Ontario Curling Association in 1939–40. It almost makes one tired just to read about this man's diverse activities, but he was also president of Sovereign Life Assurance Company and Canadian General Electric, later chairman of its board, and a director of numerous other leading corporations. He was, in addition, a director of the Ontario Club and a member of the Toronto Club, the Rideau Club, Ottawa, and the Mount Royal Club, Montreal. Needless to say he was also an invaluable member of the Granite board.

First Annual

Skating Carnival

March 22-23, 1929

~

GRANITE CLUB
63 St. Clair Ave. West
TORONTO

PROGRAMME
~ ~

1. "THE FAIRIES' GARDEN"

*A Fantasy from Fairyland, including many characters
from the Books of Childhood*

Under the direction of GEO. AND LEAH CROGER MULLER

The Story

Darkness Prevails—The Day Breaks—Flowers Asleep—Elves Awaken
Flowers—With Flowers Dancing, Mother Goose and Children from Story-
land Appear—Snow-White Enters with Her Bunnies and Brownies—
Butterflies Usher in the Queen of the Fairies—The Pied Piper and His
Children Arrive—TABLEAU.

Interpreted by

MOTHER GOOSE	Mrs. D. M. O'Meara
QUEEN OF THE BUTTERFLIES	Leah Croger Muller
THE WITCH	Mr. J. B. Kennedy
THE PIED PIPER	Mr. O'Meara
RED RIDING HOOD	Betty Baird
BO PEEPS	Mary Holme and Marion Vanstone
HANSEL AND GRETEL	Harry and Mildred Banfield
CINDERELLA	Philippa McPherson
THE UGLY SISTERS	Jack Robertson and John Scott
PRINCE CHARMING	Bob Tamblyn
PUSS-IN-BOOTS	Ann Murray
HANS AND FRITZ	Dorothy and Hazel Caley
JACK AND JILL	Ruth Paul and Mary McKnight
JACK OF THE BEANSTALK	Pat Sword
BLUE BEARD	Herman Kirk
HIS WIVES	Ruth Coffey, Jean Kirk, Catharine Gaby, Mary Vigeon, Elizabeth Sutherland, Evelyn Henderson.
PETER PANS	Joyce Hopkins, Margaret Page, Velma Ireland, Doreen Warburton
SNOW WHITE	Eleanor O'Meara

Mrs. Medland, and Edith Pepall), and Allie Agar (with Mrs. Victor McWilliams, Emily Woolley and Josephine Robertson.)

In October that year, Tankard-winning Granite skip Charles Bulley changed curling for the better when, at the Ontario Curling Association's Annual Meeting, he moved "that curling stones used in competitions by the OCA should be limited to forty-five pounds." The motion was adopted and the days of curlers carrying their own stones of varying sizes and weights to competitive bonspiels came to an end. Clubs like the Granite scrambled to buy standardized rocks, eight per sheet, for their members and visiting curlers.

In the world of figure skating, sisters Dorothy and Hazel Caley began their illustrious career in 1933 by winning the Toronto and District Pair Championship. They had been Granite members since the St. Clair club opened in 1926 and had performed in its first annual skating carnival in 1929 as Hans and Fritz in "The Fairies' Garden."

The Depression reached new depths in 1934. Membership at the club had decreased by more than a third from its 1928 high and, for the third year in a row; principal payments on the second-mortgage bonds had been missed. Desperate times called for desperate measures and the incoming president was just the breed of high-stakes player the club needed.

CHAPTER NINE

LAST YEARS OF THE DEPRESSION

1935–39

HERBERT RENNIE saved the Granite Club. He had been chairman of the finance committee during Thomas Rennie's term of office and was well aware of the club's financial position that was at best, precarious, and at worst, perilous. As soon as he took over as president in November 1933, he set out to relieve the concerns of the second-mortgage bondholders and forestall any possible action on their part to foreclose. He took a truly astonishing step. He gave his personal guarantee as security for these bonds—a courageous, selfless, and, some might say, imprudent act. Once the threat of foreclosure had been cleared away, Rennie began looking around for other sources of money. The club needed $220 000 to retire the first-mortgage bonds and $105 000 for the seconds. In a two-step operation, Rennie retired the first-mortgage bonds during his second year in office and, in his third year, paid off the seconds. With the aid and support of Hazlett Lemmon (later president of both the Canada Life Assurance Company and the Granite Club) Rennie arranged a first mortgage of $225 000 with Canada Life, secured by the club's land and buildings, and at a favourable rate of interest of 5.5 per cent. (The rate on the first-mortgage bonds had been one per cent higher.) The refinancing was approved at a Special General Meeting of Shareholders, at the end of which T.N. Phelan rose to make a motion:

> "That the thanks of the meeting be tendered Mr. G.H. Rennie for his work in securing a first mortgage at five and a half per cent replacing the present six and a half per cent mortgage."
>
> Mr. George H. Ross said that he had great pleasure in seconding the motion and he thought that we should always pay tribute where tribute was due and that was to our President, Mr. G.H. Rennie. Mr. G.H. Rennie thanked the meeting for their sincere and hearty appreciation which amply and generously repaid him for any work he done in the matter.

The following year Rennie negotiated, also at 5.5 per cent, an advance from the Dominion Bank and retired all the seven per cent second-mortgage bonds. Everyone could now breathe easier. The default had been made good and the financial pressures had been eased. Under the terms of the new Canada Life mortgage, principal repayments were just $5000 per year for the first five years compared with $28 000 on the previous bonds. Interest payments were also substantially lower because of the reduced rate. With the exception of legal fees there had been no costs to the club for this massive refinancing.

Even membership figures were showing signs of improvement. *The Mail and Empire* reported, "Granite members [are] returning to club. Many forced out by the depression are now back." Rennie's fellow directors were delighted and showed their appreciation by electing him as their president for a third term.

Canadian Department Stores Limited was an ambitious, but ill-fated, venture formed by twenty independent stores in Ontario, and one in Montreal, in an attempt to match the mass buying power of Eaton's and Simpson's. Within two years it was bankrupt and Eaton's bought the lot (except the Montreal store) for $4.5 million. The stores were located in Brantford, Brockville, Chatham, Hamilton, Hanover, Huntsville, Lindsay, Midland, Napanee, North Bay, Ottawa, Pembroke, Peterborough, Picton, Port Arthur, St. Catherines, Sault Ste. Marie, Stratford, Sudbury, and Woodstock. Eaton's never made a profit from the chain either, and sold it in 1965.

HERBERT RENNIE had begun his business career as a retailer and had ended up as a stock broker and financier. He had joined the Robert Simpson Company in 1915, and eight years later had been promoted to assistant general manager. In 1925, he became president of Canadian Department Stores* with its 21 large outlets across Ontario. In 1931 he joined forces with Granite board member David C. Haig to form the brokerage firm of Haig, Rennie & Company (later G.H. Rennie & Company).

During the Second World War Rennie served as executive director of the Wartime Prices and Trade Board. For his outstanding contribution to the war effort, he was named a Member of the British Empire (MBE).

When he retired from the Granite board in 1967, he held the distinction of being the last of the original St. Clair directors. He had served an astonishing 42 years—from October 1925 to January 1968—longer than any other director, before or since. The club named him an honorary patron.

John Rennie recalls his grandfather fondly as an astute, charming, charismatic, and fearless gambler, who "loved horse races and card games," and whose favourite quip was, "I'll bet you 8-to-5 on that one."

At a testimonial dinner held in Herbert Rennie's honour in 1963, Chairman Robert Rae recalled,

> I can remember in the early thirties that this club, along with others, had many problems in financing…. Herb spent a great deal of his time reorganizing the funded debt of the club. I can remember this quite clearly…. The success of this club is due in no small measure to his efforts. We owe him a debt of sincere gratitude.

Club Trophy for curling presented by G. Herbert Rennie

Rennie's three-year stint as president was eventful in other ways, too. It was the city's centennial in 1934 and celebrations, in spite of the Depression, were carried on throughout the year. Hollywood stars Mary Pickford, "America's sweetheart," and Walter Huston returned to their city of birth and were entertained at the club at a dinner held in their honour. Earlier in the day they had been given a tour of the club and had seen, for their first time, a game of badminton being played. "It is very much like the game of gardminton played in Hollywood," one of them remarked. Even the president of the United States, Franklin Delano Roosevelt, marked the centennial by magnanimously returning the speaker's mace, plundered by American troops during the War of 1812 when they had burned down our parliament buildings.*

In 1934 the SOLCA changed the Ladies Tankard from a double rink format to single rink. "This enabled clubs with smaller memberships to compete in the annual competition." In spite of the larger number of rinks entered, Granite women were again champions in 1934 and 1935. By that time the club had won more than half of these annual competitions—12 out of 22! In 1934 the victorious rink was Allie Agar, Mrs. Victor McWilliams, Edith Pepall, and Emily Woolley. Agar and Pepall repeated the following year and were joined by new teammates, Mrs. Lindsay and Josephine Robertson.

In badminton there were two pieces of good news. At the Toronto and District Tournament held in January at the Granite Club, Rod Phelan won his first men's singles championship and captured the men's doubles title for the second consecutive year. He went on to win the Ontario singles championship in Kitchener the following month. According to the *Toronto Star*, "a crowd of one thousand spectators watched the final." In a different vein, the *Granite Club News* reported, "Styles in badminton change. We have noticed some very snappy numbers in shorts." Badminton was becoming a more interesting spectator sport.

In 1934 the lovely Eleanor O'Meara won her first major title—the Toronto and District Championship and was given a solo spot in the Granite Club Skating Carnival. She had started her career just five years before when she played Snow White in the club's first annual carnival, with her mother skating the role of Mother Goose and her father David, as the Pied Piper.

British Open Champion Nathan Walley was hired to replace Howard Nicholson as club skating professional in 1934 and successfully defended his British title the following year.

Eleanor Wilson won the Canadian Junior Ladies Championship in 1935 and former Junior Figure Skating Champion Stewart D. Reburn brought glory to the club when he teamed up with Louise Bertram to win the Canadian Pair. They later placed fourth at the World Championships. (Reburn is perhaps best remembered for his role in the 1940 movie *Second Fiddle* with Sonja Henie and Tyrone Power.)

In May 1935, "close to one hundred curlers of the Granite Club competed in the first annual [golf] tournament. George Meech with an 85 won low gross honours."

Culminating a year's negotiations between the curling associations of the West, Ontario, Quebec, and the Maritimes, representatives from each region met at the Granite Club on March 6, 1935 and the Dominion Curling Association was founded as the supervising body for all the regional associations. Ontario's six representatives at the meeting included Granite members Thomas Rennie and R.G.L. Harstone.

For the ninth consecutive year the Canadian curling championship of Canada, the Brier, was held at the Granite Club. After a long drought (the West had been victorious for the previous seven years), the Campbell brother's Hamilton Thistle rink captured the cup—the first Ontario rink in Brier history to do so.* Attendance for the championship game was about 200 and, as Donald Campbell recalled 50 years later, "They filled the Granite Club. They had people behind the glass and some others along the side on the ice, where the figure skaters usually practised"—a far cry

Eleanor O'Meara, Toronto and District Champion of 1934 and soloist in the 1936 Skating Carnival

The Brier champions in 1935 were Gordon Campbell, skip; brother Don Campbell, vice-skip; Gordon Coates, second; and a third brother, Duncan Campbell, lead.

After that one victory for the East in 1935, the West went on to win 10 out of the next 11 Brier competitions.

Eleanor Wilson, Canadian Junior Figure Skating Champion, 1935, and soloist in the 1936 Skating Carnival

from the hundreds of thousands of spectators glued to their television sets more than half a century later.

There never has been an eight-end in Brier competition. So shed a tear for poor Charlie Kerr, the lead on Ken Watson's winning Manitoba rink the following year. Seven rocks were counting when Watson delivered his last rock. As it approached the house, ash from Charlie's cigar fell in front of the rock causing it to grind to a halt—inches short of an honoured place in curling history. And it happened at the Granite Club.

Shortly after the Brier, in April of 1936, there was a near disaster at the club. Engineer William Gallan was in the basement repairing a cylinder of chlorine gas, a germicide used to purify the water in the swimming pool. Inadvertently, while disconnecting a pipe, he neglected to fully close a valve and the poisonous, yellow-green, pressurized gas escaped and spread throughout the building. Chlorine gas is two and a half times heavier than air. Given this and the fact that the valve remained open, the concentration of gas in the basement must have been extremely high. *The Evening Telegram* reported the event:

The fumes were so strong that [Gallan] was forced to abandon his attempt to shut off the valve. He beat a hasty retreat, and was given medical attention. Later he returned to duty. Firemen under District Chief Thomas Tate were called, and ordered everyone from the building. Lieutenant Harry Hamill searched the building to see that everyone was out and was driven back by the fumes. Firemen McCarroll, Blaney, and Head were almost overcome when they opened windows in the basement. When the four firemen returned to Balmoral Avenue [fire] hall they became ill and were attended by Dr. Lawrence Hill, physician for the fire department.

Fortunately none of the men suffered any permanent injury from their exposure to this often fatal chlorine gas—first used by German forces during World War I when they released clouds of it against Allied soldiers at the battle of Ypres.

Later that month tragedy struck the club. It was a Monday morning and the club's famous coach, Johnny Walker, was starting his first swimming class of the week when he collapsed from a heart attack. He was taken home and his physician Dr. J.M. Hazlett warned him not to exert himself. But Walker disobeyed and returned to work the next day, spending five hours in the pool. On Friday he collapsed again and died at his home two days later, at age 60. News of his death appeared on the front pages of three of Toronto's four newspapers, the *Globe, The Mail and Empire,* and *The Evening Telegram.* The *Toronto Daily Star* also published a feature article, inside the paper.

The club's general manager Hector Donnelly, obviously distraught, stated: "He was highly thought of here. He had been with us since we opened, and everyone realized with pride how he threw himself heart and soul into the work, particularly where youngsters were to be trained." Vice-President David C. Haig concurred, adding, "he had no equal in Canada as a swimming coach." Ted Reeve, sports columnist at *The Evening Telegram,* agreed, hailing him as "the most successful coach we have ever known. Year after year he produced champions…until he had a record of almost uninterrupted victories that could not be duplicated by any other instructor." "Recognized internationally as the greatest swimming coach of all time [Walker] earned and maintained the title of 'maker of champions.' He was the perfect coach [with] a personality that inspired friendship and confidence," eulogized the *Globe.* "He was the world's greatest swimming coach,"

Stewart Reburn and
Louise Bertram

Stewart Reburn starred in a movie playing at the Parkdale Theatre

Nathan Walley, Granite Club skating professional and British Open Champion

echoed *The Evening Telegram*. One of his protégés, world champion Marvin Nelson,* was "at the bedside…when the end came." Misty-eyed, he declared, "We won three times together in Toronto and twice at the Chicago World's Fair, and every win I had I owed to him. He was more like a dad than a trainer and coach." Margaret Ravior, wife of world champion George Young, the "Catalina Kid" of 1927, and herself winner of the CNE Women's 10-mile swim—a record-setting three times in a row—was inconsolable. Walker had coached both her and her husband and she looked back with fondness to the memory of this tall, powerfully built, ruddy-faced coach who, in a rich Scottish brogue, handed down from on high his rigorous maxim, "A winner never quits and a quitter never wins." "He had preached this philosophy to hundreds of swimmers [and] he had died by it. If he had rested after the first heart attack, physicians said, he might have pulled through."

"He will be hard to replace," said Donnelly, in the understatement of the day. As a matter of fact it took two men, Andy Carmichael and Don MacKay, to fill the seven-league boots of the larger-than-life John Allan Walker.

A month later a more cheerful event came along to gladden the hearts of Granite members. With the unanimous approval of the board, the slim, handsome, red-headed Roderick Gerard Phelan was awarded its first honorary life membership for outstanding athletic achievement. The date was May 2, 1935. Roddy (as he was then known) and his father Thomas N. Phelan, KC, were at the celebratory banquet held to honour this remarkable 22-year-old, the winner of every badminton championship in which he had competed during the 1935 season—the Toronto and District Championship (once again held at the Granite Club); the Ontario Singles; and the Canadian Singles Championship in Ottawa, as well as the Niagara Falls International Tournament; and the State of Ohio Championship.

Director J.M. Bullen, KC chaired the event and nearly 200 members were on hand to acclaim the young champion. Badminton convener J.J.C. Downey rose to speak and began by tracing Rod's career from that first day in 1926 when club director T.N. Phelan had brought his young son to the badminton courts. Downey went on to recount Rod's exceptional victories over the past few months and throughout his address he emphasized "Phelan's unquestionable conduct on all occasions," and also assigned a "great deal of credit to Alf Ablett, coach of the club, for Rod's sterling performances." Downey concluded his remarks by praising Rod's contribution to both the sport and the club:

Rod Phelan receiving the club's first honorary life membership for athletic achievement in 1935 from President Herbert Rennie

> For the most popular victory in the history of the Granite Club the Badminton Section says "Well done, Rod," and extends its warmest congratulations on your success in winning the highest crown in Canadian badminton—The Men's Dominion Singles Championship—an honour richly deserved by your achievement in previously winning the Toronto and District and Ontario titles, but more so by your steadfast adherence to all that is manly in sport and deportment both on and off the courts.

After the banquet, most of the guests lingered to dance the night away to the music of Stanley St. John and his orchestra. Later that month, Alf Ablett, who had coached Rod Phelan over the past decade, was promoted from racquets professional to sports director.

Having won two Ontario Singles championships, young Phelan went on to win another four and, in addition, four Ontario Doubles titles and two Canadian Doubles Championships. He was also a top golfer—Canadian amateur champion and winner of the Rosedale Golf Club championship twelve times over a 25-year period.

The Stanley St. John Orchestra

The final year of Herbert Rennie's presidency—1936—was a watershed year for the country, the city and the club. King George V died at the beginning of the year. The news was announced at 7:14 p.m. EST, and Ottawa decreed that all Canadian radio stations remain silent for the balance of the evening. The new king, Edward VIII, was on the throne for less than 11 months; he then abdicated to marry American divorcee Wallis Warfield Simpson. His brother, George VI, succeeded him in December. One of the few public acts Edward performed during his brief reign was to unveil the Vimy Memorial on the 250-acre site that France had deeded to Canada, in perpetuity, in recognition of this country's enormous sacrifice in World War I.

Rod Phelan was Ontario Singles Champion in 1934, 1935, 1936, 1939, 1940, and 1941. Jack Storey of the Granite Club won the championship in 1937 and 1938; between the two of them they established a record of eight wins in a row for the Club. Phelan was Ontario Doubles Champion in 1933, 1936, 1940, and 1941 and Canadian Doubles Champion in 1937 and 1938.

The Depression was starting to taper off and the construction industry was showing signs of recovery. The new post office on Yonge Street north of Eglinton, built on the site of Montgomery's Tavern where the Rebellion of 1837 was hatched, officially opened. It is perhaps the only public building in Toronto bearing the coat of arms of Edward VIII. The Park Plaza Hotel opened for business on Dominion Day (now Canada Day) at the beginning of a real scorcher of a summer. A little more than a week later, a record high temperature reading for Toronto was set. The new Stock Exchange building on Bay Street was nearing completion and trading began early the following year. George McCullough merged *The Globe* with *The Mail and Empire* to form *The Globe and Mail*. Parliament passed an act to control broadcasting in Canada by creating the Canadian Broadcasting Corporation (CBC) as a Crown company to replace the previous Canadian Radio Broadcasting Commission. And at their Annual General Meeting in October, grateful shareholders of the Granite Club applauded when they learned that operating profit had risen during the year.

The Brereton-Raw bonspiel moved to the Granite Club in 1936. It had begun in 1922 and was probably, until its demise in 1995, the oldest mixed bonspiel in North America—certainly the oldest in Ontario. According to one of its founders, J. Frank Raw, here's how it came about:

> In the winter of 1921-1922, the curling committee of the Oakwood [Curling] Club allotted some afternoons to mixed curling; both Dr. Brereton and I participated and a competition with prizes was established. The winning rink was skipped by Dr. Brereton, who, in accepting the prizes, suggested that a cup be provided for the event. This was the origin of the Brereton-Raw cup. The cup was played for each year as a club event until the Oakwood Club fell upon evil days at the beginning of the depression. The various trophies were thrown into a lumber room where Dr. Brereton found our cup but without its base. He brought the cup to me and I took it out to the Standard Silver Ware Company, who fixed it up with a new base. This is the cup as it is today. In the meantime, the Oakwood Club had been reorganized and called the Strathcona Club. The event was then thrown open to entries from clubs anywhere in the city, and played on the Strathcona ice until, in 1936, this club went into liquidation. Dr. Brereton now joined the Granite Club, and it was only natural that the event should be played on Granite Club ice. The Granite Club has, as you all know, made this mixed bonspiel an outstanding event in the curling world.

J. Frank Raw's company was the leading supplier of mathematical and surveying instruments, drawing materials and draughting supplies. His 1928 catalogue contained 272 pages, an indication of the extent of his business. He, his wife, and their daughter Margaret all joined the club shortly after it opened on St. Clair.

The original Stock Exchange Building at 234 Bay Street was once one of the city's most evocative Post Modern Art Deco landmarks. Its hazy pink and beige granite façade featured five columnar windows below which Charles Comfort's 74-foot stone frieze depicted the workers of Canada.

Dr. Charles Brereton (left) studies
a shot with opposing skip Tom
Beattie in 1967.

Born in Bethany, Ontario in 1888, Dr. Charles Hulse Brereton came to Toronto after receiving his medical degree from the University of Western Ontario. He opened a practice in the St. Clair-Oakwood area and was a general practitioner there for 54 years. Before retiring at 82, "he was treating the great-grandchildren of his young patients of 1916." He was one of the first persons in the area to own a car, but "it was not always an asset. Many times he was stuck in Oakwood mud while people in buggies passed him by."

Brereton was a natural athlete, playing basketball, tennis and soccer in his high school and college days. According to Edwin Allen, sports editor of *The Mail and Empire*, he "was one of the best basketball players that ever played for Western University." He was an excellent curler and a superb lawn bowler as well. He made the Canadian lawn bowling championship finals several times and once won the open pairs U.S. championship.

His wife Marjorie was an avid curler too. Their daughter, Kate Lindsey, hails her mother as "one of the first liberated women" and credits her with being the initiative behind the birth of the Brereton-Raw. Charlie Brereton curled until he was almost 80. The last known year that he participated in the Brereton-Raw was 1967, but it is possible that he took part after that.

The bonspiel, in its early years at the Granite Club, was a five-day event with a full complement of 64 rinks. In later years it became much smaller, although teams still came from across Canada and the Northern United States—Alberta, Ontario, Illinois, New York, Ohio, and Wisconsin—to enjoy the fellowship of one of the country's most genial and hospitable bonspiels.

Dr. Charles Brereton died at 83 at his home on Heath Street West. He doubtless would have been gratified to know that the bonspiel founded by four old friends—Frank Raw and his wife, and Charlie Brereton and his wife, Marjorie—carried on for so many years. He might have been even more delighted to discover that his grandson Charles Lindsey was a member of the Royal Canadian Curling Club rink that won the Brereton-Raw trophy three years out of four between 1992 and 1995.

In figure skating, Eleanor O'Meara became the 1936 Senior Canadian Ladies' Champion and Dorothy Caley won the Canadian Junior title. The following year Caley took the Canadian Senior title away from her clubmate O'Meara, who then turned around in 1938 and took it back again.

From a public relations point of view 1937 could not have started off any better for the club, but the accolades and adulation came from an unexpected quarter. The famous (some would say infamous), irascible, and outrageous newspaper reporter and radio (later TV) commentator Gordon Sinclair wrote a feature article about the club in the *Toronto Daily Star*, every paragraph of which was more fulsome in its praise than the one preceding it:

Hazel (left) and Dorothy (right) Caley pictured in the 1939 Granite Skating Carnival program

WORLD'S ACE WINTER CLUB HAVING BIGGEST SEASON

By Gordon Sinclair

The largest winter sports club in the world is not in Switzerland. It's not in London or New York…. It's right here in town…the Granite Club. I'm sitting in a movie a few nights back and what flashes on the screen but one of those short [films] on winter sport [in which the commentator said] "The Granite Club, in Toronto, Canada is the largest winter sports club in all the world." Now this of course is highly exciting so I hurry up to see how the Granite boys are getting along. They have not only played but won titles at practically every winter sport in the calendar, including the biggest hockey honours in the amateur world. To look the spot over for the first time, especially on a January afternoon, is to find yourself in a vast and friendly sports department store…. Here on the ice surface, the largest indoor ice surface in the world, some little kids are skating and they skate up Granite way the same year they learn to walk. Jane Taylor, for instance, is only four but she'll have a star spot in the club Carnival at Varsity Arena next week. On the other half of the ice curling men are chucking those 42-pound rocks down the alley. Among them, sweeping the ice furiously is a tall grey veteran who every Ontario curler knows about. He's Douglas Simpson and on the first day of February he'll be 80 and still full of the old pep…. The curling crew, as you suspected long ago, have won every competition they ever went in for. Every one!! They didn't win them all, all the time, of course, but no Canadian trophy has ever been put up for annual competition which has not, at some time or other, been won by a Granite rink. Hockey, well you know about that. The Granite team of 1923–24 is still looked on as the greatest amateur team to strap on skates. They not only won the senior OHA title, the Allan Cup, and the world's championship at the Olympic games but have since become the subjects of mystic legends…sort of legendary supermen who swept everything from their path and did it with a gay and smiling good comradeship. But to a reporter who wandered around the club's premises…the charm and secret of the Granite's success is in the kindly attention given the children. Never have I, for one, seen a spot where the whole family can play at some game suitable to their age and temperament and do it in the same building at the same time. Club officials…don't want to talk about achievement and conquest and victory. They like to talk about family companionship and good clean fun. And they are the biggest of their kind on earth.

The coronation of George VI in December 1936 provided, among other more important things, the theme for the Granite Club's 1937 *Coronation Skating Carnival*. It was one of the most lavish revues ever produced by the club with Luigi Romanelli and his 50-piece orchestra providing the music. Less than a week before their own show at Varsity Stadium, 20 Granite stars travelled by private train to Chicago to take part in the Carnival of Champions for the opening of the Chicago Arena, the largest rink in America. Among those who took part in the carnival in the "windy city" were sisters Dorothy and Hazel Caley, Audrey Miller, Eleanor O'Meara, carnival director Cecil (Smith) Gooderham and her sister Maude (Smith) McDougald, Eleanor Wilson, and club professional Nathan Walley. The *Chicago Times* praised the Granite skaters in an article headlined: "Canadian Stars Add to Glitter of Ice Carnival." The *Chicago American* paid warm tribute to them as "twenty of the most talented young ladies seen here on skates." British and Olympic skating

Since that evening honouring Rod Phelan in 1935, a number of life memberships have been awarded to Granite athletes who have distinguished themselves nationally and internationally in their respective disciplines. They include Canadian Senior Ladies Figure Skating Champions Eleanor O'Meara (1936 and 1938) and Dorothy Caley (1937); World Champion and Olympic Gold Medalist Barbara Ann Scott, honoured by the Club in 1947; and curling champion Emily Woolley.

Granite skaters also performed in Atlantic City. (l-r) Eleanor O'Meara, Cecil Smith, Maude Smith, Eleanor Wilson, Dorothy Caley and Hazel Caley posed outside the Atlantic City Auditorium.

champion Jack Dunn, trained by Howard Nicholson as Sonja Henie's movie partner for four years, and known as "the best looking man in Hollywood" praised the Granite group, stating, "I've never seen finer skating anywhere." And dancers from the Ziegfeld Follies said "it was the best show ever." Expatriate Torontonians living in Chicago lined up to congratulate the skaters after the performance. Some remembered the old Church Street quarters where they had experienced their first thrill on skates, and asked about old friends." The *Chicago Herald and Examiner* was also lavish in its praise:

More than 3500 socialites impeccably attired for a social occasion applauded the *Ice Carnival of Champions* at last night's Chicago Arena premiere, a glittering presentation. Flanked by an orchid barrier and with the ice tinged in myriad hues [red, white and blue]…the Granite Club of Toronto presentation [was] at once striking and original…the best drilled, talented and rhythmic organization of its kind yet to appear in Chicago.

Incoming Granite president Frank Harrison Littlefield was no doubt pleased to have his year in office begin with all that favourable publicity. And things continued to go well throughout the rest of the year. "The entire club radiated a brighter and even more glowing air of hospitality." "Toronto

Mayor W. D. Robbins and other civic dignitaries were on hand to watch the first stone thrown in the 1937 [Brier] title meet." It was the 11th consecutive year that it had been held on Granite ice. The day before the event began, "H.P. Donnelly, general manager of the Granite Club gave visiting curlers a splendid demonstration of hospitality at a luncheon. He introduced staff members of the club, putting them at the service of the curlers, who are here from all parts of Canada for the Dominion championships." As spectators began to fill the gallery for the first game of the series they were fascinated to watch a 69-year-old Scot show the curling champions from across Canada "how it's done:"

Frank H. Littlefield,
President, 1937

He lays a half dozen or so shots on the button. Funny part of it is, he doesn't miss. He stands at the tee and runs a rock up the ice and the rock stops on the button. Slowly he trudges after it, turns around and shoves it back. Again it stops in the exact centre of the ring. The old man moves over and repeats the performance in another ice lane…. He's the Granite Club ice maker—Andrew Harvey from Scotland—and he's just testing the sheet to see "there's no falling off on the out-turn…. I would na' like to say I can put them on the spot ev'ra time, but in most cases—yes—in most cases," he says. Andy can find nothing surprising in his expertise—he been at it so long, since he was a boy in Lanark.

In women's curling, the Granite Club retained its stranglehold on the Ladies' Tankard competition. Granite rinks were victorious in 1937 and again in 1938, establishing a record of 10 wins over the 13-year period.

By the end of 1937 the country was clawing its way out of the Depression, but war clouds were on the horizon. Commercial air travel was ushered in with the founding of Trans-Canada Airlines

Josephine Robertson skipped the 1937 Tankard winning rink, with Allie Agar, Emily Woolley, and Gertrude Young. In 1938, the team remained the same except that Allie Agar took over as skip and Edith Pepall replaced Josephine Robertson.

Thomas N. Phelan,
President, 1938

(since 1965, Air Canada), to provide service across Canada and throughout the world. Malton Airport (now Toronto-Lester Pearson International) was opened to receive Trans-Canada's planes and those of other airlines. Ontario voters reelected Mitch Hepburn and his Liberals to govern the province for a second term. And parents of young children were terrified when a polio epidemic swept across the country during the summer. Ontario kids, of course, thought it was a great lark to have their schools not open until the 12th of October. It would take 16 more years before the Salk vaccine put an effective end to this disease.

Granite members attending the 1937 Annual General Meeting were encouraged to learn that, for the first time in nine years, enrolment at the club had gone up by a substantial 10 per cent from the previous year. Frank Littlefield was complimented for keeping a steady hand on the tiller and Thomas Phelan was elected as the next president.

Thomas N. Phelan, KC, was a barrister in the firm of Phelan, Richardson and Haines (later Phelan and Richardson), established in 1924. He specialized in counsel work, insurance and motor vehicle law. A past president of the Ontario Motor League, he had been its legal counsel since its inception. He had joined the Granite board in 1928 and served as a director for the rest of his life.

Early in Phelan's term as president—April 13, 1938, shortly after midnight—dense smoke billowed through the club, and the night staff rushed to turn in the alarm and rouse the third floor residents from their beds. "I have everybody's clothes on but my own," said Dr. Freemont W. Doan. "I never saw such heavy smoke," said T. Cornelius, newly arrived from London, England. "We grabbed the first things handy and got out pretty quickly." These were but a few of the excited, yet good humoured, statements from the 20 residents who had been wakened from a sound sleep and were now huddled together in the water-soaked lobby. They had had no time to dress. Clad in overcoats and dressing gowns, the men had evacuated the building via a fire escape. "Donald M. Springer, president of Toronto Fuels Limited, who [had] been living at the club for the past five years, was among those forced to leave their quarters." Fortunately no one was injured in the two-alarm blaze. The garrulous Mr. Cornelius went on to tell how he and resident R.J. Brownell had carried a crippled resident down the fire escape, and how night foreman Mike Meegahan and other staff members, covering their faces with handkerchiefs and towels, had dashed into the lounge and halls and carried valuable oil paintings to safety. So impressed was Cornelius with the "efficiency of the staff on the night of the fire" that he wrote a letter of commendation to the board.

"Fire trucks clogged St. Clair Avenue and caused a streetcar tie up for nearly two hours." Under the direction of Chief George Sinclair, firemen from all parts of the city laid down 12 hoses and poured tons of water into the building—first on the badminton courts in the new (1929) east wing where skating carnival sets stored in the gallery were aflame. They quickly extinguished this particular fire, but smoke continued to pour from the bowling alleys and lounge below. Before firemen could locate the source of the blaze (defective wiring in the ice-machine room adjoining the basement sports lounge) the flames had spread through the ceiling to the bowling alley that was consumed almost instantly by what had become a raging inferno. "After a stiff battle…the outbreak was controlled and finally extinguished." "It was nearly 4 a.m. before the fire trucks pulled away from the club."

All three Toronto newspapers gave the conflagration prominent coverage. *The Evening Telegram* ran it as a section feature with the banner headline "GRANITE CLUB FIRE DRIVES OUT SCORE IN NIGHT CLOTHES."

General manager Hector Donnelly and the directors reacted promptly and efficiently. Donnelly reassured members through a paid advertisement in the *Toronto Daily Star* announcing that: "Notwithstanding last night's fire, there will be no interruption in the club's services, excepting the alley bowling and badminton departments."

Canadian figure skaters were judged according to tests devised by the National Skating Association of Great Britain. For the First Class Gold Medal Test competitors had to complete sixteen school figures including variations on rockers, counters, three-change-three, loop-change-loop and bracket-change-bracket. There was also a four-minute free program. The Granite's Eleanor O'Meara and Eleanor Wilson became Gold Medalists in 1935. In 1937, Dorothy Caley, Hazel Caley, Virginia Wilson and Audrey Miller passed the First Class Gold Medal Test.

The board established a Fire Committee chaired by Honorary President Herbert Rennie. Other directors on the committee were President T.N. Phelan; Chairman of the Board D.C. Haig; Finance Committee Chairman Frank Kennedy; and House Committee Chairman John Westren.

Within 19 days they reported to the board that the restoration costs would largely be covered by insurance and recommended that, concurrent with the repairs, additional funds be spent on a new kitchen and dumbwaiter; air conditioning for the sports lounge and bowling alley; sound-proofing of the bowling alley; and a new floor in the sports lounge.

The work was completed not only on time and, but even better, under budget. It took just six months and the board extended its thanks to the Fire Committee "for the very efficient way that

The sports lounge at St. Clair, renovated after the fire in April 1938

the reconstruction and furnishing had been carried on." On a Friday evening in October, members poured into the club for its formal reopening. They danced until midnight, with Stanley St. John's Orchestra playing such hit tunes as "A Pocketful of Dreams," "A Tisket, A Tasket," and "The Lambeth Walk" from the movie, *Me and My Girl*. And then, when the dancing was done, they dug into a sumptuous buffet supper.

A special souvenir edition of the *Granite Club News*, "extra copies [available] from the office at the cost of fifteen cents…to mail to friends," praised the renovations. "The Promenade…to the Sports Department is now a corridor deluxe," with splendid furnishings, and paintings by renowned Canadian artists Homer Watson and F.M. Bell-Smith. The air-conditioned sports lounge was singled out as the "*pièce de résistance* of the remodelling." The walls had "gone modern in the smartest manner—large squares in two-tones of silvery-beige wood veneer to match the pattern of the new parquet flooring.... A new soda fountain, serving pantry and kitchen...for speedy and attractive service...and new rugs, furniture and smart little tables with easy chairs and chesterfields," rounded out the new decor.

The fire had been, in fact, a blessing in disguise. The advent of the Second World War ensured that it would be many a year before any further renovations could be made.

When Eleanor O'Meara won the Canadian Senior Ladies' Skating Championships for the second time in 1938, the fact that her fellow skaters from the Granite Club—Dorothy Caley, Eleanor Wilson, and Hazel Caley—placed second, third, and fourth respectively was almost as impressive. In the summer of 1938, former club skating professional Howard Nicholson, acting as agent for the Granite Club, engaged French superstars, Monsieur et Madame P. Brunet, as club skating professionals. It was a remarkable coup. Brunet and Joly, as they were known professionally, were World Pair Champions four times—in 1926, 1928, 1930, and 1932; Olympic

Granite skaters won the top spots in the Canadian Senior Ladies' Skating Championships in 1938. (l-r) Eleanor Wilson (third), Dorothy Caley (second), Hazel Caley (fourth), Eleanor O'Meara (first).

European and Olympic Champions M. and Mme Brunet became the Granite Club's skating professionals in 1938

Champions in 1930 and 1932; European Champions in 1932; and held 15 championships in France for single and pair skating.

Ruby Fisher joined the pantheon of racquets stars in the club's Sports Hall of Fame when she captured the 1938 Canadian Ladies' Doubles Tennis Championship, and repeated that outstanding feat 10 years later.

The second year of Phelan's term was a year in which the world held its breath. Following close on the heels of the Munich crisis of September 1938 came Hitler's final destruction of Czechoslovakia in the spring of 1939. By then it was clear that war was imminent and King George VI and his wife Elizabeth made a cross-Canada tour to elicit support for the mother country in the event of war. On June 7, 1939, Queen Elizabeth officially opened Ontario's first controlled-access expressway, the magnificent 91-mile road linking Toronto to Fort Erie, and named in her honour—the Queen Elizabeth Way. After Hitler's troops invaded Poland on the first day of September, it took just two days for Britain and France to declare war. Canada joined them a week later.

At the beginning of 1939 skip Emily Woolley, curling with her sisters Cathleen, Dadie and Jean, won the Ontario Ladies' Curling Championship in the eighth annual Robertson Bonspiel. A little later in the year they won again—this time, the Ladies' Tankard. Em Woolley went on to win the Robertson again in 1940 and 1941—three years in a row—and won the Tankard one more time in 1941. And in figure skating, Dorothy and Hazel Caley won the North American Fours competition, skating with Ralph McCreath and Montgomery Wilson.

During the year a Presentation Dinner was held to honour some of the club's outstanding athletes. Special guests of honour Senior Ladies' Canadian Figure Skating Champions Eleanor O'Meara and Dorothy Caley were awarded honorary life memberships. Also recognized at the banquet with gifts of luggage were Jack Storey, 1937 and 1938 Ontario Singles Badminton Champion; and in skating: Dorothy's sister Hazel Caley, 1937 North American Fours Champion and fourth in the 1938 Senior Ladies' Championships; Audrey Miller, runner-up, 1938 Junior Ladies' Canadian Championship—she had missed taking first place by just one-fifth of a point; Eleanor Wilson, 1935 Canadian Junior Ladies' Champion and third in the 1938 Senior Ladies' Championships; and her sister Virginia Wilson, an up-and-coming young skater who would be member of the Canadian Fours Champions two years later. And to end the magic evening, a breathtaking bouquet was presented to skating professional Mme Brunet.

As the year drew to a close, more and more uniforms were in evidence at the Saturday night dances. The club had prospered during Phelan's two years in office. Membership had increased for the second year in a row and was more than 15 per cent above its 1934 low.

In 1939, Eleanor O'Meara (left) and Dorothy Caley (right) received honorary life memberships (Col. J.G. Weir, standing; Skating Convener Stanley Reid, centre)

Thomas Phelan had many loves: his family, his profession, his role on the board, golfing at Rosedale, puttering at his Lake Simcoe cottage, and curling at the Granite Club. He was curling convener the winter before his death. He died in 1964, at 82, and is affectionately remembered as "a kindly and dignified gentleman [whose] sound judgment was always available when needed."

As David C. Haig took over as president of the Granite Club in December 1939, war had been declared and six years of conflict lay ahead.

CHAPTER TEN

A SECOND WORLD CONFLICT

1939 – 1945

THE END OF 1939 found Granite Club members—and everyone else in the country—in a state of shock, as they faced a second world war, just two decades after the "war to end all wars" had come to an end. Fathers who had served in the first war knew that their sons would almost inevitably be called upon to put their lives on the line in this new conflict.

In Canada, the war put an end to "the Depression with its grey, aching unemployment, its insecurity, and its national drift," wrote historian Michael Bliss.

> War brought full employment, fat pay cheques, busyness everywhere, a sense of national purpose—and for Canadian industry a huge surge of capital investment…. Canada's gross national product increased from $5.6 billion in 1939 to $11.9 billion in 1945. The production of war materials totalled almost $10 billion.

Jack Storey, Toronto and District Badminton Champion

Among the allied countries, Canada was the fourth most important supplier. Its automobile factories produced more than 800 000 transport vehicles and more than 50 000 armoured fighting vehicles. Its production of aircraft was dazzling— in 1939 eight small aircraft plants employed 4000 people and produced about forty airplanes a year. Five years later, 116 000 workers had assembled an astonishing 4000 planes. By war's end, Canada had produced 16 418 military aircraft.

By May 1940, Europe was a disaster. The German blitzkrieg had overrun Poland, Denmark, Norway, Belgium, Luxembourg, the Netherlands, and France, and had surrounded all that remained of the Allied armies in the small port of Dunkirk on the north coast of France. There, a miracle took place. A fleet of 1000 British ships—naval vessels, private yachts, fishing schooners, motor boats, even row boats—under constant German bombardment from land, sea, and air, evacuated more than 300 000 troops across the channel to England and safety. Great Britain, with troops from Australia, Canada, India, New Zealand, and South Africa, now stood alone against Germany. Undaunted, Winston Churchill growled the words that reverberate across the century,

We shall defend our island; we shall fight on the beaches; we shall fight on the landing grounds; we shall fight in the fields and in the streets; we shall never surrender. Let us therefore brace ourselves for our duties, and so bear ourselves that if the British Empire and its Commonwealth last for one thousand years men will say, 'This was their finest hour.'

By 1942, 110 Granite members had joined the armed forces. During the course of the war 288 club members were granted leaves of absence. Ten did not return—killed or missing in action.

Sports and social activities were not high on any member's list of priorities as the war effort geared up, and so the club was rather quiet during David C. Haig's first year in office. A major roof repair that could not be postponed was completed; Jack Storey won the Toronto and District Badminton Championship in January; and the club hosted the Ontario Badminton Championships as scheduled, and again the following year. At the 1940 Ontario Championships, Rod Phelan beat Jack Storey for the singles crown.* Then in 1941, Phelan laid aside his racquet, became a lieutenant in the Canadian Army, and was posted overseas. In spite of a number of members enlisting in the armed forces, "membership showed a small increase over that of a year ago," Haig reported to the Annual General Meeting in December 1940.

Because of the war, there were no World Figure Skating Championships from 1940 to 1946. The 1940 Olympics were also cancelled. The Canadian and North American competitions, however, continued to be held. In 1941 Eleanor O'Meara, skating with Ralph McCreath, won the Canadian Pair Skating Championship, and then went on to win the North American championship

as well, bringing to Canada the newly inaugurated David T. Layman Trophy designed by Tiffany. Granite skaters Virginia Wilson and Donald Gilchrist were also victorious that year as two of the Canadian Fours Champions.

A month later O'Meara and McCreath displayed their prodigious talent at Madison Square Garden in New York City, then

GEORGE HOOEY AND THE DA COSTAS WILL INTRODUCE THE NEW ENGLISH DANCE SENSATION "BOOMPS-A-DAISY"

See and learn this new dance the first time professionally shown in Toronto. Saturday Night Dance December 15th—Notice in The Granite Club News, *1939*

Badminton Courts at St. Clair

The Ontario Badminton Championships did not take place again at the Club for 35 years. They returned to the Granite courts in 1976, after the Club had moved to Bayview, and came back again in 1981.

DAVID C. HAIG, PRESIDENT, 1939–41

David C. Haig, president of the Granite Club during the first years of World War II, served as a loyal and diligent director for almost twenty years. One of his many significant contributions was his introduction of Hector Donnelly to the provisional directors in 1925, the year before the club opened its doors on St. Clair Avenue. At the time, Haig was a director and chairman of the house committee at Mississauga Golf and Country Club and Donnelly was its manager. Donnelly became general manager of the Granite Club in 1926 and, for almost twenty-five years, fearlessly and efficiently implemented policies generated by the board.

Before he became president in 1939, Haig had served on the board as honorary secretary, 1926-31; vice-president and chairman of the finance committee, 1933-37; and chairman of the board, 1938. As finance chairman, he and President Herbert Rennie worked as a team during the dark depression years of 1934-36 to resolve the club's precarious financial situation—a task made somewhat easier by the fact that they were also business partners in the firm of Haig and Rennie, stock brokers.

Haig, his wife Helen (née Muirhead), and children Gordon, Douglas, and Helen lived at 143 Spadina Road in the 1920s and 257 Russell Hill Road in the 1930s and 1940s. In addition to the Granite Club and Mississauga Golf and Country Club, Haig also belonged to the Ontario Club, the Canadian Club and the RCYC.

hurried back to Toronto to perform in *Spring Follies*, the club's 13th annual skating carnival. They held the audience spellbound. "When the North American pair skating champions burst through the entrance curtains, a hush pervaded the arena, and the 2000 spectators remained silent throughout their dazzling exhibition." They finished to thunderous applause that persisted until the stars generously returned to the ice for three encores. It was Ralph McCreath's final performance before reporting for active service as a lieutenant in the Canadian army. Eleanor O'Meara went on to a professional career, joining the Ice Capades in 1943.

In November 1942, near the end of the first year of Max Bullen's term as president, Douglas Simpson, dean of Granite Club curlers, died, just two months short of his 98th birthday. Born in Montreal in 1845, Simpson's business career had been with the Bank of Commerce, but when he retired around 1910 he was able to concentrate on more important things, such as curling, for the next three decades. Originally a member of the Queen City Curling Club, he joined the Granite Club on Church Street in the early 1920s. In 1932 President Thomas Rennie, "presented that old veteran curler, Douglas Simpson, with a basket of flowers in commemoration of his 87th birthday."[7] Simpson curled until he was 93 and after that attended, as a spectator, all the major bonspiels at the club. He was "regarded as number one 'rooter' for Mrs. L. E. [Emily] Woolley's Granite rink."[8] When his health failed in 1942, he sent a letter of resignation to the club, which the board refused, granting him instead an honorary life membership. He lived to enjoy the honour for just six weeks.

Wartime labour and material shortages, along with declining membership and revenues, left the directors little choice but to postpone all

Eleanor O'Meara and Ralph McCreath

When the IOC cancelled the 1940 Olympics because of the war, the Caley sisters—Hazel and Dorothy— turned pro. In New York City they appeared on stage at the Center Theatre in a duet skating routine. "Fortunately, they had removed the first eight rows of seats," recalls Dody (Caley) Klein, "because when we did one jump, Hazel stopped at the edge of the stage, but yours truly flew through the air and landed on this poor man's lap. I said, 'Oh, excuse me.' And they boosted me back up on stage."

"We went right on," says Hazel (Caley) McTavish. "There was just a brief musical interlude. But we finished the number."

JOSEPH MAX BULLEN, PRESIDENT, 1941–44

Joseph Max Bullen, KC was elected to the Granite Club's board of directors in 1934 to replace charter member and director William King Pearce, assistant general manager of the Dominion Bank, who had died earlier that year. Bullen served as club president from 1941–44, and as honorary president until his death in 1947.

Born in Toronto and educated at Parkdale Collegiate, he graduated from the University of Toronto in 1913 and from Osgoode Hall in 1916. He joined the practice at which he had worked as a student, later becoming a senior partner in the firm of McMaster, Montgomery, Bullen, Steele, Robertson & Willoughby, barristers and solicitors. He was a bencher of the Law Society from 1932–47.

Bullen and his wife Gracia (née Winchester) lived at 303 Kennedy Avenue, just west of High Park, and vacationed at their summer home in Muskoka Lake where Bullen was president of the Northern Muskoka Lakes Association. He was also a member of Lambton Golf Club and Forest Hill United Church. The Bullens had two daughters, Mrs. William Potter and Mrs. Murray Gordon.

major additions and alterations to the club until after the war, thus eliminating the task of future planning ordinarily addressed by the board. Granite curler George Stronach initiated Sunday trips to Niagara Falls for airmen stationed at the Manning Depot at the CNE grounds. Air Force recruits from across the country took their initial training there, and for many of them it was a chance to see one of Canada's most famous natural wonders. The Ontario Curling Association "voted $250 as a contribution to his expenses and passed a resolution eulogizing his work. As a token of the gratitude of the airmen who profited by it, he received from them a handsome illuminated address.

Bullen was faced with two sensitive issues during his tenure as president. The first was relatively minor, but nevertheless disagreeable. At the annual Curlers' Banquet in 1942, prominent lawyer Irving Stuart Fairty KC, a member since the club's opening on St. Clair, rose to his feet and voiced his displeasure with the board in a series of "derogatory remarks concerning the directors, the gist of his remarks being:

Christina Bulley's rink (with Ruth McCleary, Mrs. N. Smith, and Edith Pepall) winners of the Ontario Ladies Tankard in 1942

1. That nobody knew who the directors were;
2. That the directors were 'proxy appointed';
3. That the club was being run 'by a lot of chiselling stock brokers';
4. That the people in the room [i.e., curlers] should be running the club."

The board instructed general manager Hector Donnelly to write Fairty advising him that his remarks were "prejudicial to the good order, peace, and interest of the club," and that "an apology is due the board and club members and this should be done without delay, failing which the board of directors will request [his] resignation as club member." The apology was evidently forthcoming since Fairty continued to be listed as a member of the Granite Club in the 1946 Society *Blue Book*.

In 1942, Ken Wadsworth skipped a Granite rink to victory in the Canada Life Bonspiel. His teammates were T.S. Kerr, vice; B.C. Edwards, second; J.L. Lynch, lead. They defeated Col. W.O. Morris of the Toronto Curling Club 10 to 5.

Colonel R.S. McLaughlin

R.S. McLaughlin was president of General Motors of Canada Limited from 1918 to 1945, and chairman of the board from 1945 until his death in 1972. McLaughlin was also a generous patron of the arts. In October 1967 an exhibition of part of his collection, including paintings by Emily Carr, Tom Thomson, and Group of Seven founder J. E. H. McDonald hung in Peacock Alley for a week. McLaughlin was named a Companion of the Order of Canada in 1967 and was more than one hundred years old when he died.

The second issue was far more serious and was raised by a determined and courageous member, Dorothy Henderson, a granddaughter of Colonel Robert Samuel McLaughlin, the president of General Motors. The confrontation was particularly awkward since "Mister Sam," as he was affectionately known, was also a director of the Granite Club. He was, at the time, in his early seventies.

Giving Hector Donnelly a week's notice, Mrs. Henderson requested permission to entertain, as her guest at the club, one of the world's most celebrated tenors, Roland Hayes, following his recital at Massey Hall. Hayes was black and Donnelly turned her down flat. Undeterred, she phoned President Bullen and after 15 minutes of heated conversation, Bullen also said no—and hung up. Mrs. Henderson phoned him again. He repeated his decision. She then demanded a meeting of the board of directors to review the decision—as soon as possible, and before the scheduled date of the concert, November 5, 1943.

Hayes was a world-renowned concert artist—the recipient of dozens of honorary degrees, awards, and citations, including the Purple Ribbon of France; a man who had given a command performance for King George V and Queen Mary, who had made his Carnegie Hall debut in 1923, and his Canadian debut at Massey Hall in 1926. Just as Mary Pickford and Walter Huston had been entertained by members at the club, Dorothy Henderson wanted to have the artist as her guest.

Because of his conflict of interest, R.S. McLaughlin predictably absented himself from the special meeting; seven others were also not in attendance. President Bullen requested "the expression of the board and, if he had erred in refusing Mrs. Henderson permission, he was quite willing and anxious to call Mrs. Henderson and give the permission requested." Donnelly reported that he had "informed her that the club did not allow coloured people in the club." Various directors offered their opinions. John A. Tory stated that "[Mrs. Henderson] should not have embarrassed the club by asking for this concession." Thomas Phelan said "he approved of the president's stand, not particularly in regard to the colour line but, Mr. Hayes being a public singer, the affair should be held in a public place." John Parker did not think that "any member should invite to the club any person who, although they might be entertained at members' homes, would not be acceptable to the general membership of the club." Disagreeing with the majority, George H. Ross stated that "Roland Hayes was the outstanding Negro tenor in the world today and had been received by the King and that his programme was of a religious nature and he was sponsored by a number of religious organizations."* Robert Rae agreed. With only 13 of the 22 directors present, it was moved by Phelan, and seconded by J.G. Parker, that the president's decision be upheld. The motion passed by a vote of nine to three with George H. Ross, Robert Rae, and John Westren opposed. Bullen, as chairman, did not cast a vote.

As historian James Walker wrote in *Racial Discrimination in Canada: The Black Experience*, "From the late nineteenth century until the middle of the twentieth, racism infused Canadian institutions, government policies, and public behaviour." The Supreme Court of Canada, for instance, in 1940 upheld the right of the Montreal Forum tavern to refuse to serve blacks. Torontonians behaved in much the same way. Throughout the first half of the century, "Toronto…was known not only for its imperialistic zeal but also for its bigotry…. What is often overlooked is that the city was not unique in these attitudes." Almost every issue of *Saturday Night* from 1900 to 1930 reflected the racism that was then endemic. A historian noted that *Saturday Night* was "anti-black, anti-oriental, [and] anti-Jewish [because] that's how good upper-middle-class British-Canadians viewed things." During the first 70 years of *Chatelaine*, the "feminine ideal was a white, middle-class, heterosexual, non Jew. Unfortunately, this class bias reflected Canadian society as a whole."

The first Book Review Tea will be held on Thursday, November the 2nd, and will begin at 3:15 p.m.… The ladies of the club are invited to bring their War knitting and sewing, if they wish, hence the meeting will afford an opportunity to hear about new and topical books, and yet to relax while not neglecting their work.
—The Granite Club News, *1939*

Carnival program, 1943

*Roland Hayes' recital at Massey Hall was "sponsored by the Ontario and Toronto Religious Education Councils under the distinguished patronage of Archbishop Derwyn T. Owen, Primate, Church of England in Canada; Rt. Rev. J.R.P. Sclater, Moderator of the United Church of Canada; Rev. Dr. H.H. Bingham, General Secretary, Baptist Convention of Ontario and Quebec; and Rt. Rev. Stuart C. Parker, Former Moderator of the Presbyterian Church in Canada."

In the 1930s the Swastika Club in Toronto's fashionable Beach district posted signs, "No Jews or Dogs Allowed." During the Depression the tension between the city's British Protestant majority and its ethnic and religious minorities grew quickly, as a third of the workforce was unemployed and competing for jobs. One steamy night in August 1933, someone brandished a huge swastika flag high above the crowd at a baseball game at Christie Pits. As if on cue, sticks swung and stones flew. Reinforcements for both sides poured in and soon more than 10 000 rioters were rampaging through the neighbourhood. It took police eight hours to quell the frenzy—a frightening harbinger of the incredible events that loomed ahead in Europe.

In 1941, black soldiers rioted when they were refused admittance to Toronto's Palais Royale dance hall at Sunnyside where Earl "Fatha" Hines' black swing orchestra was playing. There was more trouble the following year when the Palais Royale again banned blacks from attending a dance featuring Jimmy Lunceford's orchestra. Then, in 1943, Roland Hayes arrived—and it was the Granite Club's turn.

The Granite Club's directors, having dealt so decisively with the Negro "problem," may have assumed that the question of admitting blacks was settled. But such was not the case. The tenacious Dorothy Henderson refused to knuckle under and, along with friend and fellow club member Ernest Warriner, drafted a petition, obtained the signatures of 35 prominent club members, and delivered it to the board:

> With regard to the entertainment of people of other nationalities as guests of members, we the undersigned, request a clarification of the rulings of our club. This request comes to you because of the fact that Roland Hayes was refused admission to the club last November 5th. Roland Hayes is a world figure, has reached the top rung of the ladder of success, has been received by royalty on many occasions—

moreover he is a Christian gentleman of very high character—but he is a Negro. If the Granite Club believes in racial discrimination...members should be made aware of the rule. This is more than a club issue. It involves our belief in democracy and in Christian citizenship. We do not believe a New Order can be ushered in, or that the sacrifices which our Canadian boys are making overseas will be worthwhile, if we at home in our private and club life accept Hitler's idea of racial supremacy in our dealings with other people. Therefore, we wish the standard set for our guests to be based on

(l-r) Claire Dickinson and Joyce Humble starring in "Double Exposure," Carnival 1941

their inherent character, their social deportment, their honesty and integrity— rather than a standard based on racial prejudice. We cannot but believe that many of the board of directors personally feel as we do on this issue, but in the case of Roland Hayes were acting in the belief that they were upholding the wishes of most of our members. Because a few members have complained of the presence of other races in the club, it does not necessarily follow that the majority of the

The troops are leaving, and spending a cold and very bleak afternoon at the Exhibition last week to get a last glimpse of a brother going overseas, we culled a few ideas ... for [those] in the club who ... don't know what the boys need, or are allowed to take. ... all officers require a flashlight ... made of black rubber, which catches no light, and is water-proof and "bounce"-proof. ... Artillery gloves, for the gunners, have no fingers and thumbs in them, and are very necessary. Sailors appreciate wristlets of navy blue wool, since their cuffs and wrists get wet many times a day and they need quite a few pairs.... —The Granite Club News, February 1, 1940

members feel the same way. Therefore we suggest…that the matter be placed to a vote of the membership: 'That we, the members of the Granite Club, be allowed the privilege of entertaining friends at the club, regardless of creed or race, so long as our guests comply with the stated rules of the club.'

The board's response was immediate and brusque. Bullen informed Mrs. Henderson that the subject was "a dead issue and the situation [might] never arise again."

Bullen's next year as president proved even more difficult than the first—the club had an opportunity to host a dinner for contralto Marian Anderson; like her idol and mentor Roland Hayes, she was black.

Hector Donnelly, using the previous board decision as precedent, refused to book a dinner in honour of the world-famous singer. Donnelly claimed that "he was sorry. He had respect for the talent of Marian Anderson, but there was a rule that had to be obeyed."

Marian Anderson's brush with bigotry in Toronto was far from being her first. Five years earlier in Washington, the Daughters of the American Revolution (D.A.R.) had refused to allow her to perform at Constitution Hall. A flood of outrage surged across the United States. Renowned violinist Jascha Heifetz cried, "I am ashamed to play there." Walter Damrosch, conductor of the New York Symphony Orchestra, and the esteemed Deems Taylor, CBS music consultant and critic for the New York *World* and the New York *American,* published vehement protests in the name of the nation's musicians. And then Eleanor Roosevelt, wife of the President of the United States, stepped in. She resigned from the D.A.R. and organized an Easter Sunday concert for Miss Anderson in Washington, to be held on the steps of the Lincoln Memorial. U.S. Secretary of State Harold Ickes introduced Anderson to the massive crowd assembled there and to the millions of radio listeners across the country, declaring, "Genius draws no colour line."

As one of Anderson's biographers noted, "The media mania surrounding the D.A.R. controversy ensured that any abuse of Anderson's civil rights from that point on would not go unnoticed by the press." In Toronto, as soon as Donnelly's decision became known, the media exploded. "Fashionable club banned Negro" charged *The Globe and Mail.* "Refusal of the Granite Club last week to entertain Miss Marian Anderson was not the singer's first experience of this kind," reported *The Toronto Star."* "Granite Club Tactics Condemned by All Law Abiding Citizens," thundered the tabloid *Hush.* Reverend Gordon Domm denounced the discrimination from the pulpit of Bathurst United Church. The U.S. press picked up on the story. "Noted Singer Barred from Exclusive Club," declared *The Chicago Defender.* Even the Sleeping Car Workers' Union got into the act. At its annual meeting in Cincinnati the union censured the Granite Club for its "infamous exclusion of Marian Anderson."

Letters to the editor in the Toronto papers were scathing:

Evidently those who control the Granite Club don't read newspapers, or they would recall the incident [of] Mrs. F.D. Roosevelt and the D.A.R.... I hope a very loud protest will be raised over the treatment of Miss Anderson by the Granite Club. If Negroes are good enough to die fighting on our side, they are good enough to eat with and to go any place where white people go. I am 100 percent Anglo-Saxon, and often feel ashamed of being one.　　　*—Toronto Star*

To think that when men, regardless of race, colour or creed, are making the supreme sacrifice, a great artist like Miss Marian Anderson was barred from a club in our fair city. As a citizen of Toronto, I bow my head in shame.

　　　—Toronto Star

When the Granite Club refused admittance to Marian Anderson, famous Negro singer, they touched off…so many protests…that I cannot find much to say other than draw the club's attention to the remarks of Mrs. Franklin D. Roosevelt when offering Marion Anderson the coveted Springarn medal,* she said in part, 'Your achievement far transcends any race or creed.'   —*Hush*

By 1944 the beginning of social change was in the wind and the Granite Club was caught up in the process. "The post-war period witnessed an articulate black Canadian reaction to the restrictions that had existed for generations, and it reached an increasingly receptive white audience," wrote historian James Walker. "Revulsion against Nazi racism, and new expressions of international opinion through the United Nations Charter…created a more liberal intellectual climate." But entrenched attitudes do not disappear overnight. In December 1946, "Viola Desmond was carried bodily out of a New Glasgow, Nova Scotia theatre after she refused to observe the 'colour line' rule and occupy a seat in the balcony." And in May 1947, only three years after the Marian Anderson fiasco, the "Toronto Police Commission scheduled a special meeting to decide whether baritone Paul Robson's appearance at a concert might constitute a breach of the peace."

Back at the Granite Club, Dorothy and Douglas Henderson continued to defend their principles and protest against bigotry. On February 14, 1949, six years after Roland Hayes had been excluded from the club, the Hendersons wrote the board regarding a newspaper photo that showed daughters of the Consuls-General for China and India attending a diplomatic reception at the Granite Club.

The other day we noticed the enclosed picture in the daily press and offer congratulations to your board for allowing these people of other races to be entertained at the Granite Club.... We were told we could only entertain people of the white race at the club—and that it would be wiser not to bring Hebrews, but certain ones would be acceptable occasionally.... We would like to know just whom we should exclude from our Granite Club groups, as our friends include many of other races and creeds.... We do feel that this is a subject every club has to face, one way or another in these days. In national, political and artistic life the intermingling of cultures has been so accepted, that it must inevitably become a consideration in our social and club life. In view of the fact that this season Asiatics have been accepted as visitors at the club, it would seem that the board of directors has faced this problem. As members of the club, we would appreciate it, if you would let us know whom we are entitled to entertain there.

The Graniteers

At the next meeting of the board the Hendersons' letter was discussed and Hector Donnelly was instructed to reply:

> Your favour of recent date was read at a recent meeting of the directors and I have been instructed to advise you that the board declines to establish any rule to meet the situation mentioned in your letter. In a club, the views of the majority must prevail. Each member is expected not to offend those views. If and when a member does so, the situation then will have to be dealt with. The above is respectfully submitted for your information.

During the past few weeks the Graniteers have been leading a very active life. On January 26th a party of 29...left for the North Country where they put on a carnival under the auspices of the Kiwanis Club of Timmins.... The next large trip was to Sault Ste. Marie... where the group put on three performances [for] the local Lions Club. ...In addition to the above trips our skaters have taken part in carnivals at Port Colborne, Hamilton and for the Finnish Red Cross at the Maple Leaf Gardens.
—The Granite Club News

The Marian Anderson incident was not soon forgotten by the people of Toronto and it cast a shadow on the club's reputation for years. During a lecture to a Unitarian congregation in 1958, Rabbi Andre Ungar accused the Granite Club of racial and religious discrimination. He spoke of a "club close at hand which refuses membership to Roman Catholics, Negroes, Jews or French-Canadians." When pressed, he clarified his remarks by saying "he had referred to the Granite Club which fourteen years ago came under criticism for refusing admittance to Marian Anderson, U.S. Negro singer." L.E. Messinger, chairman of the club's board of directors, issued an immediate rebuttal to Rabbi Ungar's charge:

> There is nothing in our constitution that prevents a person from becoming a member of the Granite Club because of race, creed, or colour. The present club president, William Fisher, is a Roman Catholic.... The Granite Club has never been known to refuse desirable individuals for membership. I cannot say if the present membership includes Jews or Negroes. We have a large membership. I know of at least one French-Canadian member of the club.

Even after half a century, the "sound and fury" still resonates. In a 1991 letter to the *Toronto Star's* TV guide, *STARweek*, octogenarian and habitual letter-to-the-editor writer Stanley R. Redman* of Midland, Ontario commented on a *STARweek* tribute to Marian Anderson which included the D.A.R.'s excluding her from Washington's Constitution Hall: "Toronto shares a dubious distinction with that pinnacle of American social life, the Daughters of the American Revolution. Readers should remember that the Granite Club, home to many members of the Imperial Order Daughters of the Empire, also barred its doors to the singer."

It should be mentioned that, while the Granite Club did indeed discriminate on the basis of colour and creed, it was among the first private clubs in the city to admit women to its member-

Stanley Redman had well over 900 of his letters published in the press.

ship, and this in 1926 when few clubs did so. Only in the 1980s was this barrier lifted in most of Toronto's male-only clubs (a change often brought about by financial imperatives). The Arts and Letters Club of Toronto, for instance, founded in 1908, never discriminated on racial or religious grounds (Paul Robeson was a guest in 1944 and countless world-famous artists of every colour and creed performed there). But not until 1985 were women admitted as members. Marian Anderson, therefore, would not have been welcomed in that club—not because she was black, but because she was a woman.

(l-r) Eleanor Wilson, Barbara Ann Scott, Eleanor O'Meara

Of course Marian Anderson was not the only person in the news in 1944. Barbara Ann Scott won her first major competition, the Canadian Ladies Figure Skating Championship, and a 10-year-old Glenn Gould was one of 7000 competitors in the inaugural Kiwanis Music Festival in February at Eaton Auditorium.

In January 1944, before 200 spectators, Ken Wadsworth and his Granite rink defeated Gerv Meech of High Park 10–9 in an extra end in the final game of the Canada Life bonspiel, held at the

Alf Ablett

Royal Canadian Curling Club. The game ended in a cliffhanger when, after three hours of play, the spectators held their collective breath as Wadsworth squeaked out a win in an extra end. "Jim Joyce, his third, [was] especially brilliant." This was the second win in three years for skip Wadsworth, but a triumphant first for his son Jimmy in only his second year of play. "Leading for his dad's quartet, he didn't miss any more than two poor shots all night. 'I feel better about the kid's game than I did about winning the trophy,' said 'Pop'"*

In October, the Canadian Figure Skating Association held its annual general meeting at the Granite Club. Also in October, Norwegian Air Force officers, then training in Ontario, received guest memberships. Racquets professional Alf Ablett taught them squash and, at war's end, they were able to take their newly acquired skills back to Norway. Even German prisoners of war benefited from the club's largesse, when member Colonel Carson McCormack, commander of the French River POW camp, took the club's used badminton racquets and birds to the camp for the prisoners' recreation.

Also in 1944, the board repealed the 1932 bylaw that had allowed people to join the club without purchasing shares. The directors became concerned when they learned that more shares were owned by non-members (members who had resigned and the estates of deceased members) than by members. (Of the 50 000 authorized shares, 28 777 were owned by non-members, 16 064 by members, and 5159 shares remained, as unissued shares, with the club.) It would therefore have been possible for "an individual or group to purchase sufficient number of shares to take control from out of the hands of the shareholder members, oust the board of directors, and run the club as they pleased." The board decided, however, that drastic action was not required, but that "restoration of the share qualification for membership would quietly meet this situation and would over a period of years have the effect of getting the club back into the hands of the members of the club." The board also decided to speed up the elimination of this imbalance between non-member and member shareholders and that "no treasury shares of the capital stock of the club [would] be

*Wadsworth's rink included James H. Joyce, vice; J.K. Webb, second; Jimmy D. Wadworth, lead.

sold to applicants for the moment, but that all applicants for membership [would] purchase their stock in the open market at whatever price the seller will accept."

With the invasion of Normandy—D Day, June 6, 1944—the end of the war was in sight. Finally, after five years, eight months, and six days, the war in Europe came to an end with the unconditional surrender of Germany on May 8, 1945. Japan surrendered in August and the United Nations (UN) was established in October. Its charter defined the UN's role in maintaining international peace and security, and the development of friendly relations between countries. The price of peace had been a horrifying 40 million casualties.

CHAPTER ELEVEN

RETURN TO PEACE

1946–1949

UNLIKE HIS PREDECESSOR, Granite president Roy McPherson had a peaceful term of office. Membership was gradually increasing, as those who had served in the war returned home. Badminton champion Rod Phelan returned and married another life member of the club, Canadian and North American figure skating champion, Eleanor O'Meara. The happy couple had their reception at the Granite Club and their wedding gifts were on display in the badminton courts. Curling and skating members continued to bring new honours to the club. Skip Emily Woolley, with her sisters Dadie and Jane, won the Ladies Tankard, although their rink officially represented the Sarnia Curling Club (Woolley's club before she joined the Granite).

Barbara Ann Scott, a pretty 16-year-old in 1945, garnered headlines as she won the Canadian Senior Ladies Figure Skating Championship for the second consecutive year. She went on to win the North American title that year, too. Nigel Stephens became "the first member of the Granite to

ROY SHARVEL McPHERSON, PRESIDENT, 1945–6

Roy Sharvel McPherson FCA was club president during the years in which the world returned to peace. McPherson had joined the club in February 1927, a few months after the move to St. Clair, and was elected as a director in 1939. Born in West Lorne, Ontario in 1890, by 1945 he was an established partner in the firm of Thorne, Mulholland, Howson & McPherson, chartered accountants, and remained there until his retirement. During those years he was a member of the RCYC and the Rotary, National, and Rosedale Golf clubs. McPherson's daughter Mary was an enthusiastic member of the skating section, and skated with John Greig as a pair. After serving as an active board member for 26 years, McPherson stepped down in October 1965, at which time the board appointed him an honorary patron of the club.

win a Canadian Senior Mens Championship, representing the Granite Club as [his] home club." Two years before, he had won the Canadian Junior Mens Championship. He and Scott starred in Ice-Sterics of 1945, the club's annual skating revue, with J. Wilson Jardine and his orchestra providing the music.

Stephens learned to skate when he was six and retired from competitive skating at age 20, after winning the senior championship. He left to pursue his studies at Trinity College, University of Toronto. His father agreed with the decision but added, "Skating has been good to you. Now it's time for you to repay the community for what you were given." Nigel Stephens has been repaying the skating community ever since.

In the business world he became a successful investment counsellor, but skating remained his first love. He served on the skating committee and performed in Granite carnivals from the mid-1940s into the 1950s, at which time he left the committee to make a life-long commitment to the Canadian Figure Skating Association (CFSA). For 30 years he served as a judge at the Canadian, Olympic, and World Championships where, in 1957, he was Canadian team manager. As the Granite Club's representative he held virtually every position in the CFSA, and was elected as its president in 1961–63—the only Granite Club member to be awarded that distinction. He was elected an honorary member of the association in 1967.

Nigel Stephens

In 1994, along with Granite members Barbara Wagner, Robert Paul, Norris Bowden, and Frances Dafoe, Nigel Stephens was inducted into the Canadian Skating Hall of Fame, joining fellow club members Sidney Soanes, Donald Jackson, Cecil Eustace-Smith, and Barbara Ann Scott who had been inducted in previous years.

In September 1994 Stephens celebrated 50 years of membership in the Granite Club. "The club means a lot to me," he said quietly during a recent interview. "It's been the one constant in my life."

Nigel Stephens at the Granite
Sports Hall of Fame wall

McPherson's second year as president was a "red-letter" year both for the country and for the club. Champion skater Ralph Scott McCreath joined the club in February 1946 and won, for the third time, the Canadian senior men's figure skating crown.

As a figure skater he was without equal, winning thirteen Canadian and three North American championships…. 'People today don't realize how good he was,' [said Granite figure skater] Donald Gilchrist, who finished second to him a few times in the 1940s. 'McCreath had the highest and longest jumps ever seen,' according to Nigel Stephens, the 1945 Canadian men's champion. McCreath qualified for the 1940 Olympic Games, but when the Second World War erupted they were cancelled…. He enlisted in the 48th Highlanders of Canada, serving in Europe and North Africa, and rising to the rank of major in the tank corps at the age of 25…. After the war, he strapped on his skates—for the first time in five years—a few months before the Canadian men's figure skating championship and won the men's event…. If McCreath wasn't able to make it to the Olympics as a skater, he did as judge—four times. He also judged six world championships. "He talked to [the skaters] as equals. He was always interested in young people." [said fellow judge Nigel Stephens]. One youngster he took under his wing was…Barbara Ann Scott, who calls McCreath her "absolute hero." For dips in the lake during summer training, McCreath wore leopard swimming trunks that made a lasting impression on her. "He was Tarzan until the day he died, to me."

McCreath had four enduring passions: his family, skating, law, and music. He played the piano and the organ by ear but, most of all, he loved to play the "gut bucket"—an instrument he concocted from a broom stick, a Venetian blind cord, and a galvanized washtub. Incredible as it may seem, this contraption actually produced music, and McCreath could thump out notes so mellow it sounded almost as though he was plucking a bass fiddle. In fact, he performed with such panache that his trio, decked out in tails, played at Toronto's Royal York Hotel. Among his musical friends were vibraphonist Peter Appleyard, pianist/composer Hagood Hardy (he wrote a song for McCreath's 70th birthday), and flugelhornist Guido Basso (who played at his funeral). McCreath was also a loyal friend of the club's orchestra leader J. Wilson Jardine who, during the 1940s and 1950s, shared musical duties for skating carnivals and for Tuesday, Thursday, and Saturday evening dances with Frank Bogart.

Ralph Scott McCreath, QC, BA, LLB, was inducted into the Canadian Figure Skating Hall of Fame in 1995, and celebrated 50 years of membership in the Granite Club the following year.

Ralph McCreath

Barbara Ann Scott's star continued to rise. In 1946, she became Canadian Ladies Figure Skating Champion for the third year in a row. Also that year, young Granite skaters Marnie Brereton and Dick McLaughlin captured both the Canadian Junior Pair and the Ten Step Championships.

For the 16th time in 33 years of competition, Granite women curlers brought home the Ontario Tankard. The winning rink was skipped by Mrs. C.S. Robertson, with Edith Pepall, Ruth McCleary, and Mrs. Fred G. Hoblitzel. Granite men were cleaning up as well. Skips R.H. "Harry" Howard and Dr. Alexander "Alex" S. Elliott and their rinks won the 1946 Men's Tankard, and triumphantly brought the banner back to the club.

Marnie Brereton and
Dick McLaughlin

On April 23, 1946, the Granite Club hosted a complimentary dinner for members who had served in the armed forces during World War II. More than 300 were invited—those who had returned to the club after a leave of absence and more who had joined the club, for the first time, after being discharged from the services.

One ex-serviceman who joined the staff in 1946 was Jim Francis, a man whose ties with the Granite Club went back a long, long way, for his father had been a member in the 1880s when the club was on Church Street. Prior to his four years in the Canadian army, Francis was a figure-skating professional at both the University and Toronto Skating Clubs. A year after the war ended, club manager Hector Donnelly hired him as ice-dancing professional and later, when back trouble began to plague him, Francis joined the club's management team.

Jim Francis was also a successful painter and art teacher. One of his paintings, *Suzanne*, hangs in the club. Over the years his works were sold by several dealers, including the Laing and Imaginus galleries, and were included in exhibitions of the Royal Canadian Academy. Past president of the club and chairman of the Art Committee George Gilmour attested to the calibre of his work saying, "Francis has extraordinary talent as an artist." The renowned British portrait artist Augustus John* once referred to Francis as "an art student of the best European tradition of painting."

Francis retired in 1986, having served the club for 40 years. He is fondly remembered not only as a skating instructor but also as a painter, art teacher, *Granite News* editor, *bon vivant,* and gentle man.

By 1946, a warm breeze of optimism was wafting across the country. Canadians were justifiably proud of the key role that Canada had played in the war and were, after the ravages of the Depression, beginning to feel good about themselves. Early in the year Paul Martin Sr. toured the battlefields of Europe and returned home convinced that the political climate was right for the establishment of a Canadian citizenship. Prior to that time, all Canadians, native-born and naturalized, were British citizens. Canada, Martin argued, should cut the apron strings and become self-sufficient. After much persuasion, Prime Minister William Lyon Mackenzie King finally agreed to Martin's proposal. The Canadian Citizenship Act was passed by Parliament and Governor General Viscount Alexander declared it law on January 1, 1947. The first person to become a Canadian citizen was none other than Mackenzie King himself.* Canadians had, at long last, awakened from their colonial slumber. Later in the year

Jim Francis

The Canadian Citizenship Act of 1947 contained a "weasel" clause emphasizing that Canadian citizens were still British subjects. The Act was amended in in 1976 and Canadians were no longer classified as such.

those who were still royalists at heart were delighted when the date for the wedding of Princess Elizabeth and Lieutenant Philip Mountbatten was announced for the following year. It was, in almost every way, the best of times to be a Canadian.

In 1947 the fourth Canada Life trophy, identical to the first, also became part of the club's permanent collection—thanks to Granite rinks winning five times out of ten in the years 1938 to

1947. Each trophy is worth in the neighbourhood of $10 000. This may explain why, in 1948, Canada Life decided to make the fifth trophy a perpetual one. Granite rinks went on to win the main event seven more times.

In December the Ontario legislature passed the "Liquor Licence Act reinstating

Ladies Tankard winners, 1946 (l-r) Edith Pepall, Mrs. G.S. Robertson, Mrs. F.G. Hoblitzel, Ruth McCleary

the sale of liquor by the glass after a lapse of thirty years" in hotels and cocktail and dining lounges, and of beer and wine in restaurants. The Royal York Hotel responded quickly to the new legislation, and its library became Toronto's first bar. It opened to the public on January 13, 1947, serving gin and rye whiskey daily (except Sunday) for one brief hour, from 6.30 p.m. to 7.30 p.m. Less than three months later, the Silver Rail at the northeast corner of Yonge and Shuter became the city's first licensed lounge and a famous Toronto landmark that operated for more than 50 years.

The Granite Club also inaugurated beverage facilities in 1947. The board decreed that all drinks consumed on the property were to be sold by the club—and the "secret bar in the squash courts for those who knew the right person" and "Rum Row" in the men's locker room closed down forever, living on only as fond memories in the minds of older members. For the first time in more than 30 years, it was possible to drink alcoholic beverages legally at the Granite Club. Members greeted the new policy enthusiastically. In 1948, the first full year of bar service at the club, bar revenues were 17 per cent of total revenues!

The discovery of the vast Leduc oil field in Alberta in 1947 provided the means for that province and its citizens to become as rich as the denizens of the East. By year's end, 30 wells were pumping out black gold at a rate of more than a million and a quarter barrels per year. In Toronto, the new CNE Grandstand (later known as Exhibition Stadium) won the 1947 Massey Medal for its designers, Marani and Morris.

The club president elected in 1947 was John Riddel—a true Scot, born and bred. And although he came to Canada as a young man, he never quite lost the burr that began at the back of his throat and rolled off his tongue whenever he pronounced his surname.

Let's Bowl!
—Carnival program 1942

Riddel was a solid and competent president of the Granite Club. By 1948, under his steward-ship, membership rebounded to 4186 (almost double the 2372 members in 1942), and continued to grow. By 1953, it had reached 5597.

Although the Granite Club *per se* did not win the Ladies' Curling Tankard in 1947, it enjoyed a vicarious victory when the unsinkable Granite skip Emily Woolley and her two sisters again car-ried off the Tankard under the banner of their former home rink, the Sarnia Curling Club. The fol-lowing year, however, curling convener Mrs. C.S. Robertson with her vice-convener Isobel Amell got the Tankard back for the Granite Club. (Other members of the rink were Marion Spooner and Kathleen Muir.) The same team repeated their victory two years later in 1950, and again in 1951.

Marcus Nikkanen

Early in 1947 club manager Donnelly hired New York Skating Club professional Marcus Nikkanen as the club's senior skating professional. Nikkanen had been Finnish Senior Men's Figure Skating Champion for 10 successive years. It was obviously a good decision for both the club and Nikkanen, since he remained in that position for the next 20 years.

Marilyn Ruth Take won the Canadian Senior Ladies Figure Skating Championship in 1947 while Norris "Norrie" Bowden won the mens. Bowden's victory made it three years in a row for the club—Nigel Stephens having won in 1945 and Ralph McCreath in 1946. Bowden and Take's moment of stardom, however, was eclipsed by Barbara Ann Scott who, having won the Canadian Ladies Figure Skating Championship in 1944–45–46, captured the European championship in Davos, Switzerland in 1947 and nine days later, the World Championship in Stockholm—the first North American to do so—her victory ended a European supremacy that began in 1896.

"Fifteen thousand Swedes exploded with obvious delight as the president of Sweden presented her with a bouquet of flowers. In a very tender scene, Barbara Ann kept one for herself and pre-sented the rest to her mother." And that year, for the first time in history, France awarded its Medal of Champions to a woman. Canada's Prime Minister Mackenzie King cabled her:

Barbara Ann Scott

JOHN HUTTON RIDDEL, PRESIDENT, 1947–49

Born at Bridge of Weir, near Glasgow, Riddel was educated at the Glasgow Academy. His first job was as an office boy in his father's engineering firm. Within four years of graduation, however, he had made his mark with the British Crown Assurance Company in Glasgow and London. With his new wife Jessie Ewing McGlashan (also from Bridge of Weir) by his side, he emigrated to Toronto in 1913 as the company's chief clerk. Within another four years he became manager for Canada, a position he held until his retirement. During the course of his business career, he also served as Canadian manager of a number of insurance interests: the Eagle Star Insurance Co. Ltd. of London, England; the British Dominions Insurance Co.; and the Universal Insurance Co. of Newark, New Jersey. Riddel also acted as president and managing director of the British Northwestern Fire Insurance Co., president of the Security National Insurance Co., and president of the Canadian Fire Underwriters Association, 1931–38.

Riddel became a director of the Granite Club in 1940 and served on the board until his death in 1963.

We are tremendously proud of you and will ever remember the honour you have gained for yourself and for our country in winning the ladies world's championship in figure skating. Your perseverance and constant application over years of training will be an enduring example and inspiration to youth of all lands.

A tumultuous welcome awaited Scott when she landed in Toronto. School children had been given the day off and, on a brisk March day, thousands of excited Torontonians jammed Bay Street for a ticker-tape parade and then gathered around city hall to honour "Canada's Sweetheart." Not to be outdone, the Granite Club hosted a second reception and awarded her an honorary life membership. An appreciative nation showered her with honours as well. She received the Canadian National Achievement Award and Canadian sports writers presented her with the Lou Marsh Memorial Trophy as the outstanding athlete of the year*—the second time she had been so honoured. The first was in 1945 after she had won the Canadian and North American championships. Not only was Scott the first woman to receive the award but she was also the first three-time winner, since she was acclaimed again in 1948, her last year as an amateur. And what a year it was. She swept all four competitions: the Canadian, the European, the World's and, best of all, in February, in St. Moritz—the Olympic Gold Medal. "When it was all over, eight of the nine judges had awarded Barbara Ann Scott first place allowing her to become the first Canadian ever to win an Olympic figure skating crown."

A few months after her Olympic win, Scott turned professional, barn-storming across Canada and performing with the Ice Capades and the Hollywood Ice Revue. In one cross-country tour alone, "there were 226 shows, playing in even the smallest towns as well as the big arenas, and the grosses were $850 000 and more than one million customers." She spent five years at this gruelling pace and then, at 25, hung up her skates for good. Skating, however, had led her to the life "she had always longed for. She had already met and fallen in love with the [Hollywood Ice] Revue's publicity manager, Thomas Van Dyke King, and in September 1955 they were married [at Rosedale Presbyterian Church] and moved to Chicago—leaving Barbara Ann Scott, the skater, to live on only in memory." At the wedding reception, family friend J.S.D. Tory couldn't resist an obvious pun in his toast to the bride: "To the Ice Queen who today becomes a King."

In 1948, after 29 years as leader of the Liberal party (22 of which he was prime minister of Canada), William Lyon Mackenzie King stepped down and Louis St. Laurent took over and carried on the Liberal's virtual monopoly of power for yet another nine years.

*The Lou Marsh Trophy, named after a former sports editor of the Toronto Star, is awarded annually to Canada's best athlete. The 75 cm high, black marble trophy can be seen at the Canadian Sports Hall of Fame in Toronto. Winners have included figure skaters Barbara Ann Scott and Petra Burka, football quarterback Russ Jackson, Lake Ontario swimmer Marilyn Bell, and hockey superstar Wayne Gretzky.

W. Reginald Shaw,
President, 1950-51

There were two other major news stories in 1949. The first was the conversion from 25-cycle to 60-cycle electric power in Ontario. This costly error had been made by Sir Adam Beck, principal founder and guiding genius of the Ontario Hydro-Electric Power Commission (now Ontario Hydro) when he introduced cheap 25-cycle hydroelectric power to Ontario, in spite of the fact that most of North America had opted for 60-cycle. During the conversion every electric motor and transformer throughout the province had to be scrapped and replaced.

The second event was a horrifying disaster. Canada Steamship Lines' *Noronic*, the "largest passenger vessel ever put in service on the Great Lakes…[was] destroyed by fire on the morning of September 17, 1949 at Toronto. The fire broke out about 1:30 a.m. when most of those on board were asleep. The flames swept quickly through the passenger accommodation on the upper decks and ultimately completely gutted the ship; 118 of the 524 passengers lost their lives." The Canadian National Exhibition was drafted into service as a temporary morgue for the victims of this tragedy.

W. Reginald Shaw was the first club president in the second half of the century. The president of Shaw's Schools, Ltd. (generally known as Shaw's Business College), he was son of William Henry Shaw, the school's founder. Reg Shaw's vice-president at the school was Granite Club member Christopher William Chant, father of Dixon Chant, who became Granite Club president in 1974. Shaw had joined the board of the club in 1944 and served for more than 20 years.

During the early months of 1950, the board was busy planning additions and renovations to the club, improvements that had had to be postponed by wartime and post-war shortages of building materials. The engineering firm of Margison and Babcock was called in to draw plans to convert the existing lounge—known as the "country club"—into an ice surface, with an extension to its south end; a men's locker room and lounge over the new rink; a third floor for a new, more spacious "country club"; additional private dining rooms; and air conditioning for the main dining room. Hector Donnelly, of course, had a major role in initiating and advancing these plans. At a meeting of the board early in the year, he declared that:

> The proposed extension would materially increase the club facilities, giving better locker space, greater accommodation in the coffee shop, private dining rooms, of which there was a severe shortage, and would give badly needed ice space to both the curling and skating sections, [and that] the added facilities would result in a substantial net profit to the club.

But Hector Patrick McCambridge Donnelly was not destined to see his plan come to fruition. On July 23, 1950, not long before construction was to begin, he died—suddenly and unexpectedly. Staff and members were stunned. Donnelly had been general manager for so long that few could imagine the place without him. "I wept all night," recalled one employee.

Donnelly epitomized all that the Granite Club stood for during its first quarter century on St. Clair Avenue. He was, said the club in its tribute to him, "the soul of honour, a tireless, competent executive who discharged his duties faithfully and with distinction."

Born in 1890 in Northern Ireland, Donnelly was the son of an Irish Catholic father and a Scottish Protestant mother. Educated in Jesuit schools in England, he immigrated to Canada at age 19. Ten years later he became secretary-treasurer and manager of the Mississauga Golf Club, a post he held for seven years, until the Granite Club, then about to build a splendid new facility on St. Clair Avenue, asked him to be its general manager.

Tall and increasingly portly as the years passed, Donnelly was an imposing and, to younger members, sometimes terrifying figure. He dressed impeccably in a navy-blue suit, sometimes worn with a boutonniere, always with a vest. One of his endearing idiosyncrasies was to slice a cigar so he could smoke it in his pipe.

Hector Donnelly

For years Donnelly had lived in the Beach district of Toronto but, in 1929, so that he'd be closer to his work, he bought a house at 36 Glengowan Road in Lawrence Park, where he was to live for the rest of his life. He worked long and hard—from 9:00 a.m. to 8:00 p.m., Monday through Saturday, every other Sunday, and on many holidays. His daughter, Denise Kennedy, recalled that, on Christmas Day, he would be at the club for the Christmas lunch, return home for a 3.00 p.m. dinner, then go back to the club immediately afterwards. He rarely took holidays. "The club was his life," said Mrs. Kennedy. "As a child I saw very little of him."

The Granite Club had long recognized Donnelly's dedication. As far back as 1933, President Thomas Rennie was lavish in his praise at that year's annual general meeting. "He has the confidence of the entire membership," said Rennie. "The success of the enterprise is due in no small measure to Mr. Donnelly's untiring zeal and efficient work."

For months after Donnelly's untimely death, every department of the club, one after another, sent flowers to his family. The board met again on July 31, 1950, and approved payment to his widow, Ellenor, of his full salary up to October 1950, plus $2500 per year for the next five years. They also awarded her a life membership that she enjoyed until she died, at 96, in 1982.

Today, nearly half a century after his death, Donnelly is still fondly remembered at the club. Brad Hatch, club president in 1978, recalled a New Year's Eve party when one young member left the celebration clutching a bottle of champagne. He sailed happily down the stairs—only to be met by the imposing Hector Donnelly standing at the bottom. "March right back up those stairs, young man," commanded Donnelly, "and put that bottle back on the table. And be in my office at 9:00 o'clock tomorrow morning." The chastened young man kept the appointment that New Year's Day, and before Donnelly could say a word, blurted out, "I don't know what you plan to do with me Mr. Donnelly, but—PLEASE SIR—don't tell my father."

For a quarter century Hector Donnelly was the *deus ex machina* of the Granite Club. He established a rock-solid foundation upon which subsequent managers have built. To this day, the respect and affection evidenced by older members is a testament to his enduring contribution to the club he loved.

CHAPTER TWELVE

LIFE IS A CARNIVAL

1950–1959

THE GRANITE CLUB'S 75TH YEAR of operation—from 1950 through 1951—was bittersweet. In spite of Hector Donnelly's sudden death in July 1950, club president, W. Reg Shaw announced that construction of the board's planned additions would proceed. In the meantime, the board advertised across the United States and Canada for a replacement for Donnelly. Forty men applied. Charles E. McWood, who had joined the staff of the club about four years earlier, was appointed as secretary-treasurer and acting manager in October 1950. After reviewing all the applications, the board appointed McWood as general manager on January 16, 1951.

At one time "the largest single covered expanse of artificial ice on the American continent," the Granite ice surface was suddenly in great demand by both the curlers and the skaters. Partly in response to Barbara Ann Scott's stunning Olympic figure skating win in 1948, but largely because of demographics (the so-called post Second World War baby boom), more and more young girls

A. Lowry A. Richardson
President, 1952-53

were clipping photographs of Barbara Ann from magazines, lining up for ice shows at Maple Leaf Gardens, and wishing to act out their own figure skating fantasies on ice.

On the expanded and improved Granite ice surface, Marcus Nikkanen taught figures and in the late 1950s Jim Francis instructed dance. Nikkanen was "highly disciplined" in his approach to figures, while Francis, who is credited with the invention of the Canasta Tango (now a compulsory component of international ice dance competition) tended to be "supportive and nurturing." Whoever was in charge, the youthful ranks of the ice skating section ballooned in the 1950s. And soon the city, regional, and national figure skating competitions were feeling the impact of skating programs at the Granite Club.

In its coverage of the Canadian Figure Skating Association Championships at St. Catharines in February, 1950, *the Granite Club News* sported the smiling faces of three up and coming figure skaters from the club. Senior women's skater Betty Hiscock was competing for the Devonshire Cup, while juniors Joyce Comrie-Palmer and an amazing 12-year-old, Charles Snelling skated in the Howard Trophy contests.

"Charles Snelling was the youngest in the competition," reported the club newsletter. "And it was his first but he performed with the air of a seasoned veteran. He put down figures that would have done a much older skater credit and provided close competition for older and much more experienced contestants. His free skating was very good and showed the results of the hard work he has done. It may not be very long before this skater will bring a prized trophy to the Granite Club."

It wasn't long. The next year, Charles was runner-up Junior Men's Champion of Canada and in 1952 he won the championship. He was six times Canadian Senior Men's Champion, earning a bronze at the World Championships in 1957 and going to the Olympics in 1956 (when he placed 8th of 18 competitors) and 1964. Later, Charles would attend medical school at the University of Toronto, pursue post-graduate studies in plastic surgery and move to Winnipeg to take his residency in the field. He would also be honoured by the club with a life membership.

Charles Snelling, however, wasn't the only member of the family involved in skating at the Granite. His sister, Sonia, won the Canadian Junior Ladies Championship in 1958. And the third Snelling, Linda, won the Central Ontario Novice Ladies Championship in 1957. Though each of the Snelling children began skating very young, the three did not skate in a program together until the Granite Club Variety Show in April, 1958. And that show involved their mother, who worked continuously back-stage getting each skater in and out of costumes smoothly.

Other Granite competitive skaters of the time included Marlene Smith (who captured the Canadian Senior Ladies Championship in 1952) Barbara Gratton (1953 and 1954 Canadian Senior Ladies Champion), Eleanor McLeod (1960 Canadian Junior Ladies Champion), Carl Harrison and Joan McLeod (1958 Canadian Junior Pairs Champions), and Barbara Bourne and Tom Monypenny (Canadian Junior Pairs Champions).

"Everybody worked toward test days," Ann Johnston (Colman) recalled of her skating practice at the Granite. Because her family were longtime members, Ann started skating very young, "but you didn't go into competition until you got up to your gold level of eight different tests. If you

(l-r) Linda, Sonia and Charles Snelling

Sporting in Toronto generally witnessed dramatic advancement during the century's fifth decade. In 1950, Sunday sports became legal in the city and that revolutionary change was celebrated along the lakeshore on May 7, when 17 388 baseball fans turned out at Maple Leaf Stadium to watch the Jersey City Little Giants play the hometown baseball Leafs.

Charles Snelling, shown in the 1949 skating carnival program

Ann Johnston

were lucky you got one a year." At age 14, Ann was the youngest person in Canada to pass her gold medal. Then she jumped to national competition at the junior level, then senior, and eventually world competitions in 1954, 1955, and 1956, and the Olympics in 1956; she reached ninth in the world. The regimen of testing or competitive training was gruelling, but "after the club championships each year, at the end of January, we began practising for the Carnival."

Whether or not they skated their way to a club title or even a national or world championship, for all Granite Club skaters the highlight of the year was the Carnival. The annual skating performances had begun in 1929, but particularly in the 1950s, when club and section membership bulged with postwar children, the skits, routines, kicklines, and production numbers of the season-ending ice extravaganza brimmed with energy and skating talent. The Carnivals were massive endeavours, involving hundreds of club skaters in the show and just as many club members behind the scenes—designing and sewing costumes, building and painting scenery flats, arranging musical charts for the live orchestra, and promoting the event. It seemed to preoccupy the club totally from January through April.

"It's hard to imagine because the ice surface was so small," remembers long-time skater and skating judge Audrey Wallace, "but we had curtains, a back-stage area, a live orchestra and bleachers—maybe 500 seats—right down on the ice."

The Wallace family had joined the Granite Club in the 1940s, partly because Audrey's father, a merchandising manager for Stedman Brothers felt it appropriate, but also because young Audrey just loved to skate. She had no aspirations to compete and although she rose through the ranks to become a figure skating competition judge, like her father, Audrey was a social skater "so the Carnivals were always my favourite part of skating.

"I remember choreographing the kids' numbers. One time the kids were all dressed in plastic raincoats and see-through umbrellas. And we had flashlights in them so when the lights went out, the umbrellas would light up the number... We had chorus lines and conga lines. There would be the kids under age 14 and some of them were only learning to skate, so the idea was to get as many of them out on the ice at once as you could, so they could do their two minutes and get off, because you really couldn't train them."

Behind the scenes at Carnival time

"Audrey was like a mother superior organizing everything," recalls Catharine Larkin, who skated in a number of Carnival kiddy production numbers. "I remember having to make my face all squiggly while all the mothers put on our make-up. One time we did a Barnacle Bill the Sailor number and I was wearing this blue dress with a big white collar and bow in the front. I was so proud of that costume. For me, dressing up in a costume with a little bit of make-up, I imagined I was skating at Maple Leaf Gardens. It was magic."

The 23rd annual Skating Carnival in 1951 opened with music and skating choreographed with a Dutch theme. As Jack Jardine gave his orchestra the downbeat, nearly 75 adult skaters emerged from behind the curtains into a Dutch garden scene to skate the opening number.

Miss Angel Food (Jan Carnegie)   Gingerbread Man (Michael Phenner)   Miss Strawberry Shortcake (Sonia Snelling)

Next, the young skating cast took the audience to "Dreamy Dream Cake Land" where a melodrama put to music told the story of Miss Angel Food (Jan Carnegie) being kidnapped by Devil's Food (Charles Snelling) and rescued by brave Gingerbread Man (Michael Phenner) who flirts with Miss Strawberry Short Cake (Sonia Snelling). In the finale of the production number, the engagement of Miss Angel Food and Gingerbread Man, the youngest members of the skating section performed as Miss Jelly Roll, the Lemon Chiffon Ballet, the Raisin Squares, the Chocolate Eclairs, the Rum and Brazil Cakes, and the Cup Cakes. Said the program notes: "The great day approaches.

Cake Land is a'glee. We take pleasure in presenting the Wedding Cake Pair. Happy dreams come true in Cake Land!"

Also part of the first act, 1949 World Team figure skater Andra McLaughlin and American dance champions Irene Maguire and Walter Muehlbronner performed several dance numbers. Following the intermission, the Granite ensemble presented two more thematic productions, including New Orleans on the Bayou and Summertime, which featured 1945 Canadian Men's Champion Nigel Stephens making a return visit to his home club, and Ann Johnston, then Granite Club Senior Ladies' Champion.

Sugar Plum (Sherry Smith) with Rum and Brazil Cakes (l-r,) Barbara Anne Buchanan, Sue Sutherland, Joanne Smith, Donna Lou Graham, Susan Brown, Diana Martyn

In the 1950s, the Granite Club Skating Carnivals saluted everything from jolly old England to raucous New York, from the Tower of London to Toronto's new Yonge Street subway system, from the Pied Piper to Robin Hood, from Jack Frost to the Four Winds, and from a Strauss waltz to Bill Haley's rock and roll. In fact, the "Rock Around the Clock" routine was so successful on Granite ice, that the six young women skaters were invited to repeat the dance at that year's Granite Review variety show in the club ballroom.

The Granite ballroom wasn't the only additional venue the Granite Carnival shows played. During the 1940s and 1950s some smaller Ontario and northern U.S. cities were anxious to find vehicles for raising money locally. And in those early spring days when the Granite season wound

New Orleans (l-r) Mr. Homer
Meyer, Miss J. Leaver, Mr. Hilmer
Meyer, Mrs. Hilmer Meyer,
Mr. C.R. DeMara, Mrs. R.F. Tilley,
Col. H.R. Harvie, Miss S. Hughes

*"One year they called and said, 'Send us your
skating group.' We went up in our own railway
coach and opened the arena in Sudbury. And
they gave every girl an alligator make-up kit
and every boy a gold watch."*—Ray Bosley

down, the Carnival hit the road to perform its shows (and fund-raise) in such communities as Kingston, North Bay, Sudbury, and Sault Ste. Marie. Arrangements were even made to provide the skaters and production crew with their own private railway car as they travelled. All proceeds went to local charities. But for some young Granite skaters it was a trip to Broadway.

The timing of the Granite Club Skating Carnival had a lot to do with the conclusion of the competitive skating season, but because the production at the St. Clair club required the entire ice surface, it also had to wait for the conclusion of the curling season. The relationship between curlers and skaters—even on the expanded ice surface after the 1950s additions—was a struggle at best. When the two active sections shared the ice surface—skaters on one side of a set of pillars and curlers on the other—the skaters had to mind the curling hacks carved into the ends of the curling surface and the curlers had to mind the ruts courtesy of the previous figure skating session.

Granite curlers were plentiful and busy during the 1950s. Across the country the sport—still an amateur pursuit—boasted more than 75 000 registered men curlers; meanwhile, the Granite was bulging at the seams with well over 800 men and women vying for the time on the club's nine sheets of ice. The 1953 records show a Granite Club house league of 100 night-time teams and "were it not for the fact that about 150 men curl in the afternoons our ice capacity would be sorely taxed."

There was curling every morning and every night of the week, at least four draws a day. And there was mixed—men and women—curling on Sundays. But the favourite was Saturday night and it was generally understood, "if you didn't get your name on the list first thing Monday morning, there'd be no room in the Saturday night draws."

Among the many first-time curlers in those years was Claire Bosley. When she gave up figure skating and the annual Carnivals, she took up curling and remembers fondly the crowded draw schedules and the cacophony of figure skating music competing with curlers' shouts to "Sweep!" There were the Sunday mixed draws, after which Granite curlers often got together at team members' homes for private parties. And if a rink had a particularly strong season on the ice, it might go to the annual Robertson Ladies Bonspiel at the Granite. In 1959, when she curled with Barb Gibson, Em Woolley, and her sister Jane Clark, Claire Bosley did just that. Her rink made it to the 48-rink bonspiel and brought home the trophy to the Granite for the first time since 1950 and for the 11th time in the bonspiel's 28-year history. Reported the newspapers: "In the tenth end, lead Mrs. Bosley, the only member of the rink who didn't curl with Mrs. Woolley's provincial title-winners, scored a double takeout on two perfect draws by the Adams rink's lead." Concluded Claire, "For me it was an honour to be in that class of curling...and representing the Granite." Claire Bosley curled as vice-skip well into the 1960s with her long-standing, regular team members: skip Jean Adams, lead Kay Grier and second Joan Mathers.

Another newcomer who felt immense pride curling for the Granite was a Toronto oral surgeon, who in the mid-1950s had established an office across St. Clair Avenue from Granite Club.

In 1952, of the 179 entries in the Canada Life bonspiel, Dr. A. W. "Whit" Matthew's rink (Alf Phillips Sr., vice skip; John T. Thompson, second; D'Alton McCarthy, lead) were undefeated.

Canada Life Winners, 1950
(l-r) Walter Tomenson, skip;
Dick Doner, vice-skip; Bill Leak,
second; Billy Bell, lead

Robertson Winners, 1959
(l-r) Claire Bosley, Em Woolley,
Jane Clark, Barb Gibson

Bob Marshall often lunched at the club and then began returning at the end of each work day to hone his curling skills. Dr. Marshall would later become curling convener, be invited to the board of the club and sit as president when the club moved from St. Clair to Bayview, but he was first attracted to the Granite's curling rinks and its reputation.

"In those days whenever we had to qualify in some way by becoming the best one or two rinks in the Granite Club," explains Marshall, "we always felt that the hardest part of the job was getting out of the Granite Club, the competition was so stiff. We would come out and play each other on Sunday mornings just for practice."

Also there those Sunday mornings were Herb Allan and A. J. McDonald. Very strong competitors in their day, the two "oldtimers" would sit behind the glass and after the draws, for those who wanted it, Allan and McDonald would dispense criticism and advice. Bob Marshall listened. He also teamed up with more senior curlers—Dick Chant, Bev Kitchen, and Dick Doner—and together their rink won the 1956 Chisholm Bonspiel at the Toronto Curling Club on Huron Street. That match was memorable because "it was my first as skip." Another notable bonspiel took place at the Tam O'Shanter Curling Club in front of CBC TV cameras, as "this was the first televised bonspiel in Canada.

"However, we got more than halfway through the game and the lights they were using had melted the ice. We had to leave the ice while they refroze it. At the time we had a 4-to-1 lead. But the TV producer said we'd have to start all over....We went back out, started all over again and won it anyway.... There was a lot of pride associated with curling for the Granite."

In the Frank Shannon tradition of companionship—that suggested "if Dad's a Granite man, Son will be certain to want to follow in Father's footsteps"—teenager Dave Thompson was eager to learn curling from his father Bill at the club. During the 1950s, whenever he could, the younger Thompson picked up curling pointers from the elder. In addition, after school, Dave and several other boys found that Alf Ablett, the curling secretary, would allow them onto the curling sheets to practise until 6 o'clock when the regular men curlers arrived for the evening draws. By 1959, Dave and his young teammates would have learned well enough to win the Ontario Junior Tankard (and earn Granite Club Gold Crests). But Bill and Dave Thompson were not the only father-and-son tandem of that era. About the same time, Alf Phillips Jr. started signing up for both curling instruction and draws. He was learning from one of the best—Alf Sr.

Born blind in one eye, Alf Phillips, Sr. overcame his disability and went on to win 18 gold medals in the Canadian diving championships from 1926 to 1934. He took two gold medals in the British Empire games in Hamilton, Ontario in 1930 and represented Canada at two Olympic Games—placing sixth in the springboard event in Amsterdam in 1928 and fourth in Los Angeles in 1932.

Turning professional, Phillips starred in Billy Rose's Aquacade at exhibitions and carnivals across Canada and the United States. Fifteen times a day he would perform a death-defying dive from a 100-foot-high platform into a canvas pool containing a mere six feet of water. He co-starred with Johnny Weissmuller (famous for his role as Tarzan in 1930s movies) at the World's Fair in New York City in 1939, and with Esther Williams in 1940. In 1942 the Granite Club appointed him Honorary Swimming Coach.

H.L. Steele
President, 1954–55

Canada Life Winners, 1952 (l-r) D'Alton McCarthy, lead; John T. Thompson, second; Alf Phillips Sr, vice; and Dr. A.W. Matthews, skip received the trophy from Graham A. Walter

In 1948, at age 40, Alf Phillips decided to take up curling. It took him just seven years to become a champion in this sport as well. In 1955, his rink was undefeated in the seven-game round robin for the Ontario title. And the following year he skipped Ontario to the 1956 Canadian championship in Moncton. There he and his rink (Reg Mooney, Stan Jones Jr., and Bill Leak Sr.) lost in an extra end of a play-off game to Manitoba. He lead the Granite's winning rink at the Ontario British Consols Trophy in 1956, and skipped the winning rink of four Ontario Silver Tankard double rink competitions between 1960 and 1964, and the winning rink of two Canada Life Trophy bonspiels in 1960 and 1964. In 1969, he and his team of George Cowan, Sandy McTavish, and Jack Young became Canadian Seniors Champions. From 1970 to 1975, Phillips' rink won the Canada Life Seniors Trophy five out of the six years. Alfie Phillips Sr. was inducted into the Aquatic Hall of Fame in 1971, and the Curling Hall of Fame in 1989. He died five years later, aged 86.

"My father was very competitive," admits Alf Jr. "He didn't like to lose, but when he did lose he always shook hands. And he taught me how to lose. He taught me to give my best, but if I didn't win, to go out again tomorrow."

"Around the Granite Club," recalls one curler of the day, Alf Sr. "won 90 per cent of the games before he ever got on the ice, because everybody would say: 'Oh Gees, we're playing Alf Phillips!'"

"Alfie had more tricks up his sleeve than you could imagine," says Walter Cassels. A relatively novice curler, joining the Granite Club in 1955, Cassels recalls playing against Phillips when "he'd light up his cigar at the far end of the ice, just as you were about to let your rock go...or flicking his broom up over his shoulder again just as you were trying to concentrate on a shot. He knew his way around."

Even so, some of Alf Phillips' prowess must have rubbed off on Walter Cassels even in his first year on the ice. In just his second season at the Granite, Cassels played second on a team skipped by Don Sisley, with Al Francis as lead and Walter's brother Martin as vice. They were all fairly new to the game. Nevertheless, they managed to win a berth at the prestigious Canada Life Bonspiel and made it all the way to the semi-final match "because the gods were with us...and then we got blasted out of the arena." Beginner's luck or not, the experience seemed to bond the four new teammates because they continued to curl together for another 10 years. Later, Walter Cassels served on the board, and became president in 1985.

Meanwhile, in 1956, in just his eighth season playing the grand old game, Alf Phillips Sr. skipped a Granite Club team that represented Ontario at the Macdonald Brier (the tournament recognized as the Canadian championship since 1927) in Moncton. After the round-robin, the rink, consisting of Alf, Reg Mooney, Stan Jones Jr., and Bill Leak Sr., finished in a tie for first place with Billy Walsh's Winnipeg rink representing Manitoba. After 12 ends of a regulation play-off game, the two teams were still tied. So a tie-breaking end was played. Alf Phillips' rink lost to Billy Walsh's rink on the last rock.

That April, as the curling season wrapped up, the Granite Club honoured its two famous rinks—Em Woolley's rink (winner of the All Ontario Ladies' Bonspiel) and Alf Phillips (runner-up at the Macdonald Brier). Four hundred club members attended the special dinner in the ballroom as guest speaker Ken Watson (who had covered the Brier) paid tribute to both rinks, in particular

"Curling is the greatest game in the world. It's the only game in the world, you shake hands with your opposition before you start the game and when the game is over."
—Alf Phillips, Sr.

TO HONOUR THE RINKS OF

Mrs. L. E. Woolley
Winner of
All Ontario Ladies' Bonspiel

and

Mr. A. H. Phillips
Runner-up Macdonald Brier

The Members of the Ladies' and the Men's Curling Sections are invited to a Dinner in the Ball Room on Tuesday, April 24th, at 6.30 o'clock, in honour of the Rinks of Mrs. L. E. Woolley and Mr. A. H. Phillips.

Cards of invitation will be mailed to all Curling Members and it will be necessary to return these to the Curling Office for dinner reservations which are limited to 400 persons.

Our Guest Speaker will be Mr. J. Ken Watson of Winnipeg, who is making a special trip to Toronto for this memorable occasion. Mr. Watson, who covered the Macdonald Brier Bonspiel in Moncton, and whose commentaries were followed with great interest by Curlers across Canada, is a recognized authority on the Roarin' Game.

Reservations for this Dinner will be recorded in the order they are received, since they are limited.

Tickets—$3.00 per person.

—Granite Club News, 1956

Lucien E. Messinger
President, 1956-57

Phillips' near-capture of the Canadian Championship, calling it "one of the best-curled games I've ever seen."

Disappointment over the Brier was momentary. Once Alf Phillips Jr. joined Sr. on regular basis, the wins came fast and furious at the Granite Club, across the city, and around Ontario and Quebec. By the end of the decade they were hitting their stride. The foursome—Alf Sr. as skip, Bill Leak as vice, Don Robinson as second, and Alf Jr. playing lead—was cleaning up.

In 1953, city politicians created Metropolitan Toronto from the adjoining 12 suburban communities, expanding the city's total area to 239.7 square miles. Granite Club member Fred Gardiner became Metro's first chairman (and later in the decade the first span of the Gardiner Expressway went up between Jameson Avenue and the Humber River.) Meanwhile, beneath Canada's longest street, work was completed on the country's first subway. On March 30, 1954, several Ontario dignitaries gathered for the pulling-the-power-switch ceremony to inaugurate service on 4.5 miles of Toronto Transit Commission subway track. One was then Premier Leslie Frost. The other was then Toronto Mayor and Granite Club member Allan Lamport.

Born in Toronto in 1903, Allan Lamport was active in sport, community work and transportation. A fascination for flying prompted his organizing the first commercial airplane business in Toronto in 1926; he would later build Barker Airfield on Dufferin and become the city's representative in building the Malton and Island Airports. First involved in politics as a city alderman in 1937, Lamport was elected mayor in 1952 campaigning for a "bigger, better and brighter Toronto" as well as "Sunday Sports." He was responsible for the move to an amalgamated Metro Toronto, the building of low-income family housing in Regent Park, the Municipal Parking Authority and (as chair of the TTC) the creation of a "pay its way" subway system under Yonge Street and along the Bloor-Danforth corridor. He was known as a most wise and cautious budget analyst and as a civic leader who always had the courage of his convictions.

The day Mayor Lamport helped inaugurate the subway, more than 100 000 Torontonians boarded the bright red train cars for a test ride. Keeping up with the pace of a modernizing Metro Toronto, Granite Club president Lucien E. Messinger reported in 1957 that the conversion in electrical power had begun at the club with the installation of 60-cycle lighting in the ballroom. Beneath those ballroom lights the Granite Club's social calendar also moved with the times. With the advent of rock 'n roll music, the club staged "sock hops" featuring Toronto musicians Bert Niosi and his Dixieland Music Makers. Otherwise, the musical entertainment at the Granite was nearly the exclusive domain of Frank Bogart. Tall and erect, with a full head of Sinatra-like hair, a broad smile and a smooth style at the piano, the man who had helped celebrate Saturday night at the Granite since the early 1940s knew how to cater to the club membership.

"Frank knew everybody," says Beryl Hatch; she and her husband Brad were regulars in the ballroom. "He always called you by name. We used to dance at the club on Saturday nights and every time Frank saw us he'd immediately break into our favourite song, 'Everything I Love.'"

"Whenever he saw us get up to dance," recalls Phyllis and Rex Parker, "it was 'Mack the Knife.' Christmas, New Year's, throughout the year, Frank was always there. He was an institution."

He wasn't always an institution at the Granite. During the Depression, Bogart had performed one-nighters so often, it seemed he was always packing and unpacking his music. However, in the summer of 1940, he boldly took his own band into the popular Brant Inn on the Burlington shoreline. Performing six nights a week, he was an immediate hit and his reputation spread. As summer waned he decided to approach the Granite Club with the idea of providing music regularly there. He was introduced to the general manager in the board room. Despite the fact that Hector Donnelly "looked like Winston Churchill" complete with striped suit and cigar, Bogart made his proposal.

STOP THE PRESS ITEM!
Bill Eagles Bowls 425 Game out of a Possible 450

The Alley Bowling Section was presented with the highest score in our history when W.E. Eagles provided us with the thrill of our lives while chalking up a 425 game in the Mixed Casual League.

Bill rolled 13 consecutive strikes— three of them at the end of the previous game and struck right into the 10th frame, picked a 5-pin on the 11th ball and spared for 425. Mr. Eagles' three-game total was 937—a marvellous score and we echo the sentiment expressed by the spectators who watched in suspenses with crossed fingers. "It couldn't have happened to a nicer fellow."
—Granite Club News,
February 12, 1957

Frank Bogart

The following Friday night, Bogart walked out onto the bandstand in the Sky Club at the Brant Inn, turned to acknowledge his audience, and realized that Hector Donnelly and the Granite Club president, A. Lowry A. Richardson, were seated at a front table with their wives. They thoroughly enjoyed the evening and "that was that," says Frank Bogart. From October 1940, Frank Bogart went on to become a fixture in the Granite Club every Saturday night.

There were many traditions associated with Bogart's performances at the Granite. As well as his own favourite tune, "Time on My Hands," Bogart would lead his orchestra through all the Cole Porter, George Gershwin, and Rodgers and Hammerstein show tunes. Birthdays among the membership were always recognized and Bogart seemed to catch every one. Eventually, Bogart added singer Helen White and filled his band with musicians who could play the standards of the day without any sheet music in front of them—a technique he picked up from orchestra leader Lester Lanin in New York—just playing ad lib from one tune to the next. It gave the impression of non-stop music and kept the Granite Club members who loved to dance satisfied from early evening until the playing of "God Save the King" when the show concluded at about midnight.

Frank Bogart's music was also an integral part of the Granite Club's annual St. Patrick's Party, "a highlight on the club's entertainment calendar." Each year in March, talented people from various athletic sections of the club presented floor-show numbers of song, dance, and comedy in the ballroom. By the mid-1950s, the variety show had grown in popularity so much that club members were even invited to be "talent scouts" and to nominate performers for awards.

"It was quite fun, but it was obvious that some sections had more talented members than others," recalls Audrey Wallace. Her husband, Jim Wallace (a badminton player and two-term board member) became deeply involved in the shows. "Eventually, you had to audition your number before getting into the show. Then, the board of education, in its wisdom, decided to have March break instead of an Easter holiday, and a lot of people began going south. So they started to call it the Granite Review and moved it to February. It became a very big annual event."

Festivities at the club were not restricted to the dance floor, the lounges and the dining rooms. In addition to the regular outlets for relaxing (and getting a drink), there was at least one unofficial watering spot for women Granite members.

Cozy, nicely decorated and located at the back of the ladies' locker room, was Dolly's Bar. Here women members could congregate and socialize in a refuge (not unlike the men's Reading Room) where the attendant, Dolly Hammersley, poured mixed drinks—usually daiquiris with plenty of sugar in them in fluted glasses. Between sips and conversation at the bar, some of the women patrons would slip back downstairs, bowl a few more frames and then return to find that Dolly had refilled the glass with more of her daiquiri concoction.

Another popular club function, catering primarily to women during these years, was the Book Review Tea in the Rose Room. Sometimes referred to as "the culture corner" of the club, the afternoon sessions were considered "an outing for women away from the home." In fact, men were not invited either to participate on committee or to attend. The Teas actually began in 1936, as a book club, through which women club members could get together to discuss published material.

—*Granite Club News*

William Clement Fisher
President, 1958-59

As the size and prestige of the book group grew, publishers regularly sent review copies; eventually the accumulation prompted the group to create a lending library. "We had a bookcase, that sort of folded together like a folding bed does," recalls Joan Mactavish, who joined in the 1960s. "One of the staff would help us pull it out of storage each month and set it up. We had our lending plan to take out books.... We maybe had a hundred titles or so."

According to the group's original mandate, "the program consists of 45 minutes of book reviews, worthwhile books new and older. The reviewer tries to interest all tastes in reading with novels, biographies, travel books and plays," but even if the books being circulated or discussed weren't the most stimulating, for some women members, the Book Review Tea was a welcome activity for club women seeking friendship and a non-athletic pursuit at the Granite.

From just 20 members in October 1936, the book club grew in the 1950s when the Teas widened their appeal by inviting authors and other arts-oriented celebrities to speak to the assembly, which often filled the ballroom with up to 400 women. In those years, tea convenor—Mrs. Junor—led discussions of such books as Thomas Mann's *Felix Krull*, Guthrie McClintic's *Me and Kit*, Elizabeth Sprigge's biography of Gertrude Stein, Gabrielle Roy's *Street of Riches*, Robertson Davies' *A Mixture of Frailties*, and Jack McLaren's *Let's All Hate Toronto*. And among those "guests of honour" invited to speak about their books were actress Pegi Brown, publisher Jack McClelland, fashion reporter Lillian Foster, author Pierre Berton, poet E. J. Pratt, and radio commentator Kate Aitken; however, rules of the event strictly forbade "any promotion of the book, nor any mention of buying or selling copies.... The author was not speaking to the group to sell books, but because he or she had something to say!"

By the 1980s and 1990s, however, the modest Book Review Tea would become the Granite Club Speaker's Luncheon—among the most sought-after stops authors and publishers could land in that vital push to promote and sell a latest book. It would not be unusual to find most of the

500 tickets per luncheon gone from the moment the roster of speakers was announced each autumn. Notable speakers would include adventurer Sir Edmund Hillary, activist June Callwood, and artist Robert Bateman.

As the 1950s drew to a close, Canadian figure skaters continued the winning ways that the Granite Club's Barbara Ann Scott had initiated at the beginning of the decade. At the World Championships, Barbara Wagner and Granite member Bob Paul took the pairs gold four years in a row—1957 through 1960. In the late 1950s, Bill McLachlan emerged from the Granite programs and, skating first with Geraldine Fenton and then with Virginia Thompson, won the Canadian Dance Championships every year from 1957 to 1962; with Geraldine, Bill placed second in the World Dance Championships in 1957, 1958, and 1960. In 1956, at the Winter Olympics in Cortina d'Ampezzo, Italy, Norris Bowden and Frances Dafoe (who had won the World Championships consistently through the mid-1950s) were just edged out of the gold. The Granite's Charles Snelling came fourth in the men's and Ann Johnston ninth in the women's.

With both the club membership and the media paying closer attention to the successes of Granite Club athletes abroad, it's perhaps no coincidence that in 1958, that Management Committee at the club established a committee "to investigate and recommend a suitable prize award for recognition of outstanding winners in all sections." Later that year the committee prepared a design and a wording for this "special award" and by the following year the Granite Club's

Bill McLachlan and Geraldine Fenton, Canadian and North American Dance Champions

STOP THE PRESS…

Our seven man team, entered in the Ontario Squash Championships, came up with a winner. … Syd Hetherington and Bill Hatch played in the singles and were beaten after some very close and strenuous matches. The five man team of: Don Boxer, Bill Boake, Bill Smith, George Mara and Brian McDonough really did themselves proud in defeating the Carlton Club in the finals by three matches to two. Our sincere congratulations to the boys for a job well done. —Granite Club News, February 4, 1958

Gold Crest Awards were a reality. Effective April 1, 1958, an embroidered crest of the club logo would be presented each year to those who, while representing the Granite Club, were winners in provincial, national or international competition.

In early 1959, the club board announced that Gold Crest Awards would be presented to Judy Jarvis and Jane Davies (who won the Ontario Junior A Ladies Doubles in badminton); to the winners of the 1959 Ontario Ladies Curling Championship: Em Woolley, Mrs. Goodwin Gibson Jr., Jane Clark, and Mrs. C.R. Mills; and to the winners of the Ontario Junior Tankard: Dave Thompson, Dennis Whitehead, Kelly O'Connor and Bob McAdam. The winners would be acknowledged at either the closing meeting or dinner of the section by the Director representative of the section.

On a sadder note, at the end of the decade, the Granite Club lost three presidents within six months of each other: William Clement Fisher while he was in office, in March 1959; Lucien E. Messinger in October 1959; and A. Lowry A. Richardson in July 1960. Robert Rae assumed the presidency as the new decade began.

During the summer of 1959, Queen Elizabeth and Prince Phillip visited Canada. On June 26, they met American President Dwight D. Eisenhower near Montreal aboard royal yacht *Britannia* and helped open the newly completed $1 billion St. Lawrence Seaway. Then on June 29, they joined the crowds at Toronto's brand-new Woodbine Racetrack to watch E. P. Taylor's New Providence win the 100th running of the Queen's Plate. It was one of several new facilities' openings that the royal couple attended while in Toronto. It was a harbinger of things to come for a new Metropolitan Toronto busting at the seams with development and well over a million residents.

Not among the royal inaugurations was the fall 1959 opening of a new service building at the Granite Club—including a new staff entrance, receiving dock, additional locker-room facilities, and a new bar for the main dining room. The magnitude of the construction didn't compare to the

St. Lawrence locks or the Woodbine grandstand, but when Granite Club board members noted in their year-end reports that "we are overcrowded at the present time" that too was a harbinger for the club's future life at St. Clair Avenue West.

CHAPTER THIRTEEN

IN SEARCH OF A NEW HOME

1960–1972

IT WAS DURING the 1960s, while on a visit to Toronto to host the CNE Grandstand show, that comedian Bob Hope jibed: "You're going to have a great town here, if you ever get it finished."

While Hope's comment probably came about as a result of getting caught in a road construction traffic jam around the city, he couldn't have been more accurate about the rapid growth in Toronto at that time. The city's downtown skyline—for years dominated by the railway yards and Royal York Hotel—suddenly sprouted elevated expressways, modern architecture and office skyscrapers. It was in 1963 that one time Granite Club member and newspaper publisher, John Bassett, moved his Toronto Telegram from its old premises on Melinda Street to a sprawling new facility on Front Street West. Meanwhile, two of the country's major financial institutions built downtown glass towers—the Toronto-Dominion (completed in 1967) and Royal Trust (ready in 1969).

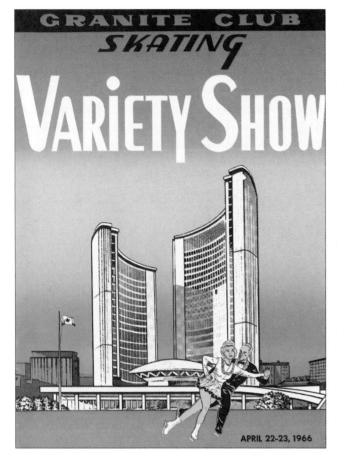

GRANITE CLUB SKATING VARIETY SHOW

APRIL 22-23, 1966

Perhaps the most talked about addition to the look of downtown Toronto, however, was the new City Hall (designed by Finnish architect Viljo Rewell). It was completed and inaugurated in 1965 on the new downtown civic square named in honour of former Mayor Nathan Phillips, who had piloted the project through to completion. Architect Frank Lloyd Wright called it "sterile" and said it would mark the spot where Toronto fell. Conn Smythe, who built Maple Leaf Gardens, thought the new city hall "would be suitable only as a place to welcome spacemen of the future." Neither occurred. In fact, it became a focal point to which many came. Most Torontonians soon accepted Rewell's futuristic design—its image even graced the cover of the program for the 1966 Skating Variety Show.

As well, in 1964, Terminal One at Toronto's International Airport (formerly Malton Airport) was opened and then christened by such notables as Elizabeth Taylor and Richard Burton en route to a premiere of Hamlet as well as John, George, Paul, and Ringo—the Beatles—who sang (if you could hear them over screaming teenagers) to sell-outs at Maple Leaf Gardens. And hundreds of thousands of new immigrants came through some of those airport gates. Metro Toronto's population in 1961 topped 1.6 million and more than a third were non-British—principally Italian, German, French, and several hundred thousand immigrants from Eastern European countries.

Growth, renovation and development were also on the minds of the Granite Club decision-makers early in the decade. At a joint meeting of the Board of Directors and the Management Committee, on March 1, 1960, those present approved the expenditure of $25 000 for air conditioning in the ballroom, and $10 000 for repairs to the third floor sunroom, new bowling alley lighting, repairs to the ceiling of the curling lounge and repairs to the rink, outside painting and new awnings.

In the early 1960s, the Granite's newsletters and presidents reports indicated that the club was indeed growing. Membership was up over 7000 for the first time. This helped to underwrite the funds required to upgrade the St. Clair Avenue West location to current building codes with such things as fire-alarm systems, emergency exits, electrical circuits, and plumbing facilities. However, in January, 1961, James H. Joyce, chairman of the management committee noted an alarming trend in club budgeting: "Proper maintenance and improvements alone require heavy expenditures... This problem is constantly in the minds of your directors."

The *Granite Club News* announcement of the arrival of Automatic Pin Setters in October of 1964 meant the end of pre-arranging for "pin staff" to be on hand. This wartime photo shows one staff member chatting with Tommy Ryan, the inventor of five pin bowling.

Among the renovations to the Granite's athletic facilities in early 1960s, the bowling alley got the go-ahead for automated ball returns and scoreboards and the squash courts received new front-wall reinforcement. An announcement in the *Granite Club News* went on to assure the squash section players that the renovated "walls of cement, applied under pressure...will withstand even your hard shot."

The racquet sports had never involved a majority of Granite members; in 1964 there were 279 badminton players and 186 squash players, versus 1488 curlers, 935 swimmers, and 354 skaters. However, what they lacked in numbers, the racquet sections made up for in enthusiasm. At an

Robert Rae
President, 1960–61

Granite squash courts at St. Clair

Ontario-wide squash tournament that took place during the winter of 1960, participants applauded the Granite's organizers, including Bill Boake, Syd Hetherington, and George Mansfield, "who made an excellent draw and was on hand all the time, keeping the tournament moving even to refereeing the semi-finals at 9:15 a.m. Sunday—that's in the morning on a Sunday, chaps!"

Originally a boxer who'd worked on the docks in London, England, George Mansfield had risen through the ranks of racquet sports, teaching squash, tennis, and badminton to wealthy families in Britain. In Canada, he promoted racquet sports and in the 1950s undertook a 10 000-mile tour, promoting his favourite athletic pursuits on radio and in television appearances. By 1960, he was on staff at the Granite Club teaching such racquet sportsmen as Brian McDonough.

"George really showed me how to play the game properly," says McDonough. A Granite member since 1936, McDonough was a regular squash player at the club. "I used to play him a lot, but he'd give me quite a shot when I first started. He'd keep telling me to hit up the lines. Finally, I listened to him and finally I beat him."

As well as grooming some Granite squash players to be highly competitive in tournaments, George Mansfield recognized his role at the club as a teacher and in expanding the section membership. When a new player joined, Brian McDonough often recalls Mansfield saying: "Play this fellow. Help him out. And if he's good, get him into the circuit."

"George worked for the players," agreed Colin Shirriff, who rejoined the Granite in 1950. His family had established the first food manufacturing firm in Toronto in 1898 and had long been members of the club. Colin came back to play squash for its speed and intensity and because "it was a quick way of getting up a sweat and getting in an enjoyable, competitive game with one of many great friends.... And George Mansfield was unique, really gentlemanly. I enjoyed the old club basically because of him."

As with many members of the racquet section, Brian McDonough and Colin Shirriff met principally through the club and their squash matches. The men shared a friendship on and off the court. For a time, the two followed a regular routine nearly every weekday—leaving their offices downtown and meeting at the club for their scheduled squash match. Then, after a refreshing shower "under those huge shower heads that made you feel like a million bucks," the two headed back downtown to their respective offices. No squash game or day was more memorable than another, except for the one day Shirriff decided to drive his friend back to work in his Oldsmobile Ninety-Eight.

"Now Brian's nose has been busted a couple of times from his days playing football. And he often wore a grey fedora. He must have looked like Lucky Luciano," says Shirriff, alluding to a well-known underworld personality of the day. "We were driving down Yonge Street around Dundas and all of a sudden a police car pulled up in front, another beside us and a third behind. The cops rushed up to us and told us to get out of the car. They were looking for a bank robber in a car that was the same description as mine. They thought we'd robbed the bank!

"So they got us to stand out in the middle of the street and opened the trunk. Of course, all they found inside was a couple of squash racquets and our sweaty gym clothes...I think it was all because of Brian's fedora."

Granite squash members actively participated in tournaments at Christmas and Easter with other area clubs, including the Carlton Club and Toronto Lawn Tennis Club. Brian McDonough, and his Granite Club teammates, such as Bill Boake, Sid Hetherington, Jim Tate, and Howard Egli,

The Granite's Dave Hetherington won the Toronto and District Junior Singles Racquets Championship on December 20, 1965

recall many hard-fought matches during the years, but especially one in which a 49-year-old Hasham Khan reigned supreme. Reported the February 1, 1961 *Granite Club News*: "The Khan family are in a league by themselves, with tremendous speed, power and beautiful drop shots.... Maybe all that's wrong with our game is that we're not old enough yet!"

In 1960, the beaming faces of the Alf Phillips rink were seen on the inside cover of the annual Skating Carnival program. They had won the Canada Life trophy over 336 other rinks, including over 1300 of the best curlers in the City of Toronto. That was also the year Marshall and Phillips, Sr. brought the Ontario Silver Tankard back home to the Granite Club.

The Phillips' rinks would win the Tankard again in 1961, 1963, and 1964, and the Canada Life bonspiel again in 1964. In 1961, with an astonishing 384 teams entered in the Canada Life bonspiel, Joe Giroux's rink won the requisite nine consecutive games to capture the cup.

Canada Life Trophy Winners, 1960 (l-r) Don Robinson, second; Bill Leak, vice; Alf Phillips Sr., skip; Alf Phillips Jr., lead

Canada's Centennial year—1967—was a big year for many of the Granite athletic and social sections. The country's hundredth birthday was celebrated at the club in a number of different ways. In March, George Mansfield organized a Granite team to participate in a Centennial badminton tournament at the Carlton Club. On July 1, Dominion Day, the lawn-bowling section ran a Centennial Mixed Tournament for the Rennie Trophy.

Ontario Silver Tankard, 1960 (back, l-r) Joe Hopper; Dick Chant, vice; Bill Leak, vice; Don Robinson. (front, l-r) Kelly O'Connor; Dr. R.W. Marshall, skip; Alf Phillips, Sr., skip; Alf Phillips, Jr.

Ontario Silver Tankard double rink winners, 1961 (l-r) W.F. Kent; C.C. Hopper; D.S. Chant; Dr. R.W. Marshall, skip; A.H. Phillips, skip; W.A. Leak; D. Robinson; F.W. Graham

The book review committee picked up the nationalistic theme and staged speakers' luncheons featuring Canadian authors. Among them was travel writer Philip Deane (whose books *Caribbean Vacations* and *The Land and Isles of Greece* took readers abroad) focused on Canadian destinations. Horticulture writer John Bradshaw explored Canadian gardens. Antique specialist, Don R. Stewart, (author of *A Guide to Pre-Confederation Furniture of English Canada*) talked about restoring and preserving old Ontario furniture. Ontario premier Leslie Frost appeared to speak about his 1967 book *Fighting Men*. And Earle Toppings, who wrote an introduction to, and edited the centennial book *Canada* spoke about writing in Canada during the centennial.

Canada Life Trophy winners, 1961 (l-r) Dr. Jack Carruthers, second; Bill Sturgeon, vice; Joe Giroux, skip; John Cathers, lead

SHIPWRECKS ON THE SANDBANKS
OF HAITI BUFFET PARTY

...Always concerned about your welfare and thinking, although not wishing that [a shipwreck] may happen, we have ... decided to organize a "Shipwreck Drill" we might call it, just as one organizes fire drills for instance, to take precautions and be certain you survive.

This instructive party will take place in the ballroom on Wednesday, January 24th. If you plan to travel next season do not fail to attend this short course to meet any emergency. You will find that a good shipwreck, as we see it, can be lots of fun.
—Granite Club News,
January 4, 1962

As well, in September, the entertainment committee staged "Bogey's 25th," a special ballroom dance to honour Frank Bogart's quarter-century association with the club; and on December 30, the Granite threw a Year End Ball, with Canadian singing star "our pet" Juliette as the guest performer.

During Centennial year, the squash section recorded its highest membership to date—285 players—and that prompted an expansion of its facilities—from two singles courts to four singles courts and a doubles court. As well, the Granite joined several other Toronto clubs in hosting the largest-ever national tournament featuring players from 44 clubs from across the country. Because the Granite was chosen to help host the tournament, the home team was made up of some skilled and some social players.

It included a wonderful cross-section of Granite squash enthusiasts. In addition to then 46-year-old Brian McDonough, there was Donny Boxer, a big man, who used his height and strength to overpower opponents; he also played with the same racquet (and, some claimed, the same unwashed shirt) for 40 years. There was "Gorilla" Mike Manley, "Shoulders" Barry Grant, and Jack Stafford, nicknamed "The Chief," because he always whooped loudly during his matches; according to section reports, "Stafford, with his hilarious anecdotes, had everyone in fits of laughter and he even competed against every speaker at every banquet." And there was an extremely competitive Steve Moysey, "who used to come in at midnight in his formal tails, take them off and practise till all hours."

"I played Steve Moysey in the finals one year," remembers Brian McDonough, who played Moysey several times a week at the club. "The match went to points in the fifth game. We fought for every point. It seemed to last forever. The last point—we knew the club championship hinged on it—and the rally would not end...till finally Steve nicked one in the back court and won the championship."

In 1967, Ontario Curling Association President Ross Tarlton revived the tradition of North American competitions and made it an annual affair. Tarlton, long remembered as "a curler of extraordinary skill and a delightful companion," began playing the game with the Hamilton Thistle Curling Club in 1929 and won (among other honours) the Governor General's Trophy twice and the Ontario Silver Tankard four times. This international bonspiel eventually named its top prize—the Ross Tarlton Shield—in his honour. Between 1967 and 1991, the Canadians won the Tarlton 16 times, the Americans eight. (The event was not played in 1973.) Longtime Granite curler, past curling convener, and past club president Ronald Grills chaired the 1991 event and was inducted as an honorary member of the Grand National Curling Club of America (founded 1867).

Centennial year curling also featured the regular bonspiels—including the men's Canada Life, the ladies' Robertson, the Brereton-Raw—as well as a new Mixed Invitational bonspiel, in which each rink comprised a Granite couple and a guest couple. In the spirit of getting together during Centennial year, couples teamed up from clubs across the province. The *Granite Club News* called "this brain-child of convener John Glenn's a huge success."

Ever mindful of its historic curling past, the Granite supported a couple of new bonspiels in mid-decade. In 1966, it recognized one of the founding members of the St. Clair club, Stuart B. Playfair, by inaugurating the Playfair Seniors Invitational Bonspiel (for men aged 55 and up). Then,

Saturday night on the dance floor at the Granite Club, 1965

J. Palmer Kent
President, 1962–63

Ross Tarlton Sr, seated between Ross Tarlton Jr (left) and Ron Grills at a dinner in 1991

(l-r) Art Hamm, Ron Grills and Ted Childs mark the 25th anniversary of the Ross Tarlton competition

following the death of Granite curling legend Em Woolley in 1967, the Southern Ontario Ladies Curling Association established a similar seniors competition for women. While both tournaments paid homage to curling's past, they overlooked the youth movement evolving in Western Canada that would overtake Eastern Canadian (and Granite Club) dominance in the sport.

"Curling was certainly a young man's game in Western Canada," recalls John Glenn of that mid-1960s period. "The game became more attractive to younger people when brooms became more efficient and with the long slide.... That's when curling became even more exciting because it had style."

As a 20-year-old in the Granite curling section, Dave Thompson remembers efforts to keep up with the latest curling innovations, including the long slide up to the hog line. First they tried tape on the soles of their shoes. Then they tried gluing tin to the sliding shoe. And eventually a friend in the automotive business suggested using a new, frictionless substance called Teflon, "so we tried every type of glue and it would work wonderfully until it hit the cold. You'd go on the ice. The glue would freeze and get brittle. And the first time you went up on your toe, it'd crack and come flying off...."

Western Canadian curlers had no such problems. In 1959, Ernie Richardson, "the King," from Stoughton, Saskatchewan, won the first world championship ever held, beating Scotland for the Scotch Cup. In fact, Richardson would win four Macdonald Briers in five years, four world title Scotch Cups and his rink would eventually be named "the all-star team for the first 50 years of the Brier." The 1960s also saw Ron Northcott's rink (of Calgary) win the Brier and the World Championship three times; Hector Gervais, creator of "the push shot," skipped a rink (from St.

James H. Joyce
President, 1964–65

Albert, Alberta) to two Brier titles and a World Championship; Lyall Dagg's rink (of Vancouver) won both the Brier and World Championship in 1964; while Joyce McKee (from Saskatoon) was among the first women to use the long sliding delivery and she skipped her rink to a Canadian Ladies' Championship first in 1960 and again in 1971, '72 and '73.

The Granite Club board reached two important decisions during its monthly meetings in the late 1960s. Each would have a profound effect on the direction and leadership of the Granite Club for the rest of the century. First, the board structure was changed so that each member was elected for a three-year term (rather than for life); each could then be re-elected for a second three-year term; however, unless on track to sit for a term as president, that board member would depart the board.

Front entrance, 63 St. Clair Avenue

This way the board would always have "new blood and fresh thinking."

The second critical decision was recorded in the January 1966 Report of the President in the *Granite Club News*. Incumbent James Joyce indicated that the "directors are still contemplating long-range plans for the provision of better facilities in the club" and it struck a building committee to research and deal with the issue.

In that same edition of the *Granite Club News*, management committee chairman (and later president) John D. Murray reported on over $116 000 worth of repairs, replacements, and improvements to locker rooms, lounges, the parking garage and the board's "continuous effort to maintain and keep the building and club equipment in good repair." The original building, which the Granite Club called home, was 40 years old and, in spots, showing her age.

For years the curling facility had been the envy of the city, indeed the continent. But partly because it had become an ice surface shared by both Granite curlers and skaters, the grooming and flooding satisfied neither section completely. The curling hacks made figure skating hazardous and the skating marks made curling shots unpredictable. Both sections began to worry openly about the "unreliability" of the ice facility. Add to that the very real problem that every minor repair seemed to escalate into a major one, and members and staff felt genuine concern that the Granite's very reputation was at stake.

"We would spring a plumbing leak in the ceiling of a room," agrees then board member Bob Marshall. "And we'd have to tear up a hundred feet of ceiling to find out where the water was coming from. The physical plant on St. Clair was aging and we had no real control over it. So we began searching for alternatives."

Indeed, it was a group of curlers—Sid Walker, John Parkin, Gay Kirkpatrick, Bill Thompson, Bob Marshall and Bill O'Connor—who formed what was known as the Forward Planning Committee. After several meetings the group came to the board with an ambitious plan to "bring the curling facilities up to the standard required by the Granite Club." The plan involved the development of the southwest corner of 63 St. Clair Avenue West, including the construction of an above ground swimming pool, the installation of 11 curling sheets (taking up the old skating surface) plus the addition of 4 more sheets. The group concluded the cost of renovations to St. Clair would cost about $2 million.

Curling rink at 63 St. Clair

In August 1965, the board initiated a feasibility study for the purchase of property west of the existing club site on St. Clair Avenue. The property was purchased the same year for $675 000 and the board considered its options: 1) do minor renovations to curling and skating facilities; 2) do the $2 million renovation to all the club's sports facilities; 3) renovate the entire club (excluding the reception area and second-floor dining room; or 4) consider moving to a new location.

Armed with a design (drawn up by the architectural firm, Page and Steele) for nearly $5 million in renovations, the special building committee called a meeting of conveners and vice-conveners in early November 1966 to discuss the proposal and invite comments. Then the board called a shareholders' meeting for November 29; to accommodate the expected crowds, one meeting was scheduled for 8:00 p.m. and another for 9:30 p.m. Following the two stormy sessions that night, it was agreed that the board would proceed with the rebuilding plan if costs did not exceed the estimate.

Artist's sketch of renovated corridor area at 63 St. Clair

When the tender price for the renovations was received on June 17, 1967, the costs exceeded the club budget by $600 000, and the rebuilding plan was dropped. Yet another group of members—the Building-Finance Committee—was assembled on February 6, 1967, and in March of the following year, this new committee advised the board that it had revised the plan's costs to come in under the budgeted ceiling. The suggested changes to the plan were, however, deemed unacceptable and the board "concluded plans for rebuilding are not contemplated at the present time."

Meanwhile, in a letter to the membership—dated September 1, 1967—club president Stan Whitehead explained that "further studies are being made and hopefully in due course we shall find answers to our pressing problems of providing improved facilities." The board had discovered that a property in North York was suddenly available and it seemed to fulfill many of the club's current and future demands.

"Brian Magee, who was chairman of A. E. Lepage, came to a board meeting," recalls Bob Marshall, who had been on the original Forward Planning Committee in 1960. "He said that he was representing the Passionist Fathers who owned 7 1/2 acres on Bayview Avenue [just north of Lawrence]. We looked at it and decided that although it was a major step for us, this was probably the direction we should be moving."

It was later that same year—November 6, 1968—when in-coming president Jack Murray released a letter to the Granite membership. In it he cited the problem of attempting to improve the 42-year-old facilities at St. Clair. Alterations to the old location, forcing it to comply with current zone and building codes, would only create premises, he said, "that had grown piecemeal over the years to meet the requirements of membership."

President Murray disclosed that for a year the board operated on the assumption that "the only economic long range solution to the problem of providing better facilities at reasonable maintenance costs, was to construct new buildings properly designed for the requirements of the membership. With this in mind, it became obvious that a new site on less valuable land would be desirable.

"After considerable searching and negotiations, the club has obtained an option to purchase approximately 22 acres on the west side of Bayview... The site is beautifully wooded and overlooks the ravine of the West Branch of the Don River and a portion of the Rosedale Golf Club...If the club is to move, it is hard to visualize that a more desirable site could ever be found."

The Board of Directors had paid $10 000 for an option (expiring March 19, 1969) to purchase and then build on the Bayview property. It had also filed for an application for the re-zoning of the site through the Borough of North York. Meanwhile, president Murray's letter concluded that the board would seek approval from the membership for the move and for the sale of the St. Clair Avenue site to help finance the move. He explained that a "special meeting of Members and Shareholders has been called to discuss the proposal, and it is hoped that as many persons as possible will attend. At the meeting, the Members will be asked to voice their opinions and will be asked to return the enclosed questionnaire within one week following the meeting."

It's unlikely a better candidate could be found to steer the club through such tempestuous times as Jack Murray. Despite obligations to work and family, in the mid-1930's Jack began supervising production of the club's newsletter, the *Granite Club News*. When he wasn't volunteering his time at the club, he and his wife, Merle, enjoyed skating. During the 1950s, at carnival time, the Murrays were regularly featured waltzing on ice. Jack Murray came to the board in the 1960s and became president in 1968 just as the club grappled with the idea of moving from St. Clair. Always working with the members' concerns at heart, Jack Murray knew it was time to make the change.

The Granite's curlers continued their winning ways, winning the Robertson again in 1968 (l-r) Kay Greer, Joan Mathers, Jean Adams, Claire Bosley

JACK MURRAY, PRESIDENT, 1968–69

Born John Douglas Murray in 1912, Jack grew up on Russell Hill Road, just blocks from the old club; in fact when the club opened on St. Clair in 1926, his family was among the original 900 founding members. Jack Murray's grandfather James Murray founded the Murray Printing Company in 1884. The business stayed in the family, run by James Murray's sons; in 1945 Jack's father, Joseph A. Murray, became president.

Jack Murray began his business career sweeping out the composing room in 1934, graduating to the office in 1937, and to president's assistant in 1945. Between 1953 and 1962 Jack negotiated the purchase of three other printing firms and in 1954 his company assumed all the printing for Eaton's catalogue, the largest printing job in Canada. In 1957, Murray moved into the president's role at Murray Printing. In 1962, Southam Press purchased a minority interest in the business; in 1967, Murray Printing was sold to Southam and Jack Murray served as that organization's president until 1969.

As word of a possible move spread among club members, a *Toronto Star* reporter interviewed Charlie Moon, a retired bank manager who lived in one of the St. Clair club residences. He'd been a member for 40 of his 79 years and was living on the top floor of the club.

"If you ask the oldtimers," said Moon, "you're going to get adverse criticism…. We'll vote it down." He paused a moment and finished by saying, "Oh, I'll be dead anyway by the time they move. I love it here. It's spotless and better than any hotel. The new place'll be all right for the young bucks, I guess."

Jack Murray tabled the results of the questionnaire on December 9, 1968. Between the membership and the shareholders, 42,691 votes were cast; 16,910 votes were cast against and 25,781 were cast in favour of the motion to empower the Executive Committee "to engage professional consultants to conduct a feasibility study of the future on St. Clair Avenue and the future on the proposed new site" at Bayview. A report completed by Woods, Gordon & Co. management consultants the following spring recommended "the Members and Shareholders should authorize the Directors to proceed with the making of plans for moving to the proposed new site."

Lawn Bowling at St. Clair, 1961

As a result of the consultants' recommendation, the board took out several options on the Bayview property through December 1969. In the meantime, the Four Seasons Hotel chain had put forward a proposal to take over the St. Clair property and manage the construction of the new buildings at Bayview. During the summer of 1969, the board passed a motion informing "Four Seasons [Hotels Limited] that the Granite Club would like to enter into negotiations, based upon their proposal, with a view to their retention as the developer of the club's new facilities, conditional upon the approval of the shareholders, re-zoning of the Bayview property, and final approval of design and agreement by the Board." Target date for the presentation of the Board's plans to the membership was October 1969. Meanwhile, on the social page of the *Granite Club News* a new monthly column entitled "B-71" (signifying a relocation to Bayview in 1971) welcomed questions and comments from the members about the proposed move. On October 23, 1969, (after a dress rehearsal the night before for directors, conveners and the B-71 public relations committee), the Board disclosed its plan for moving the club to Bayview. A vote, requiring a two-thirds majority to pass, would be taken at the end of the evening.

Swimming pool at 63 St. Clair

"It fell to me to make the presentation to the members," explains Bob Marshall, who showed slides at the meeting. "We explained what was wrong with the current plant and why we felt the best thing to do was build a new club. Well, there were people very much opposed. There were some retired members who had purchased homes in the St. Clair area. We felt keenly for those people, but still knew something had to be done. The city was growing. And we were growing out of our current premises."

"How will I get to the new club?" one elderly member is reported to have asked president Jack Murray.

"I'll drive you there, Mother," responded the president.

"It'll bankrupt the club," claimed one member, referring to the projected millions it would cost to build a new facility.

There were rumours of a huge assessment to be paid by the existing membership. Interest rates at the time were 8.5 per cent and some financial experts were recommending the board "delay, until the rates [came] down." Some worried aloud about many of the 7000 members quitting the club. Another suggested the club had "enough wealthy members that it was going to survive regardless if some quit or if fees went up."

"We can't afford not to move," suggested another member, who was aware of the costs to repair the St. Clair building.

As the meeting moved toward the vote, Dr. Marshall reminded those present that "the Granite is first and still the finest family club. There are other family clubs, but none in the world equal to ours. And we have to move with the times."

Ultimately the resolution was read and voted upon: "That the club do sell or exchange all its lands and premises situated on the south side of St. Clair West, in the City of Toronto, at a value of not less than $5 800 000, which together with a payment of not more than $1 150 000 shall be payment for the new club premises on Bayview Avenue in the Borough of North York at any time before December 31, 1973."

The vote was taken. The results were announced: 76.9 percent in favour.

As the Special Shareholders meeting finally wrapped up, members filed out of the club. Among those there to listen and vote were Rex and Phyllis Parker. They had been members since the Second World War. Phyllis would later join the board of directors and serve as the club's first woman president. The couple noticed another long-time member, Stewart Reburn, standing beside the ice surface. In the 1930s he had teamed up with Louise Bertram to win the Canadian Pairs in figure skating and later the two had placed fourth at the World Championships. But this night in November 1969, Reburn was clearly upset. He had tears in his eyes as he stood by the ice surface full of memories.

"I learned to skate here," Reburn said to the Parkers. "I've been involved in this club all my life."

With better than two-thirds of the membership supporting the move to Bayview, a Plans Committee made up of representatives from each section was formed in November, 1969. As well, the board inaugurated a committee for the selection of furniture and equipment for the new club. By April, 1970, the Building Committee had been formed to receive section recommendations and

Granite Club Variety Show, 1968
Even as major changes were being planned, some traditions continued

T. Millar Chase
President, 1970–71

The cover of the December 1984 issue of Granite News announced the retirement of the last of the Granite Club Notes. The event was commemorated with the planting of three Douglas Firs as a tribute to the three men who had devised the financing strategy: Grant Ross, George Scott and Sam Paton.

that same month, the proposal presented by Four Seasons and their architects—Webb, Zerafa and Menkes, designers of The Inn on the Park—was approved for the design of the clubhouse and its facilities.

Along the way to securing the property on Bayview, drafting architectural plans for the new club and presenting the plans to both the Council of the Borough of North York and the Ontario Municipal Board (OMB) for approval, the club's Executive worked out the financial arrangements of the transaction. Four Seasons Hotels Ltd. would be hired to complete the design and construction of the new Bayview club and acquire the old St. Clair property as part of the payment. In other words, Four Seasons would pay nearly $6 million for the St. Clair property. The turnkey amount for the Bayview property (including construction and cost of the land) was about $9 million. That left a shortfall of approximately $3 million.

The Board came up with an innovative plan to finance the shortfall without assessing any levy on the membership. The club would accept loans—in $1000 units—from interested members. And in return, the club would discount those members' annual dues by $50 per year per $1000 unit. It took a little while to work out the details, but once approved by the Ministry of Finance, the plan helped the club raise $2.4 million of the $3 million needed. In the years that followed, there was an annual party in the Granite ballroom for all the note holders—initially there were 140 members who attended—and within twelve years each $1000 unit was paid back and the debt was completely discharged.*

While getting its financial house in order, the club faced a new complication at North York Council that threatened to scuttle the entire project. In the course of applying for the re-zoning of the property to allow club construction, the proposal was challenged by a petition from the Anti-Defamation League of the B'nai B'rith. In January 1969, North York alderman Murray Chusid tabled the Jewish organization's assertion that the Granite Club "discriminated against minorities in its membership policies" and should therefore not be allowed to go ahead.

Representing the Granite Club, lawyer Donald Steele responded that "the club has nothing in its bylaws, in any form, restricting membership because of religion or race" and that "each application for membership is dealt with on its own merits." Steele went on to say he understood that the club did have Jewish members.

Regardless, the re-zoning application was sent off to North York's Parks Committee, where it was hotly debated through the winter and spring of 1969. Alderman Ian Rogers insisted the club's membership policy was irrelevant to the re-zoning, while Alderman Chusid simply wanted the Granite Club to "sit down with the Ontario Human Rights Commission and discuss if it discriminates...." The delays prevented the re-zoning proposal from reaching the Ontario Municipal Board and gave the media more time to report and comment on the story, which did not help the club's reputation.

One newspaper headlined its editorial: "How private is bias?" Another editorial commented on the OMB hearings: "The club is asking a favour of a community, yet it refuses from the outset to become a full member of that community by offering its services to everyone."

Behind the scenes, Toronto businessman Lou Ronson (and several other members of the Jewish community) met with club board members to deal with the Granite Club's membership criteria. Ronson was also vice-chairman of the Ontario Human Rights Commission and wanted to diffuse any apparent confrontation between B'nai B'rith and the club. So, in mid-January 1970, he (and his ad hoc committee of B'nai B'rith) met privately with the Granite board to discuss the issue.

Allie Agar Trophy

In 1968, the Allie Agar Bonspiel was established to commemorate one of the early members of the Granite Club. Mrs. T.J. Agar was an excellent curling competitor whose name could be found on many of the club's plaques and trophies. She also served as a mentor for many of the Granite's novice curlers.

Mrs. Agar was a former president of the Southern Ontario Ladies Curling Association and an active curler until her death in 1973.

Dr. R.W. Marshall presented the contract signing pen to T. Millar Chase, president of the Granite Club after the deal for the new club on Bayview was signed on October 23, 1970. Four Seasons president Isadore Sharpe is on the right

T. Millar Chase and Isadore Sharpe share the groundbreaking ceremonies on November 9, 1970

Rather than engaging in a long debate on whether bias existed, the Granite accepted the outside community's criticism based on their observations and moved forward. The club's position was: "Let's put it on the table. You think we've been anti-Semitic. What would you like?" Ultimately, the board of directors passed a resolution formally saying that the club would not discriminate against a prospective member on the basis of race, creed or colour. Then, Lou Ronson and representatives of the Granite board agreed to appear publicly to make simple joint statements on the issue.

The two sides appeared at a press conference on January 19, 1970, to set the record straight.

"Acceptance [in the club] is based on the character of the proposed applicant," explained club president Millar Chase, reiterating the recent board of directors' ruling. "As race, religion, and national origin are deemed to have no proper bearing on an individual's worth, they are not considered in the determination of the acceptance of applications for membership."

An artist's rendering of the new premises on Bayview as presented to club members.

David Bronstein of the B'nai B'rith explained that his organization was not interested in scoring legal points, but simply in arriving at an understanding with the Granite Club. He congratulated the club for its "forthright" statement of the issue and the resulting benefit it gave "the entire community. He concluded by saying: "We are particularly pleased with their willingness to meet again in the future in the event we encounter any further questions or difficulties."

No further difficulty was ever encountered.

Ultimately, early in 1970, the OMB chairman, J. A. Kennedy "ruled that [North York] Council went beyond its powers" by attempting to rewrite the bylaw over use of the Bayview property. But by that time, the Granite board had passed the resolution satisfying the B'nai B'rith and the re-zoning was approved.

"At Last!!" read the headline in the *Granite Club News* of November 1, 1970. On October 23, 1970, club executives—T. Millar Chase, Bob Marshall, Dixon S. Chant and Jack Murray—and the president of Four Seasons Hotels, Isadore Sharpe, posed for the prerequisite shots over the contract and then exchanged the historic signing pens. The story went on to say: "While the Board of

Skating instructor
Wallace Distelmeyer

Directors was acutely aware of the restlessness of the club members over the delay, it did not seem prudent to jeopardize the negotiations by the publication of premature statements." Projections were for turning of first sod November 9, laying of the cornerstone in 1971, and completion in the summer of 1972.

Despite the uncertainty over facilities, swimming, racquet sports and skating programs continued to grow at the Granite Club. In October 1967, the club brought an additional coach onto the skating staff from Buffalo, New York. As new senior skating pro, Wallace Distelmeyer had a long list of credentials including numerous championships in singles, pairs, and dance skating around the world and a bronze in pairs (with Suzanne Morrow) from St. Moritz in 1948. Together with Marcus Nikkanen and Jim Francis, Coach Distelmeyer helped young club skaters reach their own standards of excellence and bask in their own sense of success.

While some club members skated with the club pros, others took art classes with Jim Francis, who by then was teaching both adult and young Granite members how to work with oil paints. From the late 1930s, Francis had been a working artist who, among other things, specialized in anatomical renderings. For several years he worked under the direction of Professor J. C. B. Grant, at the University of Toronto Anatomy School, creating the illustrations for Grant's Anatomy texts "which are still being used by millions of physicians around the world."

"To start, he taught a couple of times a week," recalls son Charlie Francis. "But later, in the 1960s, when he was working there all the time, he would work with groups of people on still-lifes and portraits, sketching and painting, anything. He used to drag me up there to pose the odd time."

For many years, Jim Francis could be seen running his art classes in the gallery overlooking the skating rink at the old club. His style—both on the ice and in an art class—was the Granite Club style. He believed in practising and teaching art traditionally. Most of the time he wore a suit and tie as he painted. He taught fundamentals before advanced or experimental work. He showed students how oils were applied in layers and might include as many as 30 or 40 layers before a painting was complete.

When back trouble began plaguing the veteran ice-dance and art instructor, Jim Francis joined the Granite Club's management team, leaving the majority of the ice instruction to the younger Wallace Distelmeyer. It was about the same time that Rocco Losole announced that he would retire from the St. Clair club barber shop and return to his ancestral home in Italy. Said the *Granite Club News*: "For twenty-one years, our Rocky has been almost competition for the sun, by way of the blinding shoe-shines he's been giving."

Between 1970 and 1971 overall club membership dropped several hundred. However, in January 1971, members felt a new excitement in the air as a display of the new clubhouse—including model, pictures, plans, and drawings—went on view in the main lounge at St. Clair.

In his 1971 president's report, T. Millar Chase reported that "approximately 38 000 cubic yards of earth [had been] excavated out of an estimated total of 80 000 cubic yards.... and the pouring

Granite art instructor Jim Francis

of cement for the foundations" was about to begin at Bayview. Remarkably, even inside the boardroom at the club, not a great deal was said about the day-to-day progress of construction. Each month when the board of directors met and it came time for building committee chairman Jack Murray to report to the group, someone would ask: "How's the building coming?"

Art classes at the Granite Club in the 1960s

"Fine," Murray would say simply.

"Yes, but how's it really coming?" someone else would repeat.

"It's going fine. Don't have to worry about it."

In the view of some board members during the period of transition to Bayview, Jack Murray's calm, matter of fact style was exactly what the transition period needed. Most recognized that "Jack Murray was the perfect guy for the job. It was the only way to handle things. Otherwise, we'd still be at the first meeting with 19 guys all asking 'What about this?' and 'What about that?'"

Jim Dinwoodie recalls this period of transition from St. Clair to Bayview vividly. He had been hired initially as secretary of the club in December 1969. But by September 1971, he remembers Millar Chase coming to his office and merely informing Dinwoodie he would be taking over as club general manager. During the move to the new premises, Dinwoodie worked closely with Jack Murray when the 15 or 20 members of the building committee assembled to report on expenditures or requirements.

"Is that everything?" Jack Murray asked.

"Not quite," piped up Dinwoodie. And the general manager then presented Dieter Haag's proposal to purchase a new oven for the kitchen. From that day forth, the oven (approved that day) was known as "the Not Quite oven."

"That budget was one of the tightest budgets I ever worked on," recalls Jim Dinwoodie of the moving fund. "We only had so many dollars in the budget and we kept within it."

By mid-1971, the scaffolds, cranes, and concrete began to rise at the Bayview site. And by the time committees were planning the final Christmas and New Year's parties at the old club, work was under way on the new club's interior. The following year, final preparations were made to close the St. Clair facilities for four months to allow staff, stock, equipment, and furniture to be moved north to the new club.

Not all of the St. Clair furnishings made the move. During the spring of 1972, a Toronto firm organized many of the old club's rugs, furnishings, and artifacts to be auctioned off to the highest bidders. The auction took place over two evenings in the ballroom. It was an extremely emotional time for long-time Granite Club members and for Freda Kretchman, the recently hired executive assistant to the general manager. She had accepted the job in 1970 as temporary work, "but it was while I was listing the furniture—the old Persian rugs, the dressers from the live-in apartments—that I really fell in love with the place. It was a fascinating time to be involved with the club."

In April 1972, the entertainment committee staged its Farewell Dinner and Dance at 63 St. Clair Avenue West. Ironically, it was the largest party ever held at the old club—more than 700 people came to say good-bye.

"It was a very big bash," recalls then food and beverage manager Dieter Haag. "Black tie and gowns. Hundreds and hundreds of people. The whole upper floor was used for dinner," as

Main entrance at Bayview, March 26th, 1972

members enjoyed a five-course dinner "featuring the famous Granite Club roast beef." The main downstairs lounge was set up with bars throughout. And following the meal, there was "dancing to Frank Bogart's music in the ballroom upstairs, and "the members danced on and on...."

"I'm going to miss the coziness of St. Clair," lamented one lifelong member.

"The old club had a men's sitting or reading room," said another. "On Saturday mornings, there were so many people wanting to curl, you often had to wait until the second draw. So you'd go into this room, pick a magazine, sit in the most gorgeous big armchairs...and go to sleep."

Despite the nostalgia of the last days at St. Clair, club members began to feel the excitement of the coming move to Bayview. They were now able to see what the new club would look like. The board had issued a four-page booklet on the new look of the Bayview club. Among other things, the booklet put the move to Bayview in context by recalling that "the move from Church to St. Clair in 1926 was wise. It was also courageous."

> At the time, St. Clair was a dirt road beyond the fringe of urban activity. The cost was astronomical. By comparison the move to Bayview is a much smaller step both financially and geographically. In terms of population density, the new site serves the present membership almost as well as the St. Clair site. This was not true of the 1926 move. In terms of cost, the move to Bayview is not astronomical—far from it. But again the move is wise for tomorrow. Bayview and Lawrence will be the heart of our children's city.

The brochure then offered a short history of the decisions that brought the club to Bayview. It introduced the developer—Four Seasons—and its architects—Webb, Zerafa and Menkes, pointing to their international reputation in the creation of hotel designs in Toronto, Vancouver and

London. The booklet also showcased artists' renderings of the foyer, the ballroom, the swimming pool and the main dining room, as well as a preliminary overview of the layout of the new club and its Don Valley surroundings and individual floor plans of the four floors of facilities. It offered a mini tour of the club facility to come.

Dr. Robert W. Marshall
President, 1972–73

> From the gracious main entrance, one enters a spacious foyer three stories high. The grand staircase soars upward, skylit by day and enhanced by night with the subtle light of great chandeliers designed especially for the Granite Club.
>
> The ballroom and main lounge are directly off the foyer. Just beyond to the left are the cocktail lounge, dining rooms and sunroom overlooking the terrace and ravine. To the right are the locker rooms. Also on the main floor is a lounge overlooking the swimming pool below with its glass wall and outdoor terrace. Indoor bowling is also on the lower level.
>
> Upward from the foyer is a second floor given over to curling, skating, squash, badminton, billiards and cards. For those in sports clothes an elevator and special staircase lead from locker rooms to the sports floor. A lounge separates curling sheets from the skating area and above, on the third floor is another lounge overlooking the ice below. A roof garden completes the top level.
>
> That is the general concept... In the months to come plans will be revised and refined until everything is exactly right.

The Webb, Zerafa and Menkes design included such modern features as provision for ten sheets of curling ice—engineered with controlled humidity and controlled sound—next to a full regulation size skating surface. (Ultimately, a redesign put the skating rink on the second level and curling ice on the third.) The design described the regulation size swimming pool (25 metres long) complete with a smaller teaching pool for children. Viewing galleries would abound, not only for the curling and skating ice surfaces, but also for the four squash courts and the new eight-lane bowling alley. Also included inside were four badminton courts and a special area for golf practice; while outside would be five state-of-the-art tennis courts "patterned after the famous courts at Coral Beach, Bermuda." Far removed from the roar of traffic on Bayview, the club's lawn bowling greens, would be a "masterpiece surrounded by acres of greenery."

The design booklet summed up the concept of the new Bayview facility by saying: "Above all the Granite Club is people. It is fun and good times together. Our new clubhouse is created with that in mind."

By August of 1972, in a *Granite Club News* feature titled, "On a clear day you can see forever," the newsletter reported all was on schedule for a fall opening. The article displayed photographs—taken by club member Gilbert A. Milne—offering some of the first glimpses of completed athletic facilities and unique views from around the Bayview facility. Wrote board member (later president) J. Ronald Grills in the newsletter:

"This is the maturation—the goal of years of dedicated effort—of dreaming, conceiving—planning—organizing—preparing—conferring—manoeuvering, driving. And now achievement is in sight!"

CHAPTER FOURTEEN

THE MARVEL

1972–1979

OCTOBER 18, 1972, was a crisp autumn day. Coats and gloves were in order for the outdoor greeting party. Despite the chill in the air, however, Granite Club president Dr. Bob Marshall and his wife Edie met a parade of dignitaries with smiles and warm words of welcome.

Arriving in limousines for the occasion were Granite Club Charter Members, the presidents of Doyle Hinton, Four Seasons and the club's architectural designers Webb, Zerafa and Menkes. The Mayor of North York, Basil Hall, attended as did past and present directors of the club and their wives. Amid the wide array of other political, business and social leaders from the city of Toronto, Governor General Roland Michener arrived with a police escort to begin the official opening of the new Granite Clubhouse.

Openings and notable construction starts in Toronto had been plentiful that year. The previous season, Ontario Place had opened on Toronto's waterfront, complete with beaches, marinas,

Granite president Dr. Robert Marshall greeting Governor General Roland Michener at the official opening of the Granite Club on Bayview

children's zoo and IMAX cinesphere theatre. That was followed by the commencement of construction of the world's tallest free-standing structure—the CN Tower; in 1975, a Sikorsky helicopter would lift the last sections of antenna and lightning rod into place atop the 1815-foot tower. Also in 1972, near the heart of the city—on Yonge just above Bloor—dignitaries had turned the sod for the $30 million Metropolitan Toronto Reference Library, which would open to book-lovers and researchers five years later.

Still, Wednesday, October 18, stood apart for thousands of Granite members as their club officially opened its new premises. Throughout the morning, the dignitaries made their way up the red-carpeted and canopied entrance into the club. Along the updated Peacock Alley they visited the club's social areas—its 50-by-50-square foot foyer and grand staircase. They strolled about the club's new 5760-square-foot ballroom and its 2800-square-foot main dining room. For those who yearned for a taste of the Granite Club's past, they found five additional dining rooms—several with familiar names carried over from the old club, including Cawthra, Heather and St. Mary. For more contemporary tastes, the special guests visited the new ravine cocktail lounge and the sun-room that opened to a cantilevered terrace overhanging the valley.

In the sports sections they viewed the six-lane main floor swimming pool; then the second-floor skating rink, the eight-lane bowling alley, coffee shop and four badminton courts; and on the third floor the 10-sheet curling rink, the five squash courts, the racquet sport galleries, and Skylite Lounge. And beneath it all was underground parking for 437 cars.

The Governor General responded by calling the club "a marvel that I am sure will be greatly enjoyed by young and old."

Most media outlets ran out of superlatives to describe the new premises. The *Telegram* reporter called Bayview "the most opulent, full-of-facilities housing that an exclusive, private recreation organization ever had." The *Star* reporter called it "a posh sports palace." Later, *Clubs of Canada* magazine said the building was "a tribute to architects Webb, Zerafa and Menkes and contractor Patrick J. Casey...in creating what is undoubtedly the most exciting new premises in this country and perhaps south of the border too...Granite Club members are lucky indeed!"

The new terrace during the first winter at Bayview

It wasn't luck at all. As the *Granite News* commented:

> Few of us could know of these feverish weeks of final preparations—detail by detail—readying for the onslaught of the long expectant members. We'll never know how the Building Committee kept their cool during these hectic days, but they could be conditioned to every conceivable problem after all these years... Thank you—Members of the Building Committee for your scrupulous attention to every detail, for your unceasing and untiring efforts which have produced this well-planned, sparkling new premises.

The Bayview location was one of the first to have elevated rinks. They were made possible by "floating slab" technology—in the form of a bowled shape of stratified concrete, polystyrene and piping, totaling four feet in depth.

The Bayview Building Committee (l-r, front row) John D. Murray, James I.D. Dinwoodie, Donald R. Steele; (l-r, back row) David Lewington (Doyle Hinton), Dr. Robert W. Marshall, T. Millar Chase, J. Stanley Whitehead, Donald S. Potter. Absent: Joseph W. Wright, Robert J. Butler, James E. Kelley, Albert C. Ashforth

CLUB BLAZERS

The official Granite Club blazer in a specially selected colour and cloth has now been approved. This jacket [comes] complete with the Granite Crest woven into the cloth…
—Granite News, 1972

The first priority as the Bayview facility was readied had been to familiarize the membership with its new club. Members were invited for special tours on September 30th, October 1st and 2nd, in advance of the formal opening. Over that first weekend in October, 8000 members attended the open house and took guided tours of the facility. Scores of junior members of the club had been organized into a crew of tour guides. In shifts they whisked groups of club members through the facilities, offering information while the adult guides listened to member reaction.

"I remember showing lots of people around," says Beryl Hatch. "We were all decked out in those green skirts that Ruth Smith had made."

"We had a reception in what they called the Crush Lobby. And it was really crushed," recalls Ray Bosley, who was elected to the board of directors that year. His wife, Claire, a former skater and a curler, had been invited to work on Stan Whitehead's decorating committee.

"The decor was very much the opposite from the old club," says Claire Bosley. "I remember the remarks about the new chairs in the ballroom—those big, huge chairs—they were like beanbags with beige corduroy on them. Everybody thought they were just covers…that they were just temporary."

"It was sort of cold compared to the old club," remembers Hazel (Caley) McTavish. A skating star in the 30s, she would learn to curl with her husband Sandy at the new Bayview rink. But, "everything was better. The ice, the swimming pool were just the top. And as soon as all the old members got together at the new location it grew on you."

GRANITE CLUB TAKES TOP
CULINARY PRIZES IN CITY

The Granite Club took First Place in the Culinary Arts Festival held at the Royal York Hotel on April 25th, and special congratulations are in order for our Manager of food and beverage Mr. Dieter Haag, our Executive Chef Mr. Wili Mingam and our pastry Chef Mr. Volker Strunk.
—Granite Club News

"It's the people that make a club anyway," agreed her sister and former skating partner, Dody (Caley) Klein.

Once the club was operational, the Granite's usual bustle of activity was quickly re-established. During that first month of operation, the tennis courts were opened for casual play. Five-pin bowling leagues began for men and women. There was a ladies round robin in the badminton hall, afternoon bridge got started, and the season's curling bonspiels were organized. For members without their own means of transportation, the club inaugurated a bus service from the Eglinton TTC station to the Granite Club grounds every 40 minutes.*

"Those were exciting times," recalls Dieter Haag, who had served as food and beverage manager with the club since 1970. He had assisted in the closing of the St. Clair location and was responsible for ensuring that kitchen and bar services at the Bayview location were up and running in time for the opening. "We moved truckloads and truckloads—the china, the glassware, the cutlery, and the liquor. It was a perfect opportunity to make an inventory, but it was really hectic.

*The bus service ran until December 7, 1974. By that time, Eglinton was no longer the north end of the Yonge Street subway line.

The first President's Ball at Bayview was hosted by Dr. Bob Marshall (left) and his wife Edie, and featured New York orchestra leader Lester Lanin (centre)

"That first week, an electrician was still working in one of the dining rooms. He went to lunch and when he came back he walked right past where he'd been working. While he was gone, they'd taken away the ladder, set up tables, linen, and china. And he didn't recognize the room. We were really pushing it."

Ready or not, the Granite's social calendar at the new location was jammed. In the final week of October, the Speakers' Luncheon welcomed *Chatelaine* magazine editor Doris Anderson to the club. The first travelogue at the new club featured Toronto Camera Club photographer, Harold Norris, offering never-before-seen shots of China during the Cultural Revolution. Buses to Argonaut football games shifted from St. Clair to Bayview without skipping a beat. The women's beauty salon and men's hairstyling centre were up and running that fall. And the Granite Club's new ballroom got its first workout on November 3rd, when members paid $40 per couple to attend The Grand Ball. The black tie event featured a full reception, gourmet dinner and continuous dancing courtesy of orchestra leaders Lester Lanin from New York and Frank Bogart until one o'clock in the morning. The event was attended to capacity and the new location was well on its way to becoming the home of great Granite parties.

On October 10, 1972, the Granite Club had christened its 10 new sheets of curling ice on the third floor with the first men's bonspiel of the season. The facility was to feature some of the best manicured and pebbled ice in the city, in an environment completely controlled by seven 30-horsepower reciprocating compressors and two brine coolers. At six o'clock that evening, Dr. Bob

Marshall threw the first rock to officially open the bonspiel. The ceremonial rocks went fine, but before long it was apparent that the rink's dehumidifiers were not working properly and the ice became heavy with condensation.

"We had 64 rinks in the bonspiel," remembers Brad Hatch. "And the team that won was the John Fitzpatrick rink. He was the skip and he never once in the whole five games got a stone over the hog line. That's how bad the ice was. And yet they won the bonspiel. Just shows you, he had a heck of a rink!" Adjustments were made to the new equipment and the facility was soon meeting the members' expectations.

FLASH: Congratulations to Alfie Phillips and his rink of George Cowan, Jack Young and Sandy McTavish who last week won the Senior Event of the Canada Life Bonspiel.—Granite News, 1972

Dixon S. Chant,
President, 1974

President's Trophy for
Men's Bowling

*In 1989, the Granite Club donated
a trophy for competition between
women bowlers at the Granite and
the Boulevard Club.

Another long-time section of the Granite Club commenced its Bayview operations in October, 1972. Five-pin bowling—originated by Toronto entrepreneur Thomas Ryan in 1908 and introduced at the Granite's St. Clair club in 1926—began its schedule at the new Bayview lanes amid a growing, active membership. Only this time their Novelty, Exhibition, Men's and Women's and Mixed League games were served by eight lanes.

"We had men's league bowling nearly every night of the week," recalls Peter Earl, who had bowled at the Granite since the early 1950s. "There were eight men's teams, each with at least ten people on a team. And we had mixed [men and women] leagues, each with ten or twelve to a team... It didn't matter whether you were a good bowler or bad, the enjoyment was the social part of the game."

Granite bowlers first competed beyond the club in the late 1960s when Boulevard Club bowlers proposed a friendly annual tournament. The five best high average men bowlers from each club would meet for three games at each club in January and February each year. Winner take all. By the early 1970s, the president of the Boulevard Club had chipped in a trophy. In thirty years of competition, Granite bowlers have brought home the President's Trophy more than twenty times.*

While Peter Earl routinely bowled well enough to be on the Granite team in the President's Trophy, it was a regular Men's League bowling night he remembers most of all. In his second game that night on lane number five, Peter hit his stride and began bowling a seemingly endless string of strikes. By the time he faced the pins in his ninth frame, word was spreading around the alley. Earl was on a perfect game pace.

"The ninth is the toughest," Syd Bentley, the bowling supervisor told Earl.

It didn't matter. Peter Earl was on a roll and he coolly laid down his ninth strike in a row. Now, nobody else was bowling. All eyes were on him as he bowled a strike in his tenth frame.

"Then with the eleventh ball," laments Earl, "I took the head-pin clean... I had one more shot, but it's pretty hard to spare it after a head-pin shot. I ended up scoring 417 points. It was…the biggest game I ever bowled at the Granite."

The final chapter of the club's exciting launch at Bayview was written in January 1973. That's when Granite Club conveners and various committees organized a dinner and dance, which they called Appreciation Night, to thank those on the Building Committee "whose dedication and hard work have brought 2350 Bayview into operation." At the banquet, MC Phyllis Parker invited each member of the Building Committee front and centre to be recognized and to receive fun tokens of appreciation—for Bob Marshall, a mounted curling broom; for former president T. Millar Chase, a

The Innuit sculpture "Sheltered" was purchased as a tribute to the Bayview Building Committee and first put on display in the Crush Lobby

J. Ronald Grills,
President, 1975

neck lei of badminton birds. Following the presentations and meal, 400 club members enjoyed Frank Bogart's music, which included songs specially chosen for the occasion: they played "My Way," for committee chairman Jack Murray; "We're In The Money," for director Bert Ashforth; "You've Got to Give a Little," for president Bob Marshall; and for the relationship of the committee and the membership, "I Never Promised You a Rose Garden."

Perhaps the highest priority when the Bayview location opened, as member David Brown remembers, was strengthening the club's focus on families—children's programs became a significant component of the activity roster. Brown had filled out a membership application for his family—two adults and four children—as the club was moving to Bayview "when there was a five-year waiting list.... When some people resigned over the move, the waiting list collapsed overnight and I got the call 4 1/2 years earlier than I expected.

"But we had kids in swimming, skating, hockey, ringette, you name it—lessons all over the city. Suddenly, we realized that here was an opportunity to cut down on car pooling and transportation and to start consolidating all our activities in one spot. For several years my Saturday morning routine became bringing the kids to the club, where they'd go off for lessons for two hours and I'd go off for breakfast.... It turned out to be a great weekend program for the family."

Indeed, the move to Bayview ensured a continuation of the dream that Granite Club president Frank Shannon had had in 1925—that of an uptown family athletic and social club, located in the centre of the population with state-of-the-art facilities for a wide variety of sports.

Among those taking full advantage of that increased family emphasis at the Bayview Avenue club, Jack Muir's children couldn't wait for Saturday mornings. First at the old St. Clair building, but even more so when the club opened its doors on Bayview, Kathleen, John, Tom, James, June and Jocelyn Muir all enjoyed the freedom of swimming in the new 25-metre pool, trying out the second-floor skating rink, and exploring the various racquet sport courts. All the Muir children learned badminton from their father, Jack Muir.* But when their father's clinic was over, the younger Muirs had the rest of the day to themselves.

"You'd have a grilled cheese or a cinnamon toast on your own in the cafeteria. It was a big deal," says James Muir. In his mid-teens when the club moved to Bayview, James relished the freedom of being dropped off for a full day's visit. "In the afternoon, you'd just sort of have a free-for-all, skating, swimming or playing more badminton. You'd spend the whole day at the club."

Another hotly contested Granite team badminton match

It was also a great time for Granite badminton fortunes. In addition to receiving tutoring from their father, the Muirs also enjoyed training under British pro George Mansfield and Pakistani star Sharif Khan, who joined the Granite staff as the head racquets professional in 1971. By late 1972, Granite badminton players, in particular its junior badminton team—comprising Tom Muir, James Muir, Brian Munro, Ian Arthur, David Bolton, and Ross Clarke Jr.—was challenging for top Canadian honours. The *Granite News* edition of December 1972 recounted the team's remarkable performance in Ontario regional eliminations.

*The Muir family has deep roots in international racquet sports. In the 1920s, Jack Muir Sr., Jack's father and James's grandfather, won the Canadian Doubles Championship three times.

Our very first match was against the Boulevard Club, one of the strongest teams and finalists the previous year. Play had hardly begun, in fact the first game was still in progress, when disaster struck through a severe injury to

Brian Munro, playing second singles. In these competitions a total of 9 points is awarded and between Brian's 2 singles and 2 doubles, we could immediately see 4 points lost.... No substitutes were permitted.

By our calculations we needed to save one of those 4 points. Even that was of no use, unless every player won some very tough matches. The highlight was Tom Muir's magnificent win against highly rated Bob Hinchcliffe which stretched out to three exhausting games, and [was] only decided by a slim 17 to 15 win in the third game. James Muir won his singles match, and Tom Muir his second, also a grueling affair. The score now stood 3 points for each side... Now, as expected, we won a doubles match as James Muir and Ian Arthur easily overcame the Boulevard's second doubles team 4 to 3 for Granite. Now came the problem since the Boulevard's first team was almost certain to defeat James and Ian, our second, tying the score. If we as well defaulted our first doubles team, versus their second, the match was lost. Still, Brian could not even walk.

But he could hop? In a display of admirable determination he did just that. And his partner, Tom Muir, laboured furiously in the back court to salvage this vital win...in two straight games, but not without a tough battle and another painful fall by Brian.

However, the drama was not quite over, for as the feathers settled, James and Ian were proving that they too could reach deeply when it counted, emerging victorious after three difficult games against Boulevard's best.... The match was over, won 6 to 3 by the Granite Club. It was really the high point to date.

The Granite juniors went on to represent Ontario that year in the National Championships, but lost to Calgary Glencoe Club. However, that same year, James Muir was Ontario Junior (under 16) Boys Singles and Mixed-Doubles Champion, which earned him his first Granite Club gold crest. The embroidered cloth award was presented every year to those competitive members who won a provincial championship or better.

"When you're presented with a gold crest, it's part of an annual Recognition Dinner where all the people who are going to receive the award are invited as well as all the conveners and the directors," says James Muir. "You have a great meal in the dining room. There's a keynote speaker. And then you go up as you're introduced and receive your award—the gold crest—that you can put on your…blazer. It's quite a thrill…quite a prestigious thing within the club."

Between them James and Tom Muir earned a dozen gold crests. Yet the Muirs weren't the only Granite Club badminton players to succeed at a competitive level. Between 1959 and 1998 members of the club's badminton section were awarded 134 gold crests. More than 80 of them were won between 1973 and 1993—an average of four per year. It was during those same 20 years that the section had the legendary Raphi Kanchanaraphi as its resident professional.

One of eight children, Raphi was born in Thailand in 1935. Both his parents and two of his seven sisters had been Thai badminton champions, but Raphi himself didn't pick up the sport until he was 17. However, it only took him four years to become Thai doubles champ; in fact, between 1956 and 1958 he was one of the best doubles player in the world and even though his Thai team lost the final in the prestigious Thomas Cup of badminton in 1958, Raphi and his partner were considered national heroes and welcomed home with a ticker-tape parade. The next year he retired from international competition, coming to Canada in the early 1970s. He was soon capturing national badminton titles and was ranked 10th in the world by 1972. It was partly his championship form that attracted the Granite Club's badminton committee, but when Raphi was hired as the club's head pro in September 1973, the Granite was seeking much more.

Granite Gold Crest Award

Congratulations to the new Senior Men's Badminton champion, Mr. James McKee of the Granite Club.
—Granite News, October 1977

The Granite Club's best international players (l-r) Raphi Kanchanaraphi, Jamie McKee, David Gibson were members of Canada's Thomas Cup Team

"His manner, his philosophy of sportsmanship were real assets," remembers James Muir. "Even though he was the best badminton player in the world, he was in fact an even better human being—being able to deal with people, getting the best out of an individual—he led by example."

The Muir boys, still in their teens, learned a great deal from the new pro, now nearly 40. They learned how to anticipate shots. They discovered the role of speed and agility on a badminton court. They marvelled at Raphi's famous offensive smash return—from a crouch position, hitting the shuttle (bird) back at an opponent with a flat offensive overhead swing. But even more important than the physical object of the game, they learned the proper attitude at a tournament, particularly at the outset when looking at the draw sheet, sizing up an opponent.

"Never look at the draw," Raphi would tell his young protégés. "But fine, if you want to look at it, it doesn't matter who you play, where you are in the draw, if you're seeded or not, or if you won the tournament last week.... You go out and play each guy the best you can, because if you don't meet the first seed in the first round, you will in the final."

Raphi always found positive aspects of a student's performance—whether they were youngsters in a junior program or adults in social badminton matches. But he wasn't patronizing in his instruction either. According to current badminton pro Mike de Belle, whom Raphi recommended that the club hire as badminton pro in 1992, "it didn't matter what level of player you were, everyone received the same approach. He'd never say 'Don't do it that way.' He'd say, 'Try this and see if it works.'

Raphi and his badminton stars, 1993 (Back row, l-r) Raphi Kanchanaraphi, Jamie McKee, Ross Clarke, Jeff Wolak. Front row: John Wright, Sarah Gibbings, Caroline Gibbings

He'd just suggest alternatives and sort of steer you. And everybody felt they got special attention from him."

Raphi inspired beginners, whether in his Saturday morning clinics or summer camps. He encouraged other senior players to share their experience with younger competitors. And during the summers of 1987, 1989, and 1992, Raphi led a Granite team of badminton players on a playing tour of Thailand. Whether James Muir, who accompanied Raphi on a Thomas Cup team, or Jamie Mckee, whom Raphi coached to two Canadian singles titles and a Pan American Games gold medal, all Granite members in the badminton section knew "we were learning the game from the finest professional there is."

As with any Granite sports section, there've been many memorable badminton matches at the Bayview facility. Among them was a demonstration game, staged not long before Raphi retired as club pro in 1993. About 150 spectators—some experienced players, others just curious—filled the gallery to watch Mike de Belle (ranked 17th in the world) and Raphi (then nearly aged 60 and described by the media as "the Gretzky of badminton") take on Lucio Fabris (Commonwealth

In 1970, Freda Kretchman took "a temporary job" at the Granite as executive assistant. Three years later, she became club Secretary and in 1996 retired after a quarter century of service. Among her legion responsibilities: updating club bylaws, processing membership applications, providing administrative support to the board, maintaining correspondence and recording all board, membership, and annual general meeting proceedings. So efficiently did Freda fulfill her duties that following one meeting, typically cluttered with awkward motions and boring debate, Freda submitted the meeting's cleaned up minutes to president Don Angus for approval.

Quipped Angus, "Did I attend that meeting?"

A. Hazlett Lemmon,
President, 1976

The Raphi Kanchanaraphi Trophy
for Badminton

Games silver medalist from Sudbury) and Mike Bitten (national team member from Ottawa). The best two out of three series exhibited plenty of quick hits, jumping, smashing and longer rallies than most badminton spectators had ever seen.

"What a treat," recalls James Muir who umpired the match. "I remember some around-the-backs and Raphi's classic offensive smash returns. It was fantastic play."

"It was really impressive with all the 'ooing' and 'ahing' from the spectators," says Mike de Belle, "especially because a lot of the people there, who were used to a paddy-cake sort of badminton, saw the game played at a completely different level...I was exhausted by the end."

Raphi and de Belle lost the match, but the true winners that Saturday afternoon were the spectators. They had witnessed a veritable clinic, featuring some of the best Canadian badminton talent of the day and a true master in a command performance at the Granite.

Raphi Kanchanaraphi's high profile in Canadian racquet sports and at the Granite was just one dimension of Toronto's growing cosmopolitan reputation. In the fall of 1972, Team Canada (a team of NHL stars) welcomed the Soviets to Montreal, Toronto, Winnipeg and Vancouver for the famous Summit hockey series. In 1976, Canadian Olympians welcomed the athletes of the world to Montreal for the XXI Summer Games. In 1977, Toronto welcomed "the great American pastime" in the form of a new American League baseball franchise; in a unique Canadian twist, the Toronto Blue Jays played their opening game—on April 7, 1977—as snow fell on the ball diamond at CNE stadium.

The international flavour of the decade wasn't lost on those organizing the Granite Club's social calendar either. The year—1976—was both the year of the Montreal Summer Olympics and also the year the club had chosen to celebrate the Granite's centennial. So, "because Olympic tickets were so hard to get in Montreal," recalls then Granite swimming instructor, Herb deBray, "we

decided if we can't go to the Olympics, why not bring the Olympics to the Granite Club? So Olympic Splashdown became the swimming section's centennial project."

Relying on contacts he had cultivated while previously employed at the Montreal Amateur Athletic Association, Herb deBray began to search out Olympic swimmers who might be interested in a brief visit to Toronto essentially for a publicity appearance. The Olympians would be invited to come to the Granite for a one-day swimming, synchronized swimming and diving exhibition. While deBray approached the athletes in Montreal, back at the club Sandy Lawson and Valerie McIntyre worked on the itinerary of the day (from a pool demonstration to a meet-the-Olympians dinner) and the promotion of the event to the club membership.

"I was on the phone all night the night before," remembers deBray, "making sure we actually had athletes to pick up at the Olympic Village and put on a plane to Toronto. The next morning

Splashdown '76: Canada's Olympians at the Granite Club Pool

we put 20 or 25 people on that plane—a big, old Air Canada DC-8—and on the flight down I interviewed them all to prepare my introductions."

That day—July 29, 1976—pool-side at the Granite Club, members of the swimming section and their families and friends got to see the cream of the Olympic swimming corps, including such top swimmers and divers as John Naber (U.S.), Lynn Rowe (New Zealand), Ricardo Valerde (Mexico) and Canadian Olympians Beverley Boys, Susan Sloan, and Nancy Garapick. For the Mexican and New Zealand athletes in particular, the side trip to Toronto was an adventure because none had ever seen Toronto. For the Granite membership "Olympic Splashdown '76" was a memorable souvenir of the Olympic Games "right in our own backyard" and another feather in the cap of the Granite Club's Centennial Committee.

Whether it had to do with the Splashdown event or just the fresh enthusiasm among sections at the new Bayview facility, the swimming program got a boost that year, such that by the end of the decade "we had a full-blown swim program," says deBray, "from learn-to-swim to competitive training programs. In my view, we were doing exactly what the club wanted to do when it decided to go down the route of comprehensive aquatics." And the Granite program produced its share of elite competitors, such as freestyler Don Dixon, individual medley swimmers Kathy Richardson and David Shemilt, freestyler Deanne Weber and breaststroker Selby Kostiuk.

In addition to the swimming exhibition, the Granite Centennial Committee planned and staged such events as invitational bonspiels and tournaments, a Centennial skating carnival, a Centennial weekend bridge tournament and a Centennial fashion show (sponsored by the T. Eaton Co.). There was a Centennial dedication of works of art, a centennial booklet was published and the dining room featured a monthly Centennial gourmet meal series. A special commemorative Centennial Medal was struck to acknowledge club excellence in all sport sections that year and a centennial year flag flew outside the club from January 1 to December 31, 1976. The 100th anniversary

themes were also prominent at such events as the New Year's Eve Ball, the President's Ball, and the Recognition Dinner.

While the club's centennial year was full of colourful ceremony and the showcasing of new club facilities and activities, perhaps the most significant moment of 1976 was the inauguration of the Granite Club Sports Hall of Fame. First discussed in committee in 1975, board members Jack Murray and Dixon Chant proposed: "that the Hall of Fame be composed of members of the Granite Club who have won honours in amateur sports for Canadian, Olympic or World Championships.... The Hall of Fame will be composed of pictures of the selected members and these will be mounted in plexiglas and mounted on the wall on the third floor at the main staircase opposite the Skylite Lounge."

Centennial Celebration Cake

Granite Hall of Famers attending the opening of the commemorative wall on January 14, 1976. (l-r) Barbara (Gratton) Kelly, Nigel Stephens, Eleanor (O'Meara) Phelan, Jack Eastwood, Hazel (Caley) McTavish, Cecil (Eustace-Smith) Hedstrom, Roderick Phelan, Dorothy (Caley) Klein, John G. Muir Sr., Jane Wright, Louise (Bertram) Hulbig, Stewart Reburn

At a ceremony held on January 15, 1976, Ron Grills, chairman of the Granite board, announced the creation of the Hall of Fame. Speaking on behalf of inductees, former figure-skater Cecil Eustace-Smith Hedstrom thanked the club for the honour. Then, the first 44 inductees were announced—they included Granite stars in rowing, water-skiing, badminton, swimming, curling, the 12 members of the Toronto Granites hockey team (1924 Olympic gold medal winners) and 20 skaters.

About a month after the inauguration of the Hall of Fame, the Granite hosted another centennial function. Her Honour Pauline McGibbon, the Lieutenant-Governor of Ontario presided as the club witnessed the unveiling of a Barbara Hepworth sculpture—"Head Ra"—purchased by the club in honour of its 100th anniversary.

Ranked with Henry Moore as one of the foremost sculptors of the 20th century, Barbara Hepworth's work (by the mid-1970s) appeared in museums and public halls in Great Britain, Europe, Canada and the United States. The artist had died the year before in a studio fire, at the age of 72. At the Granite ceremony, William Withrow, director of the Art Gallery of Ontario, spoke about the contemporary art scene, Barbara Hepworth's status within it and then he congratulated the club on what he regarded was an important acquisition. Following the event, Hepworth's sculpture was put on display in the Crush Lobby.

The Hepworth acquisition highlighted the continuing growth of the club's collection of art. Immediately following the opening of the new facilities at Bayview in 1972, in order to comple-

Barbara and Elizabeth Gratton, Granite skating stars in the 1950s

ment the modern furnishings adorning Peacock Alley, the Crush Lobby and the walls of the dining rooms and ballroom, the club had begun to display some of the more modern art pieces in its collection. At the same time, however, the chairman of the furnishing committee, Stan Whitehead, had asked board member (and later club president) George Gilmour and three others to act as art advisors, to assess the Granite's art collection and make suggestions about display. Gilmour, who would serve as president of the Art Gallery of Ontario in 1980-1, and his advisors recommended a policy that took into account the old and the new. Noting that the "contemporary design of the new club combined with the much larger scale of public areas, demands art which is compatible with these factors," they went on to suggest that "all art purchased [or displayed] need not be abstract or non-objective."

"Head Ra" by Barbara Hepworth

As a result, back from storage came "The Young Visitor," a Victorian painting by James Hayllar (of the Society of British Artists), and a long-time favourite of many members. The Hayllar painting and the Hepworth sculpture characterized the two distinctive areas of the Granite Club art collection—19th and 20th century works from the old clubhouse on St. Clair Avenue and the contemporary works acquired during and after the move to Bayview Avenue in 1972. The combination provides members with a spectrum of art—from realist to abstract—and artist—from Canadian to international.

The collection includes "Hotel Cecil," painted by Canadian artist Frederic Marlett Bell-Smith, one of Canada's most prominent artists at the turn of the century. Despite being later overshadowed by the Group of Seven, his rendering of the landmark along the London embankment was inspired by a trip to that city in 1891. The work was donated to the club by 1930s president G. Herbert Rennie—the man who initiated the collection.

"The kind of art we had at the [St. Clair] club was the kind you could imagine being in Casa Loma," once commented George Gilmour. One such piece was "Curling Match at Linlithgow

Samuel T. Paton,
President, 1977

"Hotel Cecil" by Frederic Marlett Bell-Smith

"White Clouds" by Homer Watson

Palace," by Charles Lees, depicting a glimpse of Scottish life in the mid-19th century and acquired in 1952. Another work that came from the old club was "White Pines," by Elizabeth McGillivray Knowles, who took up painting in the late 19th century when (for women) it was considered one of "the polite arts." As well, Homer Watson's "Clouds" was an early club acquisition. Watson's work, capturing the beauty around his home in western Ontario, caught the eye of Oscar Wilde (who dubbed Watson the "Canadian Constable") and Queen Victoria purchased two Watson paintings for the royal collection, thus making any Watson painting a valuable addition to the club's collection.

Once the club decided to acquire newer artwork (about the time of the move to Bayview) the objective was to identify artists showing promise, but whose works were not astronomically expensive. Among those acquisitions was "Moving Clouds," painted by 20th century artist Dorothy

Knowles. The club added the piece to its collection in the 1980s.

Another piece acquired after the move to Bayview: Claude Breeze's abstraction "Pacific Arbutus and Fir Tree Shadows" painted in 1978 to depict the treescape surrounding his family cottage on Bowen Island, British Columbia. Early critical acclaim in the 1960s and 1970s, combined with the prestige of being included in the collection of the National Gallery, propelled Breeze into a successful career in the Canadian art scene.

In 1997, David Milne's "White Chiffonier" was acquired by the club. Born in Ontario in 1882, but trained in modernist painting in New York City, Milne painted the watercolour in 1913. Shortly after, he returned to Ontario where he continued to develop his own style and was ultimately recognized as one of North America's foremost artists of the 20th century. Another acquisition was Jack Shadbolt's painting "Breakaway,"

"Church at Dusk" by Fred Varley, circa 1948

noted for its cerebral quality and complex imagery of rebirth. Working almost exclusively in British Columbia, Jack Shadbolt became one of the most widely revered artists in Canada and therefore considered worthy of inclusion in the Granite collection.

How valuable is the Granite Club art collection? When asked George Gilmour said, "Not inordinately, although I suppose if you were talking about our most important [works] historically, it would be all those drawings on the way down to the lobby, simply because they're all Group of Seven. There are no artists more historically significant in Canada than the Group of Seven were in their day."

"We also had a painting stolen," continued Gilmour. "It was donated by Jack Murray in 1978. It was the Jack Shadbolt painting 'Fishing Fleet, Rainy Morning,' stolen from the hallway leading to the dining room in October, 1986. It was the best painting of that group given by the directors. The thieves knew what they were doing." Although the club held out some hope "that the removal of the painting was a prank that now finds the prankster in an embarrassing position," reported the December 1986 issue of *Granite News*. "If such were the case, we would hope that concern for

"White Chiffonier" by David Milne

the club and the honour of those concerned would overcome any embarrassment and that the painting would be returned.... Any information at all would be welcomed by the general manager and would be treated in a confidential manner." Neither prankster nor painting emerged.

Elsewhere during the decade, in their 1978 season, club lawn bowlers invited American greens expert Dr. Edgar Haley to lecture at the Granite, while the badminton section invited 25 players from the Herlev Badminton Club of Copenhagen. The Granite Carnivals featured the regular array of international skating talent. An unexpected, but well-remembered event, took place in the late 1970s, when during a private party one day at the club, a guest arrived at the front entrance and turned his late-model Lincoln Continental over to the club's valet service.

"We'll park your car for you, sir," said the attendant.

"Can you drive a car with hand controls?" asked the guest, now seated in his wheelchair and about to enter the club.

"Certainly," the valet assured the guest.

Apparently, the valet spoke prematurely, because according to one Granite Club member, "he drove the car around the building and just kept on going, through the tennis courts and down into the valley."

The next day, the *Toronto Sun* quoted one witness as saying: "I couldn't believe my eyes. Here was a car going right through the tennis courts and then it disappeared over the edge." The newspaper photograph showed the car upside down in the boughs of a tree and the reporter concluded by saying: "The [valet] was treated at hospital and released.... The tennis players ran to the top of the ravine for a look...then hooked up the downed net and resumed play."

The ballroom was busy at the Granite in this period. The Merrymen from Barbados and New York band leader Lester Lanin, "the undisputed king of high society dance music," attended several Granite dance parties during the 1970s. And Granite Club members continued to discover the world each wintertime with the weekly "Salute to the World."

"Sometimes we featured warm countries on the coldest days of the winter...but we always had a movie, music, decorations and the food and wine of the chosen country," says Dharma Ruttan, who helped Frank Stark and his group organize the Salutes. "I guess, the Salutes gave people who came a sort of escape.... But the big draw was we always gave two [airlines] tickets for a trip to that country."

Longtime members of the Granite Club, Dharma and her husband Dr. Henry Robertson Ruttan often enjoyed dining and dancing at the club, particularly at the St. Clair location. When Stark asked for help on the Salute nights, Dharma immersed herself in these evening events. For more than 20 years, they seemed to take over her life.

"The planning began every September," recalls Dharma. "We would book the ballroom around the weddings and other parties and then organized each Salute.... It was always on a Saturday night. And the ballroom was always full."

Through the fall of each year, the Salute committee contacted each consulate of the countries to be saluted, invited the ambassadors or their representatives, and sought whatever assistance they could provide—posters, paintings, artifacts, and emblems. For the Salute to Greece, the Greek consulate offered artifacts for decoration. And at the Salute to Mexico night, the Consul General spoke about the migration of monarch butterflies from Canada to Mexico "comparing the romantic story of the butterflies to our lives and our countries' relationship."

"They were among the best-attended events of the year," recalls one Granite Club member. "You'd pay a small amount and have an unbelievable evening. And then somebody would win a trip."

No sooner was the Salute to the World season over each winter, when another Granite Club production took centre stage, at least for the club's women curlers. Each February or March

NEWS FROM THE BAR

In a recently held international competition in Yugoslavia a Scarborough resident, Charels Rendes, was awarded a Gold Medal for his newest cocktail "Charlies' Angels."

During February you may order this heavenly cocktail in the Valley Bar, Dining Room or Cawthra Square.

Contents—rum, Liqueur D'oro, Banana liqueur and Pina Colada.
—Granite News, *February 1978*

Rehearsal for the Granite Revue

since 1932, the Granite hosted the Robertson Invitational Bonspiel. Over the years, the Robertson became among the province's most prestigious bonspiels for women. But equally important to the three-day curling event was the Robertson variety show, an evening of unique entertainment put on by some of the more outgoing women of the Granite Club's curling section.

"People came from Chicago and Montreal and all over," recalls curler and Robertson show director Patricia Stocks. "The ice at the Granite was always full. We'd have three games on Monday, then two games Tuesday and the finals were on Wednesday.... But the Robertson show was always on the Monday night during the big dinner in the ballroom.... Some thought it was the best part of the bonspiel. I think that's why half of them came."

While there were singers, dancers, and comediennes in the Robertson show troupe, none of the all-female cast was a professional. Even though the costumes and make-up always helped make each production number or skit believable, the seamstresses and make-up artists were all volunteers. And despite the fact

In addition to the Robertson, Granite members also took to the stage for the annual Granite Revue

Announcing Our Annual Dinner, Dance and Show

THE GRANITE REVUE 'RAGTIME'

A Roaring Twenties Musical Show
Featuring Granite Club Members

Saturday March 4th

Plan to join us!

6:30 Happy Hour

7:30 Superb Dinner

9:00 Dancing to Frank Bogart and his Orchestra

9:30 **GRANITE 'RAGTIME' REVUE**

followed by dancing until 1:00 A.M.

18.50 Per person   Call Dining Room Office for Reservations

that the staging and lighting generally happened on cue, the backstage crew was usually made up of husbands, sisters or other family members doing the grunt work.

"One time I hauled my kids in to move the props and the furniture and open and close the curtains," recalls Patricia Stocks. "Even though we always started rehearsing around Christmas, the dress rehearsal on the Sunday before was always a schemozzal. I'd think, 'This'll never come off.' But somehow it pulled itself together. Maybe everybody just had the right amount to drink so they were really mellow."

When the curtain went up on the 30- to 40-minute show, the Robertson curlers were usually in for a treat. Generally, the show focused on a theme or two—saluting Hollywood, Walt Disney, the Olympics or some nation of the world. There were always short skits and black-outs to break up the bigger numbers. One year, Dottie Large (one of the originators of the show) included a can-can number in the production; however, come Robertson show night, she was short one dancer. It was an hour before the show. Dottie phoned a relatively new curler at the club, but none other than former Granite skater and life member Dody (Caley) Klein.

"Dody," Dottie said. "You used to skate, didn't you? We need a can-can dancer."

"But it's tonight!" said Dody.

"Don't worry about it. You'll be fine."

"If I can get a baby-sitter," said Dody, "I'll be there."

An hour later, Dody Klein found herself in a locker room adjacent to the Granite ballroom. She was being hastily fitted into the one remaining dancer's costume while learning the can-can routine from the three other women in the number. Minutes after that, the four women dashed out on stage and began "what wasn't too much like a cancan," remembers Dody. "I know we ended up lying on our backs. And I thought, 'A fine way for a crown attorney's wife to behave.' But it was lots of fun," and she found herself permanently in the Robertson show crew every year after.

T. Brad Hatch,
President, 1978

Dr. G.A. Morgan in the poker room of the new Granite Club drew a Royal Straight Flush in 5-card stud poker. The odds against this are 649 740 to one.
—*Granite News, 1975*

Toronto District and Ontario Curling Champions in 1975, (l-r) Jean Hardy, Joan Mathers, Patty Hamilton, Barb Whitman

Not long after, her husband, Art Klein, got involved. He played saxophone in a hobby band with guitarist Wally Pryce, banjo player John Northcott, violinist Barney Reilly, clarinetist Don Pounsett, and a pianist named Gerry Day. Together they were known as "Gerry and the 'Atrics" and played at Granite Club parties and in the Robertson show.

"We thought we were wonderful," says Barbara Clarke, who joined the Granite with her husband Tom in 1972. She remembers the Robertson shows as some of the best times at the club. "We were lots of chiefs and very few Indians. Everybody got into the act."

Canada Life Senior Trophy winners, 1975 (l-r) Alf Philips Sr., skip; George Cowan, vice; Sandy McTavish, second; Murray Patullo, lead

In addition to the continued strong annual performance of younger curlers at the Granite, the club's older curlers continued to amass honours in their own right. It was during the 1970s that PARTICIPaction was launched in Canada. The pro-fitness advertising goaded adult Canadians into physical activity by pointing out that a 60-year-old Swede was fitter than a 30-year-old Canadian. The campaign captured the nation's imagination and seniors or masters tournaments broke out all over the country in a variety of sports.

For some, little goading was required. The March 1975 *Granite Club News* captured the smiling faces of yet another winning Granite Club rink at the Canada Life bonspiel, only this time the foursome was composed of four elder statesmen of the sport—five-time Canada Life Seniors Trophy winning skip Alf Phillips Sr., four-time Seniors winning vice-skip George Cowan, four-time Seniors winning second Sandy McTavish, and twice Seniors winning lead Murray Pattullo. The newsletter went on to say "there is, without question, a renewed interest in curling at the Granite."

While the Granite's first 100 years had clearly produced elite performers in each of its athletic sections, competitive Granite skaters led the way. In April 1976, the Granite Club's Centennial Skating Carnival also paid tribute to the club's rich heritage on the ice. Among others starring in the show were Canadian Dance Champions Barbara Berezowski and David Porter, Canadian Pairs Champions Candy Jones and Don Fraser, Olympian Stan Bohonek and special guest, former Canadian World Figure Skating Champion Donald Jackson. Very much responsible for the anniversary skating show and for the strong competitive showing of Granite Club skaters during the 1970s, was yet another tandem of skating talent—staff professionals Marijane and Louis Stong.

At age 18, Louis Stong had been a double gold medalist and had won every sectional title culminating in a third-place finish

> *"We were used to skating and training in arenas where you'd usually freeze to death. But coming to the Granite was the ultimate in luxury. A rink on the second floor! An elevator to the rink! Unbelievable!"*
> —Skating professional Louis Stong, 1973

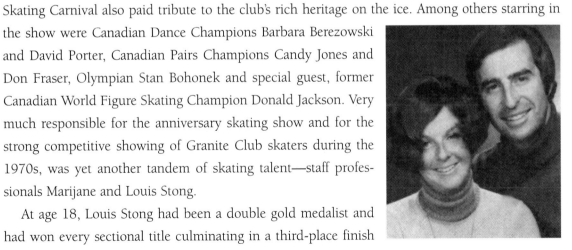

Five Granite Club skaters [are] off to "Skate Moscow," an international skating competition for top world contenders. Mr. Stan Bohonek, Miss Candy Jones, Mr. Don Fraser, Miss Barbara Berezowski and Mr. David Porter.
—Granite News, *December 1975*

Marijane and Louis Stong, 1973

Stan Bohonek

The Granite's Candy Jones and Don Fraser were the Professional Pair Skating Champions of the World in 1979

at the Senior Canadian Men's Championships and a berth on the World Team in 1960. Marijane too had won every section dance championship and skated to third place at the Senior Canadian Dance Championships in 1960. They both had begun coaching in 1960 and were married in 1963. By 1973, when the Granite Club hired them as staff professionals, between them Louis and Marijane had already acquired 35 gold medals.

"It was about our third year at the club when the carnival came along, we came up with a bold idea," recalls Louis Stong. "It would become a monster, but we thought, 'Let's try it.' A three-act version of 'A Mid-Summer Night's Dream' with our own cast. This would be a terrific production."

Right from the start the Stongs' approach was unorthodox. They took the entire skating cast to a National Ballet of Canada production of the Shakespearean romantic comedy so they could see their own characters in action. They pushed the skating section to bring in extra seating around the Granite ice surface for their Shakespeare on ice. They spent additional funds on lights and staging. And on April 18, 1978, several hundred club members sat in specially arranged bleachers for a full-length production of "A Mid-Summer Night's Dream" at the Granite.

Barbara Berezowski and David Porter, 1979 Senior National Champions, with Marijane Stong (right)

"We had Canadian champions—Heather Kemkaran, John Dowding and Lorna Wighton—playing Puck, Oberon, and Titania. And we had Olympic team [and Granite] member Stan Bohonek as the King of the Night Spirits," says Louis Stong. "It was an artistic outlet for all that training...and the club was so generous in allowing it to happen."

While the Stongs' fantasy on ice was in part a throwback to the days of "Dreamy Dream Cake Land" of the 1950s, it also heralded a new era in Granite Club skating. The bar of artistic interpretation on ice had just been raised to a remarkable new height. It would make greater demands on both the Granite coaches and their students. At the same time it would quickly bring to the surface the kind of skating expertise the Granite had cultivated in the Caley sisters, Barbara Ann Scott, the Snellings, Bill McLachlan, and Stan Bohonek. And by bringing the Stongs' combined skating connections on site at the Granite, the skating section would soon open the door to more "special memberships" (elite level skaters invited to train at the Granite with membership privileges).

Granite skaters won three National titles in 1979, John Dowding and Lorna Wighton became 1979 Senior Dance Champions of Canada; Kay Thomson, 1979 Junior Ladies Champion of Canada; Robert Burk and Karen Taylor, 1979 Novice Dance Champions of Canada.

George H. Scott,
President, 1979

Looking back over the last six years in the club, Barbara Berezowski and David Porter, club members and former Senior Dance Champions of Canada are now starring in the Ice Follies. Candy Jones, with partner Don Fraser, former Senior Canadian Pair Champions are currently the Professional Pair Champions of the World.
—Granite News, March 1979

SKATING CARNIVAL

A Mid-Summer Nights Dream

FRIDAY and SATURDAY
APRIL 28th and 29th
8:00 p.m.

SUNDAY
APRIL 30th
2:00 p.m.

Before long, the Stongs would be extending invitations to other up-and-coming skaters to train on Granite ice, to share their experience with younger potential figure-skating talents and to reintroduce the phrase "skating from the Granite Club" to the lexicon of elite competition.

Just two years after Louis and Marijane's artistic experiment with "A Mid-Summer Night's Dream," the annual Granite Skating Carnival featured such outside talent as Barbara Underhill and Paul Martini, who would one day become World Champions. And a few years later, the Stongs would introduce a young man who would eventually skate to four Canadian championships and four World Championships—Kurt Browning. The Granite was on the verge of yet another skating dynasty.

CHAPTER FIFTEEN

FITNESS, FAMILY AND SPORT

1980–1989

THE GRANITE CLUB management and members entered the club's second century in an upbeat mood. Not only were prospects good for club skaters to return to the international winners' podium, but the general health of the club's board, administration and membership also appeared strong. In early 1980, 1979 club president George H. Scott turned in an optimistic review of the year just past and a forecast for a prosperous decade to come. He reported that membership was just below 9000 and that cash flow was in excess of $6.5 million. He pointed out that renovations were complete on the Presidents' Lounge, and that for the first time in years food services had operated at a profit.

Donald L. Angus, president in 1980, noted in his annual report that while the planners of the Bayview facility had done an excellent job in anticipating the club members' needs, eight years of growth and a more youthful and active membership meant the club was bursting at the seams.

In the move to Bayview, familiar names were chosen for facilities to maintain traditions that were vivid in the memories of long-time members. The Bayview club, like the St. Clair club, had a Heather Room, a Crystal Room, a Peacock Alley and a Cawthra Square. One exception, at the beginning, was the executive lounge adjacent to the curling section. To most it was "Bob's Bar" in honour of the first president at Bayview, Dr. Bob Marshall, but in subsequent years it became more formally known as the Presidents' Lounge.

Donald L. Angus,
President, 1980

The club tartan of hunter's green, white, yellow, red and black became the official tartan, approved by the Board of Directors in January of 1985.

The quest for a tartan was initiated by the Business Girls Curling Committee in the winter of 1982 and pursued during 1983 by the Ladies Curling Committee. Jack Richardson of Richardson's Tartan Shop prepared the design, which was reviewed under a variety of lighting conditions— particularly out on the ice—before approval. The first bolt of cloth, made by West Coast Woolens of Vancouver, was available in the fall of 1983.

Total section registration in 1980 was 8000—nearly twice the number of members in all sections in 1972. Major changes to the third floor, in particular an expansion of the health and Fitness Section, and snack shop renovation were planned. Experience with previous renovation had shown that a more efficient use of space and resources created savings and better revenues—the board was confident that they were an excellent investment for the club.

The final paragraphs of Angus's "President's Report" pointed to "an unusual item...

> We have applied for armorial bearings, or a coat of arms, for the club. This is a grant from the Queen through the offices of the Lord Lyon of Edinburgh. Our petition has been granted. In the spring the appropriate parchments will be complete and it is expected that they will be presented to the club by one of Her Majesty's representatives.

President Angus acknowledged that the idea for creating a coat of arms for the club was initiated by long-time member Geoffrey Agar, one of whose hobbies was heraldry. Hamilton artist Gordon MacPherson had been hired to come up with the artwork for the coat of arms.

The design reflected the club's strengths and origins. Since the official colours of the club were green and white, the shield would consist of a green background with a white chevron to represent the clubhouse. Displayed on the green would be: in the upper left, the York Rose emblematic of the origin of Toronto as the Town of York; in the upper right, the Trillium to represent Ontario; and at the centre of the chevron, the Maple Leaf for Canada. Then, at the base of the shield, to symbolize the club's curling roots and its name, there would be a representation of Ailsa Craig, the Scottish island source of ailsite, a special granite from which curling stones are made. Below the shield, the club motto—*Inter-Familias* (among families) reflected the Granite's family orientation.

Granite Coat of Arms

Presentation of the Granite Coat of Arms at the President's Ball, (l-r) Donald Angus, George Gilmour, Dr. Pauline McGibbon

By April of 1981, the club had received the Letters Patent, granting the armorial bearings; the board had begun planning a Grant of Arms ceremony and invited the Lieutenant Governor of Ontario to the President's Ball for the coat of arms presentation. The Honourable Dr. Pauline McGibbon, the country's first woman lieutenant governor, attended the ceremony and participated in the unveiling of the club's official coat of arms on June 18, 1981.

Well-maintained facilities plus the ability to cater to contemporary tastes were the keys to keeping the club at capacity in both sports and social sections. In the case of the hospitality staff, that meant

Dancing at the Granite has a long history—over the decades the club has been the site of numerous popular (and sold-out) events such as the President's Ball, New Year's Eve, section "bashes," and the many "Salute to..." evenings. The club has also been the place where many members came to learn to dance. Lessons included evenings of Scottish Country dancing, led by pipers and drummers from the 48th Highlanders and square dancing with up to 150 club members taking part during the 1950s. In later decades, rhythmic, tap, and ballroom dance lessons became popular.

making the dining and drinking experience at the Granite memorable for both members and private customers. Dieter Haag and his hospitality staff were able to meet the challenge. Once the staff settled in the Bayview premises, menus were professionally printed. When mixed drinks were in vogue, there was always a bartender who could prepare dozens of cocktails; when wines were preferred, the club appointed a wine committee. At private functions, the budget was the only curb on decorating creativity. One wedding featured a star-filled night sky overhead—lights were strung from the dining room ceiling, then covered with sheer drapes. For another, a massive ice block was sculpted to hold bottles of champagne on top with hollowed out pigeonholes full of caviar beneath. A catered corporate function's decoration began with a car in the centre of the ballroom; a wedding's $20 000 flower budget meant the Granite hospitality staff could arrange banana leaves and Bird of Paradise flowers as centre-pieces for each table.

Annual events got just as much time and attention. "On Christmas Day we served 1200 meals at the club," says Haag, who had started with the club in 1973. "Every room, every lounge was stripped and we moved furniture into storage and rented tables just to serve Christmas dinner to members all over the club.... But then there was Mother's Day. On Christmas, if you didn't have

The Graduation Class — "Square Dancers" — 1950 Granite Club — Toronto Ont.

The Granite Square Dance class of 1950

cranberry sauce right away, it was forgivable because it was Christmas. But not on Mother's Day—everything had to be perfect. It was the toughest day of the year."

"We always felt at home at the club no matter what social function and I always remember how original the menus and food were," says Phyllis Parker. In 1941, she and her husband Rex were married at Eaton Memorial Church and held their reception at the old St. Clair club. In 1973, Phyllis joined Bob Marshall's planning committee and began serving on the board.*

While the club's food and beverage service was among the priorities during the years Phyllis Parker was on the board, much larger financial issues swirled around the club—and the country—in the early 1980s. Suddenly, Canada's economy (and that of all the G-7 nations) fell into recession. The prime lending rate seemed astronomical—in 1981 interest rates hit 23 per cent—and there was double-digit inflation. Ottawa imposed wage and price controls. There were more people unemployed in Canada than were in the armed services during the Second World War—close to half a million Canadians under the age of 25 were out of work. It was the worst economic setback in Canada since the Depression of the 1930s.

When Granite Club Board member and former president George Scott invited Phyllis Parker to join the board, it wasn't something she had pushed for. She admits she was "a professional volunteer...doing forty hours a week of volunteer work," but she wasn't interested in making a political statement.

Before accepting Phyllis said, "if you're looking for a token woman, I'm not your lady."

She went on to become the club's first woman president in 1983.

William S. Storey,
President, 1981

In 1982, a music hall to replace old Massey Hall on Shuter Street—the new 2850-seat Roy Thomson Hall—opened at King and Simcoe Streets. The hall was named for Granite member Ken Thomson's father, and in recognition of the Thomson family's support, which had helped make the facility possible.

In 1982, Phyllis Parker was second vice-president and responsible for delivering the 1981 financial statements at the Annual General Meeting. Perhaps because of the economic tensions of the times, but also because the club's AGMs had often been rather stuffy affairs, the board worked hard to encourage members to attend. In return, Parker recognized the need to be fully prepared. As the first woman ever to sit on the board, she knew she had to arrive at the meeting with all her facts and figures in order and with something extra. So, instead of just plunging into the details of the club's improved surplus, the increased use of food and beverage services that year and the budget for planned physical improvements at the club, she stepped up to the lectern and said:

"I feel a little like Elizabeth Taylor's fifth husband.... I know what to do, but I don't know how to make it interesting."

"At first there was a slight giggle," recalls her husband Rex. "Then it developed into a roar of laughter."

"I think it was the first time a joke had ever been told at an annual general meeting," says Phyllis Parker.

The statements themselves reflected a great deal of serious thought on the part of the board. As president William S. Storey noted in his report, "We have been concerned about the future direction of our club. Should we be larger or smaller? We have decided that our present facilities are well used and would not support additional members." To that end, the board issued a renewed mission statement for the club:

> The Granite Club is a Family Social Club of a controlled size of membership maintaining the traditions of the past and building its prestige while providing the best social and athletic facilities and maintaining a proper balance between social and athletic activities with general use by the membership at large taking precedence over specialized training program and events.

The board set the maximum number of senior members at 4500; the directors also laid out budget and plans for two years' worth of building renovations to accommodate membership activities.

While Phyllis Parker was setting a precedent in the boardroom, another Granite Club woman was setting a precedent in the water. Granite Club swimmer Jocelyn Muir, instructed by club pro Herb deBray and encouraged by every member of her family, challenged Lake Ontario to a marathon and won.

"It is Jocelyn's good fortune," reported *Granite News* in the fall of 1981, "to be part of a large sports-minded family. Her parents June and Jack, brothers James, Tom and John, and sisters Kathleen and June are all longtime members of the Granite and active in a number of sport sections. Jocelyn's grandfather Jack is in the club's Sports Hall of Fame....

"At 5:05 p.m. [September 4, 1981], after 15 hours and 56 minutes and 32 miles from her point of entry at Niagara-on-the-Lake...having endured the hostilities of Lake Ontario's 7-foot rollers and the mind-numbing distance, Jocelyn Muir walked out of Lake Ontario at Ontario Place. She had done what she had set out to do. [At 15, she was] the youngest person ever to swim across Lake Ontario."

By the late 1970s, the Granite's professional ranks in the pool included Herb deBray, an experienced coach from a strong aquatic club in Montreal, and he began to develop a comprehensive swimming program. "[A lot of] focus in the aquatics section was competitive swimming," recalls instructor Joan Russell. In 1976, Russell had been hired at the Granite pool to put her physical education degree and special interest in synchronized swimming to good use. She noted that at the time much of "our instruction programs were funnelled toward competition.... There seemed to be a lot of emphasis on winning."

George W. Gilmour,
President, 1982

The theme of the 1982 Granite Revue was "Around the World in 80 Minutes." The casting call went out in the December 1981 issue of the Granite News *and the show went on March 6, 1982.*

Thanks to that emphasis, as the 1980 Summer Olympic Games approached, the Granite Club was well represented in the battle for berths on Canada's swim team. At 15, Deanne Weber had already won provincial titles in breaststroke and freestyle swimming; by 1980 she had qualified for the Olympic trials in the 200-metre breaststroke. A year younger, Selby Kostiuk was preparing to compete in the trials in the 100-metre and 200-metre breaststroke. With numerous international trials to his credit, 22-year-old Don Dixon had qualified for the 1980 Olympic trials in the 400-metre individual medley and the 100-metre and 200-metre backstroke. Similarly, with plenty of international experience under her belt, Katharine Richardson was just 16 as she prepared for the trials in the 200-metre butterfly, the 200-metre breaststroke, the 400-metre and 800-metre freestyle, and the 200-metre and 400-metre individual medley. And with two Canadian records and one British record to his credit, 15-year-old David Shemilt* had qualified for the Olympic tri-

*Granite member David Shemilt won the 1500 metre freestyle event at the Canadian National Swimming Championships in August, 1983.

als in the 400-metre individual medley and the 200-metre and 100-metre backstroke events.

None of this talent made an appearance at the Olympiad in Moscow. First U.S. President Jimmy Carter announced that the U.S. Olympic team would boycott the 1980 Games because of the USSR's invasion of Afghanistan, and then Prime Minister Joe Clark decreed that the Canadian Olympic team would follow suit.*

In October 1980, deBray left the Granite to accept a position at Brock University in St. Catharines and his departure accelerated a transition already underway in the Granite pool programs—the one that was later articulated in the president's report of 1982.

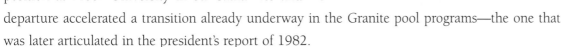

"There were really three different programs [in the pool] and they were all at odds back then," recalls club member Alan Taylor. "There's the teaching program, the competitive program, and what you might call a general program for the fitness swimmer," which included Alan Taylor. He'd first come to know the Granite when he and his new wife Nancy Milburn held their reception at St. Clair in 1962. Then he curled with his father-in-law and eventually began swimming lengths at noon hour to keep fit. However, it was during his volunteer time (from 1978 to 1988) in the Granite Club swimming section that Taylor came to understand that "the two mandates—one for the casual swimmer and the competitive program—clashed. And you can't keep the pool open 24 hours a day because of the huge cost associated with it."

During the 1980s, the Granite Club swimming section tried to strike a balance among the various demands for pool and staff time. Consequently, the staff professionals and volunteer conveners worked long days organizing a Granite swimming program that included everything from parent-and-tot programs to marathon training to scuba diving to fitness swimming. It was also

The aquatics staff worked hard to find new challenges for the club's fitness swimmers. Over the years, section members were challenged to "swim" from Vancouver to New Zealand or from St. John's to Vancouver. In 1989, it was the Great Lakes Challenge Swim.

"We're still stroking along through the cool waters of the Great Lakes. It looks like a few people have really picked up the pace in the new year and are heading towards Lake Michigan, our third lake of the challenge."—"Aquatics," Granite News

In 1984, at the Los Angeles Olympic Games, Canadians reaped more gold medals at the pool than ever before—Alex Baumann in the men's 200-metre and 400-metre medley, Victor Davis in the 200-metre breaststroke, and Sylvie Bernier in spring-board diving.

Aquacise classes were offered three times a week in the Granite pool

AQUACISES —NEW!

A new fitness program for adults. All you need is water and the willingness to try out a whole new way of exercising!

This program utilizes the natural resistance of the water to help tone and shape muscles. It's fun and it's certainly a refreshing way of exercising and keeping cool at the same time.—Granite News, *March 1986*

WE GET RESULTS!!

On Sunday, June 1, [1986] synchro teams from around the province— from as far away as Ottawa and Thunder Bay—arrived here to challenge the Granite swimmers. Challenge they did, but top honours went to our girls, winning the overall trophy.—Granite News

during this period that the section changed its name. The "aquatic section" was more inclusive and in keeping with the inclusive nature of the activities.

Still, Joan Russell hadn't forgotten the Granite's winning tradition in the pool. Three mornings a week (from 6 a.m. to 7:30 a.m.) and two evenings a week (beginning at 8:30 p.m.), she coached the young women of the club in competitive synchronized swimming. She expected the synchro team to be prompt and prepared for a thorough workout.

"My first day swimming synchro was Joan's first day coaching synchro," recalls Janice Taylor, who began the underwater ballet-style swimming routines at age 10 and was coached by Joan Russell into her teens. "I wanted to win. And Joan wanted someone to win.... She pushed me pretty hard, because she knew I wanted and needed to be pushed.

The relationship yielded personal successes for both women. Joan coached Janice (and her synchro partner Nancy Ginn) through B level and A level competitions and up to provincial championships. One year, during the club championships, all 27 members of Joan Russell's synchronized swimming team "put on a tremendous display—Synchro on Parade" at the Granite. And eventually Janice earned the Granite Club's Award of Merit.

Swimming at the Granite meant just as much to average members as it did the professional staff. For longtime casual swimmer Alan Taylor it was the luxury of swimming his lengths (at the St. Clair club) "in an enclosed place—a natatorium—that had a plaster wall with a frieze on it." Even though he left Toronto for a swimming scholarship in the United States in the late 1970s, Don Dixon regularly returned to the Granite Club for swim meets and social gatherings. Perhaps the

Granite pool meant most to club member Catharine Larkin. In July 1984, she was critically injured in a head-on car crash outside Ottawa. Following temporary paralysis and months of hospitalization, she was encouraged to take up swimming in the Granite pool as therapy. The physical exercise worked well, but the psychological lift proved even greater.

Joan Russell, synchro coach (right), presents most improved synchronized swimmer award to Lisa McLatchey and Janice Taylor

The Ontario Masters Championships were held in Etobicoke Olympium on April 25, 26 and 27 [1986].... The Granite contingent of 13 masters won a total of 12 medals (5 gold, 4 silver, 3 bronze,) resulting in a 12th place finish overall.
—Granite News

"While I was recovering, I created an incredibly close bond with the people doing master swimming at the Granite," recalls Larkin. "They encouraged me to go with them to the Canadian Masters Championships in 1988. I was dead last in every heat. It was the most humiliating and most wonderful experience of my life. I can still see them all at the end of the pool yelling 'You can do it, Catharine!' And I remember looking up and thinking, 'This is the only thing in the world that matters.'"

Just as it had been involved in Toronto's evolution and growth in previous decades, the Granite Club remained well connected to the city in the 1980s. Late in the decade, the Toronto Ontario Olympic Committee (TOOC) was formed to prepare a bid for the 1996 Summer Games. Naturally, the organizers of the TOOC bid wanted to convince the members of the International Olympic Committee (IOC) that Toronto was a perfect fit with the Olympic ideals of friendly competition and celebration. Not surprisingly, TOOC organizers Paul Henderson and David Crombie decided to include a tour of the Granite Club during a Toronto visit by IOC president Juan Antonio

Phyllis L. Parker,
President, 1983

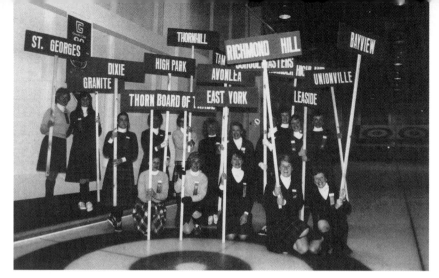

The Granite Club hosted (and welcomed) the 1985 Canada Life Bonspiel competitors

Four Granite Club skaters— Lorna Wighton and John Dowding, National Dance Champions, and Barbara Underhill and Paul Martini, National Pairs Champions—domi- nated the six-member Canadian skating team that competed at the Lake Placid Winter Olympics in the U.S.—Granite News, April 1980

"Sitting around the boardroom talking through an agenda... it's hard to get a feeling of the heart and soul of the place. When you're sitting around at dinner and there's reminiscing about the earlier days...there's a great transference of institutional memory of the club."—David Brown

Samaranch. Not long before the expected visit to the Bayview facility, the Granite Club received a phone call from IOC headquarters in Geneva, Switzerland.

"Who is going to host the tour of the club?" the caller asked.

"It will be the president of the club," explained the Granite Club representative. "Mr. David Brown."

That seemed to satisfy the caller for the moment; the conversation ended. However, a few hours later another call came through.

"The IOC calling," said the voice from Geneva. "How tall is the president, Mr. David Brown?" Somehow, the club representative was able to find out quickly: "Mr. Brown is five foot, seven inches tall."

There were calculations at the IOC end of the line. Finally the voice said: "That will be alright. Mr. Brown is an acceptable host for Mr. Samaranch."

As David Brown discovered later, when the IOC delegation arrived at the Granite Club, "with the place crawling with photographers and TV cameras, I guess [the diminutive Samaranch] never wanted to be standing beside anybody who towered over him."

Action on the Granite bowling green

A variety of swimming classes offered for all levels of participants

There was just as much pre-planning and maneuvering on the TOOC side. As President Brown showed the dozen or so IOC members around the Granite Club, there were staged events going on in the swimming pool, on the lawn-bowling greens, and the tennis courts. And when he spoke, apparently off-the-cuff, about the Granite Club being a microcosm of Toronto—where everybody seemed to be athletically inclined—Brown was actually speaking from a series of notes the TOOC organizers had asked him to memorize. The only part of David Brown's tour of the Granite that wasn't staged was the atmosphere at the club, because "we are truly a club devoted to families and sports." Still, the several hours the IOC and TOOC people spent at the club went smoothly right up to the final detail.

"We also discovered at the last minute," recalls Brown, "that I would be expected to give him a gift. We very hastily gift-wrapped a Granite Club medal, or something like that, and he presented me with an Olympic flag."

Arthur D. Sisley,
President, 1984

OLYMPIC STARS WORK OUT AT THE
GRANITE CLUB

On Sunday, April 16th, [1989] a group of bystanders began to grow as word travelled through the club that Katarina Witt and Brian Boitano practised routines under the watchful eye of choreographer Sandra Bezic. A certain group of gentlemen were pleased...to receive autographs from charming Katarina.—Granite News

In the fall of 1989, club president John Brooke paid tribute to longtime member Frank Stark. Not only had the Stark family been with the club for 25 years, but Frank had initiated the Salute Nights some 20 years earlier.

The head of the IOC was one of many celebrities the 1980s brought to the Granite Club. Thanks to its growing membership and some proactive conveners, the Speakers' Luncheon group managed to bring a who's who of Canada to the monthly events at the Granite, scheduling high-powered personalities and celebrity writers. Although some were question marks right up to the last minute.

"Scheduling these people was like fitting together pieces of a jigsaw puzzle," remembers Joan Mactavish, who by the late 1970s had become convener of the luncheons. "For a long time we wanted to get Judy LaMarsh. But it was difficult. She wouldn't commit herself. And I didn't really want to slot anybody else until I knew when she would come."

The former cabinet minister in Lester Pearson's Liberal government finally committed and kicked off the 1978–79 Speakers' Luncheon season "arriving by cab at the last minute. When [Judy] saw that it was a sell-out, she was very apologetic and quite enjoyed her visit...talking about many of the political personalities she had known. And she didn't pull any punches."

During the 1980s, the Speakers' Luncheon planning committee began to include men in its membership—and attendees, broadening the topics and

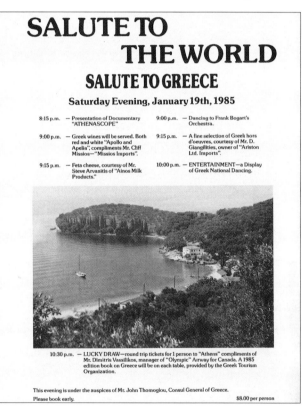

SALUTE TO THE WORLD

SALUTE TO GREECE

Saturday Evening, January 19th, 1985

8:15 p.m. — Presentation of Documentary "ATHENASCOPE"

9:00 p.m. — Greek wines will be served. Both red and white "Apollo and Apelia", compliments Mr. Cliff Missios—"Missios Imports".

9:15 p.m. — Feta cheese, courtesy of Mr. Steve Arvanitis of "Ainos Milk Products."

9:00 p.m. — Dancing to Frank Bogart's Orchestra.

9:15 p.m. — A fine selection of Greek hors d'oeuvres, courtesy of Mr. D. Giangilities, owner of "Ariston Ltd. Imports".

10:00 p.m. — ENTERTAINMENT—a Display of Greek National Dancing.

10:30 p.m. — LUCKY DRAW—round trip tickets for 1 person to "Athens" compliments of Mr. Dimitris Vassilikos, manager of "Olympic" Airway for Canada. A 1985 edition book on Greece will be on each table, provided by the Greek Tourism Organization.

This evening is under the auspices of Mr. John Thomoglou, Consul General of Greece.

Please book early. $8.00 per person

speakers. Among those with universal appeal in those years were speakers such as explorer Sir Edmund Hillary, contralto Maureen Forrester, wildlife painter Robert Bateman, actor John Neville, news anchor Knowlton Nash, and publisher Anna Porter. Each guest helped build the reputation of the event and each generally left a lasting impression.

CANADIAN INTERNATIONAL BRIDGE TOURNAMENT HELD IN MALLORCA, SPAIN
November 1984

Overall winners were Helen Catley and Vie Beaton. Another member, Jessie Hill was runner-up
—Granite News

"Investigative journalist Stevie Cameron arrived perhaps thinking she was going to speak to a little ladies' group of a dozen or so," recalls 1980s convener Margaret McBurney. "When I walked her into the ballroom with about 500 people there, she was dressed very casually in a heavy sweater. And she said, 'Ahhh,' recognizing this was more than a small ladies' group. And then she said 'Oh well, here I am.' She gave a great talk."

"When I found I was standing by the curling rink freezing and thinking, 'Five more ends and I can have a coffee,' I realized I shouldn't be curling. So I stopped and got interested in the speakers' luncheons."—Margaret McBurney

Luncheon regulars remember Terence Kavanagh, the heart specialist, being very uptight and dropping a tray of slides, but it seemed to break the ice and his visit proved memorable. Betty Oliphant, the founder of the National Ballet School, not only spoke eloquently about the evolution of classical dance in Canada, but she also brought a pair of young dancers along to prove it. When Peter Dalglish came to the Luncheon to share his dream of eradicating poverty, sickness and exploitation from the lives of Third World children, "we had people lining up to sign cheques for his Street Kids International," recalls McBurney. "That had never happened before."

The 1982 board's plans to renovate the third floor to add international squash courts, build a new racquets lounge, enlarge the Skylite Lounge, and alter the Curling Lounge and Bar meant construction and disruption for long-term gain. The long process of planning, budgeting, and clearing

Walter Gibson Cassels, Q.C., President, 1985

1986: The first phase of construction involved structural work to
support the addition

Robert M. Ginn,
President, 1986

Training on the indoor Fitness
track before the renovation

municipal rezoning hurdles meant delays, but not an end to the scheme. In a radical move, the board planned to use two of the ten curling sheets to upgrade the indoor racquets section and build an addition to the club to make room for the Fitness Section.

The Fitness Section was established soon after the Bayview facility opened. It evolved from a growing interest in aerobic exercise and a greater awareness of the benefits of warming up before full exertion in a sport. At Bayview, the fitness gymnasium took over what had originally been a nursery for the pre-school children of Granite members. There were mats for floor exercises and yoga. There were ledges on the walls for stretching and doing chin-ups. There were several stationary bicycles. And surrounding the 1000-square-foot room was a track for runners.

"It was 62 laps to the mile," recalls David Brown, who had joined the Granite about the time the Bayview facility opened. He ran circuits on the track to keep fit, but "you got sore ankles running around it, because you were constantly turning. So the routine was, every five minutes the direction would reverse on the track. You'd get this horde of people running around this tiny track and then suddenly changing direction."

"You ran in circles and got really dizzy," adds Bill McLatchy. He and his good friend, Joseph Sorbara, took up jogging on Sorbara's birthday, in April 1982. But before venturing out-of-doors each day, they would warm up with a few laps on the fitness-room track, which Sorbara says "at best could hold about 12 people."

"You had to be really careful," says Bob Hunter, a Granite member since the mid-1980s. "If you weren't using any kind of fixed piece of equipment, if you were, say, trying to share a mat, you'd go back to do a sit-up and people would crash into you."

The growing popularity of the fitness and health section, the limited space in which to work out and the board's recognition of the problems all pointed to the need for a new fitness facility. But where? The building was at capacity. At the time, David Brown was on the board and remembers

the decision to put the new fitness room "on top of the ballroom. Problem was, the ballroom wasn't built to support anything on top of it. In frustration, we hired a firm of architects and engineers, who told us to build it over the dining room, but on stilts."

In his president's report, Walter Cassels outlined plans for the new fitness complex. Inside the 10 000-square-foot facility, the section would have sufficient space to accommodate

Health and Fitness [1986] Annual meeting
"… a sociable half hour followed by a quickie annual meeting and a delightful full-course dinner. Then settle back for our own brand of future shock!… see an in-depth show-and-tell presentation featuring slides, architectural drawings and expert commentary on the new fitness facility."—Granite News

The newly expanded Fitness facility was ready for participants in May, 1987

Novice Granite squash players
learning the fine points

*There was standing room only as
over 160 members crowded into the
Sun Lounge recently for the Speaker's
Night on nutrition and stress.
Elizabeth Snell, Director of Nutrition
at the Fitness Institute Medical
Centre, gave a most instructive and
entertaining talk on how excessive
stress, whether mental, emotional or
physical, can exert a significant effect
on our nutritional needs and well-
being.*—Granite News, April 1986

David A. Brown,
President, 1987

exercise, aerobics, dancercise, and an array of weight and fitness training devices (including rowing machines, computerized stationary bicycles, and weight training equipment). Suspended around the upper level of the centre, a new track would allow runners to cover a mile in 21 laps. There would be a four-inch separation between the floor of the fitness centre and the roof of the ballroom, ensuring that "work-out music or dropped weights will be of no bother to the ballroom dancers." However, there was some controversy over the plan to glaze two full sides of the facility, thus making the upstairs gym and its occupants visible from Bayview Avenue. Given the later trend toward storefront fitness shops, the club was clearly ahead of its time.

Perhaps recalling the agony of his sore ankles from running on the old track, David Brown's summary of the May 1987 opening of the new fitness facility, noted that it "was attended by over 700 masochists who jammed the third-floor lobby to witness the unveiling of the latest instruments of torture about to be inflicted on us by the Fitness Section." But he also noted that "four years ago, aerobics classes at the Granite were unheard of. In 1987 we offered 14 classes per week...

We now employ six aerobics instructors who weekly lead over 200 members in regular and low-impact aerobics."

"It's been an amazing evolution actually," says Bonnie Mactavish Hunter. At about age 10, she started coming to the Granite on a family membership. Early on at the Bayview club, she began fitness work-outs "in that dingy green room" where, even then, the rigid dress code required white shorts and T-shirts for men and black leotards for women. But with the new facility, "things loosened up and even the opening and closing hours changed with the times. First it was 6:30 a.m., then 6:00. Now, because members want to use it, it opens at 5:30 a.m. And it's open till 10 o'clock at night."

There were also growing pains on the clay courts at the Granite in the 1980s. Aside from the explosion in the Fitness Section membership, at that time the only other section with increasing numbers was the Tennis Section. During her tenure as president Phyllis Parker recalls "tennis wanting more space" as the most pressing problem. Indeed, the Tennis Section submitted a precedent-setting petition to the board in 1983. By the next year, the tennis pavilion (an atmospherically controlled bubble over several of the outdoor courts) was under construction adjacent to the clubhouse.

With some of the Granite's tennis courts open to year-round play, enthusiasm for the section continued to climb. The arrival of "special member" Carling Bassett didn't hurt either. Then ranked fifth in the world, "Carling asked for time to play here in the winter, because she needed practice time," recalls Ron Joshua, tennis convener at the time. "And we gave her a week because her courts at home were not bubbled."

Among her sparring partners was Granite tennis pro Gary Caron. During his competitive days, Caron had climbed to 12th best men's player in Ontario. He had also coached for some years, and in 1985 replaced Eleanor O'Gorman on the Granite pro staff. Carling Bassett had a soft spot for the

Our congratulations go to Scott Dulmage who won the U.S. Under 18 Hardball [squash] Tournament at Yale.

Scott is now playing for the Canadian team in the World's Junior Championships in Brisbane, Australia.
—*Granite News, May 1986*

The erection of the Winter Tennis Bubble is an annual task which begins at 5:30 a.m. on a misty October morning. First the bubble is removed from the storage shed at the south end of court #5 and then spread over the court surface. Twenty-eight men are utilized to shift close to 7000 pounds into an inflatable position. It takes approximately an hour to inflate and secure the doors. By 6:00 p.m., this momentous job is completed by a weary staff.
—*Granite News, December 1985*

The 1981 Carnival featured Kay Thompson, winner of Skate Moscow and 1981 Canadian National Ladies Champion, and Barbara Underhill and Paul Martini, winners of America Skate. The 1985 Carnival showcased the talents of Canadians Brian Orser, Charlene Wong, and Kevin Parker.

Kay Thomson, Canadian Senior Ladies Champion 1981-83

Granite. On numerous occasions she added to the draw by attending Tennis Section parties. She attracted hundreds of spectators when she participated in specially arranged matches on the Granite Club courts.

Two other athletes came to the Granite as special members during the 1980s, but they carried figure skates, not tennis racquets. Since their World Junior Pairs victory in 1979, Barbara Underhill and Paul Martini had been searching for the next level of performance. However, they faced nagging injuries, long commuting distances in the Toronto area, and the retirement of their one-time coach. That's when the duo was approached by Louis and Marijane Stong to come to the Granite. The Stongs were already re-establishing the club's reputation as a home of champions; they coached John Dowding and Lorna Wighton (Canadian Dance Champions), Heather Kemkaran and Kay Thompson (Canadian Women's Champions), and (Olympic team skater) Stan Bohonek.

"They were my babies," recalls Louis Stong. "They were probably the people I became most subjectively involved with."

"The combination of Louis Stong and the Granite Club, we figured, were second to none," says Paul Martini. "Most places I had skated in were rinks, you know, freezing, ruddy cold. But the

Granite was a definite step up in the world. It was strictly a skating facility. No boards. Just ice dedicated to skating. It was like going to Mecca.... And Louis makes a building come alive. He just has that ability to walk into a facility and bring up everyone's spirit with his enthusiasm."

As with his other skaters, Louis Stong introduced Martini and Underhill to the Granite experience by incorporating them in the club's annual "Fantasy On Ice" carnival. That got creative juices going. Then he prescribed special attention to their stroking and jumping techniques and introduced them to renowned choreographer Sandra Bezik who fashioned a new program for them. For music, the group chose "Concerto in F" (George Gershwin's sequel to "Rhapsody in Blue") and while choreographer Bezik planned the creative side, coach Stong organized the technical components so that the four-minute program would dazzle all who witnessed it.

Barbara Underhill and
Paul Martini

The Chairman's Bonspiel took place the week after the Canada Life affair with 40 curlers participating in this exciting and ever-popular event. Our chairman, Harry Ross, expressed his concern over the fact that the very expensive cup for this event seemed to have been lost. While this announcement at the beginning of the first game cast a bit of a damper over things, it also set off a wide-spread hunt, resulting in a successful discovery by the end of the second game.—Granite News, *March 1987*

Martini and Underhill took the bronze medal at the World Championships in 1983. However, at the Winter Olympics in Sarajevo, Yugoslavia, during the short program Barbara fell in a sit-spin and Paul came down too; they finished the competition in seventh place. The Granite team contemplated the pair's next move. Martini and Underhill already had a handful of national championship titles to their credit. Should they turn professional? Or should they take one more crack at the Worlds? They chose the latter, although Paul and Barbara had mutually agreed that

Kenneth G. Belbeck,
President, 1988

Brian Orser

whatever happened in 1984, they would turn pro when the season was done.

"The 1984 period from January to the World Championships in March was drudgery," laments Martini. "Barbara [still] had an injury from the fall in Sarajevo. But she was also struggling with her new skates. And the performance level was nowhere near what we wanted. At the Granite, Louis would sit in his office in the corner, watching us and being at a total loss what to say or do."

With only a week to go before the Worlds in Ottawa in March, 1984, Martini and Underhill were totally disheartened. Nothing was working. Repetition made it worse. The skaters were tired. Barbara's skates wouldn't soften or break in. The excitement, once inspired by the Gershwin score, was fading. The Stongs, Sandra Bezik, and all the Granite staff that had always been so supportive were mum. Not even appearing on the cover of *Maclean's* magazine with the headline "The Olympic Promise" boosted their morale. The pair was about to call Ottawa to cancel, when national men's champion Brian Orser came to the Granite to work on his figures with Louis Stong. He too observed his friends' frustration and agony. But then he said: "Why doesn't Barbara just go back to her old skates?"

Martini and Underhill stopped cold.

"You're going nowhere in a hurry," Orser said. "What have you got to lose?"

Whether psychological or physical, Martini remembers the immediate change "was like some-one went over and flicked a light switch on the wall. It was like a brand-new person. The confidence was back. Leading up to Ottawa, skating practices were just like heaven, cranking off the run-through, not missing a thing. I remember vividly how much fun the Worlds were, not just because we won, but because it had been such a huge relief...skating at the level we knew were capable of."

"We had our fingers crossed every second," recalls Christine Hindson. Because of her own interest in skating and knowing the frustration that Martini and Underhill had experienced, Christine and 20 other Granite Club supporters made the trek to Ottawa to be in the audience. "We sat through everything. But Paul and Barbara were fabulous. It was a proud moment for them and for the Granite Club."

The World Pairs Champions long savoured their triumph over adversity in Ottawa, but retired from amateur competition almost immediately. There were plenty of thrills and challenges ahead for Martini and Underhill as professionals, but among the most cherished was the Granite's Skating Section dinner that spring, when "they presented us with a wonderful silver plate. There was obviously a very strong feeling amongst the Skating Section. And over the years, even though we were no longer members, we've felt that the door at the Granite was always open."

John W. Brooke,
President, 1989

As Time Goes By

1990–1999

ON OCTOBER 24, 1992, the night of the annual President's Ball at the Granite, the club was a mix of timeless images. Against the usual backdrop of contemporary elegance, the organizers of the evening had arranged a collection of 1950s cars. There were three 50s Cadillac convertibles on display, with a 1958 Corvette at the entrance to the club. On the ballroom floor sat a 1952 MGTD and a Nash Metropolitan. And along with Frank Bogart and his big band, the revellers that evening were treated to songs such as "Bo Diddley," "Blue Suede Shoes," and "Johnny B. Goode" courtesy of Canadian rock 'n' roll legend Ronnie Hawkins.

It was a 50s theme but, recalls then president Ron Besse, "we also had television sets all over the place, because that was the night the Blue Jays won the World Series."

It was past midnight Saturday and into Sunday morning when the TV sets seemed to be winning over the dancing in the ballroom. The game was tied and had gone into extra innings; in the

Barbara Underhill and Paul Martini, inducted into the Granite Hall of Fame in 1997

Garry G. Gale,
President, 1990

In March of 1996, the club's board announced a reciprocal arrangement program that would allow members to visit sports clubs in other cities and use the facilities for up to two weeks during a stay. As the program grew, clubs from across Canada, the U.S. and as far away as Australia were added to the list.

11th, Dave Winfield drove in two runs. The Jays needed both, as Atlanta came to bat in the bottom of the inning down by just one run, with two out and the tying run on third. Reliever Mike Timlin scooped up Otis Nixon's drag bunt and threw him out at first. Joe Carter leaped off first base with the ball in his hands and the Granite Club (and Toronto) exploded with joy over the Jays' first-ever World Series win.

"I came back into the ballroom," says Besse, "and Rompin' Ronnie was the only guy in the room, playing and singing."

It was an important time in the history of Toronto and at the Granite Club. The city, along with Blue Jays' president (and Granite member) Peter Widdrington, celebrated the Canadian team's capture of the top prize in "America's favourite pastime," and the team had done it by drawing more than four million fans to Toronto's newest sporting venue—the SkyDome. Its retractable roof and stadium (budgeted at $150 million) had cost $500 million, but meant no pro team in Toronto would ever get rained or snowed on again. The Blue Jays' World Series pennant was also one of a number of professional sport milestones during the decade.

In 1991, after eight years, the Toronto Argonauts brought home the Grey Cup, the first of three CFL titles in the decade. That same year, former Chicago Cubs pitcher Ferguson Jenkins became the first Canadian ever voted into Baseball's Hall of Fame. In 1993, the upstart Blue Jays made it two World Series wins in a row. By 1995, the National Basketball Association had awarded the first non-American franchises to Vancouver and Toronto, and while the Grizzlies and Raptors remained cellar-dwellers through the 90s, in Toronto a new facility—the Air Canada Centre—was in the works; it opened in February 1999, not only as the home of the Raptors but also of the Toronto Maple Leafs of the NHL.

The appearance of professional sports celebrities was almost commonplace at the Granite Club during the 1990s. In particular, club members had access to some of the greatest names in figure skating. Despite turning professional in 1984, Paul Martini and Barbara Underhill revisited club ice from time to time to rehearse their competitive and showcase routines. Brian Orser held seminars to coach young Granite skaters. Skating stars Katarina Witt (twice Olympic gold-medalist) and Jayne Torvill and her partner Christopher Dean (1984 Olympic ice dance gold-medalists) had also visited. As well, in 1992, the Granite Club gave special membership status to a couple of Canadian newcomers about to establish their own reputations on the world figure-skating stage—Karen Preston and Kurt Browning.

For Browning, the summer of 1992 was late in the process to be making crucial changes in the lead-up to the 1993 World Championships and the Olympic Games, scheduled for Lillehammer, Norway, in 1994. He already had three World Figure Skating Championships to his credit, but Browning was coping with a back injury and there was some pressure on him as the first athlete in the history of figure skating to successfully complete a quadruple jump in world competition. It was time for him to leave his Alberta roots behind and lift his skating to a new level. That's when he contacted Louis Stong at the Granite Club and the two made arrangements to meet with the board about a "special membership."

In 1992 the first President's Annual Snooker Tournament was held in the refurbished Billiards Room with over 30 participants.

The Granite's Michelle McDonald and Martin Smith become Canada's Ice Dance Champions in 1991.

"I remember taking Kurt for that interview with the board and members of the skating committee," recalls Stong. "I picked him up and he wasn't dressed properly. He's always been pretty casual. So we got him all duded up and sat waiting in a meeting room on the main floor. Then the directors walked in and Kurt conducted the best interview I've ever seen."

With the formalities complete, the Granite coaching team scrambled to find and develop two new programs for Browning almost overnight. Granite coach Marijane Stong came up with the idea of setting Kurt's long program to music from the 1943 Humphrey Bogart and Ingrid Bergman movie classic *Casablanca*. Together with choreographer Sandra Bezik, the Stongs felt that the "As Time Goes By" theme would broaden the scope of Kurt's musicality and showmanship.

Meanwhile, Louis Stong spent a day in a downtown Toronto music store listening room and came up with the drum solo from Led Zeppelin's "Bonzo's Montreaux" for Kurt's short program. He hired hip-hop music specialist Clarence Ford to don skates and help Kurt develop a robotic style of dance movements. Then, after months of rehearsal on and off the ice at the Granite, the Stongs decided to unveil Kurt Browning's new routines in front of friends, judges, media, and club members at the Granite.

Kurt Browning premiered his *Casablanca* program at the Granite

"We actually had a debut night," says Louis Stong. "We had the press, major skating officials and probably 150 invited guests at the club. Suddenly, Kurt's two new programs were big news... I remember driving to the club thinking, 'What have I done?'"

Everything was set up to showcase the Browning charm. Upon arrival, the reporters, judges, and club members were treated to wine and then escorted to seats around the ice surface. The lights dimmed. The romantic strains of the

Casablanca love theme began and Kurt premiered his new freeskate program. As the long routine was completed, the audience was on its feet applauding and calling for more. But Kurt needed a break before the short program, so he approached an open mike and announced, "I do need a little rest, so let's have a glass of wine and talk."

About half an hour later, after greeting and chatting with his audience, Kurt invited everyone to re-assemble by the ice surface, saying, "I hope you don't think I'm going to be a star in my second routine. Frankly, I'm really tired, so you're not going to see a triple axle, triple toe loop…"

"He was setting them up," says Stong, "because he gave them that and more in 'Bonzo's Montreaux.'"

"I was worried that the music wouldn't be accepted," Browning admitted later. "But it seemed to work."

"This is not music that you can count 1-2-3-4, and there are no moods in the music. It has rhythms," explained choreographer Ford. "But Kurt has a natural knack for it."

The press thought so too. The *Toronto Star* showered praise over his "freeskate to music from *Casablanca*, where he did a turn as Humphrey Bogart on blades, white jacket and all, complete with a brief stop for a smoke." Meanwhile, *The Globe and Mail* reported of his short program that "the son of a former rodeo rider has ridden into the street-dance style with ease."

In competition, the judges—at least at the 1993 Canadian and World Championships—loved the two programs as well. At Copps Coliseum in Hamilton, Browning's *Casablanca* routine scored 6.0s, as he took the national title. In Prague, he dazzled everybody and

Following a dinner to honour Kurt Browning and Frank Bogart with special Granite Club jackets, the skater suggested a performance featuring himself and the club's favourite musician. The "Bogart and Browning" evening was born. When the lights came up on the Granite ice surface that night, there was Frank Bogart on a riser in the middle of the ice with his grand piano playing the Casablanca theme while Browning skated his World Championship routine.

One of the hundreds of members watching said, "It was truly a Granite Club moment."

Over 450 members attended the "Bogart and Browning" evening in 1995; afterwards, they mingled with Kurt Browning, Josée Chouinard and Martini and Underhill

Kurt Browning on his way to the Winter Olympics in 1994

Granite member Rebecca Salisbury skated for the Canadian Junior National Team in 1994 and she placed first in the Junior World Trials that year. By 1995 she was Junior Ladies Champion of Canada. Granite skater Marcus Christensen won the 1995 Senior Men's Silver at the Canadian Championships.

won his fourth World title. And even though the 1994 Lillehammer Olympics were not as successful (Browning placed fifth), his short program and freeskate routines established new standards for creativity and innovation.

Kurt Browning continued his involvement at the Granite Club after the success of his campaign in the early 1990s. On September 1, 1999, he was appointed as the club's Skating Consultant, ready to put his World Championship experience to work developing the Skating Section.

Just as the skating program roared into the 1990s, the Tennis Section went from strength to strength. The sport remained a mainstay at the club and the section membership among the most active. However, facilities had not kept pace with the increase in members nor the resulting demand for court time.

In his "Report of the President," Garry Gale noted that upon moving to Bayview, "we built five outdoor courts and created a new Tennis Section. Since then, we have added another court and have enclosed four of them for winter play. The demand for court time is still enormous. Singles play is only allowed during off-peak times. Court bookings are issued only to those who are the first callers at 8:30 a.m. each day. Teaching time and time for junior play is restricted and some of our tournaments are held elsewhere."

The club's planning group was at its wits' end over the Tennis Section's space and scheduling dilemma, and the expansion of the fitness facilities the previous decade had made it clear that there wasn't much room to grow. Suddenly, several houses immediately north of the Bayview site came up for sale. Recalls Barbara Clarke, then incoming president, "The properties came up for sale on a Thursday afternoon.... We had to move on them right away... and we had made the purchase by Monday."

"I felt we should grab them while we had the chance," adds Ron Besse, then first vice-president. "We had a chance to buy two of them at one time. But it was a very controversial move."

The board met quickly to discuss the availability of the land. It debated ways and means of financing the purchase. It decided to assess the membership—$700 per family. It was not the best of times for such a move. Even though the club's 1990 budget showed a surplus, that fiscal year the club had made major expenditures to refurbish the fitness facility, the dining rooms, and the tennis bubble, as well as to complete a makeover of the ballroom and main lobby. On the larger financial front, the national economy seemed on the brink of another recession, the markets were in decline, the Goods and Services Tax had just become law, and the number of bankruptcies in Canada was the highest ever recorded.

Under normal circumstances, the annual general meeting of the club was not a heavily attended affair. Four hundred chairs would regularly be set up and many of those would not be filled. However, at the 1991 AGM, former board member David Brown remembers, "It was standing room only."

Granite members starred at the 1996 Ontario Masters Badminton Championships. Ross Clarke (left) and Jamie McKee won the Singles Championship in their respective age classes and then teamed up to win the Over 35 Men's Double. Molson Robertson won the Over 50 Men's Single Championship

After Granite chef Peter Oldfield joined the staff, the Granite began to offer cooking classes that showcased visiting chefs and a variety of cuisine, as well as offering recipes in the Granite News. By 1996, a take-out service had also been added.

Former president and director Walter Cassels sat on both North York municipal council and the Granite board and though he could remember heated debates in each, "I always enjoyed the Granite meetings because they weren't the least bit adversarial; we always came away friends."

When club Badminton pro Raphi Kanchanaraphi retired in November 1996, Tom Muir (left) and James Muir (right) joined in the farewell party and presented him with one of his custom built racquets

Barbara J. Clarke,
President, 1991

"The entire club rose up on its hind legs," says Phyllis Parker, "because [the board called for] an assessment and we'd never had an assessment."

Many felt, as former president Parker did, that the club took great pride in never having had an assessment in its 100-year history. Those members also felt the board had no right to spend that much money and assess a extra fee without first putting it to a vote among the membership. Christine Hindson saw the assessment from the other side. She was a relative newcomer on the board that year and while she didn't speak at the meeting, she favoured the purchase of the lots because she sensed "it was a great investment...that it would give us a future.... But I was surprised at the depth of feeling expressed."

"Still, sometimes you just have to go ahead and do what you know is right for the club," says Ron Besse. "There was a lot of controversy, but in the long term, I think it was one of the most significant moves we ever made."

Ultimately, the Granite Club purchased the 2372 and 2374 Bayview Avenue properties and it was expected that the assessment would fund the purchase by November 1992. While she commented in her "Report of the President," that "1991 was a year most people want to forget," Barbara Clarke emphasized that the club "now has some flexibility in planning the improvements of our existing physical plant to provide our members with the first class facility you have every right to expect." It would be a while—not until September 1994—but the tennis section would eventually see five new state-of-the-art courts and a protective bubble rise on those north properties, nearly doubling the amount of tennis that could be played year round by Granite members.

The 1990s were a time of the largest growth in tennis in the history of the club: by 1999, the section housed nearly 2400 members (750 men, 750 women, 460 junior boys and 380 junior girls) distributed among 11 courts and nine staff professionals. And just like the heyday of curling, if tennis players hadn't booked courts within an hour of 8:30 in the morning, there were few openings left. House leagues flourished. Pro-am leagues became busy. Clinics abounded. And junior programs were solidly booked. There were even inter-club leagues that allowed Granite players to compete in tournaments at other clubs in Toronto, Ottawa, or Montreal.

Club president Christine Hindson cut the ribbon to officially open the new tennis courts in 1994, while director Bob Torrens (left) looks on

"Our membership is more competitive than people realize," explained general manager Peter Fyvie. "These are successful people who have been successful in life, successful in business, highly competitive people by nature. Their children have the same genes. And when we started providing that kind of teaching level, they started rising to the occasion."*

"Through it all, we emphasize the social side of the game," says long-time tennis convener Ron Joshua, "You get to know a lot of people inside and outside the club just by 'hitting the ball.' That's as important an experience as winning."

"From our end," adds staff pro Gary Caron, "we're trying to strike a balance between the social, competitive, and instructional sides of the game," and both his attitude and regimen at the club

The Norman White Memorial Cup was inaugurated in 1999, and awarded annually for Sportsmanship at the Master's level in squash

The Granite's Sarah Gibbings won a place on the Ontario Badminton Team for the 1991 Canada Winter Games in Charlottetown. The young team came home with a bronze medal. By 1995, Granite members Caroline Gibbings and Carolyn Smith were helping Ontario win the Badminton Gold Medal at the Canada Winter Games.

The Munchkin Sports program for four- to six-year-olds introduced the kids to a variety of sports

In February 1993, the Granite hosted the Lapham Grant Cup, North America's oldest international squash tournament, which had rotated between Canadian and U.S. sites for 60 years. When the competition was over, the cup was on its way back to the U.S. However, as tournament vice-chairman David Hetherington noted, "We may have lost the cup, however in true Canadian style we still managed to spend more on beverage than we did on food."—Granite News

reflect that philosophy. Caron insists on making professional staff available to all ages and all calibres of players. Consequently, he's been there—racquet in hand—to work with daytime groups, with those who want to play casually after work, and to instruct junior members who are on the courts before and after school, because "we think juniors are the future of the club."

The Granite Club has always recognized that young members represent the core of the "family club" philosophy as well as future membership. The tennis conveners, committees, and professionals cultivated a kind of global view of sport. When the Munchkin players (those age four to six) attended Granite tennis programs, they also received professional instruction in badminton, squash, and curling, with a bit of bowling and fitness thrown in. And for those individual young players with exceptional talent, during the 1990s the club developed the T.E.A.M. Granite program, for Training Elite Athletic Members. The idea was to assemble 45 to 50 of the club's most promising young athletes regularly and to "surround winners with winners."

To be a T.E.A.M. Granite member, the young athlete had to be provincially or nationally ranked in one of the section sports—skating, aquatics, curling or the racquet sports. At least once a month, the club brought the young members together for presentations from fitness, nutritional, or motivational speakers. Initially, the goal was to inspire the young athletes to greater success, but ultimately, the concept has instilled pride, team spirit and confidence among the club's potential high-performance athletes.

The broader, more inclusive tennis programs of the 1990s at the Granite have gone further than that. With more court time allotted to the junior programs than ever, occasionally other Tennis Section members have felt crowded by the more than 800 junior members. To turn the situation into something positive, Pro Gary Caron and the tennis committee invited older, more seasoned members like John Elms to share their experience with the up-and-coming juniors.

Elms, a Granite Club member since his emigration from Trinidad in the 1950s, made full use of the club over the years—swimming and playing badminton, but his favourite recreational pursuit was tennis. In 1998, he was awarded a Granite Club Gold Crest for his achievements as a masters tennis player. He even became a member of the Tennis Umpires Association, officiating at provincial and national matches. When Caron introduced Elms as the "Over 70 provincial singles champion" the younger players suddenly took notice.

"I work with the kids," explains Elms, "and I try to put across to them that they've got ability and talent. All they have to do is harness it and work at it."

"Right now, in terms of programming," concludes Gary Caron, "we're looked at as the top in the country. There's a sense of pride because other clubs in Toronto are basically copying us.... But the membership and the management are tough on us. They set the standard and when we feel like we've almost reached it, they raise the bar. But we love the challenge."

In recent years, the Granite's professional staff have made much the same kind of initiative at the curling rink. Taking into account the long-standing family atmosphere of the club on weekends

The March 1995 meeting of the Ontario Tennis Association awarded the Granite Club Tennis Committee and staff the O.T.A. Junior Development Award for their extensive programs. The Granite program won the award four times during the decade.

After weeks of intensive training the Boys Under 16 Doubles Badminton team of Adam Culliford and Jeff Wolak won the gold in the [1992] Canadian Junior National competition.

In February 1993, Ann Davidson Purves and Jane Stodgell won the women's doubles event at the Ontario Tennis Association's Senior Provincial Indoor Championships.

and the fact that curling's profile was enhanced by becoming an official sport at the 1998 Nagano Olympics in Japan, the curling section inaugurated a "Little Rock" program. These Saturday sessions were designed to attract children to the Granite Club's founding sport. They were originally organized by parent volunteers on their own, but curling supervisor Kristine Moore got her staff involved too by providing instruction, arranging bonspiels, and drumming up prizes for the children who participated.

"The majority of the kids are nine to twelve years old," says Moore. "They throw smaller, 18-pound stones instead of the regular 42-pounders. We want to keep the sport social. In a lot of sports—figure skating and swimming—once a certain level of competence is reached, you either go competitive or you stop. With curling, we think it can remain social for as long as you want it to."

The Little Rock program for junior curlers

Deborah Scott became a curling convener at the Granite in the 1990s, but right from the beginning, curling was an important part of her family's social life. As a child in the 1960s, she learned curling from her father—Robert Tamblyn—by sliding coffee cans filled with cement on the outdoor rink at Eglinton Park in north Toronto. Then she curled with her father, brother, and sister at the Granite. Eventually she got her husband Jamie interested enough to try it and now their children—Geoffrey, Lindsay, and Emily—are playing at the Granite.

For Deborah, any time on the curling ice is pleasurable, whether it's the Business Girls house league play or the annual Robertson Bonspiel in March. It's the strategy of the game, its unpredictability, and the social interaction she enjoys, particularly with her regular rink mates. For four years, Scott has skipped a team with Dianne Hatch as vice, Barb Robertson-Mann as second, and Jayne Waggonner as lead. Each of the four has a different personality, each a different work and

Ronald D. Besse,
President, 1992

family schedule. Nevertheless, the rink's chemistry—on and off the ice—makes for a lot of fun and enough wins to satisfy their competitive drive.

"Funny, but the games I tend to remember are the ones when the wheels came off," says Deborah Scott. "One game, a house league game, we were up by six. The game was in hand. Then all of a sudden, not one of us could make a shot. I mean the front end missed, the second missed, my vice missed. And she said, 'Okay Deb, it's up to you.' And I'm thinking, 'Right. No problem. So why am I worried? I'm curling beautifully today.' And we ended up losing the game."

As humbling as the game can sometimes be, curling for the Granite has many positive aspects. The atmosphere of the club allows Deborah Scott's rink to be as social or as competitive as it wishes. Each season, during opening weekends at the Granite, the club invites national and world-calibre players to talk and teach strategy, delivery, release, sweeping, take-outs, and angles of the game. Not surprisingly, when her rink travels to out-of-town bonspiels, Deborah has come to realize there's a cachet attached to her home club and a reputation that must be upheld. Once an opposing curler finds out she's from the Granite, there's a short pause before Scott's opponent usually says, "Oh-oh. We're in trouble now."

In 1993 the Canada Life curling legacy came to an end. The year before, the Granite Club seized two final moments of Canada Life glory. Skip John Francis's rink (Bob Hollingshead, vice; John Bowlby, second; and Ray Murray, lead) won the Beacon event for curlers forty and older, and the Ross Solomon trophy, for men 65 and over, was won by Jack Coulter's rink (Tom Crouch, vice; Sandy McTavish, second, George Clarke, lead. Coulter was unable to make the final game, so Crouch moved up to skip and Orville "Woody" Wood took over the vice-skip position.) Both rinks won all six games in their events. Solomon, after whom the seniors' event was named, had been the bonspiel's popular draw master for more than 20 years. The Canada Life was replaced by a bonspiel sponsored by Investors Group.

William H. Gleed,
President, 1993

In February 1992, Alf Phillips Jr. won the Granite Men's Invitational, and during league play the same month, Alf did something he hadn't done in over 35 years of curling. He and his team scored an eight end— the "hole in one" of curling.

Over the years, the reputation of Granite Club curlers, swimmers, skaters, and racquet sport players may well have preceded them. However, intimidation was rarely a factor when club runners entered outside competitions. Indeed, when one group of Granite Club runners—known affectionately as Joe's Joggers—ventured beyond the grounds of the club, the glory was not in the winning, but in the participating.*

Originally group founder Joe Sorbara had been determined to go into the Royal Ontario Museum's 24-hour relay race and had pulled together the minimum 20 runners to do it. Sorbara's team managed to arrive with "Joe's Joggers" T-shirts and bags, and had a tent near the start-finish line and a room with a shower at the Park Plaza. Joe's Joggers raised about $15 000 during their

first formal competitive run, but didn't stop at the end of the ROM relay. A corps of runners continued to meet mornings at the fitness room of the club, to stretch, and then head out onto Bayview Avenue to jog.

"At any one time there would have been 10 or 12 of us," recalls Bonnie Mactavish Hunter. "We'd do a bit of a warm-up at 6 or 6:30 in the morning and then run down Bayview. The friendships formed in that group became a very important part of my life."

Joe's Joggers made quite a sight. Few wore colour-coordinated outfits; they were just a rainbow of shorts, shirts, scarves, and sweat pants. Some wore toques (or balaclavas in the winter); others

Modern lawn bowling and badminton facilities remained popular in the 1990s.

baseball caps and in the rain, green garbage bags were thrown over top. Sometimes they ran along sidewalks; in one snowstorm they ran right down the centre of the street. If there was ever a fire in the area, they'd be sure to run past it. Mactavish Hunter frequently brought her golden retriever, Cavu, along for the run and fellow jogger John Hamilton, his Jack Russell, McGriff. Most often the run took them into the park behind Sunnybrook Hospital and then along a three-, five-, or seven-mile route, depending upon how ambitious they were or how close they were to running a marathon.

In November of 1993, the Fitness Section announced a twelve-month program known as the Century Club to reward members who did 100 workouts during that period. By April 1994, two members—Mac Cuddy and Stewart Henderson— were ready to claim the honour.

On January 5, 1998, club members gained access to a new in-house sports injury clinic operated by King's Health Centre. The clinic featured chiropractic and physiotherapy services, as well as a nurse on duty during weekdays.

M. Christine Hindson,
President, 1994

*Former Granite Club swimming
coach Tommy Walker was inducted
into the Swim Ontario Hall of Fame
in 1991. Out-of-town member Harry
Class was also honoured for his
success as a Master Swimmer, as
well as for his support of the sport.*

*In April 1994, two Granite Club
swimmers were inducted into the
Swim Ontario Hall of Fame—Betty
Tancock for her success as a competitive and synchronized swimmer and
Alf Phillips Sr., for competitive
swimming and diving.*

"Joe ran with me in my first Toronto Marathon," recalls Mactavish Hunter. "We had a pact that we would run a marathon when we were 40, and he's 10 years older than I am. So when I was 40 and he was 50, he ran the last 10 kilometres of the Toronto Marathon with me."

The friendships created among Joe's Joggers have been lasting and deep. Despite an injury to his thigh, one year Bill MacLatchy persisted in joining the morning jog, riding alongside on his bicycle. When her sister died suddenly, Mactavish Hunter found great comfort and support from her jogging friends. And when the son of another runner in the group died, Joe Sorbara remembers, "many mornings as we ran that's what we talked about. We ran about the same speed, so we spent a lot of time together and talked."

"If you came to the run feeling lousy," adds Bill MacLatchy, "you'd get it that day, because everybody'd get on your back, razz you, or boost you up, whatever was needed. We never gave anybody a chance to be too depressed."

In fact, about 1993, when time constraints and personal stresses forced Sorbara himself to miss weeks of Joe's Joggers sessions, the group knew it had to do something to bring him back into the fold. One morning they ran to Sorbara's house, assembled on the driveway and called for him to come out. They threatened to change the name of the group to "Hammer's Hounds" in honour of runner John "Hammer" Hamilton. Then they dowsed a Joe's Joggers shirt with lighter fluid and set it on fire as they chanted, "It's over, Joe. It's over, Joe." Sorbara came back.

In recent years, members of Joe's Joggers gathered for breakfast too. At first, they just shared muffins and sometimes secretly drank champagne and orange juice. Then they formalized things by meeting in the SkyLite Lounge after their early morning jog for a meal before going about the day's business. Other early-rising members began joining, among them, squash player Scott Dulmage, swimmer Shirley Larson Minot, runner Rod McClelland, and fitness enthusiasts Joan and Ian Mactavish.

"We call ourselves the Breakfast Bunch," says Joan Mactavish, who's been taking fitness classes at the Granite since the 1960s. "There can be as many as 30 of us in the SkyLite... Of all the groups we've had around us throughout our lives, this one is probably my favourite...the most comfortable to be with."

The Granite Club—from its board to its staff to its membership—has always taken great pride in filling the calendar with a continuing parade of events to attract and involve the greatest number of members.* One of the gaps in the year—the week-long March break, when students and their families were looking for something to do—was traditionally kicked off with the club's annual live stage show in the ballroom. The Granite Revue (known until 1972 when the club moved to Bayview as the St. Patrick's Day Show) grew in the 1980s and 1990s to become one of the club's most highly attended and anticipated events.

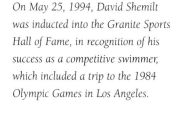

"Each year about Christmas, a notice would go out in the *Granite Club News*," says Alex Hainey, producer of the Granite Revue for a dozen years. "It was sort of a casting call for any members who wanted to perform in the show."

That was the way Hainey himself first got involved. About 1981, when the notice appeared in the club newsletter, he rented a kilt and arrived at the audition prepared to do an imitation of British entertainer Sir Harry Lauder. He sang a medley of Scottish tunes and got the nod to appear in the Granite Revue, entitled "Broadway and Burlesque."

On May 25, 1994, David Shemilt was inducted into the Granite Sports Hall of Fame, in recognition of his success as a competitive swimmer, which included a trip to the 1984 Olympic Games in Los Angeles.

The Granite's Executive chef Jim Edwards joined Canada's team at the Culinary Olympics in Luxembourg in the fall of 1998.

Rollerblading class at the Granite

In July 1993 the Granite's activities office offered its first clinic on inline skating—provided members were properly outfitted in protective gear. In 1994, in addition to two-year program to bring new Cybex machines in the Fitness area, the Granite announced the commencement of line dancing classes in the ballroom.

Dance instructor Shirley Temple (left) with The Uptown Strutters, who have performed at the Granite as well as Roy Thompson Hall

Robert W. Torrens, President, 1995

From that first Granite Revue on, Alex Hainey found himself deeply involved as the show's producer—casting singers, dancers, and individual acts each December, then choosing a theme and writing the script, and finally working with the behind-the-scenes crew to pull the show together by the beginning of March break.

During his years as producer, Alex Hainey worked with many dedicated volunteers. Donna-Dale Smith organized the music; rhythmic dance and tap instructor Shirley Temple sorted out the dancers.

"We'd get a lot of people involved, even if they couldn't sing. We'd put them in a group around those who could. The same with the dancers. We tried to let anybody who wanted, to be in it..."

In March of 1999, the Granite Club hosted perhaps its most celebrated squash competition—the Canadian Mixed Doubles. Fifty teams from across Ontario, Quebec and parts of the U.S. came to the Granite Club. The club was festooned in maple leaf flags and red and white balloons. The programs were red and white. And the tin on the two Granite courts was also coloured with red and white. Each of the 100 competitors received white track suits and the competition garnered rave reviews as "the most successful national mixed doubles in the history of the event."

Largely responsible for these accolades was one of its organizers—Granite Club member Lolly Gillen. She and her fellow co-ordinators managed to attract some of the best names in the game—including Melanie Jans and Pat Richardson, Jane Powell and Ted Ruse.

"We really dug deep to pull in the talent," said Gillen. "We did a bang up job. It was great for the Granite. It was great for the sport." What's more, a Granite Club member made it through to the finals in every open event: Michael Pirnak in the men's open, Mike Manley in the men's 50 and Lolly Gillen in the women's 40.

Lolly Gillen began playing squash about 1972. During a doubles match on the Granite squash courts, Lolly (who had never played squash) stood on the sidelines and watched a friend, John Shales, in competition. Gillen's right leg was almost completely cast in plaster, the result of reconstructive surgery to repair a knee damaged in a horseback riding accident.

"Do you play squash?" Lolly Gillen was asked by another spectator.

"No, I don't." She pointed down at her leg.

"Well, come on," said the man.

Dubious of the invitation, Gillen joined the man in an adjoining singles court. He showed her how to hold and swing the squash racquet and (despite her leg cast) how she could play the game from one spot. Not having to move made the exercise that much more enticing and Gillen came off the court invigorated and truly enthused about the game. Her friend then told her who her partner had been. "One of the greatest squash players in the world," he said. "Sharif Khan!"

The Granite's Scott Dulmage and his partner Brendan Clark of Montreal won the Canadian Men's Squash Doubles Championship in the open draw in March 1997.

Lolly Gillen and Sharif Khan, 1993 Ontario Veterans' Mixed Double Champions

Lolly Gillen (left), Andrew Slater (floor), Alan Grant (airborne) and Susan Smeaton (right) battle for points in the 1989 Convener's Cup competition

In 1995, the Squash Section inaugurated the Elaine Misurka Memorial Award, for the Ladies' Handicap Singles Champion. The first winner was Jill McCutcheon.

Before long, Gillen was out of her cast and eager to get involved in the Squash Section at the Granite. Despite being younger than most of the club's house league players, she took to the game and to fellow Granite squash players and was soon invited to tournaments and helping to organize them. By the late 1980s, she was competing nationally and internationally. She won the B.C. Open Mixed Doubles (with Alan Grant) championship in 1988 and 1989, the Ontario Open Mixed Doubles in 1990 (with Alan Grant) and 1993 (with Sharif Khan); and she won the World Women's 40+ Doubles championship in 1996 and 1998—two world titles and six Canadian titles and, just as important, eight Granite Club Gold Crests.

In January 1993, when he wrote the final edition of his "President's Corner" column in the *Granite News*, Ron Besse had a long list of accomplishments to look back on, and one big item left on his wish list: an 18-hole golf course within 30 kilometres of the club.

"I believe the board should never be planning today and tomorrow. It should be planning twenty years from today...a vision of the club in the future. And in my mind the Granite Club, going into the next century, [has] to have a golf club. It's the only thing we're missing."

Golf was not new to the Granite. For years there had been golf instruction at the clubhouse, particularly a winter golf school. But the idea of adding a Golf Section and a course had only been

entertained occasionally. (The last serious opportunity to buy a course had been turned down in 1932, when the club was in dire financial straits.) Besse's remarks sparked a lot of serious conversation around the club. Board member Milton Hess received several calls from Granite members who suggested the club go out and acquire an existing golf course. Indeed, one had just opened in the Toronto area, but because of insufficient membership and depressed real estate values at the time, it appeared to be available for purchase.

"Knowing a golf course was available," says Hess, "we raised the concept of a golf course, informally, following a board meeting. There was consensus that this wasn't a bad idea, one we ought to pursue."

Also on the board at that time and very familiar with golf course development was Paul Lavelle. He picked up on the idea and during a subsequent trip through Calgary, visited the Glencoe Club

J. Michael Horgan,
President, 1996

L. Milton Hess,
President, 1997

to determine what the acquisition of a golf course had meant to their club and its membership. The Glencoe was similar in size to the Granite, with comparable athletic facilities and a similar "family club" program. Like the Granite, a large number of Glencoe members were members of other golf clubs prior to the Glencoe's own golf expansion. In his report to the board in June 1993, Lavelle summarized the Glencoe experience:

> in 1984 the Glencoe Club acquired a partly completed golf course facility.... The proposal to the members required subscriptions from 400 golf members as a condition of purchase...and [was] approved on a 93 per cent favourable vote.... The addition of a fine golf course to the club's facilities has been an unqualified success, not only for those members who use it, but also for the Glencoe as a whole.

Encouraged by the Glencoe experience, the board launched a club-wide survey that included questions about a proposed golf course option. By 1994, the club had queried every member household about incorporating a golf course into the Granite Club. More than 41 per cent of the questionnaires were returned and they contained nearly 2000 paragraphs of responses. It was clear to the president at the time, Christine Hindson, that "there are many active golfers in our club. And the majority of respondents like the concept of golf as an athletic activity for the Granite Club." The board formed the Golf Planning Committee to analyze the survey responses and to formulate criteria for a golf initiative.

Board member Milton Hess worked on the Golf Planning Committee. He wasn't a golfer, but was convinced that the golf course proposal was a wise one, principally because of the Glencoe report, but also because "three out of four of our boys were playing golf and I never introduced them to it. I felt it was something young people across North America were taking to. And it seemed like our timing was right." The Golf Planning Committee also sought the advice of past presidents, including Bob Marshall, who had presided over the Granite's transition to Bayview in the early 1970s. He was a lifelong golfer and had been on the boards of several golf clubs in Toronto.

In the two years that followed, the Granite bid on a number of existing golf courses in the Toronto area, but since any offer to buy a course was conditional on support from a majority of Granite members, none of the offers to purchase could be immediate. None panned out. In order to give itself more flexibility, the board organized a special meeting—in November 1996—at which "the proposition was put forward to approve the addition of golf to the club facilities on the basis that it would be financed by those who wish to play golf and not by the club itself." The resolution was carried.

"That was an important milestone in our progress," says Paul Lavelle. "That approval gave the board and its committees the ability to deal from a much stronger position in any further negotiations for a property."

In effect, the board was asking the membership how many would pay $500 as an expression of serious interest in golf. More than 400 Granite members and/or families responded. In the spring of 1997, with the endorsement and the financial backing from Granite members, the board dis-

In November 1996, the club launched its website: http:www.graniteclub.com Shortly after, computer classes became part of the Activities roster.

World renowned golf architect Thomas McBroom (centre) and associates review construction plans.

Paul M. Lavelle,
President, 1998

cussed a golf course property being developed in Uxbridge, northeast of Toronto. The board went so far as to show the property to Granite members who had pre-invested in the Granite golf initiative. However, the 45-minute driving time from the Bayview clubhouse proved prohibitive.

Not long after, an engineering, planning and environmental firm—Dillon Consulting—notified the Granite board of another property northeast of Toronto, near Stouffville. The Wilson property was under 35 minutes from the Bayview clubhouse. It seemed ideal, if slightly smaller than what the board wanted for an 18-hole facility. However, between January and June of 1998, as approvals and financing of the purchase were being put in place, additional, adjacent properties that would fill out the course to a more appropriate size became available.

With the sale complete, the Golf Development Committee attended to "a host of approvals needed before construction could begin," explains Paul Lavelle. "That took us from the summer of 1998 through the spring of 1999. But we started construction in April 1999...with golf scheduled to begin July 1, 2000."

Hired to design the Granite course was renowned Canadian course architect, Tom McBroom, three-time winner of *Golf Digest*'s "Best New Course in Canada" award. He was asked to design a facility that could be played and enjoyed by both a learning golfer and an experienced low-handicapper; that meant building multiple tees on every hole, as well as including a variety of skill challenges. The other criterion Granite golfers demanded was that the course be "walkable"—not requiring powered golf carts, and that it be as much shaded as sunlit. As a result, the McBroom

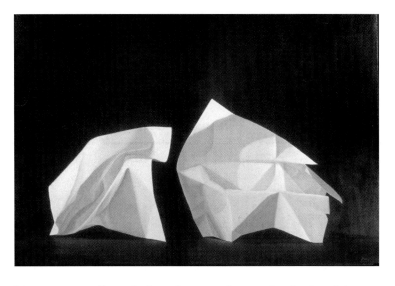

"Locked in Migration, to Petrus Christus" by David Bierk

design included plenty of open fairways as well as sheltered areas, the gently sloping fairways meant that it would be playable on foot. McBroom obviously enjoyed the challenge of the project; not only did he answer all the demands the Golf Development Committee put before him, he and his family joined the Granite Club.

"I think the single biggest differentiating factor between Granite Golf and any other golf club," continues Paul Lavelle, "is that it's a family oriented golf club, right from scratch. It will be gender neutral and will cater very much as the Granite Club does to the whole family. There'll be practice facilities for children as well as adults. We hope to have a mini-course the children can learn to play golf on before they're capable of playing on the full course. And husbands and wives, mothers and fathers, all members of the club can use the club in the same way they do the Granite."

As in other projects at the Granite, not only did the golf initiative move smoothly and comfortably into the club's "family club" mandate, it also served broader purposes. In summer, the course lands provide a summer camp-like atmosphere for children, with golf lessons and nature walks. In

In 1990 the Art Committee was delighted to receive a 1925 Christmas card designed by Frank Johnson, as a welcome addition to the club's "Group of Seven Collection," courtesy of members Esther and Ralph Reiner.

The first Granite Golf event, "Swing Club" took place on January 16, 1997. The ballroom was transformed into a 9-hole golf activity course; members could take part in a clinic, meet the course designer or chat with CPGA golf professionals

Peter D. Singer, President, 1999

the winter, the course offers an ideal setting for cross-country skiing, skating, or hiking. The Granite Golf site was planned as a year-round facility for members and their families who have more varied athletic interests than ever before, and a desire to enjoy the club in all four seasons.

As the golf club design was taking shape in the late 1990s, so were plans for a complete make-over of the Bayview location. After nearly 20 years of operation, "the property was physically not in the best shape" says general manager Peter Fyvie. "It was tired and had a look from another era. Something had to be done." After receiving a number of submissions, the Granite board chose Kuwabara Payne McKenna and Blumberg Architects to take the club facilities beyond the year 2000. The firm had seven Governor General's Awards for Architecture to its credit, with designs that included buildings at the University of Toronto and Queen's University and Kitchener City Hall.

"The prime objective of the current master plan," explained the K.P.M.B. Architects' 1998 renewal document, "is to re-invigorate, freshen and re-imagine the club for the eve of the new millennium and years to come....In design and expression, the new architecture of interior design, protects the club's traditional image of elegance, sophistication and prosperity, while creating a contemporary classic look; lighter, brighter, more materially rich, yet timeless in design."

In terms of the Granite Club building, the architects planned to remove some interior walls in order to create more space, while adding more glass to perimeter walls to invite more light in and

The architect's rendering of a proposed bistro for dining with a view to the terrace

The dining room in the late 1990s

increase the facility's contact with the nature around it. They also planned a re-design of the club's main north-south corridor (Peacock Alley) into a series of galleries; the addition of a new terrace, complete with awnings and lanterns; the reworking of windows in the dining area; the redecorating of the dining areas, the addition of a wine-tasting room and aperitif bar; and the installation of a food promenade in the club's main restaurant. The resulting atmosphere, in the words of the

On Thursday, January 28th, 1993, 56 Scots arrived at the club for a party to wind up their tour of Canada. The Strathcona Cup, contested every five years since 1909, alternates competitions between Scotland and Canada. In 1988, Canada had beaten the Scots in Scotland. Seven Scottish teams visited the west and seven took an eastern tour, and the Scots recaptured the 17th edition of the Cup.

L. Peter Sharpe,
President, 2000

architects, "will be warm, up-scale and stylish...a restaurant of the highest calibre to contend with the likes of the best restaurants in Toronto...one in which members will naturally be inclined to dine and entertain with a sense of pride."

Pride in their club is a given among Granite members. It's been that way since the beginning. Whether it was athletic achievements or the longevity of a tradition such as Frank Bogart's Saturday-night big-band music, or the enthusiasm of the volunteers who participated each year in the Skating Carnival, the Robertson Bonspiel variety show or the Granite Revue, members of the institution have always spoken in glowing terms of their club. Each has an unforgettable memory. Each has a favourite place or time in the club. Each has a personal achievement or experience that wouldn't have happened without the Granite Club. Each returns to the club again and again because it offers comfort, familiarity, recreation, service, and pleasure. The Granite Club has left deep impressions on those who've enjoyed the privilege of membership.

PRESIDENTS

TORONTO GRANITE CURLING CLUB

St. Mary Street, 1875—1880
Church Street, 1880—1926

Year	President	Year	President
1875-78	James Lamond Smith	1893-94	Robert M. McClain
1878-80	William Ramsay	1894-95	Arthur Brindley Lee
1880-81	W.F. Davison	1895-96	Wilbur Cassius Matthews
1881-82	Thomas McCraken	1896-97	Bernard Jennings
1882-83	Donald M. McEwan	1897-98	W.J. McMurtry
1883-84	Walter Gibson Pringle Cassels, Q.C.	1898-99	George Ross Hargraft
1884-85	Robert Jaffray	1899-1900	William A.J. Littlejohn
1885-86	Walter Taylor	1900-01	Robert Lawrence Patterson
1886-87	Charles C. Dalton	1901-02	Edward A. Badenach
1887-88	Daniel Robert Wilkie	1902-03	C.P. Smith
1888-89	James Alexander Hedley	1903-04	George Horace Gooderham
1889-90	Robert Henry Bethune	1904-05	Charles Boeckh
1890-91	William Badenach	1905-06	George Horace Gooderham
1891-92	Adam Henry Wright, M.D.	1906-07	Benjamin Elmore Hawke, M.D.
1892-93	Adam Rutherford Creelman	1907-08	Spencer Love

Year	President	Year	President
1908-09	G.D. Shields	1958-59	William Clement Fisher
1909-10	A.E. Trow	1960-61	Robert Rae
1910-11	Thomas Rennie	1962-63	J. Palmer Kent, Q.C.
1911-12	Robert Chisholm Davison	1964-65	James H. Joyce
1912-13	M. Rawlinson	1966-67	J. Stanley Whitehead
1913-14	Holcombe Thomas Wilson	1968-69	John D. Murray
1914-15	E.L. Williams	1970-71	T. Millar Chase
1915-16	Arthur Elliott Dalton	1972-73	Dr. Robert W. Marshall
1916-17	T.H. Brunton	1974	Dixon S. Chant
1917-18	Edward Bentley Stockdale	1975	J. Ronald Grills
1918-19	Harold Eastwood Beatty	1976	A. Hazlett Lemmon
1919-20	Sam Harris	1977	Samuel T. Paton
1920-21	Edward Bentley Stockdale	1978	T. Brad Hatch
1921-22	W.G. Lumbers	1979	George H. Scott
1922-23	William Austin Suckling	1980	Donald L. Angus
1923-26	Frank Shannon	1981	William S. Storey
		1982	George W. Gilmour
		1983	Phyllis L. Parker

GRANITE CLUB

St. Clair Avenue 1925—1972
Bayview Avenue 1972

Year	President	Year	President
1925-31	Frank Shannon	1984	Arthur Don Sisley
1932-33	Thomas Rennie	1985	Walter Gibson Cassels, Q.C.
1934-36	George Herbert Rennie	1986	Robert Ginn
1937	Frank Harrison Littlefield	1987	David A. Brown
1938	Thomas N. Phelan, K.C.	1988	Kenneth G. Belbeck
1939-41	David C. Haig	1989	John W. Brooke
1942-44	Joseph M. Bullen, K.C.	1990	Garry G. Gale
1945-46	Roy Sharvel McPherson	1991	Barbara J. Clarke
1947-49	John Hutton Riddel	1992	Ronald D. Besse
1950-51	W. Reginald Shaw	1993	William H. Gleed
1952-53	A. Lowry A. Richardson	1994	M. Christine Hindson
1954-55	H.L. Steele	1995	Robert W. Torrens
1956-57	Lucien E. Messinger	1996	J. Michael Horgan
		1997	L. Milton Hess
		1998	Paul M. Lavelle
		1999	Peter D. Singer
		2000	L. Peter Sharpe

SPORTS HALL OF FAME

BARBARA BEREZOWSKI AND DAVID PORTER   Senior Dance Skating Champions of Canada - 1975; Members of World Team - 1973, 1974, 1975

LOUISE BERTRAM (MRS. S.M. HULBIG) AND STEWART REBURN   Canadian Pair Skating Champions - 1935; represented Canada in Olympics at Garmisch - Partenkirchen, Germany - 1936; 4th in World Pair Championship, Paris, France - 1936

DOROTHY ANNE CALEY (MRS. ARTHUR O. KLEIN)   Canadian Junior Ladies Figure Skating Champion - 1936; Canadian Senior Ladies Figure Skating Champion - 1937

HAZEL CALEY (MRS. JACK MCTAVISH)   North American Fours Skating Champion - 1939

MARY CASSON   Canadian Free Style Swimming Champion (880 yards, 1,000 yards, 1 mile) -1928

HARRY CLASS   Canadian 3-metre Board Diving Champion - 1935, 1936, 1938, 1943

FRANK A. CREAGHAN   Canadian Light Heavyweight Boxing Champion - 1949

FRANCES DAFOE C.M, O. AND NORRIS BOWDEN   Canadian Pair Skating Champions - 1952, 1953, 1954, 1955; Canadian Dance Champions - 1952; North American Pair Champions - 1953-54, 1955-56; Silver Medalists World and Olympic Pair Competitions - 1956; World Pair Champions - 1953, 1954

SCOTT DULMAGE   Canadian Men's Open Doubles Squash Champion - 1991, 1995, 1997; U.S. Intercollegiate Hardball Champion - 1989; U.S. Open Hardball Champion - 1988; Canadian Junior and Senior Hardball Champion - 1987; Ontario Junior and Senior Hardball Champion - 1987

JOHN C. (JACK) EASTWOOD   Canadian Fours Skating Champion, 1926, 1927; represented Canada in Olympics, 1928; represented Canada in World's Championships, 1928-29, 1932; Canadian Waltz Champion 1931; Canadian Tenstep Champion 1936

CECIL EUSTACE-SMITH (MRS. CECIL HEDSTROM)   Silver Medal World Skating Championship - 1924, 1930; Canadian Senior Ladies Skating Champion - 1925, 1926; Canadian Fours Champion - 1926, 1927; represented Canada in Olympics - 1924, 1928

MAUDE EUSTACE-SMITH (MRS. JOHN A. MCDOUGALD)   Canadian Four Skating Champion -1926, 1927; represented Canada in the Olympics - 1924, 1928; Canadian World Team - 1928, 1930, 1932

F. ROBERT FISHER   Swimming, Canadian Record Holder, 200-yard Backstroke - 1959; 220-yard Backstroke - 1959; Canadian Intercollegiate Champion, 200-yard Backstroke - 1959, 1960, 1961, 1962

RUBY (MRS. FRANK H.) FISHER   Canadian Ladies Doubles Tennis Champion - 1938 and 1948

PETER HAROLD FROST   Canadian Mixed Doubles Squash Champion - 1979, 1981, 1982, 1985

THOMAS H. GRAHAM   Canadian Senior Men's Doubles Badminton Champion - 1965; Canadian Mixed Doubles Badminton Champion - 1972, 1973

TORONTO GRANITES   Olympic Hockey Champions - 1924: Peter G. Campbell, Harry Ellis Watson, William A. Hewitt, Duncan Brown Munro, Frank J. Rankin, Harold McMunn, Albert J. McCaffery, Reginald Joseph Smith, William Beattie Ramsay, Ernest J. Collett, Cyril Slater, Jack A. Cameron.

BARBARA GRATTON (MRS. B. KELLY)   Canadian Senior Figure Skating Champion - 1953, 1954; 3rd North American Figure Skating Championships - 1953; 4th World Figure Skating Championships - 1954

RICHARD (RICK) GRUNEAU   Water Skiing, Gold and Silver Medalist, Jumping and Figures, Canada Summer Games - 1969; Runner Up, Jumping in U.S. Masters (Petersburg) - 1970; 1st Figure and Overall, Canadian-American Invitational - 1973; Canadian Senior Men's Figure Championships and Canadian Record Holder - 1975

MICHAEL L. GUINNESS   Canadian Open Games Champion, 400 and 800 metre - 1972; 5 previous Canadian records

DAVID CONBOY HETHERINGTON   Canadian Doubles Champion, Squash - 1982

SIDNEY C. HETHERINGTON   Canadian Veterans Singles Champion, Squash - 1951

DONALD JACKSON   Canadian Senior Champion - 1959, 1960, 1961, 1962; North American Champion - 1959, 1961; Olympics Bronze Medal - 1960; World Champion - 1962; International Athlete of the Year - 1962

CANDACE JONES   Canadian Senior Pair Skating Champion - 1975; Member of World Skating Team - 1975

GAY KIRKPATRICK   Quarterback, Balmy Beach Football Team, Grey Cup Champions - 1930

RALPH S. McCREATH   Canadian Fours Skating Champion - 1938; North American Skating Pair Champion - 1937, 1941; Canadian Pairs Skating Champion - 1936, 1941; Canadian Senior Skating Champion - 1940, 1941, 1946; North American Fours Champion - 1939; North American Skating Champion - 1941

JOAN F. (MRS. ALAN) McDONALD   Canadian Ladies' Archery Champion - 1962, 1963, 1964, 1965, 1966; represented Canada in World Championships - 1965, 1967, 1975; Silver Medal -1976

JAMES K. McKEE   Canadian Men's Singles Badminton Champion - 1977-78; Pan American Games Men's Singles & Doubles Champion - 1977; Pan American Games Men's Singles & Doubles Champion - 1978; Pan American Games Men's Doubles Champion (Badminton) - 1979

WILLIAM G. McLACHLAN   Ice Dance Champion of Canada - 1957, 1958, 1959, 1960, 1961, 1962; North American Ice Dance Champion 1957, 1959, 1961; Runner Up, World Ice Dance Championship - 1957, 1959, 1960

DR. PETER MINGLE   Canadian Champion, 100-yard Backstroke - 1947, 1948, 1950, 1951; represented Canada in the 100-metre Backstroke - 1948 Olympics

SUZANNE MORROW (DR. SUZANNE M. FRANCIS)   Senior Canadian Skating Pair Champion - 1947, 1948; North American Pair Champion - 1947; Senior Canadian Dance Champion - 1948; World Championships Bronze Medal - 1948; Olympics Bronze Medal Pair - 1948; Senior Canadian Singles - 1949, 1950, 1951; World Team Member Singles - 1950, 1951, 1952, 1953; Olympics 6th Place - Singles - 1952

JOHN G. MUIR SR.   National Open Doubles Badminton Champion - 1926, 1927, 1929

ELEANOR O'MEARA (MRS. R. G. PHELAN)   Canadian Singles Figure Skating Championship - 1936, 1938; Canadian Pair Champion, 1941, 1942; North American Pairs Championship 1941

RODERICK G. PHELAN   Canadian Singles Badminton Champion - 1935; Canadian Doubles Badminton Champion - 1938, 1939

ALFRED PHILLIPS, JR.   Skip, Canadian Curling Champions - 1967

ALFRED PHILLIPS. SR.   Canadian 3-metre Springboard Diving Champion - 1926, 1927, 1928, 1929, 1930, 1931, 1932, 1933, 1934; Canadian Platform Diving Champion - 1928, 1929, 1930, 1931, 1932, 1933, 1934; British Empire 3-metre Springboard Diving Champion - 1930; British Empire 3-metre Platform Diving Champion - 1930; represented Canada in Olympic Games Amsterdam Holland - 1928; represented Canada in Olympic Games - 1932; Inducted in Aquatic Hall of Fame, Winnipeg - June 19th 1971

ALFRED PHILLIPS, SR., W. George Cowan, Jack (Sandy) McTavish, Jack Young National Seniors Curling Champions - 1969

STANLEY G. REID   Canadian Champion War Canoe - 1910, 1911, 1912, 1913; Canadian Champion Tandem, 1911

BARBARA ANN SCOTT (MRS. T.V. KING)   Canadian Figure Skating Champion - 1944, 1945, 1946, 1948; North American Skating Champion - 1945, 1947; European Skating Champion - 1947, 1948; Olympic Champion - 1948; World Skating Champion - 1947, 1948

DR. J.M. (MAC) SHELDON   Played Defence on two Canadian Senior Hockey Championship Teams: Allan Cup Winners, Toronto Dentals - 1917; Allan Cup Winners, Toronto Granites - 1922

DAVID SHEMILT   Canadian Swimming Champion, 1500-metre Freestyle - 1983 Summer, 1985 Summer; Canadian Champion 400-metre Freestyle - 1985

Winter, Summer 1985; Olympic Trials Champion, 1500-metre Freestyle - 1984; represented Canada in the 1984 Olympics, Placed 7th in final; C.I.A.U. Champion (Intercollegiate): 200-metre Freestyle - 1983; 1500-metre Freestyle 1983; 1500-metre Freestyle - 1984;

CHARLES F.T. SNELLING   Canadian Senior Men's Skating Champion - 1954, 1955, 1956, 1957, 1958, 1964

NIGEL STEPHENS   Canadian Senior Figure Skating Champion - 1945

MARLENE STEWART (MRS. J. DOUGLAS STREIT)   Canadian Ladies Golf Open Amateur Champion - 1951, 1954, 1955, 1956, 1958, 1959, 1963, 1968, 1969, 1972, 1973; Canadian Ladies Closed Invitation Champion - 1951, 1952, 1953, 1954, 1955, 1956, 1957, 1958, 1959, 1963, 1968; British Ladies Amateur Open Champion - 1953; U.S. Ladies Amateur Open Champion - 1956; Australian Ladies Open Champion - 1963; Marlene Streit is the only title holder to win all four Open Championships

MARILYN RUTH TAKE (MRS. WITTSTOCK)   Canadian Senior Figure Skating Champion - 1947

BARBARA UNDERHILL AND PAUL MARTINI   World Pair Champions - 1984; Five Times Canadian Pair Champions; Seven Times World Professional Pair Champions

BARBARA WAGNER (MRS. J.D. GROGAN) AND ROBERT PAUL   Canadian Pair Skating Champions - 1956, 1957; North American Pair Champions 1957; World Pair Champions - 1957, 1958, 1959, 1960; Olympic Champions - 1960

JANE WRIGHT   Canadian Swimming Champion - 100-metre breast stroke 1969, 1970; Member Commonwealth Swimming Team - 1970; Member Pan American Team, Gold and Silver - 1971; Member Olympic Team - 1972; Member World Championship Team - 1973

GOLD CREST WINNERS

1958 — CURLING: Dennis Whitehead; Alfred Phillips; Kelly O'Connor; Robert McAdam.

1960 — BADMINTON: Jane Stanfield Davies, Judith Anne Davies; John Lawson. CURLING: Dr. R.W. Marshall; D.S. Chant; C.C. Hopper; Kelly O'Connor; A.H. Phillips Sr.; W.A. Leak; D.C. Robinson; Alfred Phillips Jr. SKATING: Eleanor McLeod. SWIMMING: Elizabeth McGoey.

1961 — BADMINTON: Jane Stanfield Davies, Judith Anne Davies. CURLING: Mrs. L.E. Woolley; Mrs. R.H. Smith; Mrs. Goodwin Gibson; Miss Jane Clark; Dr. R.W. Marshall; D.S. Chant; C.C. Hopper; W.F. Kent; A.H. Phillips Sr.; W.A. Leak; D.C. Robinson; F.W. Graham. SKATING: Sonia Snelling.

1963 — CURLING: Mrs. L.E. Woolley; Mrs. R.H. Smith; Miss Jane Clark; Mrs. C.R. Mills.

1964 — SKATING: Dr. Charles Snelling. SWIMMING: George Goldsmith.

1965 — CURLING: A.H. Phillips; W.A. Leak; W.G. Cowan; C.R. Forsyth.

1966 — BADMINTON: Pat Daly. SQUASH: David Hetherington.

1967 — SWIMMING: Mary Lou Hawkins.

1968 — BADMINTON: Pat Daly; David Gibson; Janet Whitten; Brian Munro.

1969 — BADMINTON: Mary Petrie; Robert McAvoy. CURLING: A.H. Phillips; W.G. Cowan; J.G. Young; J.A. McTavish.

1970 — BADMINTON: Cathy Clarke, Ian Arthur, Brian Munro, Pat Daly, James McKee. CURLING: A.H. Phillips; W.G. Cowan; J.A. McTavish; J.G. Young. SQUASH: Stephen Moysey. SKATING: Stan Bohonek; Arlene Hall. SWIMMING: Alannah Campbell.

1971— BADMINTON: David Gibson, Thomas Muir, Ross Clarke, Ian Arthur, Cathy Clarke. SKATING: Stan Bohonek. SQUASH: Stephen Moysey.

1972 — BADMINTON: James Muir. SQUASH: Stephen Moysey.

1973 — BADMINTON: James Muir Doubles, Cathy Clarke, Tom Muir, Jennifer Rodgers, Clifford Jansen. SQUASH: John Shales.

1974 — BADMINTON: James Muir, Cathy Clarke, Tom Muir, James McKee. SKATING: Stan Bohonek, Kevin Robertson.

1975 — BADMINTON: James Muir, Jamie McKee, Tom Muir, James Muir, Lori Bishop. SKATING: Barbarta Berezowski, David Porter, Stan Bohonek.

1976 — BADMINTON: James Muir, Tom Muir, James McKee. SKATING: Donald Dixon. SQUASH: Peter Frost, Barry Grant, David Hetherington, Peter Heatherington, Thomas McCarthy, John Shales.

1977 — BADMINTON: James McKee, Lori Bishop, Clifford Jansen. LAWN BOWLING: Gerda M. Pryor. SQUASH: Jan Taylor. SWIMMING: Don Dixon, Katharine Richardson, David Shemilt.

1978 — BADMINTON: James McKee. SQUASH: Jan Taylor.

1979 — BADMINTON: James McKee, Ross Clarke, Cathy Clarke, James Muir, Bruce McDonald. SQUASH: Peter Frost, David Hetherington. SWIMMING: Katharine Richardson.

1980 — BADMINTON: Cathy Clarke; Ross Clarke; James McKee. SWIMMING: Peter Shemilt; Katharine Richardson; Deanne Weber; David Shemilt.

1981 — BADMINTON: James McKee; Linda McDonald; Edward Prittie. SQUASH: Garry Gale;: Peter Frost; Steven Jacobs; Catherine McKenna; Gabriella Lanzarini. TENNIS: Carling Bassett; Victoria Bassett.

1982 — BADMINTON: James McKee; Edward Prittie. SQUASH: Peter Frost; Garry Gale; David Hetherington.

1983 — BADMINTON: Ross Clarke; Peter Higgins; Jeffery Hess. LAWN BOWLING: Donald M. McBey; J. Maynard Dacey; Richard P. Wright. SKATING: Barbara Underhill; Paul Martini; Kay Thomson. TENNIS: Carling Bassett.

1984 — AQUATICS: Rob Steen. BADMINTON: Annette Argamasılla; Linda McDonald; John Wright. SKATING: Barbara Underhill, Paul Martini; Kay Thomson; Kelly Johnson; John Thomas. SQUASH: Scott Dulmage. TENNIS: Annette Argamasilla; Cynthia Mitchell.

1985 — BADMINTON: Jeffrey Hess; James McKee. SQUASH: Scott Dulmage: Peter Frost. TENNIS: Annette Argamasilla.

1986 — AQUATICS: F. Robert Fisher. BADMINTON: Sarah Gibbings; James McKee; Allison Vuchnich. SKATING: Kevin Parker. SQUASH: Janice Taylor. TENNIS: Ruby Fisher; Jonathan Tredgett.

1987 — AQUATICS: F. Robert Fisher; Katherine Von Offenheim. BADMINTON: Ross Clarke; James McKee. SKATING: Lindsay Fedosoff. SQUASH: Robin Colman; Scott Dulmage; Jonathan Tredgett. TENNIS: Annette Argamasilla.

1988 — AQUATICS: F. Robert Fisher; Katherine Von Offenheim; Richard M Willemsen; Ralph N. Ades. BADMINTON: James K. McKee; H. Bruce McDonald; Thomas B. Aikenhead; S. Molson Robertson. CURLING: Gerda Glenn; Olive Bates; Donna Jarrell; Muriel Gorrie. LAWN BOWLING: Edward D. Douglas; Ernest S. Hyus; J. Maynard Dacey. SKATING: Rebecca S. Salisbury. SQUASH: W. Mark Barber; S. Scott Dulmage; Lolly D. Gillen; Jonathan P. Tredgett; Garry G. Gale; Catharine Reid.

1989 — BADMINTON: Thomas Aikenhead; Ross S. Clarke; Sarah A. Gibbings; James K. McKee; Gio T. Tan; Allison A.Vuchnich; John W. Wright. SQUASH: S. Scott Dulmage; Lolly D. Gillen; Michael S. Pirnak; Jonathan P. Tredgett.

1990 — AQUATICS: Dick M. Willemson. BADMINTON: Sarah A. Gibbings; Adam J. Culliford; Gio T. Tan. SKATING: Jo-Ann Borlase; Martin Smith. SQUASH: W. Mark Barber; Lolly D. Gillen; Catherine Reid; David C. Hetherington.

1991 — AQUATICS: Henry Vehovec. BADMINTON: Sarah A. Gibbings; Caroline E. Gibbings; Carolyn E. Smith; Jennifer M.Wismer. SKATING: Martin Smith; Michelle McDonald. SQUASH: Michael S. Pirnak; S. Scott Dulmage; W. Mark Barber; Garry G. Gale; David C Hetherington.

1992 — AQUATICS: Henry Vehovec, Dick Willemsen. BADMINTON: Jamie McKee; Ross Clarke; John Wright; Sarah Gibbings; Caroline Gibbings; Adam Culliford; Jeff Wolak. SQUASH: Michael S. Pirnak; Lolly Gillen. TENNIS: Jane Stodgell; Ann Davidson-Purves; Brian Saunders.

1993 — AQUATICS: Henry Vehovec; Sarah Clark; Dick Willemsen. BADMINTON: Caroline E. Gibbings; Sarah A. Gibbings; Adam Culliford; Jeff Wolak; John Wright; Jamie McKee; Ross Clarke. SKATING: Kurt Browning; Karen Preston.

1994 — BADMINTON: Sarah A. Gibbings; Caroline Gibbings; Martha Gibbings; Jeff Wolak; Ross Clarke; Jamie McKee. SKATING: Kurt Browning; Josée Chouinard; Julie Hughes; Karen Preston.

1995 — AQUATICS: Robert Fisher; Henry Vehovec; Dick Willemsen; Tim Carter. BADMINTON: Caroline Gibbings; Sarah Gibbings; Adam Culliford; Ross Clarke; Molson Robertson. SKATING: Marcus Christensen; Rebecca Salisbury. SQUASH: Scott Dulmage; Lolly Gillen-Hannah; David Hetherington; Molson Robertson. TENNIS: Tony Ross; John Swinden.

1996 — AQUATICS: Robert Fisher; Henry Vehovic; Tim Carter; Dick Willemsen. BADMINTON: James Carnwath; Ross Clarke; Caroline Gibbings; Sarah Gibbings; Chloe Lennox; Jamie McKee; Molson Robertson; Andrew Wismer. SKATING: Josée Chouinard; Marcus Christensen; Kara Rijnen; Michael Pollard. SQUASH: Lolly Gillen; Michael Pirnak; Cathy Reid; Michael Manley.

1997 — AQUATICS: Harry Class; Robert Fisher. BADMINTON: James Carnwath; Ross Clarke; Caroline Gibbings; James McKee; Molson Robertson. SQUASH: Scott Dulmage; Lolly Gillen; Colin West.

1998 — AQUATICS: Harry Class; Sue Danniels; Robert Fisher. BADMINTON: Chloe Lennox; Molson Robertson; James Carnwath. SQUASH: Scott Dulmage; Michael Pirnak; Lolly Gillen; Michael Manley; David Hetherington; Ryan Forster. TENNIS: John Elms.

1999 — AQUATICS: Harry Class; Robert Fisher; Geoff Polci; Dick Willemsen. BADMINTON: Cara Cheung; Tommy McKee; Martha Gibbings; Fiona McKee; Chloe Lennox; Sarah Gibbings; Caroline Gibbings; James Carnwarth. SQUASH: Lolly Gillen; David Hetherington; Michael Manley; Michael Pirnak; Molson Robertson; Colin West. TENNIS: Fraser MacDonald; Brain Saunders.

PHOTO CREDITS

Founders: **page** 1: Lamond Smith, courtesy of Toronto Golf Club. **page** 2: Thomas McCraken, Toronto Reference Library; William Bain Scarth, National Archives of Canada, neg. no. PA198534. **page** 5: William Barclay McMurrich, Toronto Reference Library, J. Ross Robertson Collection, T15048. **page** 7: Robert Carrie, Toronto Reference Library.

Charter Members: **page** 10: Robert Henry Bethune, *Canadian Bankers' Association Journal, 1894-95.* Vol. 2. **page** 11: Archibald Hamilton Campbell, Toronto Reference Library. **page** 12: Robert Jaffray, *The Globe and Mail,* #38100. **page** 14: William Mellis Christie, Toronto Reference Library. **page** 15: Christie's Biscuit Factory, Toronto Reference Library, *Special Number of The Dominion Illustrated Devoted to Toronto,* 1882. **page** 16: James David Edgar, National Archives of Canada, neg. no. PA25632. **page** 17: Simeon Heman Janes, *Municipality of Toronto, A History* by Jesse E. Middleton, p. 89. **page** 18: Benvenuto, Toronto Reference Library, T11350. **page** 19: Alexander Nairn, Toronto Reference Library, J. Ross Robertson Collection, T34666. **page** 20: James H. Richardson, Toronto Reference Library, from *The Medical Profession in Upper Canada 1783-1850,* Wm. Canniff, MD, MRCS eng, 1894. **page** 21: Frederick Wyld, *Toronto Old and New,* 1890, by G. Mercer Adam, p. 161.

Chapter One: (Unless otherwise noted, all photos are the property of the Granite Club.) **page** 25: Sir John A. Macdonald, Toronto Reference Library, J. Ross Robertson Collection, T14958. **page** 26: Map of Toronto, 1878 (detail), Toronto Reference Library, *Illustrated Historical Atlas of York and Co.,* Toronto, 1878. **page** 28: 999 Queen Street West, Toronto Reference Library, J. Ross Robertson Collection, T10964, from a watercolour by John G. Howard. **page** 29: Robert Jaffray's store, *Toronto Past and Present until 1882,* Mulvany, p. 304.

Chapter Two: (Unless otherwise noted, all photos are the property of the Granite Club.) **page** 34: Jarvis Street lacrosse grounds, Toronto Reference Library, J. Ross Robertson Collection, T15188. **page** 35: Granite Club on Church Street, Toronto Reference Library. **page** 36: Norman Bethune Dick, Toronto Reference Library, *Outing, An Illustrated Monthly of Sport, Travel and Recreation,* Vol. XV, p. 38. **page** 40: Souvenir Booklet, Toronto's Semi-Centennial, Toronto Reference Library. **page** 41: Tennis field, Toronto Reference Library, *Outing, An Illustrated Monthly of Sport. Travel and Recreation,* Vol. XV, October 1889-March, 1890. p. 29. **page** 42: Charles C. Dalton,

Curling in Ontario, 1846 to 1946, John A. Stevenson, Ontario Curling Association, Toronto, 1950. **page** 43: Granite Tennis players, Toronto Reference Library, *Outing, An Illustrated Monthly of Sport. Travel and Recreation,* Vol. XV, October 1889-March, 1890. p. 37. **page** 44: Daniel Robert Wilkie, Toronto Reference Library, J. Ross Robertson Collection, T34824. **page** 46: Ontario Tankard Winners, Toronto Reference Library, *Outing, An Illustrated Monthly of Sport. Travel and Recreation,* Vol. XV, October 1889-March, 1890. p. 38. **page** 48: William Badenach, *Curling in Ontario, 1846 to 1946,* John A. Stevenson, Ontario Curling Association, Toronto, 1950. **page** 49: The Red Jacket Rink, *Curling in Ontario, 1846 to 1946,* John A. Stevenson, Ontario Curling Association, Toronto, 1950. **page** 51: R.K. Burgess, Toronto Reference Library, *Saturday Night,* Vol. I, 1887, Dec. 31, p. 10. **page** 52: Edmund Boyd Osler, Toronto Reference Library, J. Ross Robertson Collection, T16796. **page** 53: Invitation, Royal Canadian Academy. **page** 55: Granite Club Bowlers, Toronto Reference Library, *Outing, An Illustrated Monthly of Sport. Travel and Recreation,* Vol. XV, October 1889-March, 1890. p. 33. **page** 56: James Carlyle, *Toronto, Old and New,* 1890 by G. Mercer Adam.

Chapter Three: (Unless otherwise noted, all photos are the property of the Granite Club.) **page** 57 & 68: Granite Senior Hockey Team, 1892, Toronto Reference Library, *Dominion Illustrated Monthly,* Vol. 2, March 1893. **page** 58: A.H. Wright, Toronto Reference Library, *Dominion Illustrated,* Vol. 1, No. 3, April 1892, p. 181. **page** 60: A.R. Creelman, Toronto Reference Library, *Who's Who and Why in Canada (and Newfoundland),* 1912, Vol 1, p. 87. **page** 62: Trolley Car, Toronto Reference Library, *Toronto as seen from the Street Cars, 1894,* Chas. E.A. Carr. **page** 67: H.D. Warren, Toronto Reference Library, *Dominion Illustrated Monthly,* Vol. 2, March, 1893. **page** 68: Granite Senior Hockey Team 1892-93. Toronto Reference Library, *Dominion Illustrated Monthly,* Vol. 2, March, 1893, p. 105. **page** 70: W.C. Matthews, Toronto Reference Library, *The Toronto Board of Trade—A Souvenir—1893.* **page** 74: W.A.J. Littlejohn, Toronto Reference Library, J. Ross Robertson Collection, T15137. **page** 76: J.C. Kemp, Toronto Reference Library, *Saturday Night,* Vol. 16, March 21, 1903, p. 7.

Chapter Four: (Unless otherwise noted, all photos are the property of the Granite Club.) **page** 79: Great Toronto Fire damage, City of Toronto Archives, SC266-16317. **page** 80: R.L. Patterson, Toronto Reference Library, *Saturday Night,* Vol. 16, March 21, 1903, p. 7. **page** 82; Samuel George Beatty, Toronto Reference Library, *The Province of*

Ontario: A History 1615-1927, Jesse Edgar Middleton and Fred Landen, M.A. Vol. IV, 1927. **page** 83: C.P. Smith, Toronto Reference Library, *Saturday Night*, Vol. 16, March 21, 1903, p. 7; James Baird, Toronto Reference Library, York Pioneer and Historical Society, 1912, p. 26. **page** 84: G.H. Gooderham, Toronto Reference Library, *Leading Financial and Business Men of Toronto*, Edward McCormick, 1912, plate 52. **page** 85; Wyld, Grassett & Darling (before Great Toronto Fire), *Toronto Old and New*, 1890, G. Mercer Adam, p. 161; Great Toronto Fire damage, City of Toronto Archives, SC266-16317. **page** 86: J.M. Macdonald, Toronto Reference Library, *Saturday Night*, Vol. 16, March 21, 1903, p. 7. **page** 88: Charles Reid, Toronto Reference Library, *The Toronto Board of Trade—A Souvenir Number—1893*, p. 209. **page** 89: Charles Boeckh, Toronto Reference Library, *The Toronto Board of Trade—A Souvenir Number—1893*, p. 193. **page** 90: C.O. Knowles, *The Curler & Bowler*, March 1910, p. 6. **page** 91: Thomas Rennie, *The Curler & Bowler*, March 1910, p. 9.

Chapter Five: (Unless otherwise noted, all photos are the property of the Granite Club.) **page** 102: Granite Ladies Team, 1919, *Memories of 75 Years*, Southern Ontario Ladies Curling Association. **page** 106: Toronto Granites, National Archives of Canada, PA50686. **page** 117: Cecil And Maude Smith, National Archives Of Canada, PA52421, R. Mitchell.

Chapter Six: (Unless otherwise noted, all photos are the property of the Granite Club.) **page** 129: St. Clair Avenue in 1919, City of Toronto Archives, James 1177. **page** 134: John A. Tory, *Toronto Year Book*, 1934. **page** 142: John Fizallen Ellis, Toronto Reference Library, *Who's Who in Canada (including) The British Possessions in the Western Hemisphere*, 1922, B.M Greene, Ed. **page** 143: Johnny Walker, City of Toronto Archives, SC 266-14710. **page** 146: William H. Alderson, Toronto Reference Library, *Who's Who in Canada (including) The British Possessions in the Western Hemisphere*, 1922, B.M Greene, Ed. **page** 149: Canadian Team in Scotland, *Ontario Curling Association*, 52nd Annual, 1927. **page** 150: Charles Bulley, *The Municipality of Toronto: A History*, Vol. III, 1923, Jesse E. Middleton.

Chapter Seven: (Unless otherwise noted, all photos are the property of the Granite Club.) **page** 153: Granite Club on St. Clair chapter opener, City of Toronto Archives, James 1946.

Chapter Eight: (Unless otherwise noted, all photos are the property of the Granite Club.) **page** 171, 174: Howard Nicholson, courtesy of Eleanor (O'Meara) Phelan. **page** 172: Ontario Ladies Tankard Winners 1930, 1931, *Memories of 75 Years*, Southern Ontario Ladies Curling Association. **page** 178: James Nicholson, courtesy of St. George's Society. **page** 180: Emily Woolley, *Memories of 75 Years*, Southern Ontario

Ladies Curling Association. **page** 182: Eleanor O'Meara, Hazel and Dorothy Caley, courtesy of Eleanor (O'Meara) Phelan.

Chapter Nine: (Unless otherwise noted, all photos are the property of the Granite Club.) **page** 187, 202: skaters in Atlantic City, courtesy of Eleanor (O'Meara) Phelan. **page** 195: Rod Phelan receiving membership, City of Toronto Archives, SC266-36557. **page** 198, Dr. Charles Brereton, courtesy of Ron Grills. **page** 207, 1938 Senior Ladies Champions, courtesy Eleanor (O'Meara) Phelan.

Chapter Ten: (Unless otherwise noted, all photos are the property of the Granite Club.) **page** 211, 227: Wilson, Scott, O'Meara, courtesy of Eleanor (O'Meara) Phelan. **page** 217: Christina Bulley's rink, *Memories of 75 Years*, Southern Ontario Ladies Curling Association. **page** 221: "Double Exposure" courtesy of Claire Bosley.

Chapter Eleven: (Unless otherwise noted, all photos are the property of the Granite Club.) **page** 237: Ladies Tankard winners, 1946, *Memories of 75 Years*, Southern Ontario Ladies Curling Association.

Chapter Twelve: (Unless otherwise noted, all photos are the property of the Granite Club.) **page** 249, Linda, Sonia and Charles Snelling, courtesy of Verna Snelling. **page** 256: Robertson Winners, courtesy of Claire Bosley.

Chapter Thirteen: (Unless otherwise noted, all photos are the property of the Granite Club.) **page** 278: Ross Tarlton Sr., and 25th Anniversary of Ross Tarlton competition both courtesy of Ron Grills. **page** 283: Robertson winners in 1968, courtesy of Claire Bosley.

Chapter Fourteen: (Unless otherwise noted, all photos are the property of the Granite Club.) **page** 304: President's Ball, courtesy of Dr. Bob Marshall; **page** 309: Badminton match, courtesy of James Muir

Chapter Fifteen: All photos are the property of the Granite Club.

Chapter Sixteen: (Unless otherwise noted, all photos are the property of the Granite Club.) **page** 373: Lolly Gillen and Sharif Khan, courtesy of Lolly Gillen; **page** 374: 1989 Convener's Cup, courtesy of Lolly Gillen.

ENDNOTES

FOUNDERS: **page** 1: "largest club of its kind": James Hedley, "The Toronto Granite Club," *Outing*, October 1889, p. 28. Hedley, an early member, wrote often about curling and lawn bowling for *Outing*. **page** 1: "It is safe to say": James Hedley, "The Toronto Granite Club," *Outing*, October 1889, p. 28

CHARTER MEMBERS: **page** 9: "The 1875 list of members": *Saturday Night*, November 7, 1925, p. 10. **page** 11: "it always reported a profit": Philip Creighton, "Robert Henry Bethune," *Dictionary of Canadian Biography*, Vol. XII, University of Toronto Press, 1990, pp. 107-108. **page** 12: "near the celebrated battlefield": "Robert Jaffray". *Representative Canadians. A Cyclopedia of Canadian Biography*, Vol. II, Toronto: Rose Publishing, 1888, p. 675. **page** 12: "he lost his father": Dean Beeby, "Robert Jaffray," *Dictionary of Canadian Biography*, Vol. XIV, University of Toronto Press, 1998, p. 528. **page** 14: "I entered upon my apprenticeship": William Christie, "Journal," Archives of Ontario, MU 7728. **page** 15: "the crescent became a row": Donald Jones, "These Victorian Buildings Are Hidden from View," *Toronto Star*, February 15, 1975. **page** 18: "As the population": J.E. Middleton, *The Municipality of Toronto*. Dominion Publishing Company, Toronto, 1923. **page** 18: "most stately mansion": J.E. Middleton, "Simeon Heman Janes," *The Municipality of Toronto*, Vol. III, Toronto: The Dominion Publishing, 1923, pp. 89-90. **page** 19: "a lover of the": J.E. Middleton, "Simeon Heman Janes," *The Municipality of Toronto, Vol. III*, Toronto: Dominion Publishing, 1923, pp. 89-90. **page** 22: "Mr.Wyld was" J.E. Middleton, "Frederick Wyld," *The Municipality of Toronto, Vol. III*, Toronto: The Dominion Publishing Company, 1923, p. 83.

CHAPTER 1: **page** 25: "fifty square feet": John A. Stevenson, *Curling in Ontario 1846-1946*, Toronto: The Ryerson Press, 1950, p. 190. **page** 26: "for the comfort": James Hedley, "The Toronto Granite Club," *Outing* , October 1889. p. 29.

CHAPTER 2: **page** 33: "transformation from a commerce": *Ontario History, Journal of The Ontario Historical Society*. September 1984. **page** 34: "exuberant Renaissance Revival building": Patricia McHugh, *Toronto Architecture. A City Guide*, Toronto: Mercury Books, 1985, p. 175. **page** 34: "handsome, commodious, costly": *Saturday Night*, December, 31 1887, p. 10. **page** 37: "on cold days": Interview, Jim Francis, December 16, 1986. **page** 38: "I knew him very well": *The Globe*, March 2, 1923. **page** 43: "The Toronto's licked us": *Outing*, October 1889, p. 34. **page** 46: "I wish you could see": John A. Stevenson, *Curling in Ontario. 1846-1946*, Toronto: The Ryerson Press, 1950, p. 95. **page** 45: "Having already defeated": *Outing*, October 1889, p. 31. **page** 47: "We ain't used to playing": *Outing*, October 1889, p. 38. **page** 48: "one of the greatest skips": *Curler and Bowler* magazine, March 1910. **page** 48:

"William Badenach used to say": John A. Stevenson, *Curling in Ontario 1846-1946*. Ontario Curling Association, Toronto, 1950, p. 207. **page** 49: "The curlers adjourned": *The Globe*, February 17, 1888. **page** 50: "by which players": *Outing*, October 1889, p. 31. **page** 52: "After forming Osler and Hammond": Gregory P. Marchildon, "Wilmot Deloui Matthews," *Dictionary of Canadian Biography, Vol. XIV*, University of Toronto Press, 1998, p. 750. **page** 52: "On the entrance gates": Katherine Hale, *Toronto*, Cassell & Company Limited, Toronto, 1956. **page** 55: "The Granite has done more": *Saturday Night*, March 21, 1903.

CHAPTER 3: **page** 58: "The scene during the fire": Board of Trade Souvenir Number, 1893, p. 107. **page** 59: "provide not less than": G.P. deT Glazebrook, *The Story of Toronto*. University of. **page** 60: "The new bylaws": They are contained in a book, Constitution, Rules and Regulations of the Granite Curling Club of Toronto. The Monetary Times Printing Company, Limited, 1892. **page** 60 "much devoted to": J.R. Seeley et al., Crestwood Heights, 1956. p. 295. **page** 60: "a splendid man": H.J. Morgan, *Canadian Men and Women of the Time*. William Briggs, Toronto 1912. **page** 61: "The Toronto Railway Company": *Toronto by Trolley Car*, Toronto 1892. **page** 61: "The new cars are": The questions from *The Globe and the Mail* appear in Bruce West, *Toronto*. Doubleday Canada Limited, Toronto, 1967. **page** 65: "In 1891 the Granite": *Saturday Night*, February 26,1927. p. 29. **page** 68: "The Granites play ": *Dominion Illustrated Monthly*, Vol. 2 1893. p. 104. **page** 69: "one of the best": *The College Times* magazine. Toronto, Easter 1895. **page** 71: "The visitors left": *The Mail*, Toronto, February 10, 1890. **page** 71: "A Toronto Granite rink": John A. Stevenson, *Curling in Ontario, 1846-1946*. Toronto, 1950. **page** 74: "to deal rapidly": H.J. Morgan, *Canadian Men and Women of the Time*. William Briggs, Toronto 1912. **page** 76: "Much of the success": *Saturday Night*, March 21, 1903, p. 7. **page** 77: "membership in the 'right'": J.E. Middleton, *The Municipality of Toronto. A History. Vol. II*, The Dominion Publishing Company, Toronto, 1923, p.35.

CHAPTER 4: **page** 80: "a man known far and wide": *The Globe*, April 1917. **page** 81: "The annual meeting": *The Toronto World*, October 27, 1902. **page** 82: "he revised the whole": J.E. Middleton, *The Province of Ontario. A History*. **page** 86: "Everything was burning": Bruce West, *Toronto*, Toronto: Doubleday Canada Limited, 1967. **page** 86: "exuberant, Renaissance Revival building": Patricia McHugh, *Toronto Architecture, A City Guide*, Mercury Books, Toronto, 1985. p. 175. **page** 86: "dour clubhouse": Ibid. **page** 89: "with a pale": Barbara J.Clarke, "Did You Know," *Granite News*, January 1985. **page** 90: "In you we recognize": *The Globe and Mail*, May 20, 1947. **page** "was the best curler": Interview, April 3, 1995. **page** 93: "means of transporting": C.L. Burton, *A Sense of Urgency*. Clarke Irwin & Co. Ltd., Toronto, 1952. **page** 95: "it was twelve minutes": *The Evening Telegram*, October

4, 1913. **page** 95: "buried under a mass": Ibid. **page** 96: "smothered by smoke": Ibid. **page** 96: "People in the homes": Ibid. **page** 96: "pretty well covered by insurance": *The Toronto World*, October 4, 1913. **page** 96: "addition of a building": Minutes of Meeting of Directors, Granites Limited, October 23, 1913. **page** 97: "for the efficient work": Ibid.

CHAPTER 5: **page** 99: "The new premises": *The Globe*, December 18, 1914. **page** 100: "had not the faintest": C.L. Burton, *A Sense of Urgency*, Toronto: Clarke, Irwin & Company Limited, 1952. **page** 100: "at home, individual companies": C.L. Burton, *A Sense of Urgency*, Toronto: Clarke, Irwin & Company Limited, 1952. **page** 101: "find the curling": Rev. John Kerr, *History of Curling*, Dirleton, Scotland, 1890. **page** 104: "But it was never forbidden": *Toronto Star*, August 9, 1992, p. D4.**page** 104: "25 million people": Andrew Nikiforuk, *The Globe and Mail*, October 25, 1997. **page** 105: "after Saturday, October 19th, 1918": Ibid. **page** 106: "The Granites had": OHA, *The Annual*, 1919-1920. **page** 106: "Granites outclassed Regina Victorias": OHA, *The Annual*, 1921-22. **page** 107: "The victory of the Granites": OHA, *The Annual*, 1922-23. **page** 108: "Granites are champions": *The Globe*, March 3, 1923. **page** 109: "The trip started": Harry Watson Scrapbook, National Archives of Canada. MG28 I 99 Volume 32, p. 42. **page** 110: "A great time was had": Ibid., p. 40. **page** 110: "One and all agreed": Ibid., p. 32. **page** 111: "Mr. Hewitt has the boys": Ibid, p. 32. **page** 111: "quite unfamiliar to Canadians": Andrew Podnieks, *Canada's Olympic Hockey Teams*, Doubleday Canada Limited, Toronto, 1997, p. 15. **page** "The weather for that": Ibid, p. 16. **page** "U.S. players evidently": *Harry Watson Scrapbook*, National Archives of Canada MG28, I 99 Volume 32. p. 35. **page** "Between the champagne": Andrew Podnieks, *Canada's Olympic Hockey Teams*, Doubleday Canada Limited, Toronto, 1997. p. 17. **page** 113. "bains de luxe": *Harry Watson Scrapbook*, National Archives of Canada, MG28, I 99, Volume 32, p. 49. **page** "Granites were probably": Bruce Kidd, *The Struggle for Canadian Sport*, University of Toronto Press, 1996, p. 61. **page** 116: "without a peer": *Harry Watson Scrapbook*, National Archives of Canada, MG28, I 99, Volume 32. p. 15. **page** 116: "There never was anybody": Milt Dunnell, "Speaking on Sport," *Toronto Daily Star*, August 27, 1963. **page** 118: The twenties in Canada": Craig Brown, editor, *The Illustrated History of Canada*, Lester & Orpen Dennys Limited, Toronto, 1987. **page** 118: "begun to establish": Randall White, *Too Good to Be True*. Toronto in the 1920s, Dundurn Press, Toronto, 1993, p. 78. **page** 119: "a womanizing impresario": Robert Fulford, "The Observer," *The Globe and Mail*, June 1998. **page** 119: "Toronto's first great gift": Randall White, *Too Good to Be True*. Toronto in the 1920s. Dundurn Press, Toronto, 1993, p. 78. **page** 121: "the dernier cri": *Saturday Night*, February 26, 1926.

CHAPTER 6: **page** 124: "decided to install": John A. Stevenson, *Curling in Ontario*. 1846-1946, p.105. Toronto: The Ryerson Press, 1950. **page** 124: "the first in": John D. Arnup, *The Toronto Curling Club* 1836-1957, p. 11. **page** 126: "for friends, relatives, and prospective": *Upper Yonge Town Crier*, May 1991. **page** 127: "with full power to act": E.B. Stockdale, "Confidential Memorandum prepared for he information of the proposed Patrons and Directors of the new Granite Club.", 25 September 1925. **page** 127: "well-known in busi-

ness": *Toronto Star*, December 15, 1926, p. 7. **page** 128: "between Havargal College"": Prospectus of Granite Club Limited, November 2, 1925. **page** 129: "the proposed objects": Minutes of Meeting, October 6, 1925. **page** 129: "lawn bowling greens": E.B.Stockdale, "Confidential Memorandum prepared for the information of the proposed Patrons and Directors of the new Granite Club" October 6, 1925. **page** 130: "His correspondence was read": *The Globe*, August 1, 1966. **page** 133: "after a very full discussion": Minutes of Meeting, October 22, 1925. **page** 134: "brilliant salesmen": Michael Bliss, *Northern Enterprise. Five Centuries of Canadian Business*. McClelland and Stewart, Toronto, 1987, p. 277. **page** 134: "legal wizard": Ibid. **page** 135: "as the time for ": Minutes, Building Committee Meeting, May 14, 1925. **page** 137: "Yes! It was quite a sight": *Granite News*, June 1972. **page** 138: "the modest dry goods": *Toronto Daily Star*, October 21, 1952, p. 4. **page** 140: "revenues available from cards": E.B. Stockdale, Confidential Memorandum prepared for the information of the proposed Patrons and Directors of the new Granite Club, October 6, 1925. **page** 141: "finest open-air tank": *Toronto Star*, May 1, 1935. **page** 141: "produce a swimming team": *Toronto Star*, November 12, 1926. **page** 141: "It would not be a surprise": *The Mail and Empire*, November 12, 1926. **page** 141: "threshed through kelp": *The Evening Telegram*, May 1, 1935. **page** 142: "one of Canada's most successful": *The Globe*, February 20, 1928. **page** 142: "It's not a surprise": *Toronto Star*, May 1, 1935. **page** 143: "a sand road that resembled": *Granite News*, June 1972. **page** 144: "he would bend over almost double": Interview with E.B. Stockdale's daughter, Betty Morrison, August 1992. **page** 144: "Privileged members": Ron MacFeeters' letter to the author, November 21, 1991. **page** 146: "Mr. Alderson has no hobbies": *The Star Weekly*, January 22, 1922. **page** 146: "received his first impetus": Ibid. **page** 146: "type of the twentieth century": Ibid. **page** 148: "We sailed": *Annual of the Ontario Curling Association for 1926-27*, pp. 21-23. **page** 149: "After the schedule of games": *Annual of the Ontario Curling Association for 1926-27*, pp. 21-23. **page** 150: "No words": *Annual of the Ontario Curling Association for 1926-27*, pp. 21-23. **page** 151: "received a number of inquiries for the purchase": Confidential Memorandum prepared for the information of the proposed Patrons and Directors of the new Granite Club, October 6, 1925.

CHAPTER 7: **page** 153: "St. Clair Avenue": *The Mail and Empire*, November 13, 1926. **page** 153: "over five thousand": *Saturday Night*, November 20, 1926. **page** 154: "a modern sporting palace": *The Evening Telegram*, November 11, 1926. **page** 154: "answer to a sportsman's prayer": *The Globe*, November 13, 1926.**page** "the only family club": *Saturday Night*, February 26, 1927, p. 29. **page** 154: "If anybody wanted to realize": *Toronto Star*, November 13, 1926. **page** 155: "the largest single covered expanse": *Saturday Night*, November 20, 1926. **page** 157: "Without a doubt the finest": *The Mail and Empire*, November 12, 1926. **page** 163: "four teams from the RCYC": *The Globe*, November 13, 1926. **page** 163: "It was a fitting end": *Saturday Night*, February 26, 1927, p. 29. **page** 163: "The Granite Club's first year": *The Toronto Star*, December 11, 1926, p.11. **page** 166: "The Prince of Wales": Donald Jones, "Historical Toronto," *Toronto Star*, March 14, 1981. **page** 169: "Sister curling clubs": *The Mail and Empire*, December 30, 1929.

CHAPTER 8: **page** 171: "In Canada, as elsewhere": Craig Brown, editor, *The Illustrated History of Canada*, Lester & Orpen Dennys, Toronto, 1987. **page** 172: "Notwithstanding the unfavourable": *The Mail and Empire*, December 13, 1930. **page** 172: "the club's operating profit": Granite Club, Limited, Balance Sheet and Statement of Profit and Loss, October 31, 1930. **page** 172: "Granted that operating profit": Granite Club, Limited Balance Sheet and Statement of Profit and Loss, October 31, 1931. **page** 175: "open to juniors": *Toronto Star*, February 16, 1927. **page** 175: "group winners from": *Toronto Star*, February 16, 1927. **page** 175: "entertained at dinner": *Toronto Star*, February 24, 1927. **page** 176: "captain of the victorious lawn bowling": *Toronto Star*, August 5, 1952. **page** 177: "from Vancouver to Labrador": *The Dominion Illustrated*, 1892, p. 57. **page** 178: "seats and benches": *Dictionary of Canadian Biography*, University of Toronto Press, 1966, Vol. I, p. xi. **page** 178: "substantial number of" : Report of the President, Mr. A.L.A. Richardson, Annual Meeting of Shareholders, Granite Club, Limited, December 18, 1952. **page** 179: "Granite Club may buy": *The Globe*, April 14, 1932. **page** 180: "superb curling ability": "Achievement Award," Province of Ontario, 1964. **page** 181: "he was personally opposed": Minutes, Board of Directors, April 28, 1932. **page** 182: "We approach 1933": "Minutes," Sixth Annual Meeting of the Shareholders of Granite Club, Limited, December 6, 1932. **page** 183: "The club realized": Balance Sheet and Profit and Loss Statement, Granite Club, Limited, October 31, 1933. **page** 183: "many branches of sport": *Toronto Star*, March 7, 1933. **page** 186: "that curling stones": John A. Stevenson, *Curling in Ontario 1846-1946*, Toronto: The Ryerson Press, 1950, p. 147.

CHAPTER 9: **page** 188: "That the thanks of the meeting": Minutes, Special General Meeting of Shareholders, Granite Club, Limited, April 3, 1935. **page** 188: "Granite members are returning": *The Mail and Empire*, December 6, 1935. **page** 190: "It is very much like": "Alf Ablett Remembers," *Granite News*, June 1972. **page** 190: "This enabled clubs": SOLCA *Memories of 75 Years*, Oshawa, Ontario: Angus Press Limited, 1988, p.43. **page** 190: "a crowd of one thousand spectators": *Toronto Star*, February 4, 1934. **page** 190: "Styles in badminton change": *Granite News*, January 19, 1934. **page** 191: "close to one hundred curlers": *Toronto Star*, May 17, 1935. **page** 191: "They filled the Granite Club": *The Globe and Mail*, March 1, 1985. **page** 192: "The fumes were so strong": *The Evening Telegram*, April 14, 1936. **page** 193: "he had no equal in Canada": *The Globe,* May 1, 1935. **page** 193: "The most successful coach": *The Evening Telegram*, May 1, 1935. **page** 193: "Recognized internationally": *The Globe*, May 1, 1935. **page** 193: "He was the world's greatest": *The Evening Telegram*, May 1, 1935. **page** 194: "at the bedside": *The Evening Telegram*, May 1, 1935. **page** 194: "We won three times together": *The Evening Telegram*, May 1, 1935. **page** 194: "A winner never quits": *The Evening Telegram*, May 1, 1925. **page** 194: "He had preached": Ken W. MacTaggart, sports writer, *The Mail and Empire*, May 1, 1935. **page** 194: "He will be hard to replace": *The Globe*, May 1, 1935. **page** 194: "With the unanimous approval": Minutes of Meeting, Board of Directors, Granite Club, Limited, April 30, 1935. **page** 197: "In the winter": Frank J. Raw, excerpt from speech at Brereton-Raw bonspiel,

1948. **page** 198: "he was treating": *Toronto Daily Star*, September 29, 1971, p. 29. **page** 198: "it was not always an asset": *Toronto Star*, September 29, 1971, p. 29. **page** 198: "he was one of the best basketball": "Sporting Gossip," *The Mail and Empire*, January 8, 1936. **page** 198: "one of the first": "Behind the Glass," *Ontario Curling Report*, April 1988. **page** 201: "Canadian Stars Add to Glitter": *Chicago Times*, January 21, 1937. **page** 201: "twenty of the most talented young ladies": *Chicago American*, January 21, 1937. **page** 202: "I've never seen finer skating": *Toronto Star*, January 27, 1937. **page** 202: "it was the best show ever": *Toronto Star*, January 24, 1937. **page** 202: "Some remembered the old Church Street": *Toronto Star*, January 24, 1937. **page** 202: "More than 3500 socialities": *Chicago Herald and Examiner*, January 22, 1937. **page** 202: "The entire club radiated": *Granite News*, December 2, 1937, p. 2. **page** 203: "Toronto mayor W.D. Robbins": *Toronto Star*, March 1, 1937. **page** 203: "H.P. Donnelly, general manager": *The Globe and Mail*, March 2, 1937. **page** 203: "He lays a half dozen": *The Globe and Mail*, March 2, 1937. **page** 204: "I never saw such heavy smoke": *Toronto Star*, April 13, 1938, p. 14. **page** 204: "Donald M. Springer, president of Toronto Fuels": *The Evening Telegram*, April 13, 1938, Second Section, front page. **page** 205: "efficiency of the staff": Minutes, Meeting of Board of Directors of the Granite Club, May 31, 1938. **page** 205: "Fire trucks clogged St. Clair Avenue": *Toronto Star*, April 13, 1938, p. 14. **page** 205: "After a stiff battle": *The Globe and Mail*, April 13, 1938, front page. **page** 205: "It was nearly 4 a.m.": *The Evening Telegram*, April 13, 1938, Second Section, front page. **page** 205: "GRANITE CLUB FIRE": *The Evening Telegram*, April 13, 1938, Second Section, front page. **page** 205: "Notwithstanding last night's fire": *Toronto Star*, April 13, 1938, p. 3. **page** 206: "for the very efficient way": Minutes, Meeting of Board of Directors of the Granite Club, September 13, 1938. **page** 206: "extra copies available": *Granite News*, Souvenir Number, September 29, 1938, p. 22. **page** 206: "The PromenadeÒto the Sports Department": *Granite News*, Souvenir Number, September 29, 1938, p. 2. **page** 206: "gone modern in smartest manner": *Granite News*, Souvenir Number, September 29, 1938, pp. 10 and 20. **page** 210: "a kindly and dignified gentleman": *Granite News*, September 1, 1964, p. 2.

CHAPTER 10: **page** 211: "War brought full employment": Michael Bliss, *Northern Enterprise. Five Centuries of Canadian Business*, Toronto: McClelland & Stewart, 1987, p. 446. **page** 214: "When the North American": *Toronto Star*, April 1941. **page** 215: "presented that old veteran curler": *Toronto Star*, February 1, 1932, p. 13. **page** 215: "regarded as number one": *The Evening Telegram*, January 8, 1941, p. 19. **page** 216: "voted $250 as a contribution": John A. Stevenson, *Curling in Ontario 1846-1946*. Toronto: The Ryerson Press, 1950. **page** 217: "derogatory remarks concerning": Emergency Meeting of the Board of Directors of the Granite Club, April 29, 1942. **page** 217: "an apology is due the board": Hector Donnelly, Letter to I.S. Fairty Esq. KC, April 30, 1942. **page** 217: "The apology was evidently forthcoming": Covington, William J., Editor, *The Torontonian Society Blue Book and Club Membership Register*. Toronto: 1946. **page** 218: "the expression of the board": Minutes, Emergency Meeting, Board of Directors, November 1, 1943. *Massey Hall Program*, Friday,

November 5, 1943. **page** 219: "From the late nineteenth century": James W. St. G. Walker, chairman, Department of History, University of Waterloo, *Racial Discrimination in Canada. The Black Experience*, The Canadian Historical Association Historical Booklet No. 41, 1985. **page** 219: "Toronto was known": Frederick H. Armstrong, *Toronto, The Place of Meeting*, Windsor Publications (Canada) Limited, 1983, Ch. X, p.115. **page** 219: "anti-black, anti-oriental, and anti-Jewish": Morris Wolfe, editor, *A Saturday Night Scrapbook*, Toronto, 1973. **page** 219: "feminine ideal was a white": Judith Finlayson, "Seventy Years of Mixed Messages," *The Globe and Mail*, October 18, 1997. **page** 222: "Hector Donnelly, using": Source note: In a recent conversation between the author and long-time member Ronald L. MacFeeters, he confirmed that "It was Hector Donnelly who made the decision to turn Marian Anderson away." **page** 222: "He was sorry.": *The Globe and Mail*, April 24, 1944, p. 4. **page** 222: "I am ashamed to play there": *Toronto Star*, April 29, 1944. **page** 222: "Genius draws no colour line": *The Sunday Star*, January 29, 1989, p. D4. **page** 223: "The media mania": Rosalyn M. Story, *And So I Sing*, New York: Warner Books, Inc., 1990, p. 52. **page** 223: "Fashionable club banned Negro": *The Globe and Mail*, April 24, 1944, p. 4. **page** 223: "Refusal of the Granite Club": *Toronto Star*, April 29, 1944. **page** 223: "Granite Club Tactics": *Hush*, June 24, 1944. **page** 223: "Reverend Gordon Domm": *The Globe and Mail*, April 4, 1944, p. 4. **page** 223: "Noted Singer Barred": *The Chicago Defender*, May 2, 1944. **page** 223: "Evidently those who": "Voice of the People," *Toronto Star*, May 3, 1944. **page** 223: "To think that when men": Voice of the People, *Toronto Star*, May 3, 1944. **page** 224: "When the Granite Club": "Letters to the Editor," *Hush*, June "24, 1944, p. 12. **page** 224: "Revulsion against Nazi racism": James W. St. G. Walker, Chairman, Department of History, University of Waterloo, *Racial Discrimination in Canada. The Black Experience*, The Canadian Historical Association Bulletin No. 41, 1985. **page** 224: "Viola Desmond was carried": "From the Archives," *The Globe and Mail*, December 3, 1996. **page** 224: "Toronto Police Commission scheduled": "From the Archives," *The Globe and Mail*, May 17, 1997. **page** 224: "On February 14, 1949": *The Evening Telegram*, January 22, 1949, p. 8. **page** 226: "he had referred to the Granite Club": *The Globe and Mail*, December 10, 1958. **page** 226: "There is nothing in our constitution": *The Globe and Mail*, December 10, 1958. **page** 228: "Jim Joyce, his third": *Toronto Star*, January 25, 1944, p. 10. **page** 228: "I feel better about the kid's game": Annis Stukas, "Wadsworth's Rink Noses Meech to Win Trophy," *Toronto Star*, January 26, 1944. **page** 228: "Also in 1944, the board": Minutes, Board of Directors, May 18, 1944, p. 3. **page** 228: "an individual or group": Minutes, Board of Directors May 18, 1944, p. 3. **page** 228: "restoration of the share": Minutes, Board of Directors, May 18, 1944, p. 3. **page** 228: "no treasury shares": Minutes, Board of Directors, May 18, 1944, p. 4.

CHAPTER 11: **page** 232: "the first member": Nigel Stephens, Letter to the Granite Club, November 25, 1993. **page** 232: "Skating has been good to you.": Nigel Stephens, Interview, January 1994. **page** 233: "The club means a lot to me,": Nigel Stephens, Interview, January

1994. **page** 234: "He was Tarzan": "Lives Lived," *The Globe and Mail*, May 26, 1997, p. A18. **page** 236: "Francis has extraordinary talent": Barbara J. Clarke, "Jim Francis Retires," *Granite News*, November 1986, p. 2. **page** 236: "an art student": Barbara J. Clarke, "Jim Francis Retires," *Granite News*, November 1986, p. 2. **page** 237: "Liquor Licence Act": "From the Archives," *The Globe and Mail*, December 6, 1996. **page** 238: "secret bar in the squash": "Alf Ablett Remembers," *Granite News*, June 1972. **page** 239: "Fifteen thousand Swedes": Frank Cosentino, *Not Bad, Eh?* Burnstown, Ontario: General Store Publishing House, 1990, p. 48. **page** 240: "We are tremendously proud": Henry Roxborough, *Great Days in Canadian Sport*, Toronto, 1957, Ch. 19, p. 171. **page** 241: "When it was all over": Barbara J. Clarke, "Granite Club Skaters Join Canadian Figure Skating Hall of Fame," *Granite News*, April 1992. **page** 241: "there were 226 shows,": Jim Proudfoot, "Golden Memory," *Toronto Star*, February 1, 1997, p. C8. **page** 241: "she had always longed": David Young, *The Golden Age of Canadian Figure Skating*, Toronto: Summerhill Press Ltd., 1984. **page** 242: "the largest passenger vessel": *Encyclopedia Canadiana*, Toronto: Grolier of Canada Limited, 1972, Vol.7, p. 349. **page** 243: "I wept all night": Interview, November 26, 1992, Lucille Workman Colson, payroll department (1946-1954). **page** 244: "The club was his life": Interview with Hector Donnelly's daughter, Denise Kennedy, January 20, 1993. **page** 244: "He has the confidence": Minutes, Granite Club, Limited, Seventh Annual General Meeting of Shareholders, December 5, 1933.

CHAPTER 12 (Unless otherwise noted, all quotes are from interviews conducted by Ted Barris.) **page** 254: "were it not for the fact": 1954 Carnival program. **page** 255: "In the tenth end": Ken McKee, *Toronto Telegram*, 1959.

CHAPTER 13: (Unless otherwise noted, all quotes are from interviews conducted by Ted Barris.) **page** 271: "Proper maintenance and improvements": *Granite News*, Jan. 3, 1961. **page** 272: "who made an excellent draw": *Granite News*, March 7, 1960. **page** 280: "directors are still contemplating": *Granite News*, Jan. 1, 1966. **page** 285: "Meanwhile, on the social page": *Granite News*, Aug. 1, 1969. **page** 288: "discriminated against minorities": *The Globe and Mail*, January 20, 1970.

CHAPTER 14: All quotes are from interviews conducted by Ted Barris.

CHAPTER 15: All quotes are from interviews conducted by Ted Barris.

CHAPTER 16: (Unless otherwise noted, all quotes are from interviews conducted by Ted Barris.) **page** 359: "...freeskate to music": *The Toronto Star*, January, 29, 1993. **page** 359: "the son of a former": *The Globe and Mail*, January 4, 1993.

INDEX